Amṛta Vāṇī

Words of Immortality

I0081712

"By reading and hearing the nectarean instructions of Oṁ Nityalīlā Praviṣṭa Paramahaṁsa Aṣṭottara-Śata Śrī Śrīmad Bhaktisiddhānta Sarasvatī Gosvāmī Prabhupāda, founder of the Śrī Caitanya Maṭha and its branches, the Gauḍīya *Maṭha*, and who was the first person to preach the teachings of Śrī Kṛṣṇa Caitanya Mahāprabhu all over the world, we will certainly achieve auspiciousness. Do not doubt the efficacy of his teachings. O sober Vaiṣṇavas! Make your life successful by reading Śrīla Prabhupāda's nectarean instructions. He is gaura-vāṇī, the personification of Lord Śrī Gaurahari's teachings."

(Śrī Bhakti Mayukha Bhāgavata Mahārāja)

Other Publications by Touchstone Media:

Bhaktivinoda Vani Vaibhava
Prārthanā
Śrī Prema Bhakti-candrika
Sārvabhauma Śataka
Hari Bhakti Kalpa Latika
Śrī Nityānanda-caritāmṛta
Pada Sevana
Sweet Pastimes of Damodara
The Dog and the Wolf
Great Heroes of the Mahabharata Series
Krishna Pocket Guide
Amṛta Vāṇī
Śrī Prema Vilasa
Uddhava Gītā
Adventures of India Series
Śrī Krishna Vijaya
Mahābharata
Bhagavad-gītā at a Glance
Vrindāvana, the Playground of God
Patramrta
Heart and Soul Connection
Srimati's Vegetarian Delight
Gita Stories from Padma Purana
Kanaya's Bull and Other Stories
Vakrtavali

If you are interested in the purchasing or the distribution of this book or any of the above publications, you may contact:

Touchstone Media
Block EC 178
Sector 1, Salt Lake, Kolkata 700064, INDIA

www.touchstonemedia.com
e-mail :support@touchstonemedia.com

ALL GLORIES TO SRI GURU AND GAURANGA

Amṛta Vāṇī

Words of Immortality

His Divine Grace
Bhaktisiddhānta Sarasvatī Gosvāmī Prabhupāda

Compiled by Śrīpāda Bhakti Māyukha Bhāgavata Mahārāja)
Produced and Published by Īśvara dāsa
Translated by Bhumipati dāsa
Edited by Kaiśorī devī dāsī

TOUCHSTONE
MEDIA
Matter for the Soul

Amṛta Vāṇī: Words of Immoratality
His Divine Grace Bhaktisiddhānta Sarasvatī Ṭhākura Prabhupāda
Compiled by Śrīpāda Bhakti Mayukha Bhāgavat Mahāraja
Adapted and Published by Īśvara dāsa
Translated From Bengali by Bhumipati dāsa
Chapter Format by Isodhyanā devī dāsī
Edited by Kaiśorī devī dāsī
Typeset by Caitanya devī dāsī
Proofreading by Sacidevi dāsī
Design and layout by Īśvara dāsa

ISBN 978-8187897439

This book is dedicated to:
His Divine Grace A.C. Bhaktivedānta Swami Prabhupāda, Founder-Ācārya International Society for Krishna Consciousness, the foremost disciple of His Divine Grace Bhaktisiddhānta Sarasvatī Ṭhākura Prabhupāda, who has spread the message of Lord Caitanya to the entire world, and he is thus the reservoir of mercy and compassion for all fallen souls. The world is forever indebted to him.

Contents

Introduction

nama oṁ viṣṇu-pādāya kṛṣṇa-preṣṭhāya bhū-tale
śrīmate bhaktisiddhānta-sarasvatīti nāmine

I offer my respectful obeisances unto His Divine Grace Bhaktisiddhānta Sarasvatī, who is very dear to Lord Kṛṣṇa, having taken shelter at His lotus feet.

śrī-vārṣabhānavī-devī-dayitāya kṛpābdhaye
kṛṣṇa-sambandha-vijñāna-dāyine prabhave namaḥ

I offer my respectful obeisances to Śrī Vārṣabhānavī-devī-dayita dāsa [another name of Śrīla Bhaktisiddhānta Sarasvatī], who is favored by Śrīmatī Rādhārāṇī and who is the ocean of transcendental mercy and the deliverer of the science of Kṛṣṇa.

mādhuryojjvala-premāḍhya-śrī-rūpānuga-bhaktida
śrī-gaura-karuṇā-śakti-vigrahāya namo 'stu te

I offer my respectful obeisances unto you, the personified energy of Śrī Caitanya's mercy, who deliver devotional service which is enriched with conjugal love of Rādhā and Kṛṣṇa, coming exactly in the line of revelation of Śrīla Rūpa Gosvāmī.

namas te gaura-vāṇī-śrī-mūrtaye dīna-tāriṇe
rūpānuga-viruddhāpasiddhānta-dhvānta-hāriṇe

I offer my respectful obeisances unto you, who are the personified teachings of Lord Caitanya. You are the deliverer of the fallen souls. You do not tolerate any statement which is against the teachings of devotional service enunciated by Śrīla Rūpa Gosvāmī.

"Absolute is sentient Thou hast proved,
Impersonal calamity Thou hast moved.
This gives us a life Anew and fresh."

(*Śrīla Bhaktivedanta Swami Prabhupāda's ode to Śrīla Bhaktisiddhānta Sarasvatī Ṭhākura Prabhupād*a)

The above verse sums up the mission of Śrīla Bhaktisiddhānta Sarasvatī Ṭhākura Prabhupāda. There is really no adequate words to properly glorify Śrīla Sarasvatī Ṭhākura; but who and what Śrīla Bhaktisiddhānta Prabhupāda was has been generously described to us by his many illustrious disciples from whom we have been privileged to hear either through their writings or directly from their mouths. Śrīla A. C. Bhaktivedanta Swami Prabhupāda, the foremost preacher of Kṛṣṇa consciousness in the Western world, described his first meeting with Śrīla Sarasvatī Ṭhākura Prabhupāda, his spiritual master, and his conclusion: "Here is the right person who has taken up Śrī Caitanya Mahāprabhu's message, and now it will be distributed."

Śrīla Bhaktisiddhānta Prabhupāda was famous as the siṁha-guru, a powerful, lionlike guru, because of his uncompromising preaching of Kṛṣṇa conscious philosophy. He considered it more compassionate to be interested in a person's spiritual welfare than in their material comforts. He said a genuine spiritual master is like a butcher who applies a sharp knife to the neck of the goat. The goat represents our innumerable material desires. The spiritual master stands behind this goat and lifts the sharp knife of spiritual instructions, ready to cut. Śrīla Sarasvatī Ṭhākura Prabhupāda considered a guru who simply flattered his disciples to be his disciples' enemy.

This book is called, *Amṛta Vāṇī*. *Amṛta* has several meanings, the simplest being "nectar." But *amṛta* also means "immortality,""deathlessness." Vāṇī means "message," speech, sound (specifically, Vedic sound), words, or teachings. Thus *amṛta vāṇī* means "the teachings that deliver the nectar of immortality." All living beings hanker for blissful immortality, saddled as they are by the miseries of this world. It is spiritual nectar that produces immortality. Such nectar is not found in this world; it is a product of the spiritual world. In an epic *Purāṇa*, the demigods and demons fought for the nectar produced by churning the milk ocean, but that nectar was not ordinary. Rather, it was the nectar that brings relief from material distress, the nectar that makes one deathless.

It is the bona fide spiritual master who gives such nectar; it is the spiritual master who brings this nectar from the spiritual world. Śrīla Bhaktisiddhānta Sarasvatī Ṭhākura is a bona fide spiritual master and can make us deathless, because he is the personification of Śrī Gaurahari's teachings. He is bhagavān, the personality of servitor Godhead. The Lord's pure devotees and associates are nondifferent from Him; they share the Lord's qualities and are thus addressed as bhagavān, the servitor God. Only through them can the conditioned souls find liberation and enter the Supreme Lord's eternal loving service, the prime and only meaning of every living entity's life.

This book was compiled by Śrī Bhakti Mayukha Bhāgavata Mahārāja, a learned and dear disciple of Śrīla Bhaktisiddhānta Ṭhākura Prabhupāda. It follows the format of Śrī Bhaktivinoda Vāṇī Vaibhava, employing the same question and answer system that was used to compile Śrīla Bhaktivinoda Ṭhākura's teachings. The questions in Śrī Bhaktivinoda Vāṇī Vaibhava were composed by Sri Sundarānanda Vidyāvinoda Prabhu, and the answers were drawn by him from Śrīla Bhaktivinoda Ṭhākura's writings. Similarly, Amṛta Vāṇī is also designed in a question-and-answer format. The questions were composed by Śrī Mayukha Bhāgavata Mahārāja, who then culled the responses directly from Śrīla Bhaktisiddhānta Sarasvatī Prabhupāda's lectures, instructions, essays and other writings. Śrī Mayukha Bhāgavata Mahārāja did not provide either dates or names of the publications from which he drew each answer, but simply assumed that his readers would be familiar enough with Śrīla Sarasvatī Ṭhākura's teachings that such references would be unimportant.

In its original Bengali, this book was published shortly after Śrīla Sarasvatī Ṭhākura's disappearance, and the compiler received the blessings of Śrīla Sarasvatī Ṭhākura's disciples in his work. Thus it appears that the author's intended audience was seasoned and well-read devotees, although it is clear that newcomers would also find the instructions useful and inspiring. Therefore no one is left out from reading this wonderful work.

Amṛta Vāṇī was, in its original, titled Śrīla Prabhupādera Upadesāmṛta, "The nectarean teachings of Śrīla Prabhupāda Bhaktisiddhānta Sarasvatī Ṭhākura." However, the title seemed to confuse a number of devotees, who thought it must be a commentary on Śrīla Rūpa Gosvāmīs famous *Upadesāmṛta*. To avoid such confusion, we have changed the title to *Amṛta Vāṇī*. *Amṛta Vāṇī* and *Upadesāmṛta* are essentially synonymous. We also created chapter headings for the book to make referencing easy, something that was not done in the original Bengali, and we thank Śrīmatī Īśodhyanā devī dāsī for assisting in that work.

It has always being the desire of those at Touchstone Media to increase the number of Gauḍīya Vaiṣṇava teachings available in Western languages, especially in English, and we are happy to know that this book will further that mission. I pray only that this book will increase its readers' enthusiasm and determination as we each strive to advance in Kṛṣṇa consciousness.

Begging for the kind benediction of all the Lord's great devotees, I present this book.

Īśvara dāsa
Completed on Śrī Kṛṣṇa Janmāṣṭhamī, September 2004
Mumbai, India.

108 Essential Advice

1. *Paraṁ vijayate śrī-kṛṣṇa-saṅkīrtanam*: "All glories to the congregational chanting of Kṛṣṇa's holy names."Śrī Mahāprabhu wrote these words in His Śikṣāṣṭakam. They are the ultimate goal of the Gauḍīya *Maṭha*.

2. Śrī Kṛṣṇa is the object of all worship. He is the only enjoyer. All others are enjoyed by Him.

3. Everyone other than the devotees of Hari are fools and killers of the self.

4. It is the duty of each resident of the *Maṭha* to learn tolerance.

5. Instead of maintaining faith in their own strength, the devotees who follow in Śrī Rūpa's footsteps attribute all their qualities to the original source.

6. Those who cultivate mixed religious principles cannot serve the Supreme Lord.

7. All of you should serve Hari together, keeping one goal in mind.

8. A holy place is wherever topics about Lord Hari are being discussed.

9. We do not perform pious or sinful activities, nor are we fools or mental speculators. We are the shoe-carriers of the non-duplicitous devotees of Hari, and are initiated into the mantra, 'kīrtanīya sadā hariḥ: "Always chant the holy names of Hari."

10. Try to rectify yourself rather than blaspheming the nature or activities of others. That is my instruction.

11. Our supreme occupation is to serve the residents of Vraja, who are afflicted by separation from Kṛṣṇa.

12. An exalted devotee or mahābhāgavata knows that all others are his spiritual masters. Therefore, an exalted mahābhāgavata is certainly *jagad-guru*, the spiritual master of the whole world.

13. If we want to attain the ultimate goal of life, we must abandon all varieties of popular opinion and hear the instructions of Vedic literature.

14. Everyone should desire the ultimate goal of life.

15. The Lord's intimate devotees have no desire other than to serve the lotus feet of Śrī Rūpa's followers.

16. There is no way to connect ourselves with the transcendental object except by aural reception.

17. The moment we have no protector, the objects around us will turn into enemies and attack us. Our only protector is *hari-kathā*, spoken by genuine devotees.

18. A person who flatters cannot become a guru or preacher.

19. It is better to live as a bird, animal, ant, or other insect than to cheat. Only a person devoid of the propensity to cheat attains auspiciousness.

20. Vaiṣṇavism is another name for simplicity. The servants of swan-like Vaiṣṇavas are simple-hearted. That is why they are the best of brāhmaṇas.

21. It is the first duty of the most compassionate souls to divert the wretched taste of the living entities. It is more beneficial to save even one soul from Mahāmāyās prison house than to open millions of hospitals.

22. The association of those who have not developed their propensity to serve the Supreme Lord is never desirable, even if it appears most pleasing.

23. Preaching, without practicing what one preaches, is a limb of karma.

24. Our attachment for material life will decrease when we simply serve the Supreme Lord and His devotees.

25. Our main disease is to accumulate objects not related to Kṛṣṇa.

26. We have not come to this material world to become carpenters or mechanics; we are simply the messengers of Mahāprabhu's teachings.

27. We will not live in this world long; our human birth will become successful if we give up our lives while chanting Hari's glories.

28. The dust from the lotus feet of Śrī Rūpa, who fulfilled the desire of Śrī Caitanyadeva, is our most desirable goal of life.

29. This material world, which is averse to the Supreme Lord, is a painful testing place. Tolerance, humility, and praising others all help us worship Lord Hari in this world.

30. We are given a father and mother in every lifetime, but we may not receive beneficial instruction in each lifetime.

31. Externally, a devotee's activities and the mischief of a pseudo-devotee may appear the same, but they are different—as different as the sky and earth, as different as milk from limestone mixed with water.

32. Those who mistakenly consider nondevotional propensities devotional will certainly get into trouble. It's like mistakenly cheating a blacksmith of steel—the end product will not be reliable.

33. As soon as we learn about the truth, we should become fixed in it. We should not waste even a moment of the time we have left in our lives on sense gratification. Rather, we should use all our time to worship Hari.

34. Many people wrongly accept imitation (anukāra) as following (anusara). They are two separate things. To dress like Nārada in a play is imitation, but to practice the devotional path Śrī Nārada displayed, is following.

35. Only those who are constantly engaged in glorifying the topics of Hari are *sādhus*. Only those who are always busy in the Supreme Lord's service are *sādhus*. Only those who aim all their endeavors at pleasing Kṛṣṇa are *sādhus*. Only those who have no business other than to serve Kṛṣṇa are *sādhus*.

36. If Nārāyaṇa personally gives Himself away, He will still have something left to give. However, the Lord's devotees can give Nārāyaṇa away completely.

37. Do not become a spiritual master in order to become envious of others. Do not become a spiritual master to remain absorbed in sense gratification. If instead you can become a nonduplicitous servant of Kṛṣṇa and attain His mercy, you have nothing to fear.

38. Unless and until we accept the spiritual master as a manifestation of the Supreme Lord—as nondifferent from Him—we will not be able to chant the holy names.

39. To teach us how to serve Him, the Supreme Lord incarnated as the spiritual master.

40. The living entities will never benefit by studying hundreds of books or by acting whimsically.

41. In the present age, it is common to be cheated by those who misguide others in the name of religion.

42. The confidential purport of the undisputed truth that is spoken boldly will be realized only after hundreds of lifetimes or even hundreds of yugas. Unless we spend hundreds of gallons of hard-earned blood, it will not be possible to make others understand the truth.

43. The Supreme Lord does not accept items offered by those who do not chant one hundred thousand holy names a day.

44. Association is the main stimulus for developing the desire to worship Hari. If we associate with nondevotees, we will make material advancement; if we associate with devotees, our propensity to worship Hari will be progressively enhanced. Association with devotees is the most important asset of the human form of life. Please do not become averse to it.

45. As soon as we feel the inconvenience of mundane life, the Lord becomes our shelter and awards us the qualification to engage in His service.

46. As long as we are filled with *anarthas* we will not become fortunate enough to attain the service of Śrī Rādhās lotus feet. Those who are unqualified by their *anarthas* but who eagerly discuss the transcendental pastimes of the supremely worshipable Śrī Rādhā are certainly sense enjoyers, covered materialists, or prākṛta-sahajiyās.

47. When all *anarthas* are removed while chanting the holy names, then the form, qualities, and pastimes of the Lord automatically manifest. There is no need to endeavor artificially to remember the Lord's forms, qualities, and pastimes.

48. All of you should preach the teachings of Śrī Rūpa and Raghunātha with great enthusiasm. Our most desirable goal is to become a particle of dust at the lotus feet of the followers of Śrī Rūpa.

49. Do not give up the worship of Hari, even if you have to face hundreds of dangers, criticisms, or harassments. Do not become discouraged by seeing that most of the world's people do not accept the truth. Neither give up your worship of Hari nor your speaking of kṛṣṇa-kathā, your life and soul. Always chant Hari's names while thinking yourself lower than a straw in the street and being more tolerant than a tree.

50. We are not interested in becoming excellent workers or devoted to religious practices. Our only goal is to become a particle of dust at the lotus feet of Śrī Rūpa birth after birth.

51. May we never become indifferent to performing the sacrifice of śrī-kṛṣṇa-*saṅkīrtana* . Simply remaining progressively and unswervingly attached to this sacrifice will bring us all perfection. All of you should boldly preach the teachings of Śrī Rūpa-Raghunātha with great enthusiasm under their guidance.

52. If I give up preaching the truth, fearing that speaking the plain truth will make me unpopular, it means I have given up the authorized Vedic path and accepted the unauthorized, non-Vedic path. I will have become godless. It means I have no faith in God.

53. The Supreme Lord has two representations in this material world: transcendental sound vibration (the holy name), and the Deity form, who enjoys eternal spiritual pastimes.

54. We serve the Lord's Deity form by chanting the Lord's holy names. Consciousness is served only by consciousness.

55. The Lord's devotees call Him by chanting His holy names for His pleasure.

56. The Deity, who performs transcendental pastimes in Vaikuṇṭha, is the merciful incarnation of the Lord's eternal, original form in this world. The Deity is the direct manifestation of the Supreme Personality of God-

head. The Vaiṣṇavas are not idol worshipers who imagine that God has either a material form or no form at all.

57. Just as the Brahma-sūtra briefly gives the purport of the Vedas, Bhaktivinoda Ṭhākura's Tattva-sūtra properly and briefly describes the purport and conclusion of *Śrīmad-Bhāgavatam*, the commentary on Brahma-sūtra.

58. Unless we study *Śrīmad-Bhāgavatam* under a Vaiṣṇava *ācārya* who himself follows the rules and regulations, we will never understand the purport of Brahma-sūtra. *Śrīmad-Bhāgavatam* is the natural commentary on Brahma-sūtra.

59. Śrī Jīva Gosvāmī has specifically revealed that *Śrīmad-Bhāgavatam* is the original commentary on Vedānta-sutra. Śaṅkarācārya's commentary is foreign to the Vedānta-sūtra. Since the author of Vedānta-sūtra wrote *Śrīmad-Bhāgavatam* to serve as its commentary, *Śrīmad-Bhāgavatam* is the commentary. We can find the actual purport of Vedānta-sūtra only in *Śrīmad-Bhāgavatam.*

60. The word *bhakti* cannot be applied to anyone other than Kṛṣṇa. Kṛṣṇa is the only object of devotional service. Brahman is the object of impersonal knowledge, Paramātma of yoga, but Kṛṣṇa the supreme object of service.

61. Every word has two types of meanings: meaning derived from an enlightened viewpoint, and meaning derived from an unenlightened viewpoint. The abstract meaning of a word that is distinct from Kṛṣṇa, Viṣṇu, or Śrī Caitanyadeva, and which indicates something else, is called the unenlightened meaning. The meaning of words derived from the enlightened viewpoint all indicate Kṛṣṇa and Kṛṣṇa consciousness.

62. The actual person behind the word "Kṛṣṇa" is not the person the multitude of blind followers understand by words like "God", "Allah", or even "Īśvara" or "Paramātmā." These words are used in various languages to indicate the separate sources of effulgence connected with Kṛṣṇa. Such persons cannot grasp the complete understanding of the word "Kṛṣṇa."

63. There is no work as beneficial as serving the spiritual master. Among all kinds of worship, worship of the Supreme Lord is topmost. Service to the spiritual master is superior to service to the Supreme Lord. Unless this conviction is firmly rooted in our hearts, we cannot take advantage of our spiritual master's association. He is our maintainer and we are his servants.

64. By taking shelter at the lotus feet of the spiritual master, we can become free from illusion, lamentation, and dependence on others. If we aspire to receive our spiritual master's openhearted blessings, then the spiritual master will award us with auspiciousness.

65. Ordinary spiritual masters cannot save us from death or give us new life. This is why their position as spiritual master is partial. But one

who has saved us from the cycle of birth and death and helped us realize the eternal truth is the complete and eternal spiritual master.

66. Do not consider the spiritual master an ordinary mortal being. He gives us unlimited life. He is the expert physician to cure our material disease and is our sole benefactor.

67. As long as a person follows the path of argument he cannot attain the shelter of a spiritual master.

68. If I surrender myself one hundred percent at the lotus feet of that person upon whom the most auspicious Supreme Lord has bestowed all auspiciousness, then he, the spiritual master, awards all auspiciousness to me. If I am deceitful and live a double standard, however, making a show of performing devotional service, then he will also deceive me.

69. It is my duty to completely follow my spiritual master's instructions, and to live according to the arrangements he has sincerely made for me. This is the symptom of a surrendered soul.

70. If we are so fortunate as to associate with the Lord's devotees, then all credit goes to the Lord, because He is the one who has provided the opportunity. The Lord makes us realize fearlessness through the spiritual master's association. The Lord arranges that a suitable spiritual master will appear before us according to our degree of surrender. Those who are truly fortunate will avail themselves of his presence.

71. Gurus who pursue impersonal knowledge, perform fruitive activities, practice mystic yoga, observe severe vows, undergo austerities, are expert in the art of magic, and who cheat, are not fit to be called guru, or "heavy." They are all laghu, light. They are not the jīvas' benefactors, but are envious of themselves and others. Only mahābhāgavata Vaiṣṇava gurus are causelessly merciful to the living entities and feel distressed upon seeing the distress of others.

72. The state of Brahman the impersonalists imagine is not actually Brahman. The conception the yogīs maintain of becoming one with Paramātmā or Bhagavān is more offensive than the idea of merging into the Brahman effulgence. The liberation attained by merging into the Brahman effulgence denies the living entity his own existence, but those who want to become one with the Lord expect to maintain their personal existence while toppling the Supreme Lord's position. Mahāprabhu has said that becoming one with the Supreme is more abominable than merging into the Brahman.

73. Those nondevotees who try to reconcile matter with spirit consider good and bad association, rice paddy and weeds, and devotional and nondevotional services equal. Otherwise, the synthesis of matter and spirit does not certainly become the perversion of impersonalism. For a Vaiṣṇava, it may become pure devotion. The synthesis of matter and spirit certainly becomes the perversion of impersonalism in their hands. The imper-

sonalists say they accept everything, but they do not accept the Supreme Lord nor His eternal names, forms, qualities, pastimes, or associates.

74. The Lord's various incarnations—Rāma, Nṛsiṁha, Varāha, Matsya, Kūrma, etc.—are all transcendental Viṣṇu-tattva forms. Their names, forms, qualities, associates, and pastimes are eternal. Each of them controls Maya. Each has an eternal abode in Vaikuṇṭha. Out of compassion for the living entities in this miserable world, and by Their own sweet will, these incarnations appear and exhibit Their opulence. Yet even though They incarnate in the material world, They remain fully transcendental and always protect Their independent natures.

75. The most auspicious activity for humankind is to become delivered from the clutches of material existence and to enter into Kṛṣṇa's eternal family. Taking shelter of the spiritual master can free us from Maya. There is no other way to achieve this freedom.

76. Devotional service to the Supreme Lord is our supreme occupational duty, but material sense enjoyers cannot understand what devotional service is.

77. Śrī Bhaktivinoda Ṭhākura considers the attainment of devotional service most desirable. The previous *ācāryas* have concluded that devotional service is the supermost goal of life. Śrī Bhaktivinoda Ṭhākura, Śrī Rūpa's follower, has revealed to the world that the attainment of devotional service is to be cherished.

78. The highest form of meditation is glorification of Hari. Meditation was prescribed for those desiring perfection during Satya-yuga, but Satya-yuga did not provide *darśana* of the most magnanimous Śrī Gaurasundara. Since Śrī Gaurasundara appears in Kali-yuga, the great meditation of glorifying Hari has been recommended for this age. Because discrepancies entered the meditation process in Satya-yuga, in Tretā-yuga, sacrifice was introduced as the chief means of perfection. Because discrepancies entered the sacrificial practices of Tretā-yuga, Deity worship was introduced as most important in Dvāpara-yuga. Because of the inevitable discrepancies that would enter the practices of Deity worship, the great worship of chanting the Lord's holy names has been recommended for Kali-yuga. Just as a dying patient is administered a potent but poisonous pill at the last moment, when he has been disappointed by all other treatments and has no other hope, so the chanting of the Lord's holy names has been recommended by those who have seen the pathetic condition of those living in Kali-yuga. The Lord has invested all His potencies in His holy name. Chanting is therefore the supreme meditation, sacrifice, and form of worship.

79. We should live only to be counted among the followers of he, the spiritual master, whose mercy has allowed us to understand the ultimate

goal of life, to attain love of God. Otherwise, it is better to die thousands of times.

80. One can never become eligible to serve Govinda by neglecting the service of he, who is Śrī Nandanandana's life and soul, or by neglecting the service of that person's servants.

81. Śrī Kṛṣṇa's holy name is eternal and full of knowledge and bliss. Therefore, we will not try to mix material contamination with Kṛṣṇa's holy names. Kṛṣṇa's holy names will continue to spread their supreme influence over all other sources of knowledge.

82. Śrī Kṛṣṇa Caitanya has repeatedly reminded the living entities that they have to become free from the clutches of material conceptions and go to the supreme abode of the reservoir of all pleasure by fully engaging in His transcendental loving service in a pure and self-realized state. They should remember that they do not have to carry the imagination and thought-flow of this world to the spiritual world.

83. Skeptics, atheists, materialists, and impersonalists all ultimately desire to merge into one godlessness.

84. Viṣṇu's steady worshipers, who are initiated into Viṣṇu mantras, know that they are spirit souls, Kṛṣṇa's eternal servants. They also know that all living entities are meant for Kṛṣṇa's enjoyment and that all objects are simply ingredients for His service. They are neither interested in material advancement like the *karmīs* nor interested in building Rāvaṇa's staircase to heaven like the impersonal monists.

85. The Lord's devotees do not become carried away by the current of materialistic thought. Because they are not greedy for money, women, or material fame, they remain equipoised when they are both praised and blasphemed. They do not indulge in faultfinding. Rather, they remain busy glorifying Kṛṣṇa in the mood of separation and remain indifferent to worldly etiquette, Vedic injunctions, social oppression, chastisement, hatred, and embarrassment.

86. The living entities have no other business than to always chant Kṛṣṇa's glories. The congregational chanting inaugurated by Śrī Kṛṣṇa Caitanya is meant simply to engage us in chanting Kṛṣṇa's holy names, realizing Śrī Kṛṣṇa's true nature, realizing the true nature of the holy name, and in understanding our constitutional position. As long as we have even a tinge of physical or mental awareness, we cannot perform Śrī-kṛṣṇa-*saṅkīrtana* . By the mercy of guru and the Vaiṣṇavas, we learn of our relationship with the Supreme Lord. The more we forget the relationship we have with body and mind, the more the Lord's holy name manifests in our heart. From our heart, the holy name will travel to the tip of the tongue and dance constantly in the form of sound vibration.

87. The holy name is by nature eternal and full of knowledge and bliss. By the holy name's mercy, a living entity revives his spiritual con-

sciousness. Śrī Kṛṣṇa, who is the reservoir of all transcendental pleasure, manifests in a heart filled with simplicity, before eyes that have been fully spiritualized, on a tongue inclined to His service, and in an ear inclined to hear kṛṣṇa-kathā. The holy name manifests in those senses that are engaged only in pleasing His senses.

88. Those who chant the holy names of the Lord should follow the following eight rules:

(a) They should keep firm faith in the words of guru and *Śāstra.*

(b) They should associate with devotees who are engaged in chanting the holy names.

(c) They should perform *bhajana* by hearing and chanting the kṛṣṇa-kathā spoken by saintly persons.

(d) Following the above rules will result in anartha-nivṛtti. In the kingdom of *sādhana*, a practitioner must follow these four basic processes of *bhajana.*

(e) Those who chant the holy names must have undivided attention when they chant.

(f) They should chant the holy names according to the taste of their personal relationship with the Lord.

(g) They should be attached to chanting the holy names.

(h) In this way, they will attain *bhāva-bhakti*, the preliminary stage of love of God, which is also called permanent *rati.*

89. Complete, uninterrupted liberation means love of God. Service to Nanda Mahārāja's son, who is one without a second, is love of God. There is no question of any inauspiciousness in this service.

90. The materialistic philosophy, whether appearing in India or in a foreign country, is certainly a failure, because it is out of touch with reality.

91. *Bhagavad-gītā* consists of eighteen chapters and seven hundred verses. *Śrīmad-Bhāgavatam* consists of eighteen thousand verses and is the natural commentary on the *Bādarāyaṇa-sūtras*. In the case of the *Bhāgavatam*, the compiler of the sūtras is also their commentator.

92. If living entities do not worship Hari, they will become *jñānīs*, *karmīs*, or materialists. That is why we should always invoke the Lord by chanting the mahā-mantra.

93. Just because mundane thoughts appear in the mind while we chant the holy name does not mean we should slacken our chanting. The useless thoughts will gradually disappear as the irrevocable fruits of chanting the holy names. Do not be in a hurry.

94. The distance between our self and our gross and subtle bodies gradually diminishes when we chant the holy name and we soon revive awareness of our original constitutional position. When we are thus

self-realized, the Lord's pure holy name will manifest in our heart and we will directly see Śrī Kṛṣṇa's transcendental form.

95. If we desire to chant Hari's name offenselessly, then we should chant constantly. Constant chanting will vanquish our offenses.

96. Serving the Lord's devotee is more profitable than serving the Absolute Truth. We will greatly benefit from serving the spiritual master and the Vaiṣṇavas. Fallen souls are delivered by engaging in such service.

97. Our only bridge is to follow in the mahājanas' footsteps.

98. Making a show of possessing transcendental knowledge by accepting initiation and actually achieving transcendental knowledge are not the same thing.

99. Only those who serve the Supreme Lord are glorious. In the midst of all difficulties, hear, chant, and remember the Supreme Lord.

100. A person who thinks even once, "O Kṛṣṇa, I will serve You. You are my only shelter," attains auspiciousness.

101. The Vaiṣṇavas and non-Vaiṣṇavas are not equal, just as rice and dāl do not in themselves equal mahāprasāda. Neither are Lord Govinda and the ordinary living entities equal. Similarly, the Lord's holy names and ordinary names are not equal.

102. We are cheated until we realize that our only duty is to serve Lord Kṛṣṇa and His devotees.

103. Only one who takes shelter of Kṛṣṇa's lotus feet attains liberation from the clutches of Maya. Living entities have no business other than to worship Kṛṣṇa. There is no other object of worship than His holy name.

104. The thirteen doctrines preached vigorously in Kali-yuga are unfavorable to the topmost, conclusive philosophy taught by Śrī Gaurasundara, the Lord of the fourteen worlds, which express *sambandha*, *abhidheya*, and *prayojana*. The thirteen useless doctrines are as follows:

(a) The theory of godless, materialistic Cārvāka, which is opposed to the Vedas.

(b) The godless argumentative theory of Buddhism, which encourages temporary worship of material qualities.

(c) The argumentative theory of Jainism, which encourages the worship of material qualities.

(d) The theory of argumentative atheistic Sāṅkhya practiced by the followers of atheist Kapila.

(e) The theory practiced by Patañjali's argumentative followers.

(f) Śaṅkarācārya's monistic theory, which tries to reconcile spirit and matter and which is apparently in agreement with the Vedas.

(g) The theory of reconciliation that appears to agree with the Vedas but that encourages the worship of material qualities.

(h) The logicians' theory that encourages the worship of material qualities and that denies transcendental sound vibration (*Śabda-brahma*) as evidence.

(i) The theory of variegatedness, which encourages the worship of material qualities and denies transcendental sound vibration as evidence.

(j) The theory of the grammaticians, which encourages the worship of material qualities and pretends to agree with the Vedas.

(k) The theory of Śaivites that encourages the worship of material qualities, rejects the path of argument, and teaches that the living entities are liberated even while living in this world.

(l) The theory of direct perception, which encourages the worship of material qualities and is contaminated by material enjoyment.

(m) Another theory of Śaivites that encourages the worship of material qualities, believes that God can be achieved through karma, and that is contaminated by material enjoyment.

105. Love of Kṛṣṇa is the most cherished object among all dear objects. In order to attain it, we need the help of our service-inclined senses—the senses greedy for hearing and chanting.

106. Lord Kṛṣṇa and His name are not two separate objects. Even though they are realized or accepted differently, Kṛṣṇa's forms, qualities, pastimes, and associates are nondifferent from His holy name.

107. Utilize everything for Kṛṣṇa's service. Beware! Do not take shelter of wealth, women, fame, or duplicity in the name of serving Hari. Such endeavors show nothing but aversion to Hari. The liberated souls who are inclined to serve Hari serve Him as their life and soul. Those whose every endeavor is aimed at pleasing Kṛṣṇa are liberated.

108. A Vaiṣṇava has no possessions. Nothing can tempt his mind. There is nothing extraordinary in this world or the next, worth coveting for him; he desires only to see the beauty of the toenails of Kṛṣṇa's lotus feet. Whenever we are not attracted to serving the Lord, we should understand that we have been attacked and captured by Maya's illusory energy.

Association

1. What is a devotee's business?

It is a devotee's business to remain in touch with the Absolute Truth twenty-four hours a day. If we associate with a living source, a Vaiṣṇava, and hear hari-kathā from him, we will certainly develop faith in the Supreme Lord and awaken our propensity to serve Him. If we wish to become devotees, we must associate with Vaiṣṇavas. Associating with and fully surrendering to Vaiṣṇavas removes our impediments. The Vaiṣṇava's duty is to make his companions and dependents fearless, free from anxiety, happy, and to deliver all conditioned souls from Maya's hands. It is a Vaiṣṇava's business to induce all materialistic living entities to become inclined toward the Supreme Lord. This is real compassion. Our spiritual success is guaranteed if we are honest in our dealings with Vaiṣṇavas, hear attentively from them, and lead our lives according to their instructions. Only then can we be said to be taking advantage of their association.

2. Is it important to always associate only with devotees?

We should always remain in Vaiṣṇava association. We are so weak that we cannot survive without Vaiṣṇava association. If we remove ourselves from that association, we will again develop the sinful mentality that we are masters. If we do not always follow the orders of guru and the Vaiṣṇavas, we will find ourselves in great danger. As soon as we remove ourselves from their shelter, Maya will capture us. Then we will again wander through the universe as Maya's servants.

3. Whose association should we desire?

He who says, "Worship the Supreme Lord," is certainly a spiritual master. Only devotees are honest and saintly; others are not. The thoughts of *karmīs*, *jñānīs*, and yogis are born from their aversion toward the Lord. We should reject their association and associate only with Vaiṣṇavas. Only then will we find benefit.

4. How can we achieve Lord Hari?

We should seek to associate only with Kṛṣṇa's devotees. Kṛṣṇa's devotees are auspicious, eternal, and compassionate. Bad association—association without Kṛṣṇa consciousness—is harmful. Thus, we should not respect anything unrelated to Kṛṣṇa's devotional service.

I am astonished to see that despite hearing so much *hari-kathā* you still admire material life and attachment. This is unfortunate. We cannot attain Kṛṣṇa by bad association. Remember, we achieve Lord Hari by associating with devotees and renouncing the association of materialists.

If we can see all material objects in relation to Kṛṣṇa, then they cannot harm us. The world is full of ingredients for the Lord's service. If, however, we consider the Lord's paraphernalia as intended for our own enjoyment, our material attachment will increase and we will have to suffer material existence.

5. Should we renounce the association of those greedy for money?

Wealth is the source of all *anarthas*. It is best if wealth is used in Kṛṣṇa's service. Otherwise, it will ruin our lives and bind us to material existence. Pious devotees should never be greedy for temporary wealth. We should hanker only after eternal wealth, spiritual life. May persons who desire auspiciousness be free of attachment to wealth, because as long as we are materially attached, we will not be able to develop attachment for spiritual life. Our lives will be useless. Please bless me so that for the rest of my life, I will not have to see the faces of materialists greedy for wealth.

6. Is it good to serve the Supreme Lord in the company of other devotees?

We should serve the Supreme Lord together under the spiritual master's guidance. It is our duty to engage in the Lord's service, in the association of those Vaiṣṇavas, who are fully devoted to their spiritual master. We should be friends with such devotees and constantly remain engaged in giving pleasure to the spiritual master and the Supreme Lord. The living entities try to gratify their senses, forgetting Kṛṣṇa's service, and thus suffer material misery, but it is our duty to always remain inclined toward the Lord's service while surrendering fully at His lotus feet.

7. How can we attain Vaiṣṇava association?

If we attentively hear *hari-kathā* from devotees, we are associating with them properly. When we associate with devotees properly, we will realize both the Lord's greatness and the insignificance of this world. Then while engaging in the Lord's service under the devotees' order, we will strengthen our faith, attachment, and love for the Lord's service. To engage in Śrī Kṛṣṇa's loving devotional service is the ultimate goal of all living entities.

8. How should we live?

People will always discuss worldly topics, and we should remain inattentive to such discussions. If we have a strong desire to advance on the spiritual path, no number of obstacles can check us. Show respect to materialists, but do not adopt their behavior. Rather, mentally reject them. Discuss literature like Śaraṇāgati, Prārthanā, and Prema-*bhakti*-cāndrikā. It is certainly good to associate with scripture. Later on, we will require association with saintly persons to learn the art of worshiping the Lord.

9. Is association with devotees the most essential element of our Kṛṣṇa consciousness?

It is extremely essential to associate with the spiritual master and with Vaiṣṇavas who are fully surrendered to the spiritual master. Unless we associate with Vaiṣṇavas, how will unqualified people like ourselves learn the proper code of conduct and come to serve guru? We always need ideal examples. If we don't associate with Vaiṣṇavas who are fixed at the spiritual master's lotus feet, attached to chanting the holy name, and fixed in the Lord's service, we cannot ourselves become fixed at guru's feet. We cannot learn to consider the spiritual master our well-wisher. We cannot understand that the spiritual master is as good as God. We cannot develop the tendency to serve the spiritual master. If genuine devotees who are fixed at the guru's feet teach us neither how to serve the spiritual master nor how to behave when we are with him, then even after receiving a bona fide spiritual master we may lose him. We would be losing a coveted jewel if we were bereft of his service.

10. Isn't it possible to serve the Supreme Lord on our own?

How can we serve the Lord whimsically or without the support of those whom the Lord has appointed as His servants? Those who desire religiosity, economic development, sense gratification, or liberation are not the Lord's servants. Moreover, those who make a show of serving the Lord and are eager to have the worshipable Lord supply their sense gratification are not His servants either. How is it possible to serve the Lord in the association of such people?

Ordinary conditioned souls can never fix the mind or discuss *hari-kathā* or the Lord's instructions because they are attached to matter. A materialist is always busy with worldly matters. That is why the Śāstras have forbidden us to associate with them. It is our duty to remain in touch with the Absolute Truth twenty-four hours a day. Vaiṣṇava association awakens our propensity to serve the Lord. A devotee is a person who when approached can destroy all our inconveniences with the weapon of his instructions. He can cut to pieces our attachment to material existence and mental speculation.

How do we associate with Vaiṣṇavas? By our ears. Any hearing other than hearing from devotees is bad association. However, hearing from devotees is useless if we do not surrender ourselves completely but remain puffed up with false ego.

11. Is it necessary to live with devotees to get their association?

Certainly association with devotees is essential. However, we attain association according to our own qualification. It is not a fact that simply by living together we can take advantage of good association, and it is true that we can associate with devotees even when we live at a distance from them. Association does not necessarily mean living in the same room. However, living with devotees makes it easier to hear from them, whereas such hearing is more difficult over a distance.

We conduct festivals in the temple to give everyone the opportunity to associate with devotees, to destroy their attachment for material life, to display compassion for all living entities, to develop a taste for chanting the holy name, and to engage in the service of Hari, guru, and the Vaiṣṇavas. The *Maṭha*'s main purpose in holding festivals, reciting *Śrīmad-Bhāgavatam*, and discussing *hari-kathā* is to awaken the soul's constitutional propensity to serve Kṛṣṇa. If we hear *hari-kathā* in the association of devotees, we revive awareness of our constitutional position and attain the ultimate goal of life.

A devotee is saintly. He is neither a material enjoyer nor a dry renunciant. By associating with saintly devotees, we can understand that just as material enjoyment is sinful, the path of dry renunciation is also sinful. Confused about what to do, the pseudo-renunciants adopt the path of renunciation. Being attached or simply detached from the material world are both signs of aversion to the Supreme Lord. Unless we give up these forms of aversion—material enjoyment and dry renunciation—we cannot attain complete shelter in devotional service. If we fail to understand the meaning of pure devotional service, we will end up either as material enjoyers or dry renunciants.

12. How should we live at home?

Proper association with exalted, swanlike personalities destroys our qualification for falling into the dark well of material life. If we associate with liberated souls, we will be qualified to become spiritual householders. Those who do not associate with bhāgavatas to discuss the Bhāgavata, knowing the two to be nondifferent, will never find fortune in household life.

It is good for devotees to live at home, because it allows them to peacefully worship Lord Hari. Such peace, however, is not available to those who are too attached to household life, who are gross materialists. It is important to enter family life resolved to serve Kṛṣṇa. This resolution is far superior to practicing false, monkey renunciation. False renunciation will not help one attain the ultimate goal of life.

One should enter family life only if it is favorable for the execution of devotional service to Hari. If family life is unfavorable, it is a dark well and should be rejected. If one becomes detached from family life just to display his expertise in false renunciation, he will not benefit. Immature renunciants soon fall down.

Association with the Lord's devotees destroys materialism. Those who enter family life only to satisfy worldly morality will become absorbed in materialism. Just as the Lord's devotee must accept the renounced order, he is also required to enter household life. Family life is favorable for devotees, because when a devotee enters family life, he enters a temple. For a devotee, there is no difference between entering household life and entering renounced life. However, household life is unfavorable for nondevotees. There is a huge difference between attached materialists entering household life and the household life of a devotee.

Because a devotee enters family life only to favorably cultivate Kṛṣṇa consciousness, he should remain aloof from bad association and idle talk. He should faithfully execute the limbs of *bhakti*—his hearing and chanting—with enthusiasm, confidence, and patience. A householder devotee must serve Hari, guru, and the Vaiṣṇavas, chant the Lord's holy name, associate with devotees, and hear *hari-kathā*. If all his endeavors are aimed at satisfying Kṛṣṇa, he will attain good fortune.

13. Is it proper to become a materialist?

We are servants of the Supreme Lord. Why should we become materialists? Material enjoyment brings distress. Sense objects, which we perceive through form, taste, smell, touch, and sound perpetually trouble us. We should not become material enjoyers. Śrī Gaurāṅgadeva said that one who wants to worship the Lord should never even see a materialist.

If we surround ourselves with sense gratification, we will forget the Lord and tend to consider His devotees insignificant. A person who is traveling on the devotional path should not see a materialist's face. Not only should he not see a materialist, he should not see even an associate of a materialist. As the physician for our material disease, Śrī Gaurasundara, advised, "Do not associate with materialists, do not associate with materialists, do not associate with the materialists."

14. Should one give up bad association?

Not everyone is fortunate enough to understand a Vaiṣṇava's activities and behavior. It is good for me if, due to ignorance, someone looks upon me with a crooked glance. My only distress is that some people go to hell along with their ancestors by becoming envious of my eternally worshipable spiritual master and the Vaiṣṇavas.

It is the duty of intelligent persons to perfect their human life. These persons should know that it is dangerous to associate with pseudo-devotees. Those who accept the path of material enjoyment or dry renunciation are walking, not toward devotional service, but in the opposite direction.

There are thirteen unauthorized sampradāyas, such as the āul, bāul, etc. Their association is bad. If one considers such abominable association along with association with hypocrites and women, good, then he will inevitably become degraded. Please do not associate with such misguided people. Associating with nondevotees ensures one's degradation.

Material enjoyers or people who are fond of material enjoyment are uninitiated and devoid of transcendental knowledge. They are pseudo-devotees or nondevotees. Please stop associating with such nondevotees and make progress in spiritual life in the association of devotees and the *śāstras*.

15. Should we reject association with attached householders?

We never desire to associate with those who want to prosper in family life. We should develop a strong desire to serve those who are attached to worshiping Hari and who are situated in family life with Kṛṣṇa in the center. It is our duty to give up bad association and take shelter of saints. Those who mistake nondevotees for devotees will certainly find themselves in difficulty.

16. How do we worship Hari constantly?

By always remaining in the association of the living source—those who are constantly engaged in worshiping Hari—we will, by the mercy of those great souls, automatically receive the good fortune to engage constantly in Lord Hari's service. Therefore the *śāstras* state, nijābhīṣṭa kṛṣṇa-preṣṭha pācheta' lāgiyā, nirantara sevā kare antarmanā hañā: "Actually the inhabitants of Vṛndāvana are very dear to Kṛṣṇa. If one wants to engage in spontaneous loving service, he must follow the inhabitants of Vṛndāvana and constantly engage in devotional service within his mind." (*Śrī Caitanya-caritāmṛta* Madhya 22.159)

Śrī Bhaktivinoda Ṭhākura has also sung:

kṛṣṇa se tomāra, kṛṣṇa dite pāra,
tomāra śakati āche
āmi to' kāṅgāla, 'kṛṣṇa' 'kṛṣṇa' bali',
dhāi tava pāche pāche

"Kṛṣṇa belongs to you. Therefore you are able to give Him to others. This is certainly within your power. I am indeed wretched and fallen, simply running behind you crying, 'Kṛṣṇa! Kṛṣṇa!'"

17. Whose association should we desire?

Our spiritual master has declared that karma and *jñāna* are the religion of cheaters. We should give up those paths and follow the path of devotional service. To do so, we should associate with those who traverse the path of devotion. It is essential to associate with devotees superior to us. Our most cherished object is the dust of Śrī Rūpa Gosvāmīs lotus feet. Śrī Rūpa established Lord Caitanya's mission in this world.

Our devotional service will be enhanced in the association of devotees. Karmīs, *jñānīs*, and yogis are nondevotees. Hence they cheat themselves and others. Their association should be rejected. All association apart from devotee association is inauspicious.

18. How can we achieve mental strength?

We are weak and need to become mentally strong. Our mental condition will become stronger if we faithfully hear kṛṣṇa-kathā from living devotees. It is not possible to strengthen our mental state without associating with devotees.

19. How can we realize the self?

I can realize myself and regain my spiritual form simply by the mercy of my spiritual master, who is an intimate devotee of Kṛṣṇa. We must always associate with devotees, because simply by associating with them we can receive information about our spiritual form, our constitutional position. Once we have received this information, we will no longer consider the material body the self and our sense desires will be destroyed. Constitutionally, we are the Supreme Lord's eternal servants. This conception will be awakened in us if we engage in the Lord's service in the association of devotees. Then we will not be tempted by material enjoyment, which is the propensity of a conditioned soul.

20. Why are we unable to serve Kṛṣṇa?

It is impossible to serve Kṛṣṇa without receiving the mercy of great souls. This is why it is so important to take shelter at the lotus feet of a bona fide spiritual master. The *Śrī Caitanya-caritāmṛta* states, *mahat-kṛpā vinā kona karme 'bhakti' naya, kṛṣṇa-bhakti dūre rahu, saṁsāra nahe kṣaya*: "Unless one is favored by a pure devotee, one cannot attain the platform of devotional service. To say nothing of *kṛṣṇa-bhakti*, one cannot even be relieved from the bondage of material existence." (Madhya 22.51)

If one associates with those devotees who continually serve Kṛṣṇa, then his propensity to serve Kṛṣṇa will also be awakened. Without the association of Kṛṣṇa's devotees, one cannot develop his own desire to engage in the Lord's service. Service to Hari is not a joke. It is dependent on the association and mercy of devotees. Simply by following in the devotees' footsteps, one receives the good fortune to engage in the Lord's service.

21. How should we think of ourselves in relation to Kṛṣṇa?

Unless one thinks himself a servant, he cannot serve. Devotional service requires a relationship between servant and master. We are trying to become masters rather than servants in this world. How then can we serve? Only a servant can serve.

"I will hear, see, chant, and remember with a spirit of enjoyment": this is the *karmīs* conception, the conception of a nondevotee. If one wishes to progress, he has to renounce this formidable mental conception and learn to remain fixed as the Lord's servant. He should serve twenty-four hours a day subordinate to a devotee and in that devotee's association. Then only will he attain pure devotional service and the ultimate goal of life. If one learns to give up independence and become completely dependent on the spiritual master and Gaurāṅga, then his troubles will vanish and he will become happily engaged in the Lord's service under his guru's guidance. If he develops a relationship with Kṛṣṇa like the relationship between wife and husband, father and son, friend and friend, or servant and master, he will certainly find fortune and Hari's eternal service. It is not possible to render service if one does not have a relationship with the one whom he is serving.

One's relationship with the Lord is revived when one engages in Kṛṣṇa's service. Even people in this world render service through one of the four relationships. This is because without knowledge of their relationship with the Lord, they developed various temporary relationships. But each of us is the eternal slave of guru and Kṛṣṇa. We are sold-out animals at the feet of our spiritual master and Kṛṣṇa. Because we have forgotten this simple truth, we have fallen into our present miserable condition. If by the devotees' mercy we can come to remember this truth, we will be saved and will make advancement on the devotional path.

22. Of what should we be careful?

Everything in this world belongs to Kṛṣṇa. If one uses anything for his own enjoyment, he will have to face the consequences. Those who are averse to hearing kṛṣṇa-kathā will become materially attached and bound to this world. Therefore, pious persons who desire their eternal benefit should take utmost care to hear kṛṣṇa-kathā from real devotees.

"I serve the Lord so much,""I have already served the Lord," or "I have become a Vaiṣṇava"these are sinful thoughts. One must give up such madness and humbly beg to attain the Lord's service.

To make a show of serving Kṛṣṇa without serving the spiritual master and the Vaiṣṇavas is like keeping water in a broken pot. Such pretense is simply pride. One must seek constant association with devotees. I am so weak that I am unable to survive without the association of devotees. If I do not associate with devotees constantly, I will certainly develop a strong desire to become the master, and various sinful thoughts will disturb me. Material existence is the gateway to hell. Even though it appears pleasing in the beginning, it will disappoint me in the end.

23. What is good fortune?

After traveling through the universes from time immemorial, when a living entity's material existence is about to come to an end, he develops a slight taste for devotional service because he receives the association of a devotee. This is the definition of good fortune.

24. Is it extremely necessary to associate with pure devotees?

Neophytes or kaniṣṭhā-adhikārīs cannot actually understand the importance of Deity worship. Their mundane conceptions regarding Deity worship do not completely go away. Neither are they aware of the supremacy and transcendental position of devotees. This is why saintly persons recommend that kaniṣṭha-adhikārīs associate with pure devotees. Without the association of pure devotees, human beings cannot attain benefit and can never properly worship the Deity.

25. Which literature is topmost?

There is no literature in the world as valuable as *Śrīmad-Bhāgavatam*. But it is difficult to study *Śrīmad-Bhāgavatam* without the association of saintly persons and the spiritual master.

26. Is it improper to associate intimately with women?

One must avoid sinful activities in regard to women. Renunciants must not associate with women at all. Even householders should not indulge in too much lusty activity. A person who forgets Kṛṣṇa and enjoys this material world is materially attached or an attached householder. It is irreligious to violate the principles of household life. Mahāprabhu said, *asat-saṅga-tyāga,—ei vaiṣṇava-ācāra*, '*strī-saṅgī*'*—eka asādhu*, '*kṛṣṇābhakta*' āra: "A Vaiṣṇava should always avoid the association of ordinary people. Common people are very much materially attached, especially to women. Vaiṣṇavas should also avoid the company of those who are not devotees of Lord Kṛṣṇa." (*Śrī Caitanya-caritāmṛta* Madhya 22.87)

The Spiritual Master

1. Who can understands the mystery of bhajana?

Only the unalloyed servants of the spiritual masters Śrī Svarūpa and Śrī Rūpa can understand the mystery of worshiping the Lord. A devotee who has firm faith in and love for the spiritual master's lotus feet is called an unalloyed servant. The Vedas declare, yasya deve parā bhaktir, yathā deve tathā gurau/ tasyaite kathitā hy arthāḥ, prakāśante mahātmanaḥ: "Only unto those great souls who have implicit faith in both the Lord and the spiritual master are all the imports of Vedic knowledge automatically revealed." (Śvetāśvatara Upaniṣad 6.23)

2. Who is an actual disciple?

"If I can fully surrender at the lotus feet of my spiritual master, in whose hands Lord Kṛṣṇa has entrusted the responsibility for my well being, then I am an actual disciple. It is my duty to obey whatever arrangements my spiritual master makes for me without fail." This is how a true disciple thinks. To think otherwise means our downfall is inevitable.

Those who instead of becoming sense enjoyers serve the Supreme Lord constantly under the spiritual master's guidance are genuine disciples. Everything in this world is meant to be used in the spiritual master's service for Kṛṣṇa's service. We will not find benefit if we think anything is meant for our pleasure. If we fail to see that all objects in this world are intended for service to guru and Kṛṣṇa, we will certainly become degraded. An ideal disciple realizes this fact and always makes service to his guru and Kṛṣṇa his life and soul.

A real disciple sees his spiritual master both internally and externally. Although he considers himself insignificant, a disciple's vision is not low. A sincere disciple certainly possesses the good intelligence to know that he has no well-wisher in this world other than his spiritual master. A real disciple is always steady in the understanding that he should serve his spiritual master; he considers his spiritual master as good as God. A good disciple possesses firm faith in and spontaneous love for his spiritual master.

A true disciple accepts the spiritual master as his most intimate well-wisher. He knows his guru is most dear to Kṛṣṇa and therefore an object of love. The guru is his eternal master, his life and soul. A disciple knows that the spiritual master is simultaneously the personification of devotional service and of the Supreme Lord. The spiritual master is dearer to Kṛṣṇa than His life. He is nondifferent from Kṛṣṇa because he is a manifestation of Kṛṣṇa. It is not possible to attain Kṛṣṇa's service without serving the spiritual master. Only those who serve their spiritual master are real Vaiṣṇavas and disciples. Others are simply bewildered by false ego. Frankly speaking, they are filled with material desire.

3. Where can we find a spiritual master?

Only the person Lord Kṛṣṇa send us as spiritual master will manifest before us as our guru. By the Lord's mercy we attain a spiritual master, and by the spiritual master's mercy we attain Kṛṣṇa. We are given a spiritual master according to our fortune. Different people have different mentalities, and the omniscient Lord sends each an appropriate spiritual master. There are those who desire the Lord's nonduplicitous mercy and who completely depend on Him for their success. These souls please the Lord with their simple sincerity. To bestow His mercy upon them, He appears before them personally. To those who want something else from the Lord, who are not actually aspiring for His complete mercy, the Lord sends through His illusory energy a spiritual master appropriate to their mentality. A sincere person never faces difficulty but quickly finds a bona fide guru.

4. Should we make disciples?

Unless we are pure devotees or liberated souls, we should not make disciples. Instead, we should first become disciples ourselves by taking shelter of a bona fide spiritual master. We should then hear *hari-kathā* from such a guru's mouth and follow his instructions in practice and humility. While glorifying those instructions, we should then become gurus. Trying to remain forever insignificant on some pretext amounts to self-deceit. To become guru means to become a devotee of Kṛṣṇa and to remain constantly engaged in the Lord's service with all our senses.

There are no hard and fast rules that tell us we must make disciples, but if the Lord desires it, then a pure devotee will give instructions for others' benefit. Such pure devotees are not selfishly motivated. Rather, their main purpose is to make the insignificant great, to make the godless inclined toward the Lord, and to make each person a devotee of Kṛṣṇa.

5. Is the spiritual master enriched by Kṛṣṇa's wealth?

The spiritual master is the proprietor of the Supreme Lord. Śrī Kṛṣṇa is the spiritual master's property or wealth. That is why only the spiritual master is able to give Kṛṣṇa. Simply by the spiritual master's mercy we can attain the mercy and *darśana* of Kṛṣṇa.

6. Who is eligible for deliverance?

As soon as we forget the Lord, various mundane thoughts and sense desires swallow us. The most merciful Śrī Kṛṣṇa is always ready to protect us from such danger provided we depend on Him completely. Lord Kṛṣṇa saves the living entities in the form of the spiritual master. The spiritual master is the personification of Kṛṣṇa's mercy. The spiritual master, Kṛṣṇa's representative, appears in this world to deliver the living entities from material existence and bring them back to Godhead. Only those fortunate souls who eagerly accept the mercy of such a spiritual master become liberated and go back to the eternal abode of peace.

7. How can we achieve Kṛṣṇa's complete mercy?

We can attain Kṛṣṇa's complete mercy simply by becoming qualified to be counted among the servants of Vṛṣabhānu's daughter as Śrī Rūpa's servant. We can achieve such good fortune simply by becoming a servant or particle of dust at the lotus feet of the guru who is a staunch follower of Śrī Rūpa. That is why it is said that we need to become lower than straw in the street. If we wish to become lower than straw in the street, we have to consider ourselves the guru's servant and serve the holy name without reservation.

8. Who is qualified to become a spiritual master?

Those who think themselves Vaiṣṇavas are not Vaiṣṇavas. Those who think themselves gurus or great personalities are not qualified to become gurus. Those who consider themselves disciples of a disciple are qualified to become spiritual masters. Only one who has unflinching faith in the Supreme Lord and the spiritual master is able to act as a guru.

9. How can we understand Vaiṣṇava philosophy?

However learned or thoughtful a person may be, until he takes shelter of an *ācārya* whose qualities personify Vaiṣṇava philosophy, he cannot understand Vaiṣṇavism. The *Bhagavad-gītā* states, tad viddhi praṇipātena, paripraśnena sevayā/ upadekṣyanti te jñānaṁ, jñāninas tattva-darśinaḥ: "Just try to learn the truth by approaching a spiritual master. Inquire from him submissively and render service unto him. The self-realized souls can impart knowledge unto you because they have seen the truth." (4.34)

We can understand the Vaiṣṇava philosophy if we possess three specific qualities: unconditional surrender, honest inquiry, and a serving temperament. The teachers of Vaiṣṇava philosophy instruct those who approach an *ācārya* to render these three qualities as *dakṣiṇā*. The *ācāryas* are not tempted by mundane *dakṣiṇā*.

10. Isn't it possible to worship Kṛṣṇa without taking shelter of the spiritual master's lotus feet?

We must cultivate Kṛṣṇa consciousness under the guidance and order of Kṛṣṇa's devotee. The daughter of Vṛṣabhānu is most favorable to Kṛṣṇa. Another name for Śrī Rādhā is anukūlyena or favorable. The spiritual masters are the dearest companions of the daughter of Vṛṣabhānu. We Gauḍīya Vaiṣṇavas worship Śrī Rādhā-Kṛṣṇa. Actually, Gauḍīya Vaiṣṇavas are more partial to Rādhā than Kṛṣṇa. The spiritual master is nondifferent from Śrī Rādhā. Cultivation of Kṛṣṇa consciousness is done under Śrī Rādhās guidance and in subordination to Her. If we fail to subordinate ourselves to Her representative, the spiritual master, we will not be able to cultivate Kṛṣṇa consciousness or even please Kṛṣṇa. Rather, we will only dance wildly for our own happiness. By renouncing such adverse mentality, such pride, and by serving Kṛṣṇa under our guru's order, we will be benefited.

But unfortunately we have forgotten to satisfy Kṛṣṇa and are busy satisfying our own senses. Alas! Instead of making Kṛṣṇa the center of our household we have made ourselves the center and have become attached householders. If we are actually interested in our own benefit, we must take special care during our present life. Otherwise, we will be cheated and will lose an excellent opportunity.

11. Is Śrī Rādhārāṇī the original spiritual master?

Śrī Rādhikā, who is the hlādinī aspect of the Lord's internal energy, is the original spiritual master of all devotees. She is even Kṛṣṇa's spiritual master. As Her disciple, Kṛṣṇa learns how to dance from Her. Pure devotees belonging to *rasas* other than the *mādhurya-rasa* accept Śrī Nityānanda Prabhu as their original spiritual master, but Śrī Rādhikā is the original spiritual master of the rasika devotees belonging to the *mādhurya-rasa* .

12. Is faith in the spiritual master's lotus feet the root of devotional service?

Before awakening pure devotional service, we must certainly learn of our relationship with the Supreme Lord. The spiritual master alone is able to bestow such knowledge. Therefore the root of devotional service is firm faith in the transcendental spiritual master. This faith is the first principle on the devotional path. The first requirement any devotee must fulfill is to give up the blind conception that there are many religions. He must also reject the path of argumentation and maintain faith in his spiritual master's auspicious instructions.

What is faith? Faith means full confidence in Śrī Gurudeva's words. We cannot rely on the words of worldly persons but trust only Gurudeva. Everyone else is a pretender. Therefore we should give up all worldly topics and have complete faith in the spiritual master's words. We cannot find success in any other way. By the spiritual master's mercy, our *anarthas* will be destroyed, our desires fulfilled, and we will certainly attain the Lord's mercy and *darśana*.

Our troubles are vanquished and we achieve devotional service when we approach and associate with guru and *sādhu*. That is why we should rely implicitly on Śrī Gurudeva if we wish to approach and serve the Absolute Person. The spiritual master will give us the highest good. If perchance we meet a real spiritual master, we must be saved. We must be able to reach our goal. The spiritual master will always supply and enrich us with transcendental knowledge and service.

"I will regulate the spiritual master": this is an atheist's conception. It comes from the offense of disregarding the spiritual master's order. We must renounce this mentality as soon as it appears. I will not listen to the words of anyone in this world. I will listen only to my spiritual master's words because he has descended from Vaikuṇṭha to deliver me.

We are minute, conscious souls. We can approach the supreme conscious Lord simply by the guru's mercy. We will give up the association of others and return to our Eternal Master. Although the spiritual master considers himself the Supreme Lord's insignificant servant, we must undoubtedly accept him as the only means by which we can go back to Godhead. He is our eternal well-wisher.

I offer everything at the lotus feet of my spiritual master, knowing that he is most dear to God; he is as good as God. I will perform all my work in his service and desire nothing in return. Then I will attain perfection.

13. What does it mean to be happy?

By taking shelter of the spiritual master's lotus feet, we become fearless, free of lamentation, and happy. When we serve him, we gain his association. If we serve the spiritual master with body, mind, and speech, we quickly attain his mercy. When he is pleased, we will find that our inclination to serve him progressively increases. This is the highest form of auspiciousness and the only gain.

14. Who is a Vaiṣṇava?

The spiritual master's servants are Vaiṣṇavas. Devotees who are initiated by bona fide gurus and who have taken complete shelter at their spiritual master's feet are Vaiṣṇavas. According to how well we serve the spiritual master, we see differences in the quality of our service to Kṛṣṇa. Those who abandon their spiritual master or who are envious of him are avaiṣṇava. They are atheists possessed of a hellish mentality. Those who are envious of the spiritual master are also envious of the Supreme Lord. Actually, they are envious of the whole world. Only devotees who are fixed at the spiritual master's lotus feet and who are free of material desire are pure. A person who is free from the influence of wealth, women, and the tigress of fame is a Vaiṣṇava. He is detached and pure and can defeat the entire world.

15. Is it possible to please Kṛṣṇa without taking shelter of the spiritual master?

It is not possible to worship Kṛṣṇa without taking shelter at the spiritual master's feet. The spiritual master is not an ordinary human being. He is as good as the Supreme Lord. That is why the spiritual master is described as God. He is the object of love and devotion. Those who know that the spiritual master is as good as the Supreme Lord are his genuine followers. Such followers are eligible for his mercy. Because the spiritual master, who is dear to Kṛṣṇa, is pleased with unalloyed disciples, Kṛṣṇa, his dearmost friend, also becomes pleased with them.

Just consider how Hari, guru, and the Vaiṣṇavas are placed in succession. The spiritual master sits in the center, placing the Supreme Lord and the Vaiṣṇavas on his lap. By firmly catching hold of the spiritual master's lotus feet, we will automatically receive the mercy of the Lord and His devotees. If the spiritual master is pleased, Śrī Hari and the Vaiṣṇavas will also be pleased. If we cannot become unalloyed devotees of the spiritual master, if we cannot make the spiritual master our life and soul, then we will spoil everything and will not be able to receive the mercy of either the

Lord or His devotees. Ultimately, we will be deceived and not attain the Lord's service.

16. Is the spiritual master an ordinary man?

The spiritual master is not a temporary, perishable lump of flesh and blood. *Śrīmad-Bhāgavatam* states that the spiritual master is the Lord Himself. He is an incarnation of the Lord. Of his own sweet will, the spiritual master mercifully descends from the spiritual world to this world. He is eternally present both in the Lord's manifest and in unmanifest pastimes. He always acts as our guide and gives us proper intelligence.

The spiritual master is an extraordinary personality. He is eternal and full of knowledge and bliss. To consider him an ordinary human being is to be possessed of a hellish mentality. To think like this is an offense against the holy name. The spiritual master is self-realized; he knows the science of Kṛṣṇa. He is dear to Śrī Caitanyadeva. He has appeared in this world to deliver fallen souls like us. He is not a *karmī*, *jñānī*, or yogī. He is an associate of the Lord in His pastimes. He is a topmost devotee. As God is eternal, so is the spiritual master. The transcendental Cupid, Kṛṣṇa, is God. The spiritual master is nondifferent from that same Kṛṣṇa. He is a manifestation of Kṛṣṇa.

When we consider the spiritual master as nondifferent from God, we recognize that the spiritual master is worshipable God. Although he is the worshipable Supreme Lord, he is most dear to the Lord. The spiritual master manifests the pastimes of worshiper God. The spiritual master and Kṛṣṇa are simultaneously one and different. The spiritual master is sheltered, and Lord Kṛṣṇa is the shelter. The spiritual master is servitor God and Śrī Kṛṣṇa is the object of service, the Personality of Godhead. The spiritual master is most dear to Lord Mukunda. In the vision of a self-realized disciple on the rāga path, the spiritual master is Kṛṣṇa's energy and a manifestation of Vṛṣabhānu's daughter. The spiritual master, who is dear to Kṛṣṇa, is part of Kṛṣṇa's internal energy; Lord Kṛṣṇa is the supreme energetic. Kṛṣṇa is the male or enjoyer, and the spiritual master is the female or beloved of Kṛṣṇa.

17. Should we render service to the spiritual master every day?

We should serve the spiritual master at the beginning of every year, every month, every day, and every moment. If we do not serve the spiritual master constantly, we will certainly face difficulty. The moment we forget our guru's service, we will forget ourselves.

Knowledge imparted by worldly teachers or instructors produces insignificant results, but the bona fide spiritual master does not bestow such insignificant results. The spiritual master bestows real auspiciousness. As soon as the living entities are bereft of the mercy of the sheltered God—the spiritual master—they are captured by material desires. If an instructing spiritual master does not instruct us how to take shelter at a guru's lotus feet and how to deal with him, then we may lose the most coveted jewel even after having received it.

Chanting the Lord's holy name is the best form of worship. The spiritual master teaches us this process. But if we do not please the spiritual master, how will we gain the strength to worship the Lord? That is why I say that those who want to attain the Lord's shelter, who want real peace and freedom from material existence, should make the spiritual master's service their life and soul. They should serve the spiritual master constantly and try their best to please him. Then they will not face any problems in life. They will attain all perfection.

Enjoyer-Kṛṣṇa is half and Enjoyed-Kṛṣṇa is the other half. The various pastimes performed by both are complete. Kṛṣṇa is the complete manifestation of the enjoyer, and our spiritual master is the complete manifestation of the enjoyed. A spiritual master is one who personally demonstrates how to serve the Supreme Lord throughout life. That spiritual master is present in every object. We have no business other than to serve his lotus feet constantly.

18. Is it essential to associate and serve the spiritual master directly?

We should certainly communicate directly with the spiritual master. Those who do not wish to serve and associate with their spiritual master personally are bound to be cheated. Direct communication with guru is the first step on the path of divine service.

We should serve the manifestations of guru in every entity. If we cannot serve the guru, we cannot serve anyone. I must not hear anything until my divine master, Śrī Gurudeva, authorizes me to hear it.

19. Can we see the Supreme Lord without the spiritual master's help?

The spiritual master is the Lord's transcendental temple. The Supreme Lord lives in that temple. Lord Śrī Kṛṣṇa, who is controlled by His devotees' love, manifests Himself in the hearts of the spiritual master and the devotees. Scripture states, śrutim apare smṛtim itare bhāratam anye bhajantu bhava-bhītāḥ, aham iha nandaṁ vande yasyālinde paraṁ brahma: "Let others, fearing material existence, worship the Vedas, the Vedic supplementary Purāṇas, and the Mahābhārata, but I shall worship Nanda Mahārāja, in whose courtyard the Supreme Brahman is crawling." (Padyāvalī 126)

Many people say that they are eager to see the Supreme Lord, but they do not understand that the Lord's *darśana* is possible simply by taking *darśana* of the spiritual master. Unless we meet the spiritual master, we cannot meet the Supreme Lord. Devotional service does not begin without first taking shelter at a spiritual master's lotus feet.

The spiritual master is certainly the via media between Kṛṣṇa and the living entity. Lord Kṛṣṇa sends His best servant, His best associate, to this world to distribute His unlimited mercy. The spiritual master is the personification of that mercy. Those who teach us to serve the Lord's Deity and to chant His holy names are spiritual masters. It is not enough to serve the spiritual master with awe and reverence only from a distance; we must serve him with strong faith and love. The best example of this is the intimate service Śrīla Raghunātha dāsa rendered to Śrīla Svarūpa Dāmodara Prabhu.

20. Will we face difficulty if we forget our spiritual master?

The moment I fall down from service to my spiritual master, who is protecting me at every moment by keeping me at his lotus feet, I will become distracted from the Absolute Truth. As soon as I fall away from my spiritual master's shelter, I will be captured by innumerable material desires. When I run to bathe, I will become busy protecting myself from cold. I will spend my time running to perform activities other than my spiritual master's service. If I do not remember my spiritual master's lotus feet—the lotus feet of that spiritual master who has always protected me from the material concept of life—at the beginning of every year, every month, every day, every moment, I will certainly find myself in trouble. I will pretend to become the spiritual master myself and expect others to adore me. This is the material conception of life. It is not that we should worship our spiritual master for only a day; we should serve him at every moment.

21. Is the spiritual master present in everything?

In order to bestow mercy on me, my spiritual master appears before me in various forms. They are all manifestations of my initiating spiritual master, who imparts transcendental knowledge. The light of the *jagad-guru* is reflected in various objects. My spiritual master is reflected in each and every object. Worshipable Kṛṣṇa is half and worshiper Kṛṣṇa is the other half. Their combined pastimes are complete. Kṛṣṇa is the complete manifestation of the object of worship, and my spiritual master is the complete manifestation of the worshiper. All cognizant objects in which the reflection of transcendence falls are my spiritual master in different forms. My spiritual master is the one who always personally demonstrates how to serve Kṛṣṇa throughout my life. He is reflected in the hearts of all living entities, and he is present in all objects as the Lord's subordinate. Thus he is present in every item.

22. When does the Supreme Lord manifest in the heart?

If, out of good fortune, we can feel the spiritual master's presence in our heart, if we can see the spiritual master traveling and walking in our heart, then the Supreme Lord will manifest in our heart too. There is no way to attain the Lord's service other than by serving and satisfying that personality who always inspires us to offer our devotion to the Lord.

23. Will we be cheated if we do not take complete shelter of the spiritual master?

We think that now that we have received mantras from our spiritual master, we are saved. But if we are not prepared to take complete shelter of our spiritual master, we will be cheated in proportion to our duplicity.

24. Who can deliver us from material absorption?

Only the spiritual master who is an intimate associate of Śrī Gaurāṅga is capable of delivering us from death in the form of material existence. Now let us consider who is a spiritual master and who is insignificant. One who constantly serves the Absolute Truth, the supreme worshipable object of all spiritual masters, is a bona fide spiritual master. I am not talking about the guru who teaches vina or bodybuilding. Such persons cannot protect us from death. *Śrīmad-Bhāgavatam* states, gurur na sa syāt sva-jano na sa syāt, pitā na sa syāj jananī na sā syāt/ daivaṁ na tat syān na patiś ca sa syān, na mocayed yaḥ samupeta-mṛtyum: "One who cannot deliver his dependents from the path of repeated birth and death should never become a spiritual master, a father, a husband, a mother, or a worshipable demigod." (*Śrīmad Bhāgavatam*. 5.5.18)

When we are illusioned, we fall into death's trap. When we have knowledge, we are delivered. The knowledge earned from this world is useless when we find ourselves paralyzed or dying. If we do not search after Absolute Truth, then we are dead matter. One who cannot deliver his dependents from death is simply cheating. One who induces us to become attracted to sense gratification is certainly a cheater. But we should serve a spiritual master who protects us from all these cheaters. We should serve him every year, every month, every day, at every moment.

25. Is it most essential to serve the spiritual master?

It is extremely necessary to worship the spiritual master. Even if we want to become a successful *karmī*, *jñānī*, or sense enjoyer, we require a spiritual master's guidance. But the knowledge imparted by spiritual masters teaching such things produces insignificant results. A bona fide spiritual master, however, does not award temporary or insignificant results. A real spiritual master awards actual auspiciousness.

As soon as we forget the compassion our spiritual master has shown us we invite material desires into our hearts. If the Vaiṣṇavas, who are fixed at the spiritual master's lotus feet, do not instruct us how to approach, serve, and deal with our spiritual master, we may lose a coveted jewel.

26. Is the spiritual master fully independent?

My spiritual master is completely independent. He is not dependent on the mercy of anyone in this world. His good wish is that everyone sincerely worships Hari. He considers giving others instruction on how to satisfy Kṛṣṇa's senses as the best form of compassion. He considers teaching others to fuel their sense gratification envy not mercy.

27. Do we get a spiritual master by the Lord's mercy?

If we ever become fortunate enough to receive a bona fide spiritual master, all credit goes to Kṛṣṇa alone. Through the spiritual master, Lord Kṛṣṇa awards us the benediction of fearlessness. Only the fortunate receive this opportunity. An appropriate spiritual master comes to an appropriate person.

28. Should we enjoy items meant for the spiritual master's service?

It is an offense to enjoy items offered to the spiritual master. If we do not engage our ears in hearing *hari-kathā*, if we engage our eyes only in measuring objects we can see, our nose in smelling fragrances, our tongue in relishing palatable foods, and our body in enjoying the sense of touch, then we must be thinking those ingredients meant for the spiritual master's service are objects of our own enjoyment. This means that we are treating the spiritual master as if he were an insignificant, ordinary human being.

29. Should everyone be respected as a spiritual master?

One should not disobey his spiritual master. We should not blaspheme the Vedic literature or disrespect the guru by considering many persons his equal. The only benefit the living entities can experience is to take complete shelter of the Supreme Personality of Godhead, Kṛṣṇa.

My spiritual master is an ocean of mercy. A single drop of that mercy ocean can drown me in an ocean of happiness. Out of great compassion, my spiritual master used to tell me, "Give up your high education, sanctity, high birth, and come to me. You do not need to go anywhere else. Whatever you need—whatever house, palace, knowledge, self-control, or renunciation—you will attain simply by coming to me. Do not run after these insignificant material objects. Do not consider them the goal of your life. Ordinary people consider such things important.

30. What quality must we possess before we make disciples?

We don't need to make disciples, we need to become disciples. In other words, we must always engage in the service of guru and Kṛṣṇa. The Vaiṣṇavas, the devotees of Viṣṇu, see the spiritual master in everything. If we are proud to be Vaiṣṇavas, we cannot serve Lord Viṣṇu or the Vaiṣṇavas properly.

"I don't do anything myself. Rather, I do whatever the Lord makes me do." Persons devoid of this mentality and engaged in the Lord's service can actually benefit other living entities by helping them become inclined toward Kṛṣṇa. Simply speaking about humility is useless. One has to be firmly convinced that "I am actually directed by the Lord."

31. Did you make disciples?

I have not made anyone my disciple. Those who are considered my disciples by others are actually my spiritual masters. To associate with others means to accept something from them. I do not accept anything from anyone except that which I received from my spiritual master. I do not engage in any activity under anyone's order except the order of my spiritual master. We should not accept anything from anyone for ourselves. If anyone faithfully and gladly gives us something we can use to serve guru and Kṛṣṇa, we should happily accept it and then use it for the Lord's service. Then we will achieve auspiciousness. If we learn the mystery of engaging everything in the Lord's service without looking at it with an enjoying spirit, we can enter the kingdom of God.

32. Can an ordinary man speak about the spiritual world?

Only those who have descended from the spiritual world can speak about the spiritual world. No one from this world can speak about the spiritual world. When the living entities are fortunate enough to hear about the spiritual world from those who have come from the spiritual world, they gain the opportunity to know about Vaikuṇṭha. We cannot understand transcendental topics by mundane consideration. It is not proper to make a compromise between the transcendental and the phenomenal. If we are fortunate, we will meet a Vaikuṇṭha man. Therefore Śrī Caitanyadeva states in *Śrī Caitanya-caritāmṛta*, *kṛṣṇa yadi kṛpā kare kona bhāgyavāne, guru-antaryāmi-rūpe śikhāya āpane:* "Kṛṣṇa is situated in everyone's heart as the *caitya-guru*, the spiritual master within. When He is kind to some fortunate conditioned soul, He personally gives him lessons so he can progress in devotional service, instructing the person as the Supersoul within and the spiritual master without." (*Śrī Caitanya-caritāmṛta* Madhya 22.47)

33. When will we achieve auspiciousness?

Only when we hear *hari-kathā* from saintly persons and the mahājanas and then follow in their footsteps can we achieve auspiciousness. In order to make pots, we must first take lessons from a potter. Then we must start to work. Similarly, if we do not follow the most experienced persons but try to achieve something by our independent endeavor, we will face many obstacles on the path to success. We will also fail to understand the purport of scripture and become controlled by mental speculation.

It is our duty to take shelter of a spiritual master. There is no other way to realize the Absolute Truth than to follow the disciplic succession. Without smearing the dust from the lotus feet of the *akiñcana mahājanas* on our body, we cannot see or realize anything. Only the mahājanas can protect us from the spell of misconception. We can realize the Absolute Truth only when we take shelter of a spiritual master and serve Kṛṣṇa under his guidance.

34. Who follows the path of argumentation?

As long as people accept the path of dry argument, they cannot find a bona fide spiritual master. The path of argument causes us to doubt the fact that there cannot be any truth superior to or separate from the spiritual master's teachings. Those who follow the path of argument disregard the spiritual master. The spiritual master alone is capable of removing all doubts and misconceptions. Dry argument has no foundation or standing. The truth received through disciplic succession does not change. The spiritual master gives us that unchangeable truth. The conception maintained in the argument-prone hearts of those who are envious of the spiritual master is disrespectful toward the guru and scriptures.

35. Is there no hope of attaining auspiciousness without serving the guru?

How can we attain auspiciousness if we reject the well-wisher who has come to bestow auspiciousness? The spiritual master comes from Vaikuṇṭha. The Lord has sent him. How can we go back to Godhead if we renounce his shelter and association? The spiritual master's mercy is the root of all auspiciousness. What have we actually done to receive his mercy? Rather, we should renounce our false ego and offer our respectful obeisances at his feet. To give up the false ego that "I am the seer,""I am the enjoyer," is called offering obeisances. That is why the word "namaḥ," obeisance, is added to mantras.

Receiving the spiritual master's mercy destroys the sinful mentality that "I am the doer." Receiving the spiritual master's mercy awakens the pride that "I am the Lord's servant." Material pride, false ego, and all sinful mentalities are removed simply by his influence.

I was not accustomed to worshiping my spiritual master every day, but by his mercy I came to know that my only duty was to serve his lotus feet. It is everyone's duty to worship the self-realized spiritual master and follow in his footsteps. We should not follow the blind. The spiritual master is our only well-wisher; our only relative, and our only protector. Only by his mercy are we fortunate enough to know this.

After attaining the lotus feet of my spiritual master, I no longer maintained the mentality that without his service I have something else to do. When my spiritual master, who is the Lord's dearmost servant, mercifully imparted knowledge of Nandanandana's service to me to protect me from false ego, I realized that the living entities have no other duty than to gratify Kṛṣṇa's senses. Nandanandana is the only worshipable Lord, the life and soul and ornament of all living entities. The spiritual master is extremely dear to that Nandanandana.

An unqualified person like me cannot serve such a spiritual master with body, mind, and speech, yet my spiritual master, who is an ocean of mercy and affection, empowers me out of his causeless mercy and treats me with an abundance of love. He is so merciful! If I can attain his mercy, if I can realize that I have no other well-wisher in this world, then simply by his causeless mercy I will be able to attain the qualification to engage in his service. He is pleased by affectionate service. On the day he bestows his causeless mercy on me and becomes pleased with me I will properly understand *hari-kathā*. Then nothing other than the service of guru and Kṛṣṇa will remain important to me.

We should always pray to the spiritual master to become qualified to accept his causeless mercy and empowerment. There is nothing with which to compare the spiritual master's mercy. I am so unfortunate that I do not consider the spiritual master great. Although the Supreme Personality of Godhead, Kṛṣṇa, is controlled by his devotion, still, I am unable to show gratitude for his causeless mercy on me.

36. What mentality should a sincere disciple have?

Sincere disciples should be completely devoted to their guru. They should know their spiritual master to be as good as God and the only object of their love and devotion. "The spiritual master is my eternal master and I am his eternal servant": this is how a disciple thinks. Service to the spiritual master is a disciple's life, ornament, and means of survival. Disciples do not know anything except their spiritual master. They always think of their spiritual master while eating, sleeping, dreaming, and serving. They are fully convinced that the spiritual master is the fully independent Personality of Godhead.

A sincere disciple has the following mentality: "Even if my spiritual master does not accept service from such an unqualified person as myself, I will always be prepared to render unalloyed service at his feet with body, mind, and words. If he kicks me, I will think it is because of my incompetence; his kick will come because of my faults. He is always right. May temporary sense desires not distract me from his service even for a moment. My only prayer is that my spiritual master mercifully accepts my service. I pray never to fall into bad association or to fall away from his lotus feet. My only solace is that my spiritual master is more merciful to unqualified persons like me. With a desire to achieve his causeless mercy, I will become greedier for his service."

37. How do pure devotees respect their spiritual master?

The spiritual master is known to ordinary people in one form and to his intimate devotees in another. The pure devotees recognize their spiritual master as the supreme well-wisher, as most dear to Kṛṣṇa, and as the object of their love and devotion, the object of their eternal service and their life and soul. The spiritual master is most dear to and nondifferent from Kṛṣṇa. It is not possible to achieve Kṛṣṇa's service without serving the spiritual master. Only those who serve the spiritual master can be considered Vaiṣṇavas.

We cannot see the spiritual master's lotus feet with sinful eyes. Considering the spiritual master an ordinary human being is a hellish mentality. The spiritual master is not an insignificant creature; he is not an ordinary human being. He is the Supreme Lord and is very dear to the Lord. He is a great personality, an exalted devotee, and an *ācārya* who can award Hari's holy names to others.

38. Why are oura obstacles not destroyed and our desires not fulfilled?

Because we think the spiritual master, who is nondifferent from the Supreme Lord, is a mortal being, our current vision is full of faults. That is why we are unable to sincerely surrender to his lotus feet. We find ourselves in our present pathetic condition because we have transgressed the words of the Vedas, the Supreme Lord, and the *Bhagavad-gītā* and considered the spiritual master a mortal being, the Vaiṣṇavas as belonging to a particular caste, and the Supreme Lord as made of material elements—stone, wood, or clay.

39. Where should we repose our faith?

We should give up topics about the material world and repose our full faith in the spiritual master's words, because without the spiritual master's mercy, our *anarthas* cannot be destroyed. We must accept our spiritual master as the only means by which we can go back to Godhead. He is our only eternal well-wisher. Faith means full confidence in the guru's words. We do not rely on the words of so-called gurus, religious reformers, or pretenders.

All our inauspicious qualities will be vanquished simply by associating with *sādhus*. By such association we will attain pure devotional service. Therefore we should rely implicitly on Śrī Gurudeva in order to approach and serve the Absolute Person.

A *sādhu* is one who will relieve us from all puzzling doubts. A *sādhu* gives the highest good. We should make friends with such a guru who truly wishes our highest good. If perchance we meet such a true guru, we cannot help but be saved and reach our goal. Such a guru will always supply and enrich us with transcendental knowledge and service.

40. If Jesus Christ was a jagad-guru and his instructions capable of bringing us deliverance, why do we need a spiritual master?

We accept both the universal spiritual master and the initiating spiritual master. By accepting only the *jagad-guru*, we may face many *anarthas*. If at present we want to follow Christ's orders by accepting him as *jagad-guru*, and we think that we do not require an initiating spiritual master, we will certainly face the doubt about how well we can follow Christ's orders. The Supreme Lord or universal *jagad-guru* delivers His instructions about the Absolute Truth only through the disciplic succession. As I sit on the bank of the Ganges in Navadvīpa, far from the Himālayas where the Ganges originates, and am able to touch her water here, the initiating spiritual master similarly brings the Ganges of pure devotional service, which emanates from the Lord's lotus feet, and places it in my hand and on my head. If the flow of the Ganges did not come to me, then because I am an ordinary, powerless, poor person, I would not have been able to climb the Himālayas to touch her water. Or if the flow of the Ganges from the Himālayas was interrupted on the way, I would have had to face the danger of accepting a polluted flow instead of the pure Gaṅgā. If the instructions Jesus Christ gave two thousand years ago do not come to us through disciplic succession, or if we have to sort them out from books, then perhaps we may create a blunder and accept a perversion of the truth taught in the name of Christianity. We may even come to accept something opposite from what he taught, thinking it his actual philosophy.

The initiating spiritual master is also *jagad-guru* because he is a manifestation of the original *jagad-guru*. Out of his causeless mercy he delivers the message of the original *jagad-guru* through the disciplic succession. He does not cheat nor flatter the disciple, nor does he yearn for any material gain from me. He is simply a messenger of the Absolute Truth.

41. Should we approach the spiritual master or Lord Gaurāṅga while holding a return ticket?

Those who join the *Maṭha* with a return ticket do not completely want the Supreme Lord. Does a person who actually wants to attain the Supreme Lord wish to return from there? If we awaken our propensity to serve the Supreme Lord, do we want to give up our direct service to the Lord so we can again become busy serving Maya? Those who have attained spiritual knowledge do not and cannot approach their worshipable Lord with a return ticket. Only those who are puffed up with false ego, who wish to become masters, who have dependents to look after, who adore someone other than God, and who instead of accepting themselves as the spiritual master's servants proudly proclaim themselves husbands, fathers, learners, foolish, poor or rich. These persons suffer anxiety and distress because they are intoxicated with the pride of accepting themselves as servants of their wives, sons, and daughters. That is why the scriptures advise us to approach a spiritual master. In approaching, there is no question of return. The Vedas state, t*ad vijñānartham sa guruṁ eva abhigacchet*—if we want transcendental knowledge, we must approach a bona fide spiritual master. Abhigacchet means "to take shelter."

42. How do we achieve the mercy of Lord Nityānanda, the original guru?

"I am an expert": this is not a transcendentalist's mentality. If we realize that there are no persons as fallen, wretched, and unqualified as ourselves in the entire world, then we are eligible to receive the mercy of Nityānanda Prabhu, the original guru.

If we live with the spiritual master out of pretense, we may find ourselves in trouble. Similarly, if we live away from the spiritual master, we may also be in trouble. But if we maintain staunch faith and love for our spiritual master and the Vaiṣṇavas, we will certainly be benefited regardless of whether we stay with them or live far away from them.

One day a gentleman's son suddenly came to see me. He had passed his entrance examination. He was so detached that he wore a piece of old cloth that only came to above his knee. He came like this every day for a few days. At the time I was residing in Śrī Māyāpur and arranging for property. On seeing my activities he lost faith in me and went elsewhere. He then fell into bad association and became degraded. Therefore if we want to measure devotees simply by their external appearance and not by understanding their actual intentions, we will certainly bring ruination on ourselves.

43. Do we attain everything by taking shelter at the feet of a bona fide spiritual master?

By taking shelter of the spiritual master's lotus feet, we can attain everything including Kṛṣṇa's holy name and the mantras in relation to Kṛṣṇa. But unless we have a strong service attitude toward our spiritual master's lotus feet, we cannot realize these transcendental topics. Unless we take shelter of our spiritual master with firm faith and devotion and proceed on the devotional path under his order, we cannot attain real auspiciousness. The materialists are naturally fond of dry arguments. No one can understand devotional service by following the path of dry argumentation. Unless we take shelter of a Vaiṣṇava spiritual master and execute devotional service under his guidance, we cannot properly utilize our own good intelligence. Therefore the *śāstra* states, *guru-pādāśrayas tasmāt, kṛṣṇa-dīkṣādi-śikṣaṇam/viśrambheṇa guroḥ sevā, sādhu-*vartmānuvartanam: "First one should take shelter of a bona fide spiritual master, then he should take initiation and transcendental knowledge from him, he should serve his spiritual master with faith and devotion, and follow in the footsteps of a saintly person." (*Bhakti-rasāmṛta-sindhu* 1.2.74)

44. Can we immediately attain Śrīmatī Rādhikās lotus feet?

It is not that Śrī Rādhārāṇī is not present. Even now we can attain Her lotus feet and service. If we can see the beauty of Śrī Rādhārāṇīs toenails at our spiritual master's lotus feet, we will no longer think about where we will find Śrī Rādhārāṇī. If we are fortunate enough, we can attain service to and *darśana* of Śrī Rādhārāṇīs lotus feet in the *darśana* of our spiritual master's lotus feet, because he is nondifferent from Śrī Rādhā and very dear to Her.

In *mādhurya-rasa* , the spiritual master is an intimate gopī friend of Śrī Rādhārāṇī. He is nondifferent from the daughter of Vṛṣabhānu. Only the sincere disciples of a spiritual master in *mādhurya-rasa* can attain the *darśana* of the beauty of Śrī Rādhās toenails in the form of their spiritual master. Only the intimate disciples of a spiritual master can realize that their spiritual master is a manifestation of Śrī Rādhā, or that he is nondifferent from the daughter of King Vṛṣabhānu.

45. What is the difference between my spiritual master and me?

I am more insignificant than the most insignificant, and the spiritual master, who is always engaged in serving the Almighty is greater than the greatest.

46. What does it mean to approach a spiritual master and inquire from him?

The word pranipāt means to surrender, to hear something with full attention. Without pranipāt the hearing process is incomplete. Without pranipāt there is no way to understand the transcendental Absolute Truth and topics about the spiritual master, Vaiṣṇavas, and the *śāstras*.

The word pariprasna means "honest inquiry," or to humbly inquire from the spiritual master. We should be prepared to hear the reply to our inquiry. Inquiring with a doubtful mind is not honest inquiry. To make a show of inquiring while under the control of false ego is also not honest inquiry. Unless we are fully surrendered, we cannot make honest inquiry. But unless a subject matter is clarified through honest inquiry we cannot begin our service.

47. Is it safe to take disciples?

Give up envy and become compassionate toward all living entities. Convert the godless living entities into devotees of Kṛṣṇa. Do not become a guru and become envious. Do not become a guru so you can drown in the ocean of material enjoyment. Do not become a guru for the sake of formality. But if you can become a sincere servant of your spiritual master and Kṛṣṇa and attain their mercy, then there is nothing to fear. Otherwise, your degradation is guaranteed.

48. How should I treat my spiritual master?

Serve your spiritual master with love and devotion just as you do Kṛṣṇa. Consider the spiritual master as good as the Supreme Lord. Do not think him inferior to the Lord in any way. It is a disciple's duty to treat, worship, and serve the spiritual master as if he were God. If a disciple does not do so, he will fall down from his position as a disciple. Only those who consider the spiritual master nondifferent from the Supreme Lord can understand the confidential purport of the scriptures, chant Hari's holy name, and preach *hari-kathā*. To teach about His own service Lord Kṛṣṇa appears in the form of the spiritual master. If we are fortunate enough, we can understand this flawless scriptural verdict. Otherwise, we will remain doubtful and continue to drown in the ocean of material existence.

The spiritual master is neither the predominating absolute nor the original predominated absolute. He is a manifestation of the original predominated absolute. Lord Kṛṣṇa is the worshipable God and the spiritual master is the worshiper God. Lord Kṛṣṇa is the predominating absolute and the spiritual master is the predominated absolute. Because the spiritual master, who is the worshiper God, is the personification of service to Kṛṣṇa Himself, he is most dear to Kṛṣṇa. This is the special characteristic of the science relating to the spiritual master. Śrī Kṛṣṇa is the energetic and the spiritual master is His complete energy. The spiritual master is not an ordinary human being. He is the master of the living beings. The spiritual master is the supreme consciousness and a manifestation of the Lord's spiritual energy. But the living entities as minute spiritual sparks belong to the Lord's marginal energy and are part and parcel of the Lord.

49. What is the difference between the science relating to the spiritual master and the science relating to Śrī Rādhā?

Śrī Rādhārāṇī is the original predominated absolute. Śrī Rādhā, the daughter of Vṛṣabhānu, is the crest jewel of all *ācāryas* of *mādhurya-rasa* and of all lovers of Kṛṣṇa. Our spiritual master, who is an *ācārya* in the line of *mādhurya-rasa* , is Śrī Rādhās dear companion. He is an eternally perfected Vraja-gopī. By discussing the writings of Śrīla Narottama dāsa Ṭhākura, which state that *guru rupā sakhī bāme*, "on the left the *sakhī* in the form of the spiritual master is situated," it is clearly understood that the spiritual master or *sakhī* is the manifestation of the daughter of Vṛṣabhānu and is nondifferent from Her.

50. How determined should we be to serve the spiritual master's lotus feet?

A real disciple accepts his spiritual master as servitor God, most dear to Kṛṣṇa. He never considers his spiritual master inferior to the Lord in any way. A sincere disciple serves and worships his spiritual master as if he were God. Those who do not follow this principle fall down from their position as disciples. Until we see the spiritual master as a manifestation of and nondifferent from the Supreme Lord, we will not be able to chant the Lord's name purely. A genuine disciple must possess firm determination and faith in his spiritual master, thinking, "I will serve my spiritual master and Lord Gaurāṅga with utmost simplicity. I will follow my spiritual master's instructions, which have come down from the Supreme Lord. I will never disobey my spiritual master's orders under the influence of anyone in this world. If following my spiritual master means I must become proud or an animal or go to hell forever, I will never hesitate. I will not follow anyone other than my spiritual master. I will destroy the current of mundane thought by the strength of his instructions. If my spiritual master showers even a particle of pollen from his lotus feet upon the world, then millions of people will be delivered. There is no knowledge or proper code of conduct in the fourteen worlds that weighs more than a particle of dust from the lotus feet of my spiritual master."

51. What instruction does a bona fide spiritual master give?

There is no scarcity of instructors in this world. People in this world advise us to pay special attention to our immediate needs, but this creates more bad than good because our needs go on increasing. While trying to fulfill our temporary needs we drown in the ocean of unlimited needs and difficulties. It is neither beneficial for us to live in this world with attachment nor to display detachment. We should become free from the cheaters who, in the guise of saints, induce ordinary people to aim for religiosity, economic development, sense gratification, and liberation and who are busy trying to make ordinary people as apparently religious as themselves. Instead, we should become intelligent enough to concentrate our mind on topics about Śrī Caitanyadeva.

Bṛhaspati is the spiritual master of the demigods. He instructs the demigods in such a way that they can enjoy a better standard of life. Both Bṛhaspati's sharp intelligence and his instructions on religious principles are meant simply to increase his disciples' enjoying propensity. There are many good instructors in human society too— family priests, community leaders, country leaders, and relatives— whose instructions are similarly meant. There are also family spiritual masters such as Vasiṣṭha who instruct their disciples to renounce sense gratification. But a Vaiṣṇava spiritual master instructs people only to worship Hari. He makes neither material enjoyment nor dry renunciation the goal of his instructions. Instead, he instructs others for their eternal benefit.

52. Don't you have many disciples?

I have not made any disciples. Everyone is my spiritual master. I learn something from everyone. My only prayer is that they may mercifully award me the opportunity to follow their non-duplicitous ideal of worshiping the Lord.

53. What does a spiritual master give to a surrendered soul?

The spiritual master gives a surrendered soul the spiritual name. The spiritual master is nondifferent from the Supreme Lord and personifies devotional service. We should never disregard the spiritual master or consider him an ordinary human being. If we disregard the spiritual master, we commit a grave offense. Similarly, there is no difference between the transcendental sound vibration and the transcendental Lord. Kṛṣṇa's holy name and Kṛṣṇa Himself are nondifferent. The holy name is not a product of the material world. The holy name is not an object of our vision; rather, He is the seer.

Only a bona fide spiritual master who is dear to Kṛṣṇa can bestow Kṛṣṇa on others. Kṛṣṇa-kathā should be heard only from the Vaiṣṇava spiritual master. No one but devotees can speak about the Lord. If we approach *karmīs*, *jñānīs*, yogīs, or worldly teachers to hear something, they will only discuss Maya. They accept neither the Lord's eternal existence nor the fact that the Lord is eternal and full of knowledge and bliss. Such people consider both the Lord's incarnations and the spiritual master to be mortal beings.

A spiritual master awards his surrendered disciples Kṛṣṇa's holy name and the mantras in relation to Kṛṣṇa. Kṛṣṇa-mantras are topmost. There is no mantra as powerful as a kṛṣṇa-mantra. If we learn to chant these kṛṣṇa-mantras perfectly, all our mental speculation will be destroyed. As long as we consider our spiritual master an ordinary being, we will not be able to understand the holy name's glories. We will not become spiritually successful if we consider Śrī Caitanyadeva an ordinary human being. Simply by the spiritual master's mercy can we understand the glories of Śrī Gaurasundara and Vraja-dhāma.

The spiritual master has an eternal kuñja on the shore of Śrī Rādhā-kuṇḍa. There he has bound Kṛṣṇa by the power of his service. Simply by his mercy we can attain the shelter of Govardhana Hill. Govardhana Hill is another form of Kṛṣṇa. If we are filled with mental speculation we will see Govardhana only as a stone mountain. But the place where Vṛṣabhānu's daughter enjoys Her pastimes is not an ordinary place made of clay in this world. It is transcendental and decorated with spiritual gems. It is by our spiritual master's mercy that we can aspire to attain the intimate service of Śrī Rādhā-Mādhava.

All our inauspiciousness is destroyed and our auspiciousness created simply by the spiritual master's mercy. It is impossible to know Kṛṣṇa either by sinful endeavor or worldly morality. We can understand Him only through pure devotional service. It is possible to learn to practice this pure devotion only by the spiritual master's mercy.

Kṛṣṇa-kathā is certainly an invaluable asset. Actually, it is the only asset as we attempt to progress on the path leading to Goloka. Kṛṣṇa-kathā is nondifferent from Kṛṣṇa Himself. Any topic not related to Kṛṣṇa is actually useless. Therefore, kṛṣṇa-kathā should be preached extensively in this world. We can hear topics about Kṛṣṇa or Vaikuṇṭha from the lotus mouth of the spiritual master who is a resident of Vraja. At present, we spend our time thinking about our body, which is a bag of bones and flesh, and have given up topics about Kṛṣṇa. Therefore, we identify with material objects and do not attain self-realization.

54. Should we discuss the spiritual master's instructions every day?

Among Vaiṣṇavas, the spiritual master is topmost. It is essential to listen eternally to the instructions of the spiritual master, who is dear to Kṛṣṇa. If we do not discuss or hear our spiritual master's instructions every day but engage in other activities, we will simply invite distress. We should not imitate the spiritual master or the Vaiṣṇavas. Such imitation constitutes bad association. Rather, we should follow in their footsteps. We should associate with those devotees in whose hearts the Lord resides. Devotees and nondevotees, liberated souls and conditioned souls, perfect souls and imperfect souls—these are not one and the same. Raw rice is not fit for our eating; it becomes fit only after it is cooked. Similarly, we should associate with perfected devotees. That is both most desirable and auspicious.

55. Why is the spiritual master called Prabhupāda or Viṣṇupāda?

Since the spiritual master is conversant with the science of Kṛṣṇa and is the personification of the highest service to the Lord, his disciple considers him just like Kṛṣṇa Caitanya or Hari Himself. Therefore the disciple addresses him as Viṣṇupāda or Prabhupāda.

56. How does a Vaiṣṇava who is fixed at his spiritual master's lotus feet think?

Unless I realize that all the people in the world are worshipable, I cannot offer my respectful obeisances to my spiritual master. My spiritual master is the spiritual master of the entire world. People who are envious of my spiritual master are also envious of the Supreme Lord and of every other human being. Until I feel this conviction in my heart, I cannot become a real servant of my spiritual master and cannot surrender at his lotus feet. Neither will I be able to understand that I am the most insignificant created being. Therefore I will not be able to chant the holy name of Hari thinking of myself as lower than a straw in the street and more tolerant than a tree. I will not be devoid of the desire for respect or prepared to offer respect to others. If I respect my spiritual master properly, I will be able to respect the whole world. This will make it possible for me to become free of the desire to receive respect for myself and thus able to glorify Lord Hari constantly.

57. Who is a spiritual master?

The spiritual master is the one who can protect me from death in the form of material existence. The bona fide spiritual master is the one who can deliver me from the fear or anxiety generated by death. When I approach my spiritual master, I do not need to hear from anyone else. He is the source of all my auspiciousness and the hands into which the all-auspicious Supreme Lord has entrusted my well-being.

By the spiritual master's grace, my mentality of false proprietorship is destroyed. The spiritual master is Kṛṣṇa's potency. He plants Vedic knowledge in our hearts, makes us feel lower than the straw in the street, makes us more tolerant than a tree, removes our desire to be respected, teaches us to offer others our respect, and empowers us to always glorify the Supreme Lord and everything in relation to Him. The spiritual master alone is capable of delivering us from the clutches of Maya.

The spiritual master is he who awards me the knowledge that everyone in this world is worshipable. He teaches me that everyone is my spiritual master and that I am Kṛṣṇa's eternal servant. He also teaches me that service to Kṛṣṇa is my constitutional duty.

58. Do the spiritual master and the Vaiṣṇavas approve all of our actions?

As a good doctor does not prescribe cures according to the patient's desire, a bona fide spiritual master does not falsely encourage or flatter conditioned souls. I have no qualification to approve the actions of those who display or will display devotion to their fathers and mothers in order to achieve worldly happiness and peace. Our hearts are not righteous like theirs. We follow Vedic injunctions. Our aim and ideal is simply to practice devotional service. Therefore we are unable to pay attention to anything else. Neither can we take anyone else's advice while becoming indifferent to the service of guru and the Vaiṣṇavas. We have no time to serve others while indulging in mental speculation, renouncing the Lord's service, which is our constitutional duty.

59. Is it proper to consider the spiritual master as God or the supreme enjoyer?

The spiritual master is not the supreme enjoyer like Kṛṣṇa. In other words, he is not Gopīnātha, the beloved lord of the gopīs. The spiritual master is the servitor God. In that sense, he is as good as God, most dear to God, and the Lord's topmost devotee. The spiritual master is the predominated God; he is not the predominating God like Kṛṣṇa or the original predominated God, like Śrī Rādhā.

The spiritual master is nondifferent from Gaurāṅga. That is, he is simultaneously one and different from Śrī Gaurāṅga. He is the manifestation of Śrī Gaurāṅga. He is the predominated Absolute Truth. If we attempt to merge him with the existence of the predominating Absolute Truth and thereby destroy the identity of the predominating Absolute Truth, we will be guilty of the offense of impersonalism. Such thinking is purely impersonalism, atheism. *Śāstra* states, yadyapīāmāra guru—caitanyera dāsa, tathāpi jāniye āmi tāṅhāra prakāśa."Although I know that my spiritual master is a servitor of Śrī Caitanya, I know him also as a plenary manifestation of the Lord." (*Śrī Caitanya-caritāmṛta* Ādi 1.44)

tāte kṛṣṇa bhaje, kare gurura sevana, maya-jāla chuṭe, pāya kṛṣṇera caraṇa: "If the conditioned soul engages in the Lord's service and simultaneously carries out his spiritual master's orders, serving him, he can become free of Maya's clutches and become eligible for shelter at Kṛṣṇa's lotus feet." (*Śrī Caitanya-caritāmṛta* Madhya 22.25)

Under the shelter, guidance, and order of the spiritual master who is dear to Kṛṣṇa, we should worship Kṛṣṇa. This is the śāstric verdict.

60. Who can act as our spiritual master?

Only that great personality who has been sent by the Lord from the spiritual world into this world to deliver fallen souls like us, who delivers people who are afflicted with the threefold miseries and sends them back to Godhead, who is most dear to the Supreme Lord and who represents Him, and who is the messenger of transcendental subject matter, is capable of acting as our spiritual master. He is an actual devotee and an actual spiritual master whose ax-like words remain always sharpened to sacrifice our propensities for material enjoyment and dry renunciation.

A spiritual master is that person who has no concept, duty, or business other than Kṛṣṇa's service, and who understand that Kṛṣṇa is the only object of service. He is not eager to hear anyone's flattery and he is a brave preacher of the Absolute Truth.

One who does not speak anything other than *hari-kathā*, who does not instruct others to do anything but serve Hari, and who does not himself engage even for a moment in any activity other than such service, is qualified to be a spiritual master. An insincere hypocrite cannot be guru. One who aspires for mundane activities cannot become a spiritual master. Pseudo spiritual masters should be exposed. If a spiritual master utilizes the ingredients collected by his disciples— the wealth, alms, etc.—for his own enjoyment or simply to accumulate gold, women, and fame, his disciples should totally reject such a spiritual master, knowing him to be a cheater. We should not hear anything from such dishonest persons. A person who usurps the ingredients meant for Kṛṣṇa's service can never be called a spiritual master. The *Nāradiya Purāna* states, *īhā yasya harer dāsye, karmaṇā manasā girā/ nikhilāsv apy avasthāsu, jīvan-muktaḥ sa ucyate*: "A person acting in Kṛṣṇa consciousness with his body, mind, intelligence, and words, is a liberated person even within the material world, although he may be engaged in many so-called material activities." (quoted in *Bhakti Rasāmṛta Sindhu* 1.2.187)

We need not associate with the atheists who have come to engage in social service rather than Kṛṣṇa's service. Such people can benefit neither themselves nor others. While performing social service, they fall into Maya's pit and make others fall into that pit also. We do not associate with those who make a show of chanting the holy names on beads just to cheat the Lord, or who raise a great hue and cry yet do not see Kṛṣṇa in every sound vibration and Gaurasundara in every utterance. The goal of all knowledge is to develop our relationship with Kṛṣṇa. If we develop a propensity to serve the Lord under the spiritual master's order, in the association of devotees, we will learn to see the entire world as made for the Lord's service. We will then utilize everything we see for that service and thus attain auspiciousness.

If we associate and serve that great personality who sees the Lord everywhere, who sees everything in relation to the Lord, who sees his spiritual master everywhere, who thinks himself humbler than a blade of grass, who is more tolerant than a tree, who does not desire respect for himself, who is always ready to respect others, and who in this way constantly chants the Lord's holy name, then the path to perfection will open. Simply out of good fortune, we obtain such a bona fide spiritual master. We cannot reach Gaurasundara's shelter by accepting a servant of Maya as our spiritual master and thus maintaining our enjoying spirit. Although Śrī Gaurasundara may not currently be present in this world, if we sincerely associate with guru and the Vaiṣṇavas, dovetailing our mentality with the mentality of such Vaiṣṇavas—if we mix our desire with their desire—then we will, by the mercy of Śrī Gaurasundara, certainly attain auspiciousness. If we can take complete shelter at the lotus feet of a spiritual master who is conversant with the science of Kṛṣṇa, then by his proper association, service, and subordination we will attain ultimate benefit.

61. How do we find a genuine spiritual master?

The first step in attaining perfection is to take shelter of a bona fide spiritual master. By the Lord's will, everyone receives a spiritual master according to his own qualification, just as the Christians received Jesus Christ and the Muslims Prophet Mohammad. Moreover, according to their luck, materialists remain attached to material life by accepting family priests as their spiritual masters. But if we are fortunate and search sincerely for a bona fide spiritual master, and if we humbly pray to the Lord to attain the mercy of such a guru, then by the Lord's mercy we will certainly receive a bona fide guru in this lifetime. Then by taking shelter at his lotus feet our life will become successful. The *Śrī Caitanya-caritāmṛta* states:

brahmāṇḍa bhramite kona bhāgyavān jīva,
guru-kṛṣṇa-prasāde pāya bhakti-latā-bīja

Out of many millions of wandering living entities, one who is very fortunate gets an opportunity to associate with a bona fide spiritual master by the grace of Kṛṣṇa. By the mercy of both Kṛṣṇa and the spiritual master, such a person receives the seed of the creeper of devotional service. (*Madhya* 19.151)

kṛṣṇa yadi kṛpā kare kona bhāgyavāne,
guru-antaryāmi-rūpe śikhāya āpane

Kṛṣṇa is situated in everyone's heart as the *caitya-guru*, the spiritual master within. When He is kind to some fortunate conditioned soul, He personally gives him lessons so he can progress in devotional service, instructing the person as the Supersoul within and the spiritual master without. (*Madhya* 22.47)

guru kṛṣṇa-rūpa hana śāstrera pramāṇe,
guru-rūpe kṛṣṇa kṛpā karena bhakta-gaṇe

According to the deliberate opinion of all revealed scriptures, the spiritual master is nondifferent from Kṛṣṇa. Lord Kṛṣṇa in the form of the spiritual master delivers His devotees. (Adī 1.45)

yadyapi āmāra guru—caitanyera dāsa,
tathāpi jāniye āmi tāṅhāra prakāśa

Although I know that my spiritual master is a servitor of Śrī Caitanya, I know him also as a plenary manifestation of the Lord. (Ādi 1.44)

śikṣā-guruke ta' jāni kṛṣṇera svarūpa,
antaryāmī, bhakta-śreṣṭha,—ei dui rūpa

One should know the instructing spiritual master to be the Personality of Kṛṣṇa. Lord Kṛṣṇa manifests Himself as the Supersoul and as the greatest devotee of the Lord. (*Ādi* 1.47)

jīve sākṣāt nāhi tāte guru caitya-rūpe,
śikṣā-guru haya kṛṣṇa-mahānta-svarūpe

One should know the instructing spiritual master to be the Personality of Kṛṣṇa. Lord Kṛṣṇa manifests Himself as the Supersoul and as the greatest devotee of the Lord. Since one cannot visually experience the presence of the Supersoul, He appears before us as a liberated devotee. Such a spiritual master is none other than Kṛṣṇa Himself. (*Ādi* 1.58) \

"O Kṛṣṇacandra! Please accept me as your servant. I will not continue to serve this temporary material world while thinking of myself as an enjoyer."

When a living entity sincerely and humbly prays to the Lord in this way, then the most merciful Kṛṣṇa appears before him in the form of a liberated devotee. Unless we are fortunate enough to receive transcendental knowledge from a bona fide spiritual master, we cannot become qualified to engage in the Lord's service. Since no human being or demigod is capable of awarding such transcendental knowledge, we must find shelter under a bona fide spiritual master.

62. Who is a spiritual master and how should he be served?

The guru and Vaiṣṇavas are the transcendental home of the Supreme Lord. The Lord does not manifest just anywhere. He appears and remains in the hearts of guru and the Vaiṣṇavas. Many people want to see the Lord, but they do not know that the Lord's *darśana* can be had only through the spiritual master's *darśana*. It is not possible to begin devotional service without a spiritual master. The spiritual master is the via media between us and Kṛṣṇa's lotus feet. This is Kṛṣṇa's mercy: He sends His topmost servant or Vaiṣṇava into this world to deliver everyone. Thus the spiritual master is the personification of that causeless mercy.

The spiritual master is our ever well-wisher. Therefore it is not enough simply to serve him with awe and reverence from a distance. Instead, we must serve him with firm conviction and love. Then only will we attain perfection. The spiritual master is more important to us than Lord Kṛṣṇa. Śrī Gaurāṅgadeva is the spiritual master of all gurus. He revealed to us that even though the spiritual master is nondifferent from the Supreme Lord, he is the Lord's principal devotee. We cannot serve the Lord without our guru's mercy, because our guru is the Lord's topmost devotee. The living entities have no way to achieve auspiciousness other than to serve the spiritual master.

63. Is the spiritual master's mercy Kṛṣṇa's mercy?

Lord Kṛṣṇa bestows mercy upon us and gives all living entities shelter in the form of the spiritual master. *Śrī Caitanya-caritāmṛta* states:

kṛṣṇa yadi kṛpā kare kona bhāgyavāne,
guru-antaryāmi-rūpe śikhāya āpane

"Kṛṣṇa is situated in everyone's heart as the *caitya-guru*, the spiritual master within. When He is kind to some fortunate conditioned soul, He personally gives him lessons so he can progress in devotional service, instructing the person as the Supersoul within and the spiritual master without." (*Śrī Caitanya-caritāmṛta* Ādi 1.45)

guru kṛṣṇa-rūpa hana śāstrera pramāṇe
guru-rūpe kṛṣṇa kṛpā karena bhakta-gaṇe

"According to the deliberate opinion of all revealed scriptures, the spiritual master is nondifferent from Kṛṣṇa. Lord Kṛṣṇa in the form of the spiritual master delivers His devotees." (*Śrī Caitanya-caritāmṛta* Madhya 22.47)

The spiritual master's mercy and the mercy of Kṛṣṇa are not two separate things. The spiritual master does not teach anything other than to worship Kṛṣṇa. Lord Kṛṣṇa also does not accept any service that has not been rendered by His devotee.

The spiritual master offers everyone's service to Kṛṣṇa. The eternally worshipable spiritual master is not an ordinary, mundane human being. In order to deliver the fallen souls he appears in this world by Kṛṣṇa's will and awards the fallen souls the seed of devotional service, the opportunity to serve the Lord. Kṛṣṇa's mercy comes to us through the spiritual master. *Śrī Caitanya-caritāmṛta* states:

brahmāṇḍa bhramite kona bhāgyavān jīva
guru-kṛṣṇa-prasāde pāya bhakti-latā-bīja

"Out of many millions of wandering living entities, one who is very fortunate gets an opportunity to associate with a bona fide spiritual master by the grace of Kṛṣṇa. By the mercy of both Kṛṣṇa and the spiritual master, such a person receives the seed of the creeper of devotional service." (*Śrī Caitanya-caritāmṛta* Madhya 19.151)

64. Does Kṛṣṇa appear in the form of a spiritual master to teach His own service?

The Supreme Personality of Godhead has hands and He is scratching His body with His hands. There is no difference between His body and His hands. He is serving Himself. In the same way, in order to teach devotional service, the Lord personally appears in the form of a spiritual master. My spiritual master is nondifferent from the Lord. The Lord is the predominating object, and the spiritual master is the predominated object. The Lord is the worshipable God, and the spiritual master is the worshiper God. Lord Mukunda is the object of service, and the spiritual master, who is most dear to Mukunda, is the topmost servant. There is no one as dear to the Lord as my spiritual master. He is certainly most dear to Kṛṣṇa. Like two halves of a chickpea, worshipable Kṛṣṇa is one half and worshiper Kṛṣṇa is the other. The pastimes between them make them complete. The complete existence of the worshipable Lord is Kṛṣṇa, and the complete existence of the worshiper Lord is my spiritual master.

Lord Kṛṣṇa is the predominating Supreme Brahman and the spiritual master is the predominated supreme Brahman. We are smaller than the smallest and the spiritual master, who constantly serves the greatest, is greater than the greatest. The spiritual master is extremely dear to Lord Mukunda. The spiritual master's lotus feet are the best form of shelter. We will attain success if we accept the spiritual master, who is dear to Kṛṣṇa, as servitor God.

65. Who can act as a spiritual master?

Only a devotee of Kṛṣṇa who knows the science of Kṛṣṇa can act as guru. Since *karmīs*, *jñānīs*, and impersonalists are nondevotees, they can never become gurus. Only one who worships the Personality of Godhead is able to become a spiritual master. Those who think proudly that they are Kṛṣṇa's servants cannot become spiritual masters unless they proudly identify themselves as disciples of a disciple. As long as we are proud to be Vaiṣṇavas, we cannot become guru. A person who acts as guru never claims to be a Vaiṣṇava or spiritual master. My spiritual master never considered himself a Vaiṣṇava. One who calls himself a Vaiṣṇava is branded a non-Vaiṣṇava.

Śrīla Bhaktivinoda Ṭhākura has sung:

āmi ta' vaiṣṇava, e-buddhi ha-ile, amānī nā haba āmi
pratiṣṭhāśāāsi', hṛdaya dūṣibe, ha-iba niraya-gāmī
tumāra kinkara āpane jāniba, guru abhimāna tyaji
tumāra uchhistha pada jala renu, sadā niṣkapate bhaji
nije śreṣṭha jāni', ucchiṣṭādi-dāne, habe abhimāna bhāra
tāi śiṣya tava, thākiyā sarvadā, nā la-iba pūjā kāra

If I think I am a Vaiṣṇava, I shall look forward to receiving others' respect. If the desire for fame and reputation pollutes my heart, I will certainly go to hell. I will give up the pride of being a guru and consider myself your eternal servant. I will sincerely accept your remnants

and the water that has washed your lotus feet. By giving others the remnants of my food, I will think myself superior and be burdened by the weight of false pride. Therefore, always remaining your surrendered disciple, I will not accept worship from anyone else. (*Kalyāṇa Kalpataru*)

Only a pure devotee can be a spiritual master. A great personality sees the spiritual master everywhere. Such a person is himself qualified to become a spiritual master because he can induce everyone to become Kṛṣṇa conscious. Unless we are devotees ourselves, we cannot make others devotees. Therefore, to become guru, we must become devotees of Kṛṣṇa. We must always engage in Kṛṣṇa's service with all our senses. We are not qualified to act as spiritual master unless we are ourselves staunch disciples of our own spiritual master.

A pure devotee thinks himself to be humbler than a blade of grass and more tolerant than a tree. He never says he has served his spiritual master enough and therefore no longer needs to offer service to his guru. He never thinks it is time for him to become guru. Although he may indeed act as spiritual master, he never becomes proud of it.

66. Is it important to take shelter at the feet of Vaiṣṇavas?

If we do not take shelter of a devotee's lotus feet, we cannot take shelter of Kṛṣṇa's lotus feet. Without the association and shelter of the Lord's devotees, we can never obtain the Lord's service. We are all fallen souls and are therefore unable to benefit ourselves. Since we are fallen, we cannot be delivered until we take shelter of the lotus feet of the deliverer of fallen souls. There is no other way to achieve auspiciousness than to associate with devotees.

67. What is the meaning of initiation?

In the beginning, we have to know about our relationship with the Supreme Lord. Initiation is another name for the kind of knowledge we gain when we come to understand our relationship with the Supreme Lord. Merely receiving instructions regarding how to chant mantras is not initiation. Initiation is that act by which we attain transcendental knowledge. The living entities cannot benefit themselves even after studying hundreds of pieces of literature or by making a show of whimsical worship. Mercifully, the spiritual master imparts transcendental knowledge unto his sincere disciples who are inclined to serve the Lord. Only a devotee who completely follows his spiritual master's orders by renouncing his independence is eligible to receive the spiritual master's mercy and become successful in attaining actual transcendental knowledge.

68. What does it mean that the spiritual master does not make disciples?

An actual spiritual master does not make disciples. Rather, he makes everyone his spiritual master. He makes godless people devotees of Kṛṣṇa. He pleases Kṛṣṇa by engaging everyone in the Lord's service. His activities and behavior are consistent with devotion. He always sees everything in relation to Kṛṣṇa and in relation to his own spiritual master. He does not see anything with an enjoying spirit or from a mundane viewpoint. As medical professors do not make students but doctors, the spiritual master does not make disciples but spiritual masters.

If the Vaiṣṇava does not execute a spiritual master's duty, then the Vaiṣṇava family, the disciplic succession, will be checked. If, however, a Vaiṣṇava acts as if he were a spiritual master, he will become a non-Vaiṣṇava. Therefore we should not try to act as if we were spiritual masters if we are not qualified to serve in that way. If we do, we will bring about our own ruination. A spiritual master does not proudly consider himself guru.

69. What is kartā-bhajā, self-worship?

Kartā-bhajā is an unauthorized sampradāya or sect. The followers of this sect are not Vaiṣṇavas. They imagine that the spiritual master is Kṛṣṇa Himself—that is, that the guru is the supreme enjoyer. Therefore, they think there is no need to worship Kṛṣṇa. This is atheism. While it is true that the spiritual master is nondifferent from Kṛṣṇa, it is not true that he is the supreme enjoyer. He is servitor god, a topmost devotee, the personification of devotional service. He is most dear to Kṛṣṇa. In order to teach us how to serve Him, Lord Kṛṣṇa appears in this world in the form of various spiritual masters. The spiritual master is not the energetic, but the Lord's energy. He is expert in rendering the Lord service. He personifies devotion. Since he is servitor god, he has no tinge of material desire. This is why Vaiṣṇavas who are attached to his lotus feet can serve Kṛṣṇa under his guidance. They adopt the process of devotional service as their life and soul. They never consider their spiritual master Rāsabihāri, Gopīnātha, or Rādhānātha.

70. Of what type of guru should we take shelter?

If I am fortunate enough, I will take shelter of a spiritual master who always worships Hari. I should surrender to a spiritual master who is cent percent engaged in the Lord's service. Otherwise, unable to follow his ideal example, I will not be able to engage myself cent percent in the Lord's service. A person devoid of proper etiquette, a platform speaker, or a professional priest cannot become guru. If we receive such a spiritual master, unfortunately, we cannot learn to worship Hari. A spiritual master must be free from material desire, self-controlled, well conversant with scripture, and self-realized. *Śrīmad-Bhāgavatam* (11.3.21) states, tasmād guruṁ prapadyeta, jijñāsuḥśreya uttamam/ śābde pare ca niṣṇātaṁ, brahmaṇy upaśamāśrayam: "Therefore, any person who seriously desires real happiness must seek a bona fide spiritual master and take shelter of him by initiation. The qualification of the bona fide guru is that he has realized the conclusions of the scriptures by deliberation and is able to convince others of these conclusions. Such great personalities, who have taken shelter of the Supreme Godhead, leaving aside all material considerations, should be understood to be bona fide spiritual masters."

71. Is it possible to remain materialistic after seeing the spiritual master?

If we proudly think we are great, we cannot become humble. Even though we are servants, we would prefer to be masters. As a result, we would bring about our own ruination because we would come to see everything as fit for our enjoyment rather than for Kṛṣṇa's enjoyment. If we can see everything in relation to guru and Kṛṣṇa, we will not see it as meant for our personal enjoyment. When we wear blue spectacles everything appears blue; by seeing everything in relation to guru and Kṛṣṇa, we come to see everything through divine vision. Everything will rightly appear worshipable. This universe is full of objects for the service of the master of this universe. Therefore, all objects are worshipable. If we are endowed with spiritual vision, we can easily see Kṛṣṇa.

Just as the mother who is meant to be enjoyed by the father and not by me, the father is meant to be served by me, similarly I am meant to serve and worship this material world, which is meant for the universal Father's enjoyment. If we actually take shelter of a spiritual master and serve him sincerely with love, we will certainly attain Kṛṣṇa's service along with transcendental knowledge about Him.

We have to act in a way that doesn't bring us into the association of gross materialists and women. Then we will be able to treat objects meant for Kṛṣṇa's enjoyment as worshipable. Our service propensity will be awakened when we stop considering ourselves enjoyers of women and matter. When we are free of this enjoying propensity, we will actually be able to realize Kṛṣṇa. Even after we accept initiation, if we continue to maintain an enjoying spirit, we are fallen. Therefore I advise those who want auspiciousness to catch hold of their bona fide spiritual master's lotus feet and serve him as their life and soul. In this way, their perfection will be guaranteed. An obedient and faithful disciple never falls down. Devotees who are attached to the spiritual master's lotus feet will certainly attain Kṛṣṇa's lotus feet.

72. Is receiving the spiritual master's mercy the only way to attain Kṛṣṇa's mercy?

The spiritual master is nondifferent from Lord Nityānanda. By his mercy we receive Kṛṣṇa's holy name, initiation into kṛṣṇa-mantras, and proper instruction by which we can attain eternal auspiciousness. Without the spiritual master's mercy we cannot receive the mercy of Lord Gaurāṅga and Śrī Rādhā-Govinda. Our previous *ācārya* , Śrīla Narottama dāsa Ṭhākura, has explained this: the jīvas' material existence is exhausted and the wealth of love of God is attained simply by their receiving the spiritual master's mercy. The spiritual master, who is our devotional teacher, is an intimate devotee of Śrī Gaurāṅga. By serving such a guru with love, our perfection is guaranteed. Those whose hearts have become hard due to material attachment cannot chant the holy name of Kṛṣṇa, who killed the Agha demon, purely. If, however, we hear Hari's holy name attentively from the mouth of the spiritual master, then the holy name will certainly intoxicate us. If the spiritual master bestows unconditional mercy upon us, seeing our sincere humility and eagerness, glorification of Hari will come from our mouth with intensity.

73. How can we understand the actual truth?

The faith, devotion, and tastes of godless people are always opposed to devotion. With such faith, devotion, and tastes, human beings will never be able to understand actual truth. When the Absolute Truth personally appears by His causeless mercy, He reveals Himself to the surrendered souls. In the form of the Supersoul, the Lord reveals to sincere souls to whom they should surrender. Actual truth comes down to us through the pure and perfect process of disciplic succession.

74. Who is the internal spiritual master?

The localized Paramātmā, the individual Godhead situated within the heart of every living entity, who is described in the Vedas beginning with the verse dvā suparṇā, is the internal, pure, unalloyed "conscience spiritual master," the *caitya-guru*.

75. How will we receive a bona fide spiritual master?

The Supreme Lord is present in our heart as the internal spiritual master and outside our heart as a pure devotee. If we are sincere, the Lord will guide us to a pure devotee. We may approach Him and beg for such mercy, but He is the sole in-charge for granting our wish. We cannot question Him if He refuses to grant it. Kṛṣṇa is not the caretaker of our garden. Our duty is to wait patiently for His mercy. In the meantime, we should give up material desire and engage in His service. If we sincerely seek His mercy, He will certainly bestow it upon us. Simply by His mercy we will obtain a bona fide spiritual master. *Śrī Caitanya-caritāmṛta* states:

kṛṣṇa yadi kṛpā kare kona bhāgyavāne
guru-antaryāmi-rūpe śikhāya āpane

"Kṛṣṇa is situated in everyone's heart as the *caitya-guru*, the spiritual master within. When He is kind to some fortunate conditioned soul, He personally gives him lessons so he can progress in devotional service, instructing the person as the Supersoul within and the spiritual master without." (*Śrī Caitanya-caritāmṛta* Madhya 22.47)

76. How can we understand the Absolute Truth?

The Absolute Truth is the Supreme Personality of Godhead. He is the cause of all causes. The Absolute Truth is self-manifest. He is not dead matter. He is fully cognizant. He manifests before us out of His own sweet will. It is impossible to know Him by mundane experience or the ascending path. The Absolute is not an object belonging to the third dimension. We can measure objects belonging to the third dimension. Anything that can be measured with our material senses belongs to the world of Maya.

As we have to open our eyes if we wish to see the sun, we have to wait until our internal spiritual consciousness is revived before we can realize the Absolute. As we cannot see the sun at night even if we illuminate the sky with thousands of electric lights—and as there is no need of artificial lighting once the sun rises in the morning—so the Absolute Truth cannot be illuminated by sensually acquired knowledge. As long as we are materially conditioned, we cannot understand the Absolute Truth's identity. We must hear about Him from our spiritual master. Thus there is no way to know the Absolute Truth except to surrender at our spiritual master's lotus feet.

77. How will I understand whether or not a spiritual master is bona fide?

The spiritual master we choose, or a person who, according to our consideration is qualified to be guru, may not be bona fide. Only a person sent to us personally by Kṛṣṇa will manifest before us as the spiritual master.

78. What is the function of the caitya-guru (Supersoul) and the other forms of guru?

The Supreme Lord regulates the living entity's good and bad propensities by residing in their hearts as the Supersoul. The Supersoul or internal spiritual master directs all living entities. The Supersoul also guides us to a spiritual master. Aside from this, the spiritual master's servants act as instructing spiritual masters.

Persons who glorify the *śāstras*, who explain *śāstra* to others, and who act according to śāstric injunctions regulate the restless, anartha-filled minds of ignorant people. Such instructing spiritual masters help people before they receive initiation from a spiritual master.

Without the mercy of the internal spiritual master (*caitya-guru*), no one can become qualified to serve the lotus feet of the initiating and instructing spiritual masters. Until we accumulate piety in the form of Kṛṣṇa's mercy, we cannot achieve the true mercy of the *caitya-guru*. As long as our hearts are filled with the desire for religiosity, economic development, sense gratification, and liberation, we cannot aspire for devotional service. If due to good fortune we desire to take shelter at the Lord's lotus feet, then the internal spiritual master will mercifully guide us to initiating and instructing gurus.

The devotee spiritual master is attained by the *caitya-guru*'s mercy. The *caitya-guru* bestows mercy in two ways, and it is because of these two forms of mercy that some people become materialists and others become devotees. Materialists are people who have accepted sense gratification as their ultimate goal. Instead of searching for devotional service, which is the ultimate goal of life, such people seek temporary happiness. This is the *caitya-guru*'s tricky mercy. Only a cheater is fit to receive such tricky mercy. Pious, sincere devotees, however, become glorious by receiving the *caitya-guru*'s true mercy. If someone who despite becoming the Supreme Lord's servant wants something other than his Lord's service, what can he be but a cheater?

An instructing spiritual master teaches a surrendered disciple to accept an initiating spiritual master. Therefore even though there may be many instructing spiritual masters, there is no difference in opinion between such gurus and the initiating spiritual master, who awards the disciple transcendental knowledge. Rather, an instructing spiritual master is the real friend of the initiating spiritual master.

A living entity's awareness of his constitutional position is revived when he receives transcendental knowledge. At that time those who give instructions regarding the process of Hari's devotional service are called instructing spiritual masters. The initiating spiritual master is situated between the commander-in-chief and the ordinary soldiers who are in the form of instructing spiritual masters.

Only a person who is favored by the Lord in the form of the *caitya-guru* receives the good fortune to understand the devotee of the Lord as his bona fide spiritual master. Only by the Lord's mercy can a living entity see the beauty of a bona fide spiritual master's toenails and thus make his life successful.

79. In spite of accepting mantras, why are our minds still unregulated?

If our minds remain unregulated after having received mantras, it means we have not actually received the mantras. Giving mantras is more than whispering something or blowing air into someone's ears. Accepting mantra initiation means to accept transcendental knowledge. This transcendental knowledge smashes to pieces the pillars of the nescience we have accumulated since time immemorial, then builds pillars of eternal truth out of transcendental knowledge. When Lord Kṛṣṇa gave Brahmā transcendental knowledge, he said, "I am the Absolute Truth." Only an empowered personality can reveal the Absolute Truth. This empowered personality is the spiritual master. Many insignificant agents or messengers come into this world, but the most powerful messengers are sent by God. Kṛṣṇa adapts them to the needs of the recipients and calls them spiritual masters. Such expert personalities reveal the Absolute Truth. Only such spiritual masters can destroy our mental speculation and bring about a radical change in our spiritual propensity.

The knowledge we receive from the spiritual master is not mundane but transcendental, spiritual. This transcendental knowledge is Kṛṣṇa. Kṛṣṇa is eternal and full of knowledge and bliss. Mantra is fully cognizant. Mantra can definitely regulate our mind. It can deliver the mind from both vice and virtue and award us the qualification to cultivate real spiritual life.

80. What do we need to do now?

We must hear from a bona fide spiritual master. When we first hear from guru his words appear revolting to us. Some unfortunate people dare to think we can correct our spiritual master by our own experience. But the current of mundane thoughts cannot attack the spiritual master; he is situated millions of miles from such thoughts. He is known as guru because his position does not shift; he is the heaviest personality.

81. What is the result of taking shelter at the feet of a bona fide spiritual master?

By taking shelter of a bona fide spiritual master a living entity can make the highest advancement on the path of worshiping Hari. By serving guru and Kṛṣṇa a living entity's mundane conceptions are destroyed and he attains Goloka. As a result of sincere service a living entity can attain an equal position with liberated souls—even eternally liberated souls. The spiritual master, who is nondifferent from Lord Nityānanda, is not a lump of flesh and blood. By taking shelter at his lotus feet a living entity can attain freedom from the threefold material miseries.

82. Is it most offensive to disobey the spiritual master's order?

To disobey the spiritual master's order is the third offense in chanting the holy name. To disregard the spiritual master means to consider him an ordinary living being, a product of matter, and an insignificant person. To neglect his service is also an offense against the holy name. If we commit offenses against our spiritual master, the holy name will not appear in our heart. Without the spiritual master's mercy human beings cannot become liberated from the influence of high birth, opulence, vast knowledge, and fame. Such persons will be unable to attain service at the Lord's lotus feet.

The spiritual master is the direct manifestation of the Supreme Personality of Godhead. He is the servitor God, yet he is nondifferent from the worshipable Lord. The spiritual master is simultaneously one and different from Nanda Mahārāja's son. Just as we cannot see the sun with the help of either sunrays or an artificial light, we cannot see Kṛṣṇa on our own. But when by the strength of the spiritual master's mercy the fire for material enjoyment is extinguished in our heart, we will be able to see Kṛṣṇa face to face.

However hard we may try to achieve knowledge about the transcendental Absolute Truth without the spiritual master's mercy, we will find that we are laboring uselessly. It will be as if we were beating a husk after the grain had been removed. Our attainment of scriptural knowledge depends on the spiritual master's mercy. To try to attain scriptural knowledge with the help of academic qualifications is as futile as pouring ghee onto ashes.

We should never be faithless when hearing the words of *śāstra* or guru. That is an offense. It is necessary to have complete faith in the words of the spiritual master and the scriptures if we are to understand the Absolute Truth. The fourth offense in chanting is to not have complete faith in the śāstric statements.

83. Isn't the dust from the feet of guru and Vaiṣṇavas worshipable?

If the spiritual master and the saintly persons mercifully allow us to take dust from their lotus feet, we should respectfully accept it. However there is a possibility of inviting inauspiciousness if we forcibly or by request try to take dust from their lotus feet. One day, when a person named Vṛndāvaṇacandra Lashkar touched my spiritual master's lotus feet, my spiritual master became upset and said, "How dare you touch my feet?

You will go to hell." When Lashkar told me about it I explained, "Even persons like Brahmā have difficulty achieving the spiritual master's lotus feet. Attaining the spiritual master's feet is rare. Therefore what right or qualification do we have to touch the guru's feet? We cannot approach the spiritual master unless we are eligible. We cannot approach the spiritual master with our sinful mentalities and offensive hearts."

One day, out of his causeless mercy, my spiritual master personally took the dust from his own lotus feet and smeared it on my head. Such was his mercy!

84. What are the initiating and instructing gurus? What is the function of the guru who dwells in the heart?

There are three types of spiritual masters, the initiating guru, the instructing guru, and the *caitya-guru*. The spiritual master is never ordinary. He is godly. It is an offense to separate the spiritual master from Śrī Kṛṣṇa Caitanya by considering him an ordinary, insignificant human being. In the form of the spiritual master, Kṛṣṇa alone awakens the living entity's spiritual consciousness and thereby helps him attain eternal benefit.

The initiating spiritual master awards transcendental knowledge, knowledge of the Absolute Truth. "Kṛṣṇa alone is my eternal master and I am His eternal servant": this transcendental knowledge or *sambandha-jñāna* is imparted by the initiating spiritual master.

An instructing spiritual master first tells us how to remove *anarthas*, then teaches us the process of pure devotion. In most cases the initiating spiritual master acts as the instructing spiritual master. A conditioned soul cannot act as an initiating or instructing spiritual master. An initiating spiritual master gives both mantras and instructions on *bhajana*. An instructing spiritual master teaches the process of *bhajana* after our *anarthas* are destroyed.

Śrī Hari, who dwells in our hearts as the Supersoul, is the internal spiritual master, *caitya-guru*. *Śrī Caitanya-caritāmṛta* states, kṛṣṇa yadi kṛpā kare kona bhāgyavāne, guru-antaryāmi-rūpe śikhāya āpane: "Kṛṣṇa is situated in everyone's heart as the *caitya-guru*, the spiritual master within. When He is kind to some fortunate conditioned soul, He personally gives him lessons so he can progress in devotional service, instructing the person as the Supersoul within and the spiritual master without." (*Śrī Caitanya-caritāmṛta* Madhya 22.47)

The *caitya-guru* awards us the qualification to realize the instructions we have heard from the initiating and instructing gurus. He also imparts the strength to follow those orders. Without His mercy, no one can understand the intention of either the initiating or instructing spiritual master. Lord Śrī Gaurāṅgadeva alone awards transcendental knowledge and pure devotional service through the initiating spiritual master, protects that pure devotion by sending the instructing spiritual masters (who are nondifferent from Him), and as the internal spiritual master personally awards the strength to follow the gurus' orders and teachings.

85. Is anything possible without the spiritual master's mercy?

I am blinded by ignorance, so who will show me the right path? Who will impart to me real knowledge? Everything is attained simply by the spiritual master's mercy. We are fallen conditioned souls and the spiritual master is our only shelter. A spiritual master is he who always serves the Supreme Lord. The spiritual master is the servitor God. Are we looking at him in that way? If not, how can we expect to benefit from his association?

86. What actions will bring us auspiciousness?

By serving the spiritual master with great faith we will definitely attain auspiciousness. Human beings work hard in this world of distress simply so they can suffer more and more. This is māyās arrangement for the conditioned souls. Those who are busy trying to attain worldly happiness certainly invite inauspiciousness. Due to their aversion to the Lord's service, human beings have developed such a mentality. They cannot understand that their distress is caused by their endeavor to achieve personal happiness. The entire fourteen worlds are a place of such inauspiciousness.

Unfortunately, we have currently developed the strong misconception that we are the doer. How can we free ourselves from such a misconception? We have to take shelter at the spiritual master's lotus feet and engage in the Supreme Lord's service. At present we are busy enjoying this world under the control of our senses. We have come to this world by opposing the Lord's service. We think, "Let everyone gratify my senses. If anyone disturbs my sense gratification, he is bad." The only way to become free of such a miserable condition is to take shelter at the spiritual master's lotus feet.

87. Is the spiritual master great?

We are smaller than the smallest and the spiritual master is greater than the greatest. The spiritual master serves the Great, and that Great is controlled by his love. Those who worship Kṛṣṇa in the mood of *mādhurya-rasa* accept the spiritual master as nondifferent from the daughter of Vṛṣabhānu. Those who are candidates for vātsalya-*rasa* accept him as a manifestation of Nanda and Yaśodā. Those who serve on the platform of sakhya-*rasa* know the spiritual master as one of Kṛṣṇa's friends such as Sudāmā or Śrīdāmā as well as a manifestation of Lord Nityānanda, who is the Lord of Kṛṣṇa's friends. Those who pursue dāsya-*rasa* consider the spiritual master a manifestation of Nanda Mahārāja's servants such as Raktaka and Patraka.

The spiritual master is the predominated Supreme Lord. No one should misunderstand him to be the original predominating Supreme Lord or object of service. There is a difference between how we see the spiritual master when we have *anarthas* and how we see the spiritual master when we are free of *anarthas*.

We have to serve the Lord in the same way our spiritual master serves Him. If we serve the Lord whimsically and independently, we will not be successful. Material existence means the mundane concept of life. Our misconceptions can be removed by the spiritual master's mercy, because the spiritual master sees everything with equal vision. The Lord's devotees know that this world is meant to be used in the Lord's service. When our hearts are free of material desire, we will see every impediment we experience as Kṛṣṇa's mercy. Our ruination is inevitable if we think that the spiritual master is an imperfect, mortal being like ourselves, or that he is little better than we are. The spiritual master is our life and soul. Without his shelter, we will not be able to understand the spiritual conception of life and our journey will be limited to the platform of direct, indirect, and beyond the direct and indirect.

Maya refers to what we can see, smell, touch, and enjoy. We have to become servants of the transcendental Lord. We cannot achieve such service through a hired priest or the representative of a hired priest.

88. What is the spiritual master's identity?

The spiritual master is as good as Lord Hari. This does not mean that he is the supreme enjoyer. Rather, he is servitor God. Kṛṣṇa remains the supreme object of service. The spiritual master is Kṛṣṇa, yet an individual, topmost devotee of Kṛṣṇa. Kṛṣṇa is the object of all spiritual pastimes, and the spiritual master is the best among the supporters of those pastimes. There is no better devotee of Kṛṣṇa in this world than the spiritual master. The spiritual master is one and not five or ten. He is an associate of Kṛṣṇa. If associates of the Lord are separated from the Lord, then the Lord's supremacy is denied. This will result in revolution against the Lord. The spiritual master is not separate from the Lord.

Although the spiritual master and his worshipable Lord are one, they possess different characteristics. We should not attempt to eliminate the object of worship from its worshiper. The nondevotees conclude that the spiritual master's position is temporary, that he is only a means to an end and not eternally worshipable. By treating the spiritual master with such an abominable, low-class mentality, however, we will certainly go to hell.

Only Kṛṣṇa can give Himself away; Kṛṣṇa gives Himself to the spiritual master, and the spiritual master can then give Kṛṣṇa away to others. The spiritual master alone can give away Kṛṣṇa. That spiritual master who gives Kṛṣṇa away to others resides eternally in Goloka Vṛndāvana. He was present before material time came into being and he will remain afterwards.

One who does not serve the spiritual master can never become a spiritual master himself, because the spiritual master teaches by his personal example how to serve guru and Kṛṣṇa. A spiritual master is that person who eternally serves Kṛṣṇa without fail. Every action the spiritual master performs is motivated by the desire to give Kṛṣṇa pleasure. It is not the spiritual master's job to become God, because opposing God is an action of low-class, insignificant creatures.

The spiritual master can never be a nondevotee. He is self-realized and expert in allotting service to his disciples according to their particular qualifications. We will certainly achieve perfection if we receive such a great personality as our spiritual master. A spiritual master who encourages our sense gratification is not a spiritual master but a flatterer. A spiritual master who does not want to see his disciple progress approves everything his disciple does. A genuine spiritual master does not do so, because he is not a flatterer.

A spiritual master is not the disciple of his disciples, nor is he their order supplier. He does not flatter others, but carries Kṛṣṇa's order to them. Lord Kṛṣṇa is the Supreme Personality of Godhead, and there is no abomination in His existence. The spiritual master is an eternally liberated devotee of the Lord; he is devoid of *anarthas*. The spiritual master imparts knowledge regarding the Lord's energies, glories, and identity. The spiritual master appears in this world to benefit us.

Our spiritual masters are eternally perfected beings. They have not attained perfection by the strength of their *sādhana* but were already perfect. If we do not serve such a spiritual master, we will become proud, remain far away from the humble vision of being lower than a blade of grass, and will not become established as Kṛṣṇa's servants.

Despite receiving shelter at the feet of a bona fide spiritual master, we have not been able to take advantage of it because we do not pay guru-dakṣinā. To not pay guru-daksiṇā after having accepted the spiritual master's shelter is cheating. Do we feel that we belong to our spiritual master? If not, how will we serve? By serving the spiritual master with love and devotion as surrendered souls, all our *anarthas* and prejudices will be destroyed. Only through serving the guru can we achieve auspiciousness. To become indifferent to the spiritual master's service is the path of degradation.

Although the spiritual master is eternally worshipable, he is the embodiment of the Lord's service. He is the personification of devotional service to the Lord. The spiritual master is full of Kṛṣṇa consciousness. He is always absorbed in thoughts of Kṛṣṇa's service. The spiritual master's name, form, qualities, and pastimes are all fully engaged in the Lord's service. Service to the Supreme Lord is his existence, his identity, his quality, and his pastime. He is expert in loving the Lord and an experienced teacher of loving devotional service. The spiritual master is the captain to help us cross the ocean of material existence. He gives us both the holy name and love of God. He is the perfect guide, an *ācārya* for teaching us how to chant the holy name and to give us knowledge of our relationship with Kṛṣṇa.

89. Is there harm in not properly following the spiritual master's orders?

By not following the orders of the all-auspicious spiritual master the living entities invite suffering. Such disobedience or neglect increases their material desires and they go to hell after death. Anyone who does not obey his spiritual master's orders is certainly a materialist and offender. Those who transgress the spiritual master's orders take birth as pigs. Those who are too attached to material enjoyment cannot attain benefit because they do not serve the spiritual master with heart and soul, even though, due to good fortune, they have received a bona fide guru. Since they do not understand the value of such an invaluable gift they consider the temporary material world eternal and suffer birth after birth.

A Devotee's Vision

1. Do we really need to be introspective?

We have to give up external vision, the vision of material enjoyment and material forms, and become introspective. Until we become introspective, we will continue to depend on external vision. External vision is illusory.

If we are eager to know the contents of a letter, we show no patience when looking at the envelope. If we see objects in this material world as ingredients only for the Lord's service, we will no longer have external vision. The Supreme Lord is situated everywhere in this world. He is situated in the hearts of all living entities.

"The Lord is always situated in the temple of my heart just to give me the opportunity to serve Him." When this conviction becomes prominent in our minds, then according to the logic, "A learned person sees everyone equally. Therefore I can perceive my worshipable Lord everywhere," we will find our external, inferior, worldly vision cleared. At that time, I will consider the entire world full of happiness.

2. Can we save ourselves?

"I will protect myself": this is what a nondevotee demon thinks. This concept will certainly get us into trouble. Instead, devotees know that Kṛṣṇa is their protector. Why should we be afraid? We should maintain this understanding taught by the great devotee, Prahlāda. As soon as we become indifferent to *hari-kathā* and become less dependent on the Lord, we will become captured by various sinful motives and false ego. Then we will be in danger.

3. How should we treat the material world?

We should see this material world and everything in it as full of ingredients for the Lord's service. Everything in this world is meant for Kṛṣṇa's service. The day when we can look at the world like this and become liberated from the material conception, we will be able to see the material world as the spiritual world, Goloka. We should treat all women as Kṛṣṇa's beloveds. They are to be enjoyed by Him. Do not look at them with an enjoying spirit. They are meant to be enjoyed by Kṛṣṇa, never by the living entities. Treat your father and mother as Kṛṣṇa's father and mother. Instead of considering your children your servants, treat them as friends of child Kṛṣṇa. Then you will not see the material world everywhere but Goloka.

4. What is a pure devotee's mentality?

A pure devotee sees that nothing is meant for his own enjoyment. All animate and inanimate objects are meant for the Lord's service. Therefore all our activities should be directed toward His unalloyed service. *Śāstra* states: sarvopādhi-vinirmuktaṁ tat-paratvena nirmalam, hṛṣīkeṣa hṛṣīkeṇa sevanaṁ bhaktir ucyate: "Bhakti, or devotional service, means engaging all our senses in the service of the Lord, the Supreme Personality of Godhead, and the master of all the senses. When the spirit soul renders service unto the Supreme, there are two side effects. One is freed from all material designations, and one's senses are purified simply by being employed in the service of the Lord." (*Śrī Caitanya-caritāmṛta* Madhya 19.170)

All our services must target Him only. All our senses should be engaged in the service of the master of the senses. All are servitors of Kṛṣṇa. Therefore we shall not deprive them of their service. Let all of them offer their services to Kṛṣṇa. Let us pray, "May the Supreme Lord accept our service." If we use the bricks for our own house, then there will be problems, but if we use the bricks to build a temple for the Lord, we will be happy and blessed. The proper use of inanimate objects is to engage them in the Lord's service, and if they are engaged in satisfying the living entities' senses, then we are misusing or exploiting them.

We should direct our senses to serve Kṛṣṇa. All objects are really the Lord's property. They are not meant for the pleasure of conditioned souls. It is wrong and misguided to think that everything we see has been created for us. Nothing is meant for our sensuous enjoyment. Everything should be properly adjusted for service to God.

If all this world's inanimate objects are engaged in Hari's service, then their purpose is served. For example, these bamboos here—if they are used to arrange a stage for propagating *hari-kathā*, then they have been properly utilized. We use these things for the service of Hari and His devotees. All the Vaiṣṇava's activities are aimed at pleasing the Supreme Lord, the spiritual master, and the other Vaiṣṇavas. A true devotee does not do anything for his sensuous enjoyment. A pure devotee does not do anything for himself or his relatives. Whatever he does, he does for the Absolute. He is always true to the Supreme Lord's service.

5. What should be the mentality of a householder devotee?

A householder devotee must remember that his house belongs to Kṛṣṇa and he himself is a pet dog that Kṛṣṇa maintains. Śrī Bhaktivinoda Ṭhākura writes, "O Lord! I do not know what is good and what is bad. I simply engage in Your service. I guard objects that belong to You." One should serve Kṛṣṇa with all that he possesses, knowing well that Kṛṣṇa is the master of his household.

Materialists who are attached to the house do not consider Lord Hari and the spiritual master worshipable. They see the spiritual master and the Lord's Deity form as ordinary objects. Only those who can offer everything to Kṛṣṇa by giving up material attachment are able to chant Kṛṣṇa's holy name. Chanting the holy name of Kṛṣṇa is not possible unless one gives up attachment for family life and offers everything in Kṛṣṇa's service.

6. Is every devotee worshipable? Who protects the devotees?

If any rich or powerful person attacks an akiṅcana devotee, Śrī Nṛsiṁhadeva will certainly take care of the devotee. Only those among the higher and lower castes in society who have taken shelter of the Lord's devotional service are proper candidates for our spiritual respect and adoration. To consider that a Vaiṣṇava belongs to a particular class is offensive.

7. What is the mentality of a devotee?

A liberated soul does not desire liberation. The devotees are liberated souls. Therefore they do not desire religiosity, economic development, sense gratification, or liberation. Devotional service is full of happiness. Everything else is devoid of happiness. Thus only a devotee is actually happy, whereas everyone else is distressed and disturbed. Because there is no devotion in the activities of *karmīs*, *jñānīs*, yogīs, bhogīs, and tyāgīs, all of them are restless. Materialists think, "Let me be happy and let others suffer," whereas those walking the unalloyed devotional path think, "Let us perform hari-kīrtana together twenty-four hours a day without cheating anyone." The path of unalloyed devotion requires no mixes, because chanting the holy name is an infallible weapon. First one hears through the ears, then gradually one finds the other senses favorably engaged. At that point one becomes qualified to see the form, qualities, pastimes, characteristics, and associates of the Lord. According to this consideration the devotees gradually make advancement on the path of devotional service.

8. What is the mentality of a surrendered soul?

Unalloyed devotees of the Lord accept all the Lord's arrangements without argument. Displaying impatience about the Lord's arrangements proves that one lacks faith and desires material enjoyment. Devotees are not concerned whether the Lord's mercy seems like punishment, cruelty, or wealth because they are fully surrendered to the Lord. No amount of material inconvenience can distract them from their surrender or from accepting the Lord as their maintainer.

The Lord is the ultimate seer of everything; but various obstacles impede the vision of the conditioned souls. By expressing displeasure at or restlessness with the Lord's arrangements, one certainly invites inauspiciousness. The surrendered devotees have no concept other than to engage constantly in Lord Hari's service by being pleased to accept the Lord's arrangements.

9. What is the mentality of a Vaiṣṇava?

A devotee of Viṣṇu considers neither his spiritual master nor his disciples to be objects of his own sense enjoyment. He is always engaged in Kṛṣṇa's service under his guru's guidance and is pleased to engage everything in his Lord's service. A sincere disciple has no desire for sense gratification. He is concerned only with serving his spiritual master. If a disciple does possess the desire for sense gratification, it can be assumed that he is not fully serving the spiritual master. In his commentary on *Śrīmad Bhāgavatam* 4.28.34, *jagad-guru* Śrīla Viśvanātha Cakravartī Ṭhākura writes, regarding the ideal of service to the spiritual master:

gūro sevāyaṁśisya śravaṇa kirtanāt anyapi bhogān taduthān premānandān api gāhān taducit vivikta sthalaṁ api naivā pekṣat.śrī guru sevaiva sukhen sarva sādhya siddharthaṁ iti upadeśo vyanjita

A disciple who is engaged in the service of his spiritual master does not mind sacrificing the happiness he derives from hearing and chanting about the Lord. In other words, he does not care about his own solitary *bhajana*, because he knows that simply by serving his spiritual master he will easily attain all perfection.

10. How does a devotee see the material world?

An exalted devotee sees the material world as the Lord's mercy. Mercy, compassion, is worshipable. It is not possible to surpass the Lord's compassion. If one sees this material world, which is meant for the Lord's enjoyment, or the personification of the Lord's mercy in the spirit of enjoyment, one will certainly be punished.

11. What mentality should a devotee maintain?

The Keṇa Upaniṣad states that having received specific powers from the omnipotent Supreme Lord, the demigods perform their respective duties. When that power is withdrawn, the demigods lost their potency. Devotees who follow in Śrī Rūpa's footsteps rather than placing faith in themselves attribute all glories to their source. We do everything for the pleasure of Śrī Kṛṣṇa Caitanya, Śrī Rūpa, Śrī Bhaktivinoda Ṭhākura, and our spiritual master. As soon as we give up the path of devotional service, the path of subordination to Kṛṣṇa, false ego and illusion swallow us.

12. Do the devotees practice worldly morality?

Actual devotees of Kṛṣṇa never encourage immorality. The lotus feet of Śrī Kṛṣṇa, who is the personification of religion, are the complete resting place of all morality. The highest form of morality for a spirit soul is to become attached to the Supersoul. The devotees of Kṛṣṇa are the ultimate limit of this pure attachment.

Being perfected and increased millions of times, the topmost morality preached by the great soul Jesus Christ is anxiously waiting to serve the morality of love of God as cultivated by the Vaiṣṇavas.

We do not confine our conception only to worldly morality. Our ambition is to attain the morality of transcendental love of God, which is the ultimate goal of everyone's life and which is beyond all forms of ordinary and extraordinary morality. When a pure soul is situated on the transcendental platform of love of God, worldly morality appears insignificant. At the same time, devotees are neither opposed nor attached to worldly morality. Rather, all forms of morality stand in attendance on spiritual morality, just as a maidservant becomes glorious by serving an exalted personality.

An exalted devotee is always moral. People opposed to morality or who have fallen from the standard can never be considered transcendentalists. Adultery, for example, can never be called devotional service.

13. What should the mentality of practitioners like us be?

A practitioner should know that anartha-nivṛtti is the last platform before attaining the goal of life. Part of that understanding is to know that unfavorable situations create situations favorable for devotional service in the next moment. If one develops the mentality that everything in this world is meant for Kṛṣṇa's service, then the propensity for material enjoyment cannot disturb him. We should all gladly accept whatever pleases Kṛṣṇa. If Kṛṣṇa is pleased by making me averse to Him, then I should accept that. Such dependence on the Supreme Lord will protect us. When hearing and chanting about the Lord become prominent in our lives, *anarthas* are gradually and automatically destroyed. We should proceed on the path of devotional service by knowing firmly that following in the footsteps of the eternally perfected spiritual master is the only alternative for attaining our ultimate goal of life.

14. Is there more to the mentality we should maintain?

We should treat those relatives averse to Śrī Caitanya as strangers. We have to give up bad association and take advantage of good association. Unless we associate with saints, we cannot give up bad association. We should understand that those who are averse to, indifferent toward, or envious of Śrī Caitanyadeva's devotees are enemies of Caitanya.

Only those who spend their time discussing Kṛṣṇa-kathā are devotees. Those who instead of discussing Kṛṣṇa-kathā spend their time discussing worldly topics and the philosophy of impersonalism are nondevotees and sinful. That the material world is meant for our enjoyment and that we are the enjoyer is a mundane conception. Actually, the material world is Jagannātha's residence, who is the Lord of the universe.

We become fortunate when we go to Vraja if we accept our spiritual master, who is an eternally perfected associate of Kṛṣṇa, to be a Vrajavāsī. Our duty is simply to approach and follow an eternally perfected personality, accepting him as guru. That will give us the shelter of Vraja. If instead we become independent and try to see things through sense perception, we will prolong our material existence and never reach Vraja. Try your best to sincerely worship Hari. You will not live long but are bound to leave this world. Engage in the Lord's service under guru's guidance. When your serving propensity becomes strong, nothing will distract you from that. Our perfection lies in desiring the dust from the lotus feet of the guru who is a staunch follower of Śrī Rūpa. By paying close attention to the pleasure of guru and Gaurāṅga, we will not be ruined by the desire for sense gratification. We must live simply to worship Hari. Do not give up hari-*bhajana* simply because you see obstacles or dangers on the devotional path.

15. What does a devotee understand to be true?

Actual devotees do not become disturbed in any situation whether it is happy or full of distress, convenient or inconvenient. Rather, they always engage in the Lord's service with body, mind, and speech. Devotees are firmly established in the principle of serving the Lord. They think, "I am the Lord's servant. Serving Him is my life and soul. Apart from service everything is material existence or death." Devotees are by nature inclined to serve the Lord. They cannot remain without service. Only service-inclined devotees are able to serve the object of their service. The object of service, the servant, and the service are sewn with the same thread.

16. What is a real disciple?

One whose life and soul is his guru, whose ideal is his spiritual master, whose aim is to serve his spiritual master, and who is more partial to his spiritual master even though he has equal love and devotion for Kṛṣṇa, is an actual disciple. Real disciples are not weak; they are strongly upheld by the spiritual master's mercy. Their strength and hope are the service and mercy of their spiritual master. Real disciples never transgress their guru's orders even when their life is at stake. Because disciples follow the guru's order as their life and soul, they are qualified to receive their spiritual master's mercy.

17. What should a disciple's mentality be?

Our object of hearing should be glorification of the spiritual master. We must humbly follow the spiritual master's orders without any reservation. For this we should gladly accept any necessary inconvenience. This is how a disciple thinks.

The spiritual master glorifies the Absolute Truth. A disciple must hear his words attentively and then apply them in his own life.

18. What is the conception of the devotees?

Devotees consider all objects to be ingredients of the Lord's service. If we see things with a service attitude rather than a spirit of enjoyment, then everything is worshipable. If there is a gap in our hearing, chanting, or remembering the Lord, then we will be swallowed by the idea that we are the enjoyer. If we become absorbed in gossip, we will lose the opportunity to associate with *sādhus* and therefore lose the serving mentality.

Hearing and chanting about Hari is both *sādhana*, the process of attaining the goal of life, and *śādhya*, the ultimate goal. By good fortune we have received a human body. By good fortune and the grace of guru and Kṛṣṇa, we have been given an opportunity to serve the Supreme Lord. If we waste our time in idle talk, then we are misusing the gift. It is our duty to always discuss *hari-kathā* and to cultivate Kṛṣṇa consciousness. By doing so we can become the Lord's devotees, become free of the material concept of life, and attain perpetual happiness.

19. Does a devotee see Kṛṣṇa everywhere?

According to a Vaiṣṇava's transcendental vision, the Lord is eternally present in water as well as on earth. He is present in each and every atom. The Lord is situated everywhere as the Supersoul. But He does not come under the purview of those nondevotees who are attached to wealth, women, and fame. Such people do not believe in the Vaiṣṇava's conviction. But Lord Nṛsiṁhadeva, who proved His devotee's words true, proved that the Supreme Lord is everywhere by appearing from a stone pillar. Śrī Nṛsiṁhadeva destroys impediments on the path of *bhakti*.

Devotional Service

1. Will whatever we do out of duty destroy nescience?

Our sense of duty and gratitude are mental functions, not characteristics of the soul. Actions performed out of duty are based on the mind, intelligence, and false ego, whereas devotional service is an activity of the soul. If we have not acted out of pure love, we cannot call our actions pure devotion. Only what we perform with love and devotion can be called pure devotion. Duty is but regulation. Devotional service is the soul's constitutional propensity, and to maintain a sense of duty is the mind's propensity. If we wish to find fortune, we must follow the soul's constitutional propensity.

2. Who is a devotee?

One who sacrifices his happiness for Kṛṣṇa's happiness and who remains always engaged in Kṛṣṇa's service by renouncing his own enjoyment for Kṛṣṇa's pleasure is a devotee. He certainly attains auspiciousness. Devotional service is the propensity to give Kṛṣṇa pleasure. The endeavor to make oneself happy is nondevotional service and is the source of misery. A nondevotee says, "I will become Kṛṣṇa and intimately enjoy the association of women." If one rejects such a mentality and becomes inspired by a Vaiṣṇava's ideal example, he is guaranteed good fortune. If he does not keep himself engaged in Kṛṣṇa's service, he will certainly become a material enjoyer or a dry renunciant rather than a Vaiṣṇava.

3. Is indulging in worldly talks harmful to devotional service?

Śrīman Mahāprabhu told us to neither hear worldly topics nor discuss them. We should neither eat palatable foods nor wear opulent clothing. He gave those instructions for those who had developed faith in and taste for worshiping Lord Hari. Eating palatable foods is harmful, but it does not inconvenience others or create obstacles in their worship of Hari. Wearing opulent clothing, however, is more harmful to others. When we dress attractively, we draw others' eyes to ourselves. The purpose of gorgeous dress is to distract people's minds and eyes from Lord Hari's worship.

The tongue's greed—its urges—harm our devotional service. Śrī Mahāprabhu said:

jihvāra lālase yei iti-uti dhāya
śiśnodara-parāyaṇa kṛṣṇa nāhi pāya

"One who is subservient to the tongue and who thus goes here and there, devoted to the genitals and the belly, cannot attain Kṛṣṇa." (*Śrī Caitanya-caritāmṛta* Antya 6.227)

Hearing worldly topics is more harmful to us than eating palatable foods. Similarly, speaking *prajalpa* is more harmful to others than our dressing opulently. When we gossip or indulge in worldly topics, we become like prostitutes. Gossip contaminates and disturbs people's hearts. The more taste one has for useless talks, the less natural taste one has for *hari-kathā*. Śrīla Raghunātha dāsa Gosvāmī said, "asad vārtā vesyā visāja mati sarvasyahārinīḥ: "Worldly topics are like prostitutes. They contaminate and disturb one's mind." Whenever a few people gather, there is bound to be idle talk. That is why devotees always glorify *hari-kathā*. If we discuss kṛṣṇa-kathā, no one will have the opportunity to gossip. Those who are serious about worshiping Hari should neither hear nor speak worldly topics, nor should they pay attention to palatable foods or opulent dress. The desire to eat and dress opulently will certainly take us away from our worship of Hari. We cannot worship Hari as long as we desire to eat voraciously and dress attractively. Moreover, if we maintain a taste for hearing and speaking worldly topics, we will become distracted from the path of worshiping Hari. Such talks will misguide us and force us to forever relinquish our worship. Therefore, persons who are interested in Lord Hari's service must be careful about such things. Otherwise, they will inevitably fall down.

4. What is devotional service?

Devotional service means trying to please the Lord. It is meant to give Kṛṣṇa happiness, not to give happiness to ourselves. Devotional service is the soul's eternal constitutional propensity, the living entity's natural characteristic. The soul has no other constitutional duty than to offer service to the Lord. Temporary material propensities are not the original characteristic of the spirit soul but only the characteristic of the materially conditional living entity. Material propensities are changeable because they are temporary, but devotional service destroys lamentation, illusion, and fear, all of which come from absorption in matter. Absorption in anything other than Kṛṣṇa and His devotees is called material absorption. Devotional service is absolute and meant only for the Lord's pleasure. Practicing devotional service helps us develop Kṛṣṇa consciousness.

5. What is the path of auspiciousness?

No path in this material world is auspicious except the path of service to the Lord. The mentality that we understand life better than the devotees do leads to hell, and therefore keeping such a mentality is harmful. The secret of success in spiritual life is to follow the path traversed by the Lord's devotees. We should follow the devotees no matter how difficult the path. If we wish to be successful in our following, we must be humble enough to realize how worthless we are. If we understand our disqualification, we can become qualified to see the beauty of the lotus feet of Kṛṣṇa's devotees. Ordinary human beings are always proposing how to get sense gratification. If we consider such topics religious, we can never become religious. Serving the devotees is the best form of auspiciousness.

6. What is service?

Service is not a function of the body or mind but of the spirit soul. There is no business or trade in service. For the service to be actually devotional, it must be intended simply for Kṛṣṇa's pleasure. One's service should contain nothing motivated by a desire for one's own happiness. Devotional service is unmotivated, causeless, and the uninterrupted propensity of the spirit soul. One cannot understand the ultimate goal of knowledge unless he engages in unalloyed service to guru. Only the Lord's devotee is eligible to become a spiritual master. This is not an exaggeration but a fact. Lord Kṛṣṇa states, "As they surrender unto me I reward them accordingly." In the conjugal pastimes, Kṛṣṇa's devotees serve Him with their entire body. Kṛṣṇa reciprocates by giving Himself to those devotees. He considers Himself indebted to them. The ultimate perfection and goal of service is found in the conjugal mellow.

7. How can we enhance our devotional service?

Our propensity to serve will increase if we simply serve. If we have no desire at all to serve the spiritual master or Kṛṣṇa, then what is the question of increasing our service? If our mind is fixed at the spiritual master's lotus feet, then wherever we may be, our propensity to serve will increase. If our mind is fixed otherwise, we will only increase our propensity for sense gratification and material life. By serving the spiritual master continuously, we attain all fortune. If instead we choose to serve Maya or become busy seeking personal happiness, we will experience various disturbances and misfortunes and find ourselves in danger.

We cannot enhance our devotional service without Vaiṣṇava association. Therefore we should serve Vaiṣṇavas. If after taking shelter of guru and Kṛṣṇa we do not care for their service, how will we be benefited? If after taking shelter of the devotional path, we do not engage in devotional service, how will we be helped?

First, we must take shelter of the guru's lotus feet and become servants. This is called āśraya. It is the business of a surrendered soul to serve his master. Are we doing that? By offering everything at guru's feet, we will obtain the Absolute Truth, but instead of making such an offering, we don't want to give him anything. Yet we want his mercy; we want him to give us the Lord.

It is impossible to cheat the Supersoul. Unless we approach a guru, how will we increase our propensity to serve Kṛṣṇa? If after taking shelter at the guru's lotus feet we maintain our enjoying spirit or increase our propensity for material life, we will again become degraded and will not make spiritual progress. If we actually takes shelter of the spiritual master and serve him with love, we will certainly attain Kṛṣṇa's service. We will attain transcendental knowledge about Kṛṣṇa and will be merged into Kṛṣṇa's ecstatic service.

We need to engage in activities that diminish our propensity for material enjoyment and worldly life. Then we will no longer consider ourselves enjoyers and will treat the material world along with everything it contains as suitable for Kṛṣṇa's enjoyment. All objects

8. Isn't it possible to serve Hari by our own endeavor?

Service to Hari is possible only if Lord Kṛṣṇa mercifully bestows such an opportunity upon us. Otherwise, it is impossible to engage in Hari's service even after taking much personal trouble. Service to Hari is not a light engagement. In the hope to serve Hari, high birth is an enemy, opulence is an enemy, vast learning is an enemy, and beauty is an enemy. Unless we engage each of these in the service of the lover of the gopīs, they will captivate us.

We have a problem when instead of seeing the material world and everything in it as intended for Kṛṣṇa's service, we see them as objects for our own enjoyment. Seeking personal happiness makes us want to become masters of the material world rather than servants of the Supreme Lord. In this world, everyone is trying to become masters, enjoyers. This is the basis of non-Vaiṣṇavism. Devotional service is the connection between servant and master. If we continue to see ourselves as due the service of others, what is the question of our learning to serve? Only servants serve.

Karmīs and nondevotees think they will see, chant, and remember as doers. Only when they engage all their endeavors in the Lord's service by renouncing the false pride of controllership will they achieve auspiciousness.

We are Kṛṣṇa's servants. We should serve the Lord twenty-four hours a day in the association of devotees and depend fully on the Supreme Lord's lotus feet. The solution to all problems or dangers is to depend wholly on the Lord's arrangements.

In this world, we serve one another through four relationships: husband and wife, father and child, friend and friend, and master and servant. Unaware of our relationship with the Lord, we developed temporary relationships. Although these may appear good at first, they always bring disappointment in the end. Life will be auspicious if we can develop any of these relationships with the Supreme Lord.

We can return to Vaikuṇṭha from this world if we engage in the Lord's service. If instead we desire to accept service from others, remaining attached to this world, we will continue to suffer the threefold miseries of material existence. We are not Kṛṣṇa; we are not supreme. We are instead Kṛṣṇa's servants and Kṛṣṇa alone is our eternal master, the eternal object of our service. We are Kṛṣṇa's eternal slaves, His sold-out servants. As soon as we forget this and rebel against His service, we are bound to perpetual suffering. Material existence is the gateway to hell; it is a world only of sense gratification and suffering. Forgetting Kṛṣṇa begins our material existence. Therefore *Śrī Caitanya-caritāmṛta* states: *cāri varṇāśramī yadi kṛṣṇa nāhi bhaja, svakarma karite se raurave paḍi' maje*: "The followers of the *varṇāśrama* institution accept the regulative principles of the four social orders [*brāhmaṇa*, *kṣatriya*, *vaiśya*, and *śūdra*] and four spiritual orders [*brahmacarya*, *gṛhaṣtha*, *vānaprastha*, and *sannyāsa*]. However, if one carries out the regulative principles of these orders but does not render transcendental service to Kṛṣṇa, he falls into a hellish condition of material life." (*Śrī Caitanya-caritāmṛta* Madhya 22.26)

9. What is the highest welfare activity?

Let everyone be devoted to Kṛṣṇa. This is the highest benediction for the world's people. The highest form of welfare is to engage people's minds at Kṛṣṇa's lotus feet. The topmost charity or altruism is to distribute

Kṛṣṇa's devotional service to everyone. The devotees are always anxious to help others in this way.

To know God is supreme knowledge. The *Śāstra* says that knowledge means to know the Supreme Lord. Śrī Caitanya Mahāprabhu states, *prabhu kahe—"kon vidyā vidyā-madhye sāra?" rāya kahe—"kṛṣṇa-bhakti vinā vidyā nāhi āra"* The Lord inquired: "Of all types of education, which is the most important?" Rāmānanda Rāya replied: "No education is important other than the transcendental devotional service of Kṛṣṇa." (*Śrī Caitanya-caritāmṛta* Madhya 8.245)

The godless education that is being disseminated does not in any way benefit the general populace. Rather, the people have been harmed by it and will continue to be harmed. Humankind can be benefited instead simply by distributing Śrī Caitanyadeva's mercy.

10. How do we achieve devotional service?

Attaining Kṛṣṇa's lotus feet is the living entity's topmost achievement, but devotional service can be attained only in the association of devotees. Only the most fortunate souls can attain Kṛṣṇa. A living entity becomes fortunate when his desire to wander throughout the universe is extinguished. Then, when by the strength of the guru's mercy his constitutional propensity is revived, he attains the seed of devotional service. There is no difference between Kṛṣṇa's and the guru's mercy. The word prasāda means "the Lord's mercy."Śrī Caitanya Mahāprabhu states, *brahmāṇḍa bhramite kona bhāgyavān jīva, guru-kṛṣṇa-prasāde pāya bhakti-latā-bīja:* "According to their karma, all living entities are wandering throughout the entire universe. Some of them are being elevated to the upper planetary systems, and some are going down into the lower planetary systems. Out of many millions of wandering living entities, one who is very fortunate gets an opportunity to associate with a bona fide spiritual master by the grace of Kṛṣṇa. By the mercy of both Kṛṣṇa and the spiritual master, such a person receives the seed of the creeper of devotional service." (*Śrī Caitanya-caritāmṛta* Madhya 19.151)

Devotional service is defined as a desire to serve the Lord as His menial servant, only for His pleasure. Serving for our own pleasure is not devotion. When the guru plants the seed of devotion in our heart, we have to sow it in the field of the heart and water it with hearing and chanting. "I am a servant and my duty is to serve": when we become established in this conviction, we are gardeners. If after receiving the *bhakti* seed from guru—the seed that Lord Kṛṣṇa awarded us out of His causeless mercy in the form of the guru—we fail to engage in Kṛṣṇa's service but become indifferent to that service, we will find ourselves in trouble.

Impediments on the devotional path are removed by the strength of the guru's mercy. Once they are removed we will make quick progress. Therefore, we should hear about the Lord from the spiritual master and the saints and study the literature under their order. "Hearing" includes studying devotional literature. If we become distracted from our guru's feet for even a moment, it is inevitable that we will become degraded.

Hearing and chanting about the Lord is like water. Persons who have taken complete shelter at the spiritual master's lotus feet are gardeners. Our only duty is to always serve the guru with love and devotion and to associate with saintly persons. It is essential to nourish and safeguard the devotional creeper by faithfully engaging in the Lord's service. Otherwise, we will face various difficulties.

11. Should we give up material enjoyment [karma] and renunciation [jñāna]?

Mahāprabhu instructed us to give up both material enjoyment and dry renunciation. Material enjoyment is defined as accepting mundane form, taste, smell, sound, and touch through our eyes, tongue, nose, ears, and skin as pleasurable. Although there is some apparent momentary happiness in material enjoyment, we later discover that sense gratification comes with more distress than happiness. That's why renunciation is more glorious than enjoyment. Renunciation or detachment, is good, but if in the process of detachment we also renounce the Supreme Lord, then such renunciation is simply another form of material enjoyment. The conception of those who consider the material world false or as worthless as the stool of a crow is defective, because that conception denies the omnipotent Lord's energies. The material world is factual, although everything in it is temporary. This is the conclusion of those who are conversant with Vedānta.

Just as material enjoyment does not allow one to understand the relationship between the Supreme Lord and the visible objects because he deceitfully sees himself as the enjoyer, renunciation does not give one the opportunity to understand that everything in this world is meant for the Lord's service. Thus he disrespects objects related to the Supreme Lord.

Material objects are this world's opulence. Objects that have form, taste, and so on, are the goal of the senses led by the eyes. The senses will never become averse to them; they will never retire from pursuing them. Although certain renunciants sometimes dress themselves as if they were controlling their external senses; their mind, the king of senses, remains absorbed in material enjoyment even without their knowledge. Moreover, if in order to become renounced someone tries to destroy his senses, which are the gateways through which he accepts material enjoyment, the affliction he suffers due to separation from his senses will hurt him immensely before he is able to attain true renunciation.

Vaiṣṇavas know that material objects are neither to be enjoyed nor rejected. Rather, they are to be used to give the Lord pleasure. That is, they are ingredients for His service. Remaining detached from material enjoyment and accepting only what is required to keep body and soul together, devotees always act as the Lord's menial servants. Karma and *jñāna* are not the soul's constitutional propensity. The souls' only propensity is devotional service.

Liberated souls are fully absorbed in the service of their worshipable Lord in Vaikuṇṭha. If one wishes to become liberated from his own conditioned state, he must not try to engage God in supplying him sense objects for his own pleasure, nor should he reject sense objects simply to be renounced. Rather, we should accept those objects that are favorable for his service and reject only those that are unfavorable.

12. How long does the living entity remain conditioned?

Until devotional service fully blossoms in the living entities, they cannot understand that they are the Supreme Lord's servants. Thus, they remain conditioned. Unless one develops transcendental pride, how can he give up material pride?

13. Who should live in the Maṭha?

Our *Maṭha* is not meant for wrestlers; nor do aristocrats need to live in the *Maṭha*. Only Lord Hari's devotees should live in the *Maṭha*. If we remove the people in the *Maṭha* who are fond of eating and enjoying intimate association with women, the *Maṭha*'s expenditures and problems will diminish. We have to send home those proud and independent people who do not follow the *Maṭha*'s rules and regulations, and who neither follow the spiritual master's orders nor display humility. If as a result we have less manpower, we are content. We should not allow those who are not interested in worshiping Hari but who aspire for profit, adoration, distinction, women, and wealth to live in the *Maṭha*. Such people are opposed to the *Maṭha* in their hearts. They think, "I have been living in the *Maṭha* for a long time. I have worked hard for the *Maṭha*, and therefore can now eat nice foods, dress opulently, demand respect from others, and be given a share in *Maṭha* administration." We should never encourage such ideas, because they are opposed to devotional service. Such mentalities develop when living entities indulge in doubt, blasphemy, and idle talk.

We should not be proud and think, "I am expert, intelligent, a good speaker, and a good singer." These thoughts are averse to devotional service. We need to feel ourselves lower than the straw in the street. If anyone attacks or criticizes us, we should tolerate it and simply chant Hari's holy name. We should think that today the Lord has mercifully awarded us the opportunity to become humbler than a blade of grass. When someone blasphemes us, we should know that the Lord is awarding us a benediction through those whose trouble is inevitable.

14. Whom should the Maṭha avoid?

The *Maṭha* does not and cannot have a relationship with anyone who takes shelter of the *Maṭha* but is under the control of duplicity— someone with the desire to misuse transcendental knowledge. Just as we need a boat and a boatman to cross the river, we need a spiritual master to cross the material ocean. With such a mentality, these people accepted me as their spiritual master. They have never actually seen me, nor did I ever associate with them. I do not wish to associate with such people ever in my life. Although these people may not have been cheating from the beginning, they committed offenses at the feet of guru and the Vaiṣṇavas and have fallen from the path of devotional service to Hari, again taking to material life.

As soon as we try to argue with our guru, as soon as we attempt to measure the guru with our mundane knowledge, and as soon as we imitate the guru rather than follow him, we invite inauspiciousness and ruination upon ourselves. We attain benefit only when we give up such a mentality. Mundane wealth, education, expertise, and knowledge are not good assets for devotees because they influence one to disregard guru and Vaiṣṇavas. As a result, one may become bereft of the guru and Kṛṣṇa's service.

15. How do we achieve strength and mercy?

Mercy and spiritual strength are invested in the heart when one takes shelter at the lotus feet of guru without deviation. The spiritual master gives strength and mercy. Nourished by devotional service, the spiritual master's gift of mercy and strength gradually destroy one's *anarthas*. If, however, one renounces devotional service or becomes indifferent to it, the *anarthas* will again become prominent and gradually dim the effect of the Lord's mercy and strength. When a seed fructifies, a small plant grows from it. By gradually watering this plant, it will eventually grow into a tall tree. It is necessary, however, to protect the plant from external attack until it reaches maturity. In the same way, one must gradually nourish the mercy and strength the guru bestows and enhance it by practicing *bhajana*.

16. How do we become free of lusty desires?

Having lusty desires means we want to enjoy sense gratification. It is the living entity's duty to serve the Supreme Personality of Godhead. Aversion to the Lord's service drowns us in an ocean of material misery. If we wish to become liberated from that misery, we must serve the nonenvious servants of Kṛṣṇa. That is the only remedy. Kṛṣṇa's servants alone can protect us from lust. We tend toward lustiness because we are not inclined to serve Kṛṣṇa, the transcendental Cupid. The slightest disturbance in the attempt to satisfy that lust makes us angry. Lusty desire is the mother of all sense gratification. The only occupation of a pure spirit soul is to gratify the transcendental Cupid's senses. One who acts for this purpose finds the seed of lusty desires destroyed by his service and surrender to Śrī Kṛṣṇa.

17. Should one serve the devotees and the Supreme Lord personally?

It is not proper to engage others to worship and cook for the Lord. We can, however, make an exception if we are in some predicament or are ill. If out of laziness we do not feed Kṛṣṇa but we ourselves eat nice foods, then our respect for the Lord's service will diminish.

It is not proper to disturb or change the thought flow of devotees who live in the *Maṭha* or temple. Dravyaḥ mulyena suddhati: "we can purchase food if we are unable, for some reason, to cook. Our paying for it purifies what we purchase." This is applicable to those who are unable to cook. It is certainly a symptom of laziness if those who are able to cook go to the market to purchase cooked food for offering. We want only to please Kṛṣṇa. Otherwise, our lives become godless. If we love God, we will want to cook for Him and distribute His remnants to devotees. If we do so, we will never become averse to serving the devotees.

18. Is it essential to serve the Lord?

Our duty is to serve guru and Kṛṣṇa, and we will continue to do so. Let Kṛṣṇa do whatever He pleases. We must accept His arrangements without reservation. The daughter of Vṛṣabhānu does not give up Kṛṣṇa's service because She is afraid of being criticized.

19. How should devotees live at home? How should they live in the Maṭha?

Whether they live in the *Maṭha* or outside as householders, devotees should live externally like materialists while remaining internally fixed in devotional service. Do not dress simply like a devotee externally while internally remaining attached to material enjoyment—house, wealth, and fame. This is duplicity, and duplicity is extremely detrimental to devotional service. Pseudo renunciation, monkey renunciation, is abominable. Those who practice it misguide the living entities from the path of devotional service and lead them to hell. Our only duty is to follow the ideal example and teachings of Mahāprabhu. Just consider what Śrīman Mahāpra-

bhu told Śrī Raghunātha dāsa Gosvāmī: *markaṭa-vairāgya nā kara loka dekhāñā, yathā-yogya viṣaya bhuñja' anāsakta hañā/ antare niṣṭhā kara, bāhye loka-vyavahāra, acirāt kṛṣṇa tomāya karibe uddhāra*: "You should not make yourself a show-bottle devotee and become a false renunciant. For the time being, enjoy the material world in a befitting way, but do not become attached to it. Within your heart, you should keep yourself very faithful, but externally you may behave like an ordinary man. Thus Kṛṣṇa will soon be very pleased and deliver you from the clutches of Maya."
(*Śrī Caitanya-caritāmṛta* Madhya 16.238-39)

20. Can a person become liberated from material existence simply by becoming a sannyāsī?

Dressing like a *sannyāsī* and becoming a real *sannyāsī* are not the same thing. We have to take *sannyāsa* from material enjoyment and the desire for liberation. One who has made Kṛṣṇa's devotional service the essence of life by renouncing the desire for religiosity, economic development, sense gratification, and liberation is the real *sannyāsī*.

To become a real *sannyāsī* means to follow in the footsteps of the mahājanas and to become attached to the transcendental Lord. In addition, dressing like a *sannyāsī* is nothing but imitation, pretense. Śrī Mahāprabhu states: *parātma-niṣṭhā-mātra veṣa-dhāraṇa, mukunda-sevāya haya saṁsāra-tāraṇa*: "The real purpose of accepting *sannyāsa* is to dedicate oneself to the service of Mukunda. By serving Mukunda, one can actually be liberated from the bondage of material existence." (*Śrī Caitanya-caritāmṛta* Madhya 3.8)

If after accepting *sannyāsa* one lovingly serves Kṛṣṇa with body, mind, speech, wealth, knowledge, intelligence, and his possessions, he can both become liberated from material existence and become a bhakta. It is impossible to attain any benefit without rendering the Supreme Lord service. Whether one lives at home or in the *Maṭha*, one must engage in the Lord's service as his life and soul. Then only can he please the Lord. He must give up miserliness and the propensity to cheat. If he can make the Lord's service the goal of life, he can attain the Lord's mercy in this lifetime.

21. Is it possible to recognize a devotee simply by examining his external activities, education, or degree of wealth?

Materialists are fond of sense gratification, dry renunciants are detached from material enjoyment, recognizing it as the source of misery. Both materialists and dry renunciants are full of material desires and therefore nondevotees. That is why they cannot understand the service attitude and spontaneous renunciation of bhaktas. If one tries to recognize a devotee by his external appearance—his high birth, opulence, education, beauty, or other material prosperity, or by his lack of these things—he is bound to be deceived. Even the most intelligent persons are unable to understand a Vaiṣṇava's activities and behavior. When *karmīs* and *jñānīs*, material enjoyers or dry renunciants, look at devotees through their gross, external vision, they do not see the devotee's true identity. A devotee who serves the Lord lacks no opulence, because the Lord Himself possesses all six opulences. Instead of enjoying their opulence, however, devotees offer it to their worshipable Lord and unlike materialists and renunciants; neither enjoy the opulence nor give it up. Therefore, whether one sees a devotee with opulence or with no apparent opulence, one should not disrespect him because that devotee knows perfectly well how to utilize everything in the Supreme Lord's service. A devotee is neither a sense enjoyer nor a renunciant. He is something other than either of these because he gratifies his beloved Lord's senses.

It is only possible to develop this conception by the mercy of a devotee. Therefore, if one engages constantly in Śrī Hari's service, constantly chanting His names, giving up false ego, and taking shelter of the Vaiṣṇava guru's lotus feet, then one's improper attempts to measure both the Lord and His devotees, as well as one's material thirst, will diminish and one will certainly attain eternal auspiciousness.

22. What kind of Vaiṣṇava has no possessions?

Those who want nothing from this world are actually *akiñcana*, devoid of possessions. Such Vaiṣṇavas have understood that there is nothing in this world that can give them eternal happiness. The material world is a prison house for conditioned souls. Because we have been averse to Kṛṣṇa, we have been imprisoned here and have suffered the material miseries.

Although Prahlāda Mahārāja was an emperor, he had no possessions. Sudāmā Brāhmaṇa was extremely impoverished, and he too was *akiñcana*. Both devotees were free of material desire.

The *akiñcana* devotees know well that the material world simply contains ingredients for the service of Hari, guru, and the Vaiṣṇavas. They do not see this material world in the spirit of personal enjoyment, nor do they become indifferent to it. Rather, they engage everything in this world in the Supreme Lord's service. Unless we worship Lord Hari, we have no right to take even a blade of grass from this world. Akiñcana devotees realize this fact.

The devotees are convinced that by rendering devotional service to Kṛṣṇa they can attain happiness and auspiciousness. By constantly and offenselessly chanting Kṛṣṇa's holy name, they realize the essential characteristics of Vaiṣṇavas, devotional service, and the Supreme Lord.

We have to hear Kṛṣṇa-kathā from the spiritual master and the Vaiṣṇavas and then preach it to others. This is how we cultivate Kṛṣṇa consciousness. If we are not cultivating Kṛṣṇa consciousness, we will certainly cultivate attitudes unrelated to Kṛṣṇa.

23. Is working for Kṛṣṇa, devotional service?

A devotee has no engagement other than to work for Kṛṣṇa. Whatever the pure devotees do for the Lord's pleasure is devotional service. A person is subject to enjoy the fruits of his work if he considers himself the doer. Therefore, there is a gulf of difference between karma and *bhakti*.

24. How can we attain Kṛṣṇa's service?

We are souls surrendered to Kṛṣṇa. We are under the shelter of the spiritual master's lotus feet. It is not possible to see the Lord with our present material eyes. The Lord's pure devotees always see Him through eyes anointed with devotion. We are conditioned souls. Our conception as servants of the Supreme Lord will be awakened if we can simply carry the shoes of Śrī Caitanyadeva's servants. By the mercy of devotees, we will receive spiritual eyes anointed with devotion and then, by the spiritual master's mercy, attain realization of and service to Kṛṣṇa.

25. What is service?

That which gives pleasure to Lord Hari is service and that which gives pleasure to ourselves is enjoyment. Duplicitous people may worship the Deity with sixteen ingredients in order to get sons and grandsons, but this cannot be called service because the purpose behind their worship is to get something from the Lord. There is so much cheating going on in the name of Deity worship and chanting of the holy name.

Actually, serving the Lord and making a show of serving the Lord are two separate things. We should be extremely careful to make sure that we are rendering service to the Deity. Not just anyone can become a servant of the Lord's Deity. Simply paying twenty rupees does not allow us to hear the Lord's holy names or a discourse on *hari-kathā*. Such purchased recitations attract people because of the melodious singing and flowery language, but they have nothing to do with devotional service or Vaiṣṇava dharma. Instead, these recitations are karma-kāṇḍa, material enjoyment. A *brāhmaṇa* priest who has been hired for ten rupees cannot serve the Lord. Until we are firmly convinced that service to Lord Viṣṇu and the Vaiṣṇavas is the highest attainment, we cannot benefit.

26. What is the living entity's ultimate goal?

Material enjoyment or liberation cannot be the living entity's ultimate goal. The living entities are servants of the Supreme Lord, so their ultimate goal is devotional service. Liberation is the other side of material enjoyment. Both material enjoyment and liberation are witches, because both pull the living entities away from righteousness. This is why God-fearing, pious people never take shelter of witchlike material enjoyment or liberation. The devotees of the Lord are already liberated souls and therefore do not hanker for liberation. We should give up karma and *jñāna* and take shelter of devotional service.

27. Is a kaniṣṭha-adhikārī superior to a karmī or jñānī?

A kaniṣṭha-adhikārī is superior because he has adopted the path of devotion, the path of auspiciousness. Karmīs and *jñānīs* do not have such fortune. Kaniṣṭha-adhikārīs are generally engaged in Deity worship. By serving the Deity, the guru, and the Vaiṣṇavas, and by serving the Lord's holy name, living entities attain supreme auspiciousness. Śrī Caitanyadeva has said that the tongue of anyone who utters the name of Kṛṣṇa even once is the best of all. A kaniṣṭha-adhikārī who worships the Deity with mantras consisting of the Lord's holy names is superior to the best of pious fruitive workers in this world. He is also better than any *jñānī*; because however great the *karmīs* and *jñānīs* may be, they do not have faith in the eternal service of the Absolute Truth, Viṣṇu. Therefore, even though they claim to be Vedic followers, they are actually atheists, whereas the worshipers of Viṣṇu regardless of their level of advancement in the kingdom of *bhajana* are faithful to the Deity form of the Absolute Truth because they have heard of His glories from the mouth of their spiritual master. The thousands of *karmīs* who have opened innumerable hospitals, old age homes, centers for the poor, and schools, and the thousands of *jñānīs* who have engaged in meditation and undergone severe austerities are insignificant compared to a single kaniṣṭha-adhikārī Vaiṣṇava ringing the bell once before the Lord's Deity. This is not sectarianism but plain truth. Atheists can never understand the confidential purport of my words, so they sometimes openly and other times covertly criticize devotional service.

28. Is praying to the Lord for a healthy life detrimental to devotional service?

Whatever way Lord Kṛṣṇa is pleased to keep us we should accept without reservation. To desire sound health in order to worship the Lord is favorable for devotional service. To desire sound health in order to engage in sense gratification is not acceptable. Devotees do not wish to follow the path of the nondevotees, who demand that the Lord serve them. Rather, they pray for good health at the lotus feet of Śrī Nṛsiṁhadeva, who destroys all obstacles, in order to worship Kṛṣṇa, and this is certainly favorable.

29. Is the desire for fame an impediment on the devotional path?

There is no point accumulating material fame. We should remember that material fame is like the hog stool. It is to be rejected. There are two paths in life, śreyas and preyas. The materialists follow preyas and desire wealth, women, and fame. Travelers on the devotional path follow śreyas and are therefore freed from material desire. That is why association with devotees is most beneficial.

30. How can we destroy dissatisfaction?

If we are devoted to the Supreme Lord, we have no cause to feel dissatisfied. Because we are averse to the Lord's service, we are compelled to enjoy the fruits of our karma in this world. As a result of our karma, sometimes we enjoy happiness, sometimes we suffer miseries, and sometimes we become envious of others. If we realize that the Lord's service is our ultimate goal, then the miseries and desires for material happiness cannot disturb us. We should always engage our mind in the Supreme Lord's service. If we do so, no harm can come to us. If we become agitated and live in this world by displaying our dissatisfaction before others, we will not remember topics about the Lord's service.

Fighting battles of speech, bodily comforts, and battles in the form of mental dissatisfaction will not allow us to serve Lord Hari. Therefore, become as tolerant as a tree and by the Lord's will continue to live at Kuruksetra. By doing so, we will attain auspiciousness. We wait for that day when Śrī Gaurahari will send us to some other place.

31. Should we have immense faith in God?

We are constantly inducing the Lord's servants to enhance their faith in God. Their success, however, depends on their respective luck. If Kṛṣṇa bestows His mercy, everyone will profit. We should always discuss topics about the Vaiṣṇavas. Then the pride that we are enjoyers will not trouble us. Our mind can help us become bound by different kinds of material enjoyment, but when devotional service, the soul's constitutional propensity, is awakened, the pure, uncontaminated spirit soul will always cultivate *hari-kathā*.

32. How should we chant and serve?

Until we develop firm faith that service to Lord Viṣṇu and the Vaiṣṇavas is topmost, we cannot attain auspiciousness. Therefore, we should first serve the Deity with firm faith and chant the Lord's holy name simply for His pleasure. If we have some ulterior motive, we will not be able to engage in the Lord's service. Therefore, we request everyone: O friends! Give up all sinful activities and engage in the Lord's service for His pleasure. What appears auspicious in this world is not actually auspicious. You do not need to artificially dress as a Nārada as if you were in a drama. Worship the Lord and chant His holy name simply to please Him. This will award you auspiciousness.

33. What is universal religion?

People in this world currently regard activities such as following religious principles or serving our fellow citizens as the topmost religion, but they are nothing but attempts at sense gratification by the atheistic community through the artificial processes of karma, *jñāna*, and yoga. Lord Kṛṣṇa says in *Bhagavad-gītā* that we should give up all varieties of religion and take complete shelter of Him, but by creating concocted religious systems in the name of synthesizing all religions, even as they transgress the Supreme Lord's instructions, the atheists are themselves cheated, just as they cheat others. Even though the people accept such concocted religious systems as truth, they distance themselves from actual truth. The endeavors of godless people, proud of their material knowledge, can never be accepted as supreme religious principles or sanātana-dharma. The only supreme religion for all humanity is unmotivated and uninterrupted devotional service to the transcendental Lord Hari. *Sanātana-dharma* is the eternal occupational duty of the spirit soul and gives benefit to all. The *Padma Purāṇa* states: *ārādhanānāṁ sarveṣāṁ, viṣṇor ārādhanaṁ param/ tasmāt parataraṁ devi, tadīyānāṁ samarcanam*: "Of all types of worship, worship of Lord Viṣṇu is best, and better than the worship of Lord Viṣṇu is the worship of His devotee, the Vaiṣṇava." Therefore, better than worship of Kṛṣṇa is the worship of the daughter of Vṛṣabhānu, of Nanda and Yaśodā, of Śrīdāmā and Sudāmā, and of Raktaka and Patraka.

34. What is the path of devotional service?

Any path that does not deal with service to Kṛṣṇa is a nondevotional path. In pure service to Kṛṣṇa, there is no desire other than the desire to please Kṛṣṇa. Pure devotional service means to favorably cultivate Kṛṣṇa consciousness. On the path of devotional service, giving Kṛṣṇa happiness is the goal. However, on the path of nondevotional service, there is no question of seeking Kṛṣṇa's happiness. The nondevotional path means seeking sense gratification.

35. How should we serve devotees of various qualifications?

We should engage cent percent in the service of the *mahā-bhāgavata*, 66.6 percent in the service of the *madhyama-bhāgavata*, and 33.3 percent in the service of the *kaniṣṭha-bhāgavata*.

36. Why do our hearts change?

If we do not always serve Hari with love, our mind will become disturbed. Service to Hari should be constant. If there is the slightest interruption in our service, the illusory energy will take advantage of it and swallow us.

37. What is devotional service or the worship of the Lord?

Whatever is done for Kṛṣṇa's pleasure is devotional service. Rendering service to the Lord is called devotional service. Dāsya-, sakhya-, vātsalya-, and *mādhurya-rasas* are each progressively superior. Favorable cultivation of Kṛṣṇa consciousness without any tinge of anyābhilāsa, karma, *jñāna*, yoga, tapa, or vrata is called *bhajana*, worship of the Lord. Nondevotional processes such as haṭha-yoga, rāja-yoga, karma-yoga, *jñāna-yoga*, and *vrata-tapasya-yoga* cannot be called *bhajana*. It is not possible to purify the heart completely by practicing karma, *jñāna*, yoga, *tapa*, or *vrata*. Only devotional service or hearing *hari-kathā* can purify the heart completely. Even the restless mind becomes purified and pacified simply by serving the Supreme Lord.

38. Is the occupational duty of Kali-yuga devotional service?

What to speak of Kali-yuga, devotional service is the occupational duty for all yugas, for all times, and for all people. Activities like karma, *jñāna*, and yoga are only temporary duties. They are not the spontaneous duties of living entities. Only devotional service is the eternal occupational duty of liberated souls. The occupational duties of conditioned souls afflicted by *anarthas* are called karma, *jñāna*, yoga, tapa, and vrata.

39. How will our material desires be vanquished?

Śrīmad-Bhāgavatam says that Lord Kṛṣṇa, who is the benefactor of devotees, resides in the hearts of devotees who are engaged in hearing His name, form, qualities, etc. He destroys all the lusty desires in their hearts totally. Thus, for one who daily hears or glorifies the most auspicious topics of the Lord, the Lord soon personally appears in his heart.

If we can hear kṛṣṇa-kathā from a bona fide spiritual master and chant the Lord's holy name constantly, then mundane thoughts will be vanquished and remembering Kṛṣṇa will become a constant affair. The influence of chanting makes remembering Kṛṣṇa spontaneous. By regularly hearing and chanting about the Lord with a simple heart, all our obstacles are destroyed and we will achieve auspiciousness.

40. What is a devotional service?

The path devoid of kṛṣṇa-kathā is a nondevotional path. Devotional service means cultivating Kṛṣṇa consciousness. The word "cultivation" means to serve continuously. When a living entity is fixed in devotional service, he is called a devotee.

Devotional service means to please Kṛṣṇa. When practicing devotional service, there is no question of desiring sense gratification. The devotees do not serve Kṛṣṇa for any other purpose than to please Him.

The first step in devotional service is to develop faith, because the *śāstra* states that faithful persons are qualified to execute devotional service. In the beginning, therefore, we should hear scripture in the association of devotees so that our faith in the purport of the scripture will be strengthened. If we have not come to understand our relationship with Kṛṣṇa, it is not possible to engage in devotional service. *Śrīmad-Bhāgavatam* 11.2.42 states: *bhakti pareśānubhavo viraktir, anyatra caiṣa trika eka-kālaḥ/ prapadyamānasya yathāśnata syus, tuṣṭi puṣṭi kṣud-apāyo 'nu-ghāsam*: "Devotion, direct experience of the Supreme Lord, and detachment from other things—these three occur simultaneously for one who has taken shelter of the Supreme Personality of Godhead, in the same way that pleasure, nourishment and relief from hunger come simultaneously and increasingly, with each bite, for a person engaged in eating."

Detachment from material enjoyment and knowledge of the Absolute Truth appear simultaneously in the course of practicing devotional service. We cannot become detached from material enjoyment and come to know the Absolute Truth without practicing devotional service. Devotional service is attained only in the association of devotees. While executing pure devotional service, there is no desire for religiosity, economic development, sense gratification, or liberation.

41. How do we attain devotional service?

If we wish to attain devotional service, we should first take shelter of a spiritual master. This is the principal limb of the sixty-four limbs of devotional service. Unless we surrender to a spiritual master, we can never become eligible to execute devotional service. Hearing and chanting about the Lord cannot produce good results unless we subordinate ourselves to a guru. If we attempt to practice devotion without submitting to a guru, we will accumulate piety but will not learn to perform pure devotional service.

We get a bona fide spiritual master only by good fortune and Kṛṣṇa's mercy. Those who completely surrender everything to their spiritual master's lotus feet are initiated into kṛṣṇa-mantras and Lord Kṛṣṇa's teachings. Partial surrender does not bring a complete result.

42. What is the difference between transcendental subject matter (adhokṣaja) and spiritual subject matter (aprākṛta)?

We can realize the Supreme Lord only by devotional service. The Supreme Lord, who is transcendental, cannot be known by any other means. We achieve devotion simply by the mercy of the Supreme Lord and His devotees. We cannot understand the science of the Absolute Truth without the Lord's mercy. *Śrī Caitanya-caritāmṛta* states: īśvarera kāpā-leśa haya ta' yāhāre, sei ta' īśvara-tattva jānibāre pare: "If one receives but a tiny bit of the Lord's favor by dint of devotional service, he can understand the nature of the Supreme Personality of Godhead." (Madhya 6.83)

There is no such thing as devotional service if the Personality of Godhead is ignored, because the Personality of Godhead is the indispensable factor in devotional service.

We understand from the following *Bhāgavatam* verse, beginning, "anartha upasamam saksat *bhakti* yogam adhoksaje," that all *anarthas* are destroyed when we engage in the Supreme Lord's service. That is why Adhokṣaja has four arms: He destroys the jīva's *anarthas* with His weapons. In the adhokṣaja conception, awe and reverence is prominent.

From the external viewpoint, the spiritual object appears mundane, but it is not. In the conception of aprākṛta or spiritual object, there is no feeling of awe and reverence; the devotee feels only intimacy. There are no *anarthas* in the conception of aprākṛta. After our *anarthas* are completely vanquished, the aprākṛta conception manifests. That aprākṛta or spiritual object is the two-armed form of Kṛṣṇa playing a flute. He is served with love and devotion.

According to the understanding of *para*, *vyūha*, *vaibhava*, *antaryāmi*, and *arcā*, the *para* cannot be anyone other than Kṛṣṇa. The word *aprākṛta* is applicable only to the Absolute Truth Kṛṣṇa. The word *adhokṣaja* is applicable to *vyūha* and *vaibhava*. The word *aparokṣa*, indirect, is applicable to *antaryāmi*. Words like *parokṣa*, direct, and *pratyakṣa*, face-to-face, are applicable to *arcā*.

43. Are the words "devotional service" applicable only to the Supreme Lord?

Lord Viṣṇu is no one's order supplier but is the master of all order suppliers. Since Lord Viṣṇu is worshipable for everyone, the words "devotional service" can apply only to Him. The words "devotional service" cannot apply to the demigods, even though the demigod worshipers falsely attribute those words to their practices. When we worship the demigods, we want religiosity, economic development, sense gratification, or liberation, but when we worship Viṣṇu we attend only to what Viṣṇu wants.

The Supreme Lord, *bhakti*, and the devotee are sewn with the same thread. Devotional service is the via media between the Lord and His devotees, the Lord is the object of the devotees' worship, and the devotees are the Lord's servants. The demigods are not god but jīvas. The *Śrī Caitanya-caritāmṛta* states: *ekale īśvara kṛṣṇa, āra saba bhṛtya, yāre yaiche nācāya, se taiche kare nṛtya*: "Lord Kṛṣṇa alone is the supreme controller, and all others are His servants. They dance as He makes them do so." (Ādi 5.142)

The *Padma Purāṇa* states:

harir eva sadārādhyaḥ sarva deveśvareśvaraḥ
itare brahma rudrādyā nāvajneyāḥ kadācana
yas tu nārāyaṇaṁ devaṁ brahma-rudrādi-daivataiḥ
samatvenaiva vīkṣeta sa pāṣaṇḍī bhaved dhruvam

"Lord Hari alone is the supreme worshipable object. He is the controller of all controllers. Demigods like Brahmā and Śiva are subordinate to Him. Yet they should never be disrespected. A person who considers demigods like Brahmā and Śiva to be on an equal level with Nārāyaṇa is to be considered an offender."

The scriptures declare that service to the Supreme Personality of Godhead Hari is devotion, but at present the word *bhakti* is being misinterpreted and misused. People have come to think that it means devotion to the father, king, or schoolteacher. If we do not know what devotional service is and through which medium it is to be performed, we will find ourselves in trouble. Serving Lord Hari, the master of all the senses, with our senses is called devotional service. The Nārada-pañcarātra states, sarvopādhi-vinirmuktaṁ tat-paratvena nirmalam/ hṛṣīkeṇa hṛṣīkeśa sevanaṁ bhaktir ucyate: "Bhakti, or devotional service, means engaging all our senses in the service of the Lord, the Supreme Personality of Godhead, the master of all the senses. When the spirit soul renders service unto the Supreme, there are two side effects. One is freedom from all material designations, and the other is that one's senses are purified simply by being employed in the service of the Lord.

Lord Gaurāṅga states in *Śrī Caitanya-caritāmṛta*: "*anya-vāñchā, anya-pūjā chāḍi*' '*jñāna*', 'karma', *ānukūlye sarvendriye kṛṣṇānuśīlana/ ei 'śuddha-bhakti'—ihā haite 'premā haya pañcarātre, bhāgavate ei lakṣaṇa kaya*": "A pure devotee must not cherish any desire other than to serve Kṛṣṇa. He should not offer worship to the demigods or to mundane personalities. He should not cultivate artificial knowledge, which is devoid of Kṛṣṇa consciousness, and he should not engage himself in anything other than Kṛṣṇa conscious activities. One must engage all one's purified senses in the service of the Lord. This is the favorable execution of Kṛṣṇa conscious activities. These activities are called śuddha-*bhakti*, pure devotional service. If one renders such pure devotional service, he develops his original love for Kṛṣṇa in due course of time. These symptoms are described in Vedic literatures like the Pañcarātras and *Śrīmad-Bhāgavatam*." (Madhya 19.168-69)

Śrīmad-Bhāgavatam 3.29.11-12 states:

mad-guṇa-śruti-mātreṇa mayi sarva-guhāśaye
mano-gatir avicchinnā yathā gaṅgāmbhaso 'mbudhau
lakṣaṇaṁ bhakti-yogasya nirguṇasya hy udāhṛtam
ahaituky avyavahitā yā bhakti puruṣottame

"The manifestation of unadulterated devotional service is exhibited when one's mind is at once attracted to hearing the transcendental name and qualities of the Supreme Personality of Godhead, who is residing in everyone's heart. Just as the water of the Ganges flows naturally down towards the ocean, such devotional ecstasy, uninterrupted by any material condition, flows towards the Supreme Lord."

44. What is actual happiness?

The *śāstras* declare that all happiness emanates from the Supreme Brahman. Lord Kṛṣṇa is the embodiment of ecstatic love. He is the personification of complete peace. The *Brahma-saṁhitā* 5.1 states: "*īśvara parama kṛṣṇaḥ, sac-cid-ānanda-vigrahaḥ/ anādir ādir govinda sarva-kāraṇa-kāraṇam*""Govinda, Kṛṣṇa, is the cause of all causes. He is the primal cause, and He is the very form of eternity, knowledge and bliss." Elsewhere, *śāstra* states: "*na alpe sukham asti*""there is no happiness to be found in insignificant objects." Material happiness brings no satiation because it is incomplete. The Absolute Truth is the only reservoir of happiness. Therefore, only by engaging in the service of blissful Kṛṣṇa can the living entity become completely happy.

45. What is enjoyment and what is renunciation?

Enjoyment refers to sense activities, and renunciation refers to remaining aloof from material objects for sense gratification. When enjoyment is prominent, renunciation is diminished, and when renunciation is prominent, enjoyment is diminished. Neither enjoyment (material variegatedness) nor renunciation (material impersonalism) are necessary in this world. Actual enjoyment means to serve the Supreme Lord; real renunciation means to reject material enjoyment in order to give Kṛṣṇa pleasure. A devotee's two primary qualities are attachment to Kṛṣṇa and renunciation of the thirst for material enjoyment. A devotee finds enjoyment in assisting Kṛṣṇa to satisfy His senses.

46. How do we attain devotional service to Kṛṣṇa?

By attentively hearing kṛṣṇa-kathā with a service attitude from sincere devotees of the Lord who have no business other than to constantly glorify Him, we can attain devotional service to the Supreme Personality of Godhead, Kṛṣṇa.

47. To serve Viṣṇu, do we need to give up our daily activities?

Perform all your duties as Vaiṣṇavas. Do not simply engage in day-today activities by giving up the principles of Vaiṣṇavism or service to Lord Viṣṇu. Vaiṣṇavas engage in activities that are favorable for devotional service to Hari.

48. What is our eternal occupational duty?

Our eternal, occupation duty is to render devotional service to the transcendental Personality of Godhead. This duty is both unchangeable and unchallengeable. Nowadays, various so-called eternal occupational duties have been proposed, but they are all unauthorized and non-Vedic. They are nothing but the physical and mental activities of the karma and *jñāna-kāṇḍīs*. If we consider such concocted religious systems the eternal occupational duty of living entities, we will be cheated and will never attain peace.

49. Is anger toward those envious of devotees a limb of devotional service?

We should display anger toward those who are envious of devotees. This is a particular limb of devotional service. A lack of anger against blasphemers is unjustified. But we need to understand who is actually envious of devotees. Those who do not serve the Supreme Lord, the Supersoul and most blissful friend of all living entities, do not benefit themselves but instead invite trouble by their envy of Kṛṣṇa and the Vaiṣṇavas. Such people are branded as envious, and we should not show them mercy. These people become intoxicated by worshiping materialists. We should both ignore them and display our anger toward them.

But before that, we have to see whether we ourselves are envious of devotees, whether we ourselves are actually serving Kṛṣṇa. Or are we serving something else on the pretext of serving Kṛṣṇa? How much are we attached to Kṛṣṇa? Are we trying to enjoy the objects meant for Kṛṣṇa's enjoyment?

I think my enjoyment-prone material body is fiercely envious of Kṛṣṇa and His devotees, because instead of thinking constantly of Kṛṣṇa's lotus feet and happiness, I am busy worrying about my own happiness, blaspheming others, and looking for faults. I do not look at myself at all. I am such an offender at the feet of devotees that I should first learn to display anger toward myself. I am so envious of devotees that I should beat myself with shoes simply to purify myself. Then I can set an example for others and sincerely engage in the service of Hari, guru, and the Vaiṣṇavas. I must remember that everyone is worshiping Hari but me. I am unable to do so. I should also remember that I may die at any moment.

So first we should show anger toward our own sinful propensities, such as our desire for profit, adoration, and distinction and our propensity to cheat others. We must correct ourselves first. Otherwise, we cannot correct others. Then we have to correct those who are related to us, who are envious of the spiritual master and Kṛṣṇa and who are pulling us toward material enjoyment by tempting us. This is the secret of success.

50. Do the devotees want anything other than devotional service?

Religiosity, economic development, sense gratification, and liberation are fit to be kicked out. Materialists aspire for such things, but devotees never want them. Devotees aspire for pure devotional service.

We should purify the heart. Otherwise, we will be cheated despite making a show of rendering service. I had many friends and well-wishers, but they are busy in other pursuits. Even though they externally show symptoms of worshiping Hari, they are engaged internally in materialistic activities.

51. Is devotional service the only path to be followed?

Apart from devotional service to the Lord, all other endeavors, including karma and *jñāna*, are foolish and sinful. All topics excluding service to ŚrīŚrī Rādhā-Kṛṣṇa are simply attempts to cover the soul's eternal propensity. It is said that Lord Hari takes everything away, but what does He take? He does not take our skin, our flesh. He wants our soul. By taking shelter of the Supreme Lord, all our responsibilities are fulfilled.

52. Is it proper to associate with women?

A householder can associate intimately with his wife only at proper times to beget children. It is improper to associate with one's wife simply to enjoy sense gratification. Sense gratification is an obstacle on the path of devotional service to Hari.

53. Do the living entities have any business other than worshiping Kṛṣṇa?

Lord Kṛṣṇa says, "It is the duty of all living entities to worship Me alone. All their activities should be executed with Me in the center. They should engage all their senses only in My service."

54. Should we engage in devotional service twenty-four hours a day?

We should remain engaged in the Lord's service twenty-four hours a day. We should not desire anything for ourselves even for a second. This stance is natural to our constitutional position. If we can dovetail all our endeavors in the Lord's service, we will then be engaged in His service twenty-four hours a day and will not engage in any other activity, even unknowingly. Real Vaiṣṇavas worship Hari twenty-four hours a day, but such Vaiṣṇavas are rare.

55. Can we call just anything devotional service?

Devotional service means to do what Kṛṣṇa likes. Doing what we like is not devotional service but sense gratification. We should become neither sense enjoyers nor dry renunciants. We should surrender our independent natures and become devotees of the Lord by seeking His complete shelter. In this way, we will work only for His pleasure.

56. Kṛṣṇa awards devotional service even to ambitious devotees, but elsewhere in śāstra it is said that "Kṛṣṇa eagerly awards material enjoyment and liberation to His devotees but generally hides His devotional service from them." How are these two statements reconciled?

Sometimes people make a show of worshiping Kṛṣṇa while internally wanting Him to give them religiosity, economic development, sense gratification, and liberation. *Śāstra* states that "as one surrenders to the Lord, He rewards him accordingly." This means that the Lord deceives him by bestowing upon him the insignificant objects he desires. He never awards such hypocrites pure devotional service.

But if out of ignorance a devotee prays to the Lord for material happiness, then the Lord mercifully awards that ignorant yet sincere person the opportunity to hear *hari-kathā* from pure devotees or attracts him with His charming sweetness. In this way, He belittles the devotee's desires. The main point is that Lord Kṛṣṇa never awards hypocrites who only make a show of worshiping Him the rarely achieved loving devotional service. Rather, He deceives them by giving them material enjoyment and liberation. The Lord certainly awards pure devotional service to ignorant but sincere devotees through the via media of the spiritual master.

57. What does the Supreme Lord want from us?

The Lord does not want anything other than full surrender. We should cultivate God consciousness and help those who are unable to cultivate God consciousness. Otherwise, they will become hostile. We should always remember that serving Maya is not the same as serving Kṛṣṇa. Materialistic or godless people do not have the privilege to serve the Lord. Only those who are alive can serve the Lord, not those who are as good as dead. Persons who are inclined to the Lord's service are actually alive.

Fear, lamentation, and illusion shadow every step. The only way to become free from the clutches of these three plunderers is to engage in devotional service to Adhokṣaja. The Deity of the Lord is also Adhokṣaja. He is not clay, wood, or stone.

58. Why do we sometimes consider godless people great?

Sinful people, pious people, fruitive workers, mental speculators, and yogis spend their lives in godlessness. We consider them great when we are out of touch with devotional service.

The Lord's Associates and Devotees

1. What is the duty of an ācārya?

An *ācārya* is the Supreme Lord's messenger. He carries the Lord's message from Vaikuṇṭha and distributes it to us. One must hear that message emanating from his mouth through service-inclined ears. If one becomes fully surrendered, by the *ācārya* 's mercy one will achieve perfection. No one other than an inhabitant of Vaikuṇṭha is able to speak about Vaikuṇṭha. We have to hear about Calcutta from a person who has seen Calcutta. Then only will we get a true message.

2. Since I know nothing other than material experience, how will I understand spiritual subject matter?

It is true that in our present condition it is extremely difficult to know anything about transcendence, but it is also true that there are genuine methods to gain such knowledge. The messenger brings news of our friend from the far distant country, and we simply have to hear.

3. What if a messenger did not bring a message for everyone?

Those for whom the messenger did not bring a message are unfortunate. But we should note that those who are eager for a message will certainly be given one.

4. How can one recognize a messenger from Vaikuṇṭha, and how can one determine whether the message is real or false?

If my prayer is genuine, then I will understand everything by the mercy of the omniscient Lord. A student can recognize a learned scholar only by the learned scholar's mercy. The Lord in my heart will help me; I need only to depend on Him. There are two ways to know anything in this world. The first is to try to understand with the help of our material experience, and the second is to receive knowledge through aural reception from an exalted personality coming from the kingdom of knowledge. To receive knowledge by this second method we must be prepared to fully surrender to that exalted personality.

5. Who is Śrīla Rūpa Gosvāmī Prabhu?

Śrī Rūpa Gosvāmī Prabhu is an eternally perfected associate of the Lord. He is *jagad-guru* and the emperor of the devotees. In kṛṣṇa-līlā he is Śrī Rūpa-mañjarī. Śrī Rūpa Prabhu is also an intimate devotee of Śrī Gaurāṅga. He does not belong to the jīva-tattva and is not an ordinary living entity. Rather, he is the master of the living entities and part of the Lord's internal energy. He is dear to the daughter of Vṛṣabhānu.

Śrī Rūpa Prabhu is special among the devotees of Lord Gaurasundara, and is extremely dear to Śrī Gaurasundara Himself. Śrī Rūpa Prabhu understood Śrī Gaurasundara's internal mood. No other follower of Gaurasundara acted as an *ācārya* manifesting the topics of the highest supreme service. Śrī Gaurasundara's confidential internal mood is shown only to those who follow Śrī Svarūpa Dāmodara and Śrī Rūpa. Therefore, we are all indebted to Śrī Rūpa. As long as the Gauḍīya Vaiṣṇava sampradāya exists, no one will deny Śrī Rūpa Gosvāmī Prabhu's extraordinary and matchless charity. Neither can anyone repay his debt to Śrī Rūpa Prabhu, even those who surrender fully at his feet. He who dwells in the lap, on the chest, and on the head of Śrī Kṛṣṇa is our eternally worshipable Śrī Rūpa Gosvāmī Prabhu. The dust from his lotus feet is our most cherished item. His lotus feet are our only hope and shelter.

How can we attain Kṛṣṇa's service? Śrī Kṛṣṇadāsa Kavirāja Gosvāmī Prabhu tells us to serve Kṛṣṇa by serving Śrī Rūpa and Raghunātha. Our realization of the Lord's service is determined by how we are cheated of the lotus feet of Śrī Rūpa Prabhu. Śrī Rūpa's followers possess all opulence. Śrī Rūpa is the ideal example of how to cultivate Kṛṣṇa consciousness. In the ordinary historians' vision, he was a disciple of his elder brother Śrī Sanātana Gosvāmī, but even Sanātana Gosvāmī Prabhu begs Śrī Rūpa's mercy. Śrī Sanātana Prabhu says that those who do not aspire for Śrī Rūpa's mercy will never see the beauty of service to Rādhā-Govinda.

When fruitive workers and impersonalists began to gather strength in their attempts to discredit devotional service, Śrī Gaurasundara required a commander-in-chief who could preach the philosophy of devotional service and defeat their arguments. Śrī Rūpa and Sanātana were His two commanders-in-chief, and all their followers formed the Lord's army. Śrī Svarūpa Damodara Prabhu is the leader of the Gauḍīya Vaiṣṇavas, and through him all armies are recruited for defeating the opponents of *bhakti*.

Śrī Rūpa's army has no weapon other than kīrtana. Śrī Gaurasundara empowered His commander-in-chief Śrī Rūpa Gosvāmī Prabhu to use this weapon when they were together at Prayāga; He taught him how to lead an expedition against those opposed to devotional service and how to protect oneself from bad association. By discussing the battle, we can also learn to fire at the conceptions of people opposed to *bhakti*. We too can learn to destroy sinful mentality, fruitive and other forms of material desire, atheism, godlessness, and any other contrary mood.

6. Who is Śrī Raghunātha dāsa Gosvāmī?

Although Śrī Raghunātha dāsa Gosvāmī was a servant of Śrī Caitanyadeva, he was extremely proud to be identified as a follower of Śrī Rūpa. He served both Svarūpa Dāmodara and Śrī Rūpa, and was especially dear to Śrī Svarūpa Dāmodara as well as other dear devotees of Mahāprabhu. Śrī Raghunātha was the beloved servant of Śrī Rādhā-Govinda, whom He served under the guidance of Śrī Rūpa-mañjarī. Even though Śrī Raghunātha proudly considered himself Śrī Caitanya's servant, his pride at being a servant of Svarūpa Dāmodara and Śrī Rūpa was more prominent. No one but Śrī Raghunātha dāsa Gosvāmī has revealed so much about the service of Vṛṣabhānu's daughter.

7. Is Śrī Caṇḍī Dāsa a pure devotee?

Because Śrī Caṇḍī Dāsa was a pure devotee, Śrī Gaurāṅgadeva used to hear his songs. Caṇḍī Dāsa considered himself the Lord's servant. A servant of the Lord thinks himself a follower of a devotee who is dear to Kṛṣṇa. There were no abominable affairs between Caṇḍī Dāsa and Rāmī. Śrī Caṇḍī Dāsa was an exalted devotee. He had no desire for personal happiness. Not understanding his position, the materialists will go to hell because they have committed offenses at his lotus feet. The pure devotee Caṇḍī Dāsa is completely different from the Caṇḍī Dāsa the great materialists have imagined. The materialists are completely unqualified to recognize a transcendental soul like Caṇḍī Dāsa.

A servant of the Lord who serves in the mādhura-*rati* in his transcendental body is not an ordinary human being interested simply in material enjoyment. There is a gulf of difference between a mundane female body and the spiritual body of the transcendental kingdom of devotional service.Caṇḍī Dāsa taught this philosophy. If those who read Caṇḍī Dāsa and Vidyāpati engage in Kṛṣṇa's service, giving up material pride and the desire for proprietorship, then rather than thinking of Kṛṣṇa as an object of their enjoyment they will understand that He is the Supreme Personality of Godhead. Then they will realize the actual purport of the songs written by Caṇḍī Dāsa and Vidyāpati and will no longer be misled by mundane misconceptions, thinking that Vidyāpati was Lakṣmīs paramour and Caṇḍī Dāsa the paramour of Rāmī.

8. Who has categorically revealed devotional service as the ultimate goal of life?

Jagad-guru Śrīla Bhaktivinoda Ṭhākura is one of those spiritual masters who have been sent to this world by Śrī Gaurāṅgadeva for the benefit of the jīvas of this world. That great personality who has given everyone the opportunity to know about pure devotional service and the disciplic succession is none other than Śrīla Bhaktivinoda Ṭhākura. He is dear to Gaurāṅga and our only shelter.

Śrīla Bhaktivinoda Ṭhākura considers devotional service to be preyas, or for the immediate good. Previous *ācāryas* have considered devotional service to be sreyas, a process to bring us ultimate good. But Bhaktivinoda Ṭhākura, as a rūpānuga, has specifically revealed that *bhakti* is preyas. Those who do not consider devotional service preyas are godless non-Vaiṣṇavas, devoid of their own ultimate good. Human beings consider sense gratification, fruitive activities, and mental speculation preyas; but one who considers service to the Lord as preyas and whose only concern is to gratify Kṛṣṇa's senses, becomes an intimate devotee. Śrīla Bhaktivinoda Ṭhākura is such an intimate associate of Śrī Gaurāṅga and is nondifferent from Him.

Accepting unalloyed devotional service as his primarily duty, Śrīla Bhaktivinoda Ṭhākura instructed everyone to practice it. People may say that all paths lead to ultimate good, but Bhaktivinoda Ṭhākura protected human society from such nondevotional propaganda. Śrīla Bhaktivinoda Ṭhākura never discussed the incomplete, nor did he discuss nondevotional topics. His philosophy is distinct from those who try to reconcile spirit with matter and who maintain that devotional service and nondevotional service are the same. Nondevotional service and devotional service are never the same. Pleasing Kṛṣṇa and pleasing Maya are not synonymous. Śrīla Bhaktivinoda Ṭhākura had no love for anything other than pure devotional service.

Before Bhaktivinoda Ṭhākura appeared, the current of *bhakti* had been obstructed by the worldly masses. Śrīla Bhaktivinoda Ṭhākura alone considered devotional service preyas and again made the current of *bhakti* flow.

My spiritual master is he whose life and soul is Śrīla Bhaktivinoda Ṭhākura's teaching. Those who respect Bhaktivinoda Ṭhākura's words are as good as my spiritual masters.

We are under the shelter of that spiritual master who considered devotional service to be the only goal and the only thing of value. We have no relationship whatsoever with those who consider Bhaktivinoda Ṭhākura, who was a dear associate of Gaura, an ordinary man. May we never see the sinful faces of any unfortunate persons who are envious of Śrīla Bhaktivinoda Ṭhākura for the rest of our lives.

9. Why do the pure devotees sometimes laugh and sometimes cry?

It is difficult to understand the activities and behaviors of pure devotees. Love of God intoxicates them. When devotees are attached to Kṛṣṇa, they sometimes laugh and sometimes cry. Devotees laugh because they see that the world is full of happiness. This is because they are seeing Kṛṣṇa everywhere. Sometimes pure devotees cry because they realize how terribly the people of this world are suffering. They do not care what other people think of them when they exhibit these behaviors.

Śrīmad-Bhāgavatam (11.2.40) states:

evaṁ-vrataḥ sva-priya-nāma-kīrtyā,
jātānurāgo druta-citta uccaiḥ
hasaty atho roditi rauti gāyaty,
unmāda-van nṛtyati loka-bāhyaḥ

By chanting the holy name of the Supreme Lord, one comes to the stage of love of Godhead. Then the devotee is fixed in his vow as an eternal servant of the Lord, and he gradually becomes very much attached to a particular name and form of the Supreme Personality of Godhead. As his heart melts with ecstatic love, he laughs very loudly, cries, or shouts. Sometimes he sings and dances like a madman, for he is indifferent to public opinion.

The following is from *Śrī Caitanya-caritāmṛta*, Ādī 7.81-83, and 86-88:

kibā mantra dilā, gosāñi, kibā tāra bala
japite japite mantra karila pāgala
hāsāya, nācāya, more karāya krandana
eta śuni' guru hāsi balilā vacana
kṛṣṇa-nāma-mahā-mantrera ei ta' svabhāva
yei jape, tāra kṛṣṇe upajaye bhāva
kṛṣṇa-nāmera phala—

—'premā, sarva-śāstre kaya
bhāgye sei premā tomāya karila udaya
premāra svabhāve kare citta-tanu kṣobha
kṛṣṇera caraṇa-prāptye upajāya lobha
premāra svabhāve bhakta hāse, kānde, gāya
unmatta ha-iyā nāce, iti-uti dhāya

"My dear Lord, what kind of mantra have you given Me? I have become mad simply by chanting this mahā-mantra!

"Chanting the holy name in ecstasy causes Me to dance, laugh, and cry." When My spiritual master heard all this, he smiled and then began to speak.

"It is the nature of the Hare Kṛṣṇa mahā-mantra that anyone who chants it immediately develops his loving ecstasy for Kṛṣṇa.

"The conclusion of all revealed scriptures is that one should awaken his dormant love of Godhead. You are greatly fortunate to have already done so.

"It is a characteristic of love of Godhead that by nature it induces transcendental symptoms in one's body and makes one more and more greedy to achieve the shelter of the lotus feet of the Lord.

"When one actually develops love of Godhead, he naturally sometimes cries, sometimes laughs, sometimes chants, and sometimes runs here and there just like a madman."

10. Do "associate" and "devotee" mean the same thing?

The word associate means one who constantly remains with the Lord. Those who do not remain constantly with Him cannot be called associates. Even though Śrī Narottama dāsa Ṭhākura did not appear during Mahāprabhu's appearance, he is considered an associate because he appeared to fulfill Mahāprabhu's desire. Narottama dāsa Ṭhākura is eternally intoxicated by serving Mahāprabhu, and as such he understood Mahāprabhu's internal moods. He nourished the viśrambha-bhāva (service performed with love and devotion). Therefore Ṭhākura Mahāśaya was also an eternally perfect devotee.

11. Who are the Gauḍīya Vaiṣṇavas?

Devotees of Viṣṇu are called Vaiṣṇavas, devotees of Kṛṣṇa are called Kārṣṇas, and the devotees of Śrī Rādhā are called Gauḍīyas.

Lord Gaurāṅga's devotees, who are under the shelter of parakīya-*mādhurya-rati* and who follow Śrī Rūpa, are called Gauḍīyas. The Gauḍīya Vaiṣṇavas follow Śrī Svarūpa Dāmodara Gosvāmī, the incarnation of Lalitā. Therefore they can be defined as followers of Śrī Svarūpa and Śrī

Rūpa. Therefore Mahāprabhu commented to Śrī Svarūpa Dāmodara Prabhu, "This is the behavior of your Gauḍīya devotees."

The Gauḍīya Vaiṣṇavas are interested in mañjarī-bhāva, and Śrī Rādhā-Govinda, Śrī Rādhā-Gopīnātha, and Śrī Rādhā-Madana-mohana are their worshipable Deities. *Śrī Caitanya-caritāmṛta* states:

śrī-rādhā-saha 'śrī-madana-mohana',
śrī-rādhā-saha 'śrī-govinda'-caraṇa
śrī-rādhā-saha śrīla 'śrī-gopīnātha',
ei tina ṭhākura haya 'gauḍiyāra nātha'

The Vṛndāvana Deities of Madana-mohana with Śrīmatī Rādhārāṇī, Govinda with Śrīmatī Rādhārāṇī, and Gopīnātha with Śrīmatī Rādhārāṇī are the life and soul of the Gauḍīya Vaiṣṇavas. (*Śrī Caitanya-caritāmṛta* Antya 20.142-143)

ei tina ṭhākura gauḍīyāke kariyāchena ātmasāt,
e tinera caraṇa vandoṅ, tine mora nātha

These three Deities of Vṛndāvana [Madana-mohana, Govinda, and Gopīnātha] have absorbed the heart and soul of the Gauḍīya Vaiṣṇavas [followers of Lord Caitanya]. I worship Their lotus feet, for They are the Lord's of my heart. (*Śrī Caitanya-caritāmṛta* Ādi 1.19)

Madana-mohan is the same Kṛṣṇa described in the eighteen-syllable mantra worshiped by Gauḍīya Vaiṣṇavas, and Govinda is that same Govinda and Gopījana-vallabha is that same Gopīnātha. Realization of Madana-mohana Kṛṣṇa is *sambandha* realization, service to Govinda is *abhidheya* realization, and attraction to Gopījana-vallabha is *prayojana* realization, because Madana-mohana Kṛṣṇa is the predominating Lord of *sambandha*, Govinda is the predominating Lord of *abhidheya*, and Gopīnātha is the predominating Lord of *prayojana*."

Generally, Lord Gaurāṅga's devotees are known as Gauḍīyas, and the devotees in Gauḍadeśa (Bengal) are also called Gauḍīyas, just as the devotees in Utkala are called Oḍiyās.

12. Who is a Vaiṣṇava?

A Vaiṣṇava is one who is aloof from the influence of gold, women, and tigresslike fame. Such a person is detached and pure. Such a person can defeat the wholeworld.

13. Who serves the Lord in the heart?

Pure devotees install the Lord in the temple of their hearts and then constantly serve Him there with love. The devotees headed by Prahlāda Mahārāja have also served the Lord by establishing Him in a temple in their hearts. It is not possible to keep a temple open at all times, but the heart temple never closes. Kaniṣṭha-adhikārīs cannot understand this type of worship.

14. Who is Śrī Rādhārāṇī?

Śrī Rādhā is Śrī Kṛṣṇa's eternal consort and the crest jewel among His lovers. There is no one as dear to Kṛṣna as Śrī Rādhā.

Śrī Rādhā is not inferior to Kṛṣṇa in any way. Lord Kṛṣṇa Himself accepts two forms, one as the enjoyer and the other as the enjoyed. In this way He relishes eternal pastimes. *Śrī Caitanya-caritāmṛta* states:

rādhā-kṛṣṇa eka ātmā, dui deha dhari
anyonye vilase rasa āsvādana kari

Rādhā and Kṛṣṇa are one and the same, but They have assumed two bodies. Thus They enjoy each other, tasting the mellows of love. (*Śrī Caitanya-caritāmṛta* Ādi 4.56)

If Śrī Rādhikās beauty were not greater than the beauty of Kṛṣṇa, who is overwhelmed by His own beauty, then She would not have been able to attract that most enchanting Kṛṣṇa. Thus She is known as Madana-mohana-mohanī. Kṛṣṇa is compared to the full moon, and Rādhā is like His effulgence. She is also the origin of all Kṛṣṇa's energies.

Servants do not have sufficient words to properly describe their worshipable Lord, but the worshipable Lord can describe the truth about those servants. That is why Lord Kṛṣṇa alone is capable of revealing Śrī Rādhikās glories to us.

Another personality who can reveal the science of Śrī Rādhā is the spiritual master who directly serves Kṛṣṇa and the daughter of Vṛṣabhānu and who is an intimate devotee of Śrī Gaurasundara.

Lord Kṛṣṇa is the reservoir of all transcendental pleasure and the origin of all beauty and transcendental qualities. He is the shelter of all opulence, heroism, and knowledge. Only He is capable of understanding Śrī Rādhās greatness. What can puny human knowledge understand about Her glories, or even the knowledge of liberated souls? It is impossible to describe Her greatness, She, whose only shelter is Kṛṣṇa and who is able to enchant the most enchanting Kṛṣṇa. Because of Her opulence and sweetness, the whole world is bewildered.

15. Who is a real devotee?

Simply by wearing matted hair or dressing like a renunciant, or even by becoming a rich householder, one is not qualified to be called a devotee. Those who are always engaged in *hari-kathā* are devotees. Devotees are always eager to serve Kṛṣṇa throughout their lives, and their every endeavor is aimed at pleasing Kṛṣṇa.

Topics that give Kṛṣṇa pleasure are called *hari-kathā*. Those for whom *hari-kathā* is their life and soul and who cannot live without glorifying Hari are devotees. One who speaks about Kṛṣṇa for His pleasure, who is not proud of being a great speaker, and who is established as Kṛṣṇa's servant, is a real devotee. Karmīs, *jñānīs*, and yogīs cannot be considered devotees. Only those with no desire other than to please Kṛṣṇa are called devotees.

16. Who are the Lord's associates?

The eternally perfected intimate associates of Śrī Kṛṣṇacandra are His eternal associates. Those who sincerely try to fulfill His mission are His primary associates, and those who, despite living in this world, try to make advancement in *bhakti* under their spiritual master's guidance are His secondary associates.

17. Weren't there many spiritual masters during the time of Śrīman Mahāprabhu?

All these spiritual masters were associates of the Lord. They were all dear to Kṛṣṇa, and as such, are nondifferent from one another. Their duty was simply to preach the glories of *bhakti*.

18. How does the Supreme Lord give protection?

The Absolute Truth is omniscient. In order to deliver the fallen conditioned souls and to change their perverted mentality, the most merciful Absolute Truth sends His most liberated representatives to this world. This is how He protects the people here.

19. What is a Vrajavāsī?

The root vraja means "to walk." Anyone who is always walking the path of satisfying Kṛṣṇa is a Vrajavāsī. One should chant the Lord's holy name after submitting to a Vrajavāsī if one does not wish to drown in the ocean of nescience. By following in the footsteps of the Vrajavāsīs, one will attain the world of Kṛṣṇa consciousness. If one is unable to worship Kṛṣṇa constantly, then one will lose the sense of subordination to the Vrajavāsīs. My spiritual master, Śrī Rādhārāṇī, Śrī Nanda-Yaśodā, and Śrī Śrīdāma, Sudāmā all are Vrajavāsīs.

Serving the Lord and His Devotees

1. How can we gain strength in devotional service?

By serving the spiritual master with respect and love, one's heart is filled with immense strength. Only by serving the spiritual master and the holy names will one gather the strength to engage in devotional service.

2. What does it mean to see the Supreme Lord?

Seeing the Supreme Lord means cent-percent engagement of the senses in His service. In other words, serving the Lord twenty-four hours a day with all one's senses means living in one's original constitutional position. In that position, one naturally sees the Lord. By guru's mercy and on the strength of one's own *bhajana* one becomes fully Kṛṣṇa conscious both internally and externally. This is called "Seeing the Supreme Lord."

3. Is it good to try to be happy without serving the Supreme Lord?

Trying to become happy is a nondevotional endeavor. Even if one gives up the service of the Lord, the spiritual master, and the Vaiṣṇavas, and remains busy pursuing his own happiness and prosperity by demanding service from others, he cannot find it. Rather, such a person becomes an object of negligence and criticism. On the other hand, if someone disregards the pursuit of his own happiness and prosperity and remains always engaged in the service of guru and Kṛṣṇa with body, mind, and words, then what to speak of millions of people coming forward to serve him, Mahāprabhu Himself will come to offer him service.

4. Is there no benefit without serving the Lord?

Being averse to Kṛṣṇa, some living entities adopt the yoga path in order to contemplate the Supersoul, and others rush to the path of impersonal knowledge to cultivate Brahman realization. However, this is not how to achieve ultimate benefit. Service to the Supreme Lord awards one the Supreme Lord. A spirit soul cannot attain any fortune without serving the Lord. The Lord is not an object for us to associate with but the object of eternal service.

Discussing mundane topics proves our lack of interest in hearing kṛṣṇa-kathā. Simply by discussing kṛṣṇa-kathā we will certainly develop a taste for it. If we do not attain liberation in this lifetime, then we will have to take birth again. Why is it that we do not even wish to become free from such an inconvenience? And if someone wants freedom only from material life, that too is a material desire—a desire for personal happiness. Serving the Lord is not about satisfying ourselves. It is not about looking for one's own happiness. Searching for personal happiness is only selfishness. The desire for material enjoyment and liberation amounts to searching for personal happiness. That is why the Lord does not help material enjoyers or dry renunciants. Instead, He gives them over to His illusory energy. The Lord only helps those who totally surrender to Him and try to please Him.

If we wish to attain pure devotion, we must be freed from material bondage by serving the Lord without duplicity and under the guru's guidance. Unless one is liberated one cannot serve the Lord properly. One must therefore always chant the holy names while surrendered to the spiritual master. Always remember that chanting is the best form of *kṛṣṇa-bhajana*. By chanting one attains all perfection. If one simply serves the holy names one can understand everything about the topmost kingdom of worship.

5. To whom should we render service?

Both the spiritual master and the Supreme Lord are transcendental. One who has begun to develop a relationship with the Absolute Person also comes to see the spiritual master as good as God. The spiritual master is servitor God, the sheltered. Thus the spiritual master is both God and a devotee. In that sense, although the spiritual master is nondifferent from the Supreme Lord he is also most dear to the Lord. The spiritual master is Kṛṣṇa's complete energy and Lord Kṛṣṇa is the supreme energetic. The Śāstras confirm that there is no difference between the spiritual master and the Lord.

One should serve that spiritual master, who is Kṛṣṇa's devotee and who serves the Lord twenty-four hours a day. It is also essential to serve Vaiṣṇavas devoted to their gurus. Nothing is gained by serving pseudo devotees who appear as Vaiṣṇavas. Due to Kali's influence, we see many pseudo devotees these days, people who pose themselves as Vaiṣṇavas but who are actually atheists. That is why I say that one must serve the bona fide spiritual master and the Vaiṣṇavas if one wishes to make spiritual advancement.

One should also note that one may serve the Vaiṣṇava spiritual master, but later find that one's guru has again become a nondevotee. If that should occur, there is no longer any need to serve such a person. Serving nondevotees invites inauspiciousness.

It is vital to serve and follow only the Lord's devotees. We must take shelter at the guru's lotus feet and serve him with great determination. The *Śāstra* states, viśrambheṇa guroḥ sevā: one should serve his spiritual master with love and intimacy. If one serves the spiritual master and the Vaiṣṇavas with firm faith and love, Kṛṣṇa will certainly be pleased. We should not consider the spiritual master an ordinary human being. The spiritual master is faultless. Do not try to find fault with him. We may not always have the same time and opportunity. As long as one is alive, take advantage and worship Hari in the association of Vaiṣṇavas.

6. Who is dead and who is alive?

The living entities are the Supreme Lord's servants, and serving Him is their eternal, constitutional duty. Fulfilling one's constitutional duty is life. Therefore only the Lord's servants are alive; and others are dead.

The jīvas have no other business but to serve Lord Kṛṣṇa and His devotees. They are the natural servants of guru and Kṛṣṇa. Leading a whimsical life does not help us to use our life properly, and therefore we are dead. People engrossed in karma-kāṇḍa practices are dead. Those engaged in sinful activities, who are inattentive when spiritual topics are discussed, are dead. To fail to cultivate Kṛṣṇa consciousness is death. Those who choose to serve illusion are dead, even though they appear to live. It is not our constitutional duty to prosper physically and mentally. Pursuing those ends is not a sign of life but of death, unconsciousness. Devotional service alone gives supreme happiness. Everything else is only an absence of happiness. Both *karmīs* and *jñānīs* are unhappy, restless, and ultimately, dead. Only the selfless devotees are alive, happy, and peaceful.

7. What is the best form of worship?

To serve the son of Nanda Mahārāja in the mellows of sweet ecstatic love is the ultimate goal and the ultimate process for achieving it. The best form of worship is to worship the son of Nanda. The cowherd girls of Vraja did not accept Nanda's son as their husband because they were not overwhelmed with His opulence. No amount of Kṛṣṇa's opulence could attract their minds. Rather, they were spontaneously inclined toward Kṛṣṇa. Their only desire was to please Him. This great, causeless desire induced them to accept Kṛṣṇa as their husband.

8. Who is the topmost servant?

In the *Padma Purāṇa* Lord Śiva tells Pārvatī:

ārādhanānāṁ sarveṣāṁ, viṣṇor ārādhanaṁ param
tasmāt parataraṁ devī, tadīyānāṁ samarcanam

Of all types of worship, worship of Lord Viṣṇu is best, and better than the worship of Lord Viṣṇu is the worship of His devotee, the Vaiṣṇava.

The Supreme Lord worships His devotees. Although the Lord Himself is supremely worshipable, His devotees are the objects of and candidates for His adoration and love. The spiritual master is topmost among the Lord's devotees. Needless to say, one whom the Lord worships must be worth worshiping. My spiritual master is the spiritual master of the whole world, and my Lord the Lord of the universe. My spiritual master's enemies are the enemies of the universal controller. Unless we root this conviction firmly in our heart, we cannot surrender fully at our guru's lotus feet and cannot become true disciples. We will not realize our insignificant position, and will not be able to chant the holy names while thinking ourselves lower than straw in the street and more tolerant than a tree.

There is nothing more auspicious than serving the spiritual master. Among all kinds of worship, worship of the Supreme Lord is the greatest, but service to the spiritual master is even greater. Unless we are fully convinced about this, we cannot properly take shelter of our guru and understand that he is our shelter, protector, and maintainer. The Vedas say, sarvasvaṁ gurave dadyāt, "Everything should be offered to the spiritual master " If we do not serve the guru by offering our lives, wealth, intelligence, speech, mind, knowledge, and body at his lotus feet, we will not become free of our absorption in matter. We will not give up our material desires; our material disease will not be cured, and our illusion, fear, and distress will not be vanquished. By surrendering completely at the guru's feet we become free from illusion, fear, and lamentation. If we aspire for the spiritual master's causeless mercy, then the spiritual master will bless us without duplicity.

The spiritual master is not a mortal being; he is immortal or eternal. The spiritual master is eternal, his service is eternal, and his servants are eternal. Therefore we have nothing to worry about if we serve him; we will be freed from death.

Since our material attachment or sense of being the doer is strong at present, we are anxious and miserable. Only the spiritual master can protect us from such formidable pride. Do we want his protection? It seems we prefer to remain trapped in material existence. If we wanted to become free we would engage in his service. Do we have such a mentality? What to speak of giving the guru one hundred percent of our energy, we are not even prepared to give him one percent.

Unless we accept the essence of everything, Lord Kṛṣṇa, as the goal of life, how can we achieve Him? Our present pathetic condition is due to our not accepting the spiritual master as if he were as good as the Supreme Lord. This is the root cause of our continued attachment to matter. That is why I say one should not consider the spiritual master an ordinary being. He is the one who can give you unlimited life; he is the doctor of your soul, your protector, maintainer, benefactor, and selfless well-wisher.

If we are not prepared to take complete shelter at his lotus feet, then we should expect to be cheated according to the degree of our negligence or duplicity. Think carefully about this. If we are not introspective, we will not be successful.

If we do not surrender ourselves one hundred percent at the feet of that personality to whom most auspicious Kṛṣṇa has entrusted our well-being, how can he bless us? If we make a pretense of devotional service or become hypocrites while maintaining material desire, then the omniscient spiritual master will be compelled to deceive us. The *Śāstra* states, yādṛśī bhāvanā yasya siddhir bhavati tādṛśī: "According to one's state of mind one attains perfection." When you cheat your spiritual master and Kṛṣṇa by serving Maya and your relatives, without taking full shelter of guru, then the *caitya-guru* will mercifully remind you that you have not yet become a true disciple. You are not yet following your spiritual master's instructions, and your heart still contains sinful desire. Since you are accustomed to listening to your duplicitous mind and adopting the ideals and conceptions of ordinary people, that's proof that you have not yet developed ears to hear My instructions. Therefore you have been cheated. Again, it is the duty of a disciple to accept his spiritual master's arrangements for his life without reservation. If you do not, degradation is inevitable.

O my friends! Do not become sense enjoyers! Everything in this world is meant for the service of guru and Kṛṣṇa. If you try to usurp the objects meant for their pleasure, you will find only misfortune. Until you learn to see everything in relation to your spiritual master, there is no question of success on the devotional path.

9. How is it possible to actually serve Kṛṣṇa?

Actual service to Kṛṣṇa is rendered simply by serving the spiritual master and the Vaiṣṇavas. The sahajiyās cannot understand this. They think that one who worships Kṛṣṇa is great, and therefore they proudly consider themselves Vaiṣṇavas, accept service from others, and renounce their guru-and vaiṣṇava-sevā. Those who have heard the teachings of Śrī Caitanyadeva and the Gosvāmīs, however, know well that it is possible to serve Kṛṣṇa by serving the guru and the Vaiṣṇavas, who are all Kṛṣṇa's dear devotees. What is the point in making a show of serving Kṛṣṇa while neglecting to serve His devotees?

Those who renounce their subordination and service to the spiritual master pretend to serve Kṛṣṇa and chant the holy name, but they commit offenses at every step. As long as one continues to commit offenses he cannot serve Kṛṣṇa or chant His holy names purely. Only the surrendered devotees engaged in guru—and vaiṣṇava-sevā attain pure devotion by their mercy. Śrī Caitanyadeva and the Gosvāmīs bestow mercy on those who serve guru and the Vaiṣṇavas with love and devotion.

I used to think of myself as a learned scholar in mathematics and philosophy, but by my good fortune I met my spiritual master. When he shocked me by pointing out that my great qualities—my truthfulness, my pure moral life, and my vast learning—were insignificant, I realized how great he must be to consider such qualities insignificant. By his push I could understand that there was no person as fallen and wretched as myself. I understood my actual position. Here was a great soul who placed no value on qualities such as learning and moral character—qualities I esteemed highly. I understood what an invaluable object this great personality must possess! I concluded that he was either extremely merciful or extremely proud. Thereafter I took shelter of the Supreme Lord with humility. By the Lord's mercy I realized that without the service and mercy of such an *akiñcana*, I could not achieve spiritual success. When I developed that good intelligence, I received the shelter and unlimited mercy of my spiritual master and my life became successful. Here I am speaking about that most auspicious personality whom I have realized by the mercy of the Supreme Lord, my own spiritual master.

The shock I received from my spiritual master made me realize that unless people are similarly shocked they will not come to their senses. Therefore I declare that I am the most foolish person in the entire world. Do not become foolish like me! Do not try to measure the spiritual master or Kṛṣṇa. Discuss kṛṣṇa-kathā and you will certainly become a great personality.

10. How can we realize our constitutional position?

If one does not realize that he has a spiritual body, then he will remain forgetful of Kṛṣṇa and consider his body the self. The Absolute Truth is beyond material sense perception. Kṛṣṇa is the master of the senses, and one must serve Him with all one's senses. Service to Kṛṣṇa is rendered through service-inclined senses, spiritualized senses. One revives one's spiritual body only by guru's mercy. The soul serves the Supersoul, who is sat-cit-ānanda, through its spiritual senses.

People devoid of service inclination toward the transcendental Lord are compared to the animals. Better one always associate with saintly persons. The Lord's devotees are constantly engaged in His service. If we associate with devotees, we will also develop the propensity to give the Lord pleasure. Simply by associating with devotees we can come to understand that we possess a spiritual body. Then we will no longer consider the material body the self and our desire for material happiness, which is all-destructive, will be destroyed forever.

A devotee desires neither material enjoyment nor liberation. Rather, a devotee is always eager to please the Supreme Lord by engaging constantly in His service. A materialist thinks, "I will enjoy by cheating the Lord." An impersonalist thinks, "I will become the Lord myself by cheating Him." Devotees do not possess such sinful mentalities. Rather, their devotional practices situate them in their original constitutional position as the Lord's servants.

11. Does serving the Supreme Lord give real freedom?

We are so dependent in this world, and so controlled by Maya, that we cannot protect ourselves. Therefore *Śrīmad-Bhāgavatam* instructs us to constantly cultivate Kṛṣṇa consciousness and asserts that to depend on worldly strength is treacherous. We are always under death's control. What freedom can we have in Maya's kingdom? Only by engaging in the service of Hari will we become spiritually healthy and be situated in eternal independence.

12. Which concepts should one understand with great care?

We should take utmost care to attain the Lord's service by awakening our eternal constitutional propensity. We should always be eager to serve the son of Nanda Mahārāja. A person favored by Kṛṣṇa has no wealth or shelter other than Kṛṣṇa. If one is proud because of his high birth, wealth, knowledge, or beauty, he cannot attain the Lord's mercy. Such a person will continue on in material existence.

If we become attracted to the path of ultimate benefit (śreyas), we will lose interest in the path of immediate benefit (preyas). Intelligent persons should accept the path of ultimate benefit and worship the Lord in the association of His devotees until death.

Everything in this world belongs to the Lord. If we are greedy to acquire material objects we will face difficulties. Only those averse to hearing kṛṣṇa-kathā remain attached to or conditioned by material existence. Such people travel in the chariot of their minds and ultimately fall into distress.

One should give up the mentality that we have become Vaiṣṇavas. Rather, we should humbly pray for the Lord's mercy and service. Simply by the mercy of Hari, guru, and the Vaiṣṇavas we can attain the Supreme Lord's service. At that time, we will no longer be filled with false ego.

Being controlled by lust and anger, human beings become proud. When one is proud, one thinks it is no longer necessary to take shelter at the lotus feet of guru and the Vaiṣṇavas. As a result, the noose of conditioned life tightens.

To protect oneself, one should remain always in the association of devotees. We cannot survive without their association. If instead we listen to mind and remain aloof from the devotees, we will not be able to master our sinful mentality. Rather, we will feed it. Then we will be in danger of disregarding the orders of guru and the Vaiṣṇavas. As soon as we lose that shelter, Maya will capture us. Making us her servant, she will force us to travel throughout the universe.

13. How can an infinitesimal soul serve the infinite Supreme Lord?

The living entity is not an infinitesimal material object but an infinitesimal spiritual object. Even though the jīvas are tiny, they have the ability to serve the unlimited Lord. It is the soul's constitutional nature and eligibility to serve the unlimited Lord. In that sense, the soul has the same power as the Lord. If a spark is supported by the fire from which it emanated, it can burn the entire world to ashes.

14. What is the relationship between the supporter and the supported?

Lord Kṛṣṇa is the only supporter and everyone else is supported. The supported is not separate or different from the supporter. The relationship between supporter and supported is a servant relationship between master and servants. The supporter, Kṛṣṇa, is one, but there are many supported, many servants. Lord Kṛṣṇa is the unique object of service.

Although there are many servants, they are divided into five principal categories under ideal devotees. In the *mādhurya-rati* the ideal is Vṛṣabhānu's daughter, in *vātsalya-rati* Śrī Nanda and Yaśodā, in sakhya-*rati* Subala and other friends, in *dāsya-rati* servants like Raktaka and others, and in *Śānta-rasa* items like the cows, flute, and cowherding stick. Each servant serves Kṛṣṇa in one of these five flavors under the guidance of their respective ideal. Only those who do not waste time uselessly discussing mundane topics can understand the confidential purport of this topic.

In our present condition, it is impossible to understand the science of Śrī Rādhā, the personification of love for Kṛṣṇa. Vṛṣabhānu's daughter is the original servitor God and She is situated on the highest platform of devotional service. In order to serve Kṛṣṇa She even climbs on His chest, scolds Him, and chastises Him. Those who are greedy to serve Kṛṣṇa can understand the confidential meaning of these topics with their pure heart.

15. How can we vanquish lust?

Inclination for the Lord's service can protect us from the inclination to enjoy matter. Lust is another way to say "aversion to Kṛṣṇa's service." It is our duty to serve the complete whole. The only way to be rid of lust is to serve those devotees who are free from material desire. Kṛṣṇa's devotees are alone capable of protecting us from lust's influence. Lust is opposed to devotional service. We experience mundane lust because we lack attraction to the transcendental Cupid. We should give our attention to gratifying His senses. Surrender and service to Kṛṣṇa destroys the seed of lust.

16. Should service be rendered personally?

Every one of us will have to become servants of the transcendental Personality of Godhead. We cannot hire a representative, even a priest, to perform our service for us. I have see that in some sampradāyas, a spokesman conducts the worship while others remain standing. This is not how we render service. We must each engage ourselves in the Lord's service under the guidance of an *ācārya* . We can perfect our lives when we associate with saintly persons, chant the Lord's holy name, hearing *hari-kathā*, and worshiping the Deity. But we will fail totally if we act out a pretense. If instead of surrendering ourselves we try to imitate these activities without heart, we will fail to achieve the goal.

Whatever wealth and assets we are given by Kṛṣṇa's will, we should engage them in Kṛṣṇa's service. We will be in trouble if we accumulate wealth either through miserliness or by remaining indifferent to the Lord's service.

Many people suggest that I make a permanent arrangement for the continuation of the *Maṭha*'s Deity worship, but I will not do that. If there is actual inclination to serve the Lord and actual surrender, then by the Lord's mercy His service will continue unhindered and Mahāprabhu's teachings will be preached boldly. Otherwise, let everything go to hell.

We should pay close attention to the welfare of others and ourselves. We will not live in this world for too long time. If we give up our bodies while chanting Hari's glories and engaging in His service, then our lives will be successful. We have not come to this material world to become carpenters and builders. We are simply messengers of Śrī Caitanyadeva's teachings.

17. Is it a mistake to consider serving one's family synonymous with serving the Lord?

One's home, which is the abode of one's enjoyment, and the temple, the abode of Hari's service, are not one and the same. Therefore it is a mistake to consider serving the family the same as serving the Lord. The mentality of an attached householder and the devotee's propensity to serve Hari are two separate things. However, for those who are actually engaged in hari-*bhajana*, there is no difference between the *Maṭha* and their home. And for those who are unable to practice hari-*bhajana* anywhere, there is no real difference between the *Maṭha* and their home; they will be disturbed by illusion in both places.

If we think serving our family is synonymous with serving Hari, there is no hope for spiritual advancement. It is impossible to serve Hari as long as we remain attached to and focused on our temporary relatives and the life we build with them. If we are bound by such temporary material affections, then affection for our relatives will become the object of our service.

When we forget who is the father of whom or the son of whom, we are bound to become degraded. Even after accepting initiation, if we feel that association with those who are averse to Lord Hari, such as our father, son, country, wife, or mother is favorable for our spiritual progress, obviously we have forgotten what it means to execute pure devotion. In such a situation we should renounce our misconceptions and restlessness and associate with the living source (guru) for some time. Otherwise, dangerous attachment for relatives, affections for children, and pleasures in the wife's company, will perpetually separate us from our actual worship. We will come to desire only material life. It is only bad association that teaches us these mistaken conceptions. If we want to free ourselves from that mess, we must associate with Kṛṣṇa's devotees and hear the scripture.

18. Who is not able to follow?

The living entities cannot benefit without serving Kṛṣṇa, the transcendental Absolute Truth. No one other than my spiritual master is able to render service to that supreme worshipable Lord. Whoever lacks this conviction cannot surrender.

19. What is the value of accepting a material body?

This body is a product of matter, a bag of flesh and bones with no relation to Kṛṣṇa. The only value in accepting a material body is if one engages it in Kṛṣṇa's service under the spiritual master's guidance. It is always profitable to engage one's worldly knowledge, education, and so on in the Lord's service.

20. What is the secret of success?

We are servants of the Supreme Lord and our only goal is to serve Him. This is the way of success. There is no duty superior to serving the Supreme Lord. We must enter into Kṛṣṇa's family, not Maya's family. We are successful when we become servants, not masters.

21. What is the main duty of those who want to serve God?

The first and foremost duty of those who want to serve the Lord is to give up bad association. Until one gives up the association of nondevotees, one cannot begin to associate properly with devotees. All desires other than the desire to serve Kṛṣṇa are considered bad association. *Śrī Caitanya-caritāmṛta* states:

'duḥsaṅga' kahiye—— 'kaitava', 'ātma-vañcanā
kṛṣṇa, kṛṣṇa-bhakti vinu anya kāmanā

Cheating oneself and cheating others is called kaitava. Associating with those who cheat in this way is called duḥsaṅga, bad association. Those who desire things other than Kṛṣṇa's service are also called duḥsaṅga, bad association. (*Śrī Caitanya-caritāmṛta* Madhya 24.99)

A sincere devotee firmly renounces association with nondevotees. He respectfully associates with and serves the devotees.

Now the question must be asked: Who is a devotee? One who constantly chants the Hari's holy name, who discusses Hari and His pastimes and instructions, and who engages in His service is a devotee or saintly person. Those who spend their time in sense gratification, planning to become happy in this world, are nondevotees or sinful.

The sincere practitioners of devotional service reluctantly accept only as much sense gratification as necessary to keep body and soul together while they eagerly engage in vaiṣṇava-sevā. As a result they gradually attain auspiciousness. *Śrīmad-Bhāgavatam* (11.26.26) states:

tato duḥsaṅgam utsṛjya, satsu sajjeta buddhimān
santa evāsya chindanti, mano-vyāsaṅgam uktibhiḥ

An intelligent person should therefore reject all bad association and instead take up the association of saintly devotees, whose words cut off the excessive attachment of one's mind.

People averse to God are nondevotees. We have to give up the association even of our near and dear ones if they are averse to God. People opposed to Śrī Caitanya are opposed to the Supreme Lord. Those who do not take shelter at Śrī Caitanya's lotus feet or follow His invaluable teachings are nondevotees. Only those who follow in the footsteps of Śrī Caitanyadeva's devotees and are faithful to them are actually inclined to serve the Lord.

As people who desire knowledge cannot avoid taking shelter of learned people, similarly those fortunate and pious persons who want to attain the Lord's shelter cannot avoid taking shelter of Śrī Gaurāṅgadeva, who has appeared in this age, and His devotees. The Supreme Lord can be attained through their mercy.

22. What is our main duty at present?

We can taste sense gratification and enjoy the fruit of our karma birth after birth. But let's set these aside and now engage in serving Kṛṣṇa. That is our most important duty, and it can be executed only in the human form of life. If we had been born demigods we would not have been given the time or opportunity to hear *hari-kathā*. Therefore until our last breath we should try our best to attain the Lord's lotus feet. There is no greater duty than this.

23. What is the duty of a brahmacārī?

A *brahmacārī* does not enter family life. On seeing the householders' distress, *brahmacārīs* remain cautious. Perhaps he will wonder who will cook for him, and such fears drive him into family life. He thinks he will somehow manage and live his life in happiness and with little distress. Such ideas get people into trouble.

Our perfection and prime necessity is to attain the Lord's service. There is nothing more important than this. Devotional service will give us ultimate peace, happiness, and fulfill life's ultimate goal. If we give up the Lord's service simply to seek personal happiness, we will find only distress in the end. Join Kṛṣṇa's family, leave Maya's family aside. Try to become a servant and forget about being the master.

24. What is the proper religious principle?

Bhāgavata-dharma, *bhakti-dharma*, and *bhāgavata-sevā-dharma* are different names for the proper religious principle. To serve Kṛṣṇa and His devotees is a proper religious principle. Apart from this, everything else is temporary or conditioned dharma, or even an improper religious principle. Devotional service to the Lord is the soul's eternal occupational duty, and that is why it is called a "proper religious principle."

When people realize that all living entities are servants of Kṛṣṇa, they will see with equal vision. This means they will be liberated from the constant need to discriminate between large and small.

To follow the path of peace means to engage in Kṛṣṇa's service. Devotional service is sanātana-dharma, eternal dharma, and is also called parama-dharma and ātmā-dharma. Without devotional service the jīva's life is useless. Without devotional service, every endeavor is aimed only at becoming the master. Devotional servitorship is on one side of the balance, and the attempt to master the material energy by practicing karma, *jñāna*, yoga, or anyalabhilāṣa is on the other. Chanting the holy name is the ultimate goal of *bhāgavata-dharma*. There is no other remedy for our material disease than Kṛṣṇa's name.

25. What is service?

Hari's servants preach: O living entities! Please engage in Kṛṣṇa's service. You do not need to do anything else. Do not engage in sense gratification in the name of serving Hari. Remember that devotional service means gratifying Kṛṣṇa's senses, whereas gratifying your own senses and materialistic relatives is selfishness. If you think they are synonymous, you have been deceived. Do not mistake serving your family for serving the Lord. After taking shelter of the Lord, do not waste time serving Maya. This will not help you. Rather, it will increase your attachment to material life and you will fall down from the platform of devotion. Be eager to serve the Lord if you wish to attain Him. Serving Kṛṣṇa is not a joke. If you try to cheat Him, you yourself will be cheated. Therefore, be clever and serious and forget everything but Kṛṣṇa's service. Then the Supreme Personality of Godhead Kṛṣṇa will be pleased with you.

26. Does the soul enjoy?

The soul serves the Supersoul as its only duty. Therefore, why should the soul renounce the Lord's service to engage in material enjoyment? It is not natural for the soul to hanker after material enjoyment. Such hankering is the nature of the mind. The propensity to taste material enjoyment binds one to matter and covers the soul's original propensity to serve Kṛṣṇa.

27. How can we prepare ourselves to serve God?

We attain the Supreme Lord's mercy by serving the spiritual master. Such service qualifies us to serve God. If we simply serve the spiritual master and the transcendental sound vibration we will be given spiritual strength.

28. We consider doing good to others our religion. What is your opinion in this regard?

Welfare work is good, but it has two defects: it directly or indirectly encourages godlessness, and it supports violence to animals and other living entities. Whatever attempts we make to help others while neglecting the Absolute are useless.

Neither are we in favor of practicing devotion in order to use the *sādhus* for our own ends. Those who want to accomplish something mundane by using the *sādhus* proves that they have no respect whatsoever for saintly persons.

Ordinary altruism is not the goal of life. There is a much more important duty while one is in the human form of life, and that is to serve God. Serving God can permanently liberate people from their material distress and allow them to taste eternal happiness. It is our intention to convert the entire human population to practicing *bhakti*.

Serving God is the soul's supreme eternal religion. Hearing Śrī Caitanyadeva's teachings on this point will forever help everyone. Śrī Caitanyadeva said:

bhārata-bhūmite haila manuṣya janma yāra
janma sārthaka kari' kara para-upakāra

One who has taken his birth as a human being in the land of India [Bhārata-varṣa] should make his life successful and work for the benefit of all other people. (*Śrī Caitanya-caritāmṛta* Ādi 9.41)

Śrī Caitanyadeva preached throughout the world for the welfare of all jīvas, but the welfare work He proposed was not of the temporary, insignificant, narrow-minded, changeable, or imaginary type—not pie in the sky—as is the welfare work proposed by so-called social reformers and mundane philanthropists. The welfare work He proposed is of the highest caliber and is neither temporary nor insignificant. The ways to uplift others as invented, being invented, and about to be invented by ordinary human beings according to their narrow considerations will in no way benefit anyone because they are each temporary. Śrī Mahāprabhu revealed the actual way to uplift others:

dharmaḥ projjhita-kaitavo 'tra paramo nirmatsarāṇāṁ satāṁ
vedyaṁ vāstavam atra vastu śivadaṁ tāpa-trayonmūlanam

śrīmad-bhāgavate mahā-muni-kṛte kiṁ vā parair īśvaraḥ
sadyo hṛdy avarudhyate 'tra kṛtibhiḥśuśrūṣubhis tat-kṣaṇāt

Completely rejecting all religious activities which are materially motivated, this Bhāgavata *Purāṇa* propounds the highest truth, which is understandable by those devotees who are fully pure in heart. The highest truth is reality distinguished from illusion for the welfare of all. Such truth uproots the threefold miseries. This beautiful *Bhāgavatam*, compiled by the great sage Vyāsadeva [in his maturity], is sufficient in itself for God realization. What is the need of any other scripture? As soon as one attentively and submissively hears the message of *Bhāgavatam*, by this culture of knowledge, the Supreme Lord is established within his heart. (*Śrīmad Bhāgavatam* 1.1.2)

The process of doing good for others described by the *Bhāgavatam* was discovered and refined by Śrī Caitanyadeva. This process destroys the threefold miseries, whereas the usual forms of mundane welfare work imagined by this world's thoughtful people are neither beneficial nor do they deliver the ultimate goal of life. They cannot even destroy the material miseries.

Miseries are the effect of a particular cause. Until the cause is destroyed, the effect will remain. Until the root of a banyan tree is destroyed, it will again sprout even if one cuts down its trunk and branches thousands of times. The thousands of manmade proposals for social welfare remind us of the attempt to empty the ocean with one's bare hands. Even if thousands of people engage continuously in such an endeavor for thousands of yugas, they will never be successful. Still, one may see that their work has caused a vast body of water to accumulate in some other place. Similarly, we cannot empty the ocean of material misery by our own strength. At most we will simply succeed in transferring the misery somewhere else. Of course, by doing that we can certainly deceive others and even ourselves.

The threefold miseries cannot be vanquished without following the *Bhāgavatam*'s instructions. There are unlimited varieties of misery. We cannot concoct a way to destroy even one of them. They are caused by nescience in the form of forgetfulness of the Supreme Lord. This nescience both covers the living entities and throws them into further pain. Until we destroy this root cause we will never destroy the miserable effect. We must propagate devotional service if we wish to help others. If the Lord's message is preached around the world, then all countries and all people will achieve the greatest success of all time.

29. Is service to Viṣṇu service to mankind?

Lord Viṣṇu is all-pervading because He is the supreme Brahman. He is greater than the greatest. If we serve Him, we are serving everyone else automatically. When someone serves a particular horse, he does not automatically serve all horses. Patriots are by nature servants of a particular country, not all countries. Paid servants are those who serve only at particular times, not at all times. Those who kill fish or goats to serve their tongue make the fish or goats unhappy and therefore do not serve all living beings. But by serving Lord Viṣṇu, all living beings are satisfied. Śrī Caitanya Mahāprabhu's mercy yields no inauspiciousness results. Devotional service benefits all beings in all countries at all times.

30. What is the constitutional duty of the spirit soul?

The spirit soul is unborn and as such, has no mother. To enjoy or to give up enjoyment is not the soul's propensity because the soul does not possess a material body. The soul is an associated counterpart of the Absolute Truth. The propensity, duty, and self-interest of the soul is to render service and to give pleasure to the Absolute Truth.

31. Don't those who serve Hari serve all living entities?

Lord Hari is the complete whole. Therefore His servants are the real friends and well-wishers of all living entities. Bewildered by the various external appearances of the living entities, those who consider service to the temporary body service to Hari are in total illusion. Their service to the living entities has no value. As they serve the material body, so they serve Maya, Lord Hari's external limb. Even if they serve Maya for unlimited years, they benefit neither themselves nor others.

When one thinks of the poor as Lord Nārāyana (*daridra-nārāyaṇa*), one is saying that Lord Nārāyaṇa is poor. With such a mentality one can neither serve Lord Nārāyaṇa nor His servants. One simply serves Maya. The illusioned serve desert mirages or shadows, not the Absolute Truth. The Absolute Truth is Kṛṣṇa, and the living entities are His eternal servants. Since we are eternal servants of Kṛṣṇa we will serve Kṛṣṇa and His devotees and will physically and mentally help those who are unable to understand the glories of either the devotees or Hari. We will also serve those who are envious of the devotees by simply ignoring them.

The Lord's servants are our best friends, so we should befriend them. Then we will preach about Viṣṇu's service to those of our friends who, not understanding the glories of service to Viṣṇu, have adopted other religious processes, provided they are not envious. We will not cooperate with atheists or the envious.

32. Please tell us something about how to worship Kṛṣṇa.

The best way to worship Kṛṣṇa is in the same way in which the gopīs of Vraja worshiped. Lord Kṛṣṇa is full of transcendental energies and is supremely independent. His transcendental energies have three principal duties. His first energy is called hlādinī, and its purpose is to give Kṛṣṇa pleasure. His second energy is called saṁvit, and its purpose is to help Kṛṣṇa feel the depth of His own self. The third energy is known as sandhinī, the energy of existence, and its purpose is to make all arrangements for the Lord's enjoyment.

Actually, all the ingredients for Kṛṣṇa's enjoyment are arranged by the sandhinī-śakti. Personified, she serves Kṛṣṇa by manifesting His abode and the paraphernalia for His pastimes. The saṁvit energy serves Kṛṣṇa by making Him feel pleasure and helping Him realize Himself. The hlādinī-śakti personified manifests Herself in various form to increase the transcendental mellows of Kṛṣṇa's ecstatic love in newer and newer ways. These forms appear as the damsels or gopīs of Vṛndāvana. The gopīs are expansions of Śrī Rādhā, who is the personification of ecstatic love for Kṛṣṇa and the supreme enchantress. Śrī Rādhā is the original shelter of all of Kṛṣṇa's transcendental energy. Although this divine young couple form a unity, they manifest Themselves as enjoyer and enjoyed. Mahāprabhu comes to establish our service through subordination to Rādhikā.

33. What is the procedure for engaging in service?

Śāstra states:

etāvaj janma-sāphalyaṁ,dehinām iha dehiṣu
prāṇair arthair dhiyā vācā,śreya-ācaraṇaṁ sadā

It is the duty of every living being to perform welfare activities for the benefit of others with his life, wealth, intelligence and words. (*Śrīmad Bhāgavatam* 10.22.35)

Serving God is the secret of success and happiness, and aversion to His service is the root of all distress. Prāṇa means "consciousness" or "love." Service to the Supreme Lord is rendered mainly through prāṇa; wealth, intelligence, and speech. Those devoid of prāṇa cannot serve properly, and that is why prāṇa is listed first. The spiritual master invokes prāṇa in his disciple.

The spiritual master teaches the sincere disciples how to serve God. He teaches the secrets of the Lord's service only to those who desire to serve the Lord.

34. What is service?

When all our propensities and endeavors are directed only to giving Viṣṇu pleasure; that is called service. Activities performed with the desire to demand service from others in the form of religiosity, economic development, sense gratification, and liberation are called disservice or atheism. Atheism can appear in various forms, even as sympathy for others.

35. How should one treat the material world?

The *Īśopaniṣad mantra*, states:

īśāvāsyam idam sarvaṁ, yat kiñca jagatyāṁ jagat
tena tyaktena bhuñjīthā, mā gṛdhaḥ kasya svid dhanam

Everything animate or inanimate that is within the universe is controlled and owned by the Lord. One should therefore accept only those things necessary for himself, which are set aside as his quota, and one should not accept other things, knowing well to whom they belong.

O sense enjoyers! Why do you think that this world is meant for your pleasure? You will not be able to worship Hari as long as you remain engrossed in material enjoyment. Why have you forgotten that this material world is meant for the Lord's service and that Lord Kṛṣṇa is the supreme enjoyer of all objects? Why do you try to enjoy, even though you are servants? It is the servants duty to serve his master; a servant's satisfaction lies in giving the master pleasure. Striving to taste matter does not bring peace. Only serving the Lord allows one to feel peaceful.

36. Who does the Supreme Lord deliver?

Fools, *karmīs*, and dry renunciants do not understand devotional service. Those who follow the path of strict renunciation, dry speculation, or argument, will not understand the glories of devotional service.

I am a servant of the Supreme Lord and service to my Lord is my eternal duty. I have no other recourse but to take shelter at His lotus feet. We learn this by our spiritual master's grace. The Lord does not forsake those who do not forsake Him. Anyone who serves the Lord will surely attain Him. But we must surrender cent percent if we do not want to be deceived. If we surrender one hundred percent, the Lord guarantees our deliverance.

37. Is it possible to serve the transcendental Lord with our blunt material senses?

We should not think we can serve the transcendental Lord with the gross material body. Lord Hari is not served either by the gross senses (the eyes and ears) or by the subtle senses (the mind). Yet these senses appear to all we have in this world. Therefore Śrīla Rūpa Gosvāmī devised a plan by which we can use our material senses to reach the transcendental kingdom. He said, "When the senses, by their own strength, want to reach the transcendental realm, they will fail. This is why those who practice the ascending path never reach their destination. But when the light of inclination toward the Lord's service illumines the senses, they become qualified to understand transcendental subject matter. Then they no longer remain hostile to spirit but can enter the transcendental realm."

38. Should one serve the Lord personally as opposed to through a hired representative?

We cannot serve the Lord by hiring a priest or other representative. Everyone should personally render service to the Lord with love and devotion.

39. Can one achieve any benefit without serving the devotees?

One who serves the Supreme Lord is a devotee, and one who accepts service from His servants as their worshipable Lord is God. The Lord's devotees are as worshipable as the Lord Himself. Thus there are two kinds of worship, worship of the worshipable Lord, and worship of His worshipable servants. The Supreme Lord is just like the sun, and the devotees or spiritual masters are just like light. The worshipable Lord and His servants, in other words, are inseparably related. The devotees are never separate from the Lord. The Lord is complete, and the devotees are dependent on Him.

The devotees are those who possess devotional service. When we speak about the devotees we must naturally speak about the Supreme Lord, just as when we discuss a man's son, it is natural to speak of the son's father. Similarly, *bhakti*, the devotee, and the Supreme Lord are inseparable. The devotees are ever dependent on Kṛṣṇa, and Kṛṣṇa is ever dependent on His devotees. They are nondifferent just as the body's limbs are inseparably connected to the body. If we try to remove the devotees when discussing the Lord, there will be nothing left as the Absolute Truth. If we stop the worship of the devotees, there is no question of worshiping the Lord.

Bypassing the devotee amounts to having a partial conception of the worshipable Lord. If the devotees are separated from the Lord, their propensity to serve the Lord is also checked, and they will be encouraged to become independent. This is how nondevotees think. The devotees not only serve the Lord but serve those who are engaged in His service. The word "Lord" here refers to His name, form, qualities, pastimes, and associates. Our attempt to worship the Lord directly may not often reach Him, but worship of the Lord performed through the devotee via medium is infallible and is bound to reach the Lord. This is because in that case, the devotee takes all responsibility for the one worshiping the Lord and ensures that the Lord receives the offering.

Hearing

1. How can we become determined and courageous?

We must hear *kṛṣṇa-kathā* from the Lord's agent. While hearing kṛṣṇa-kathā we have to lock up our worldly experience and arguments. By hearing the powerful glorious topics of the Lord from a living saintly person, all our *anarthas*—our weakness of heart—are destroyed and our heart is filled with strength. Then our nature, which is to surrender to the Lord, will be awakened. In the surrendered heart, the self-manifest truth of the transcendental kingdom will automatically manifest. This is how to know the truth. It is impossible to know the Absolute Truth by any other means.

2. How is it possible to hear hari-kathā in the association of devotees if we live far from the devotees or at home?

There is always discussion of *hari-kathā* in our *Maṭha*, and the residents there are also engaged in Lord Hari's service. It is our duty to associate in all respects with devotees for whom the Lord's service is their life and soul. That place where there is no kṛṣṇa-kathā is extremely unfavorable for *bhakti*, even if it is filled with relatives and items for comfortable living. I simply think of Mahprabhu's mercy when I see the devotees in the *Maṭha* continually discussing *hari-kathā* and being eager to serve the Lord at all times.

Pious persons who desire their own good should visit the *Maṭha* from time to time and hear kṛṣṇa-kathā from the spiritual master and the Vaiṣṇavas. If we have a taste for kṛṣṇa-kathā and a propensity to serve Kṛṣṇa, then that taste will keep us aloof from bad association. By always reading spiritual magazines and studying the literature written by the mahjanas while constantly begging for Śrī Guru-Gaurāṅga's mercy, we can attain the result of hearing kṛṣṇa-kathā from the mouths of the devotees. Although in this material world we cannot always meet with devotees from the spiritual world, the pastimes and conversations of the devotees who were contemporaries of Mahāprabhu have been permanently recorded in books. Therefore there is no need for disappointment. If we live somewhere and discuss kṛṣṇa-kathā, we will certainly attain auspiciousness and nothing can harm us.

If we simply engage in discussing topics of the Lord while living anywhere by the Lord's mercy we can realize the glories of devotional service, the Lord's mercy, and come to remember the Lord in our day-to-day life. A devotee should live wherever the Lord is pleased to keep him and should forget his own material miseries. When the propensity to serve the Lord is awakened in the heart while discussing *hari-kathā* in the association of devotees, then we will automatically remember Hari under all circumstances. In order to test us, the Supreme Lord is always present behind what we can see. If we see the Lord's mercy behind each and every incident, we will no longer feel distress. The material world, material existence, is the place where we are tested. If we wish to pass the test, we must hear kṛṣṇa-kathā from the pure devotees. Even though at present we may not always have the opportunity to hear *hari-kathā* in the association of devotees, if we continuously hear it in the form of discussing Vaiṣṇava literature, we will not feel the absence of Vaiṣṇava association.

The Lord's devotees always see the Lord everywhere, whereas those who are envious of Him do not even believe in His existence. Being situated in the marginal position, sometimes we display a taste for serving Hari and at the next moment become busy with sense gratification. If we simply develop a strong desire to become intoxicated by serving Hari our propensity for material enjoyment will be vanquished. Material enjoyment includes both temporary happiness and distress, but service to Hari pleases Lord Hari. We should always remain eager to please the Lord.

3. From whom should we hear topics about Kṛṣṇa?

We should hear topics about the Supreme Lord from a bona fide spiritual master. For the Lord's pleasure we have to preach those topics to the inquisitive, not to the faithless, but we should hear from a spiritual master, not an atheist. If by mistake we have accepted a nondevotee as guru, we should renounce him and take shelter of a Vaiṣṇava.

4. From whom should we hear Śrīmad-Bhāgavatam?

We should hear *Śrīmad-Bhāgavatam* from exalted spiritual masters and pure devotees who are fixed at their own spiritual masters' lotus feet. We cannot achieve auspiciousness if we hear *Śrīmad-Bhāgavatam* from those who are not bhāgavatas.

A person with loose character, who is always thinking of sense gratification, and who is only interested in wealth and fame, can never recite *Śrīmad-Bhāgavatam*. In fact, *Śrīmad-Bhāgavatam* does not manifest in his mouth. Such a person simply gratifies his senses on the pretext of reciting the *Bhāgavatam*, and he cheats himself and others. Rather, we should hear *Śrīmad-Bhāgavatam* from a spiritual master who is constantly engaged in worshiping Hari or from a pure Vaiṣṇava whom the spiritual master recommends. Then we can attain auspiciousness and devotional service to the Lord.

Those who have accepted *Śrīmad-Bhāgavatam* as their life and soul actually recite it, serve the Lord, and chant Hari's holy name. We should associate with such devotees and offer everything to them. Because such devotees do not engage in sense gratification they do not deceive themselves or others on the pretext of serving the Lord, and they do not accumulate mundane fame like pseudo renunciants by giving up objects meant for the Lord's service, thinking them material.

A person from whom I would want to hear and with whom I would want to associate must be a follower of the disciplic succession. The saintly person and the spiritual master never accept the path of sense gratification. They follow the path of disciplic succession. The teaching that we should lead the life of devotion the followers of our disciplic succession have received from their respective predecessor ācaryas is, in turn, taught to others. Our ācaryas neither speculate nor concoct. People often accept spiritual masters or associate with saints not for their ultimate benefit but to fulfill some self-interest. Nowadays it is fashionable to accept a spiritual master, just as it is fashionable to keep a personal barber or washerman. Associating with sadhus and hearing kṛṣṇa-kathā from them is fashionable too. How will we benefit? Is it possible to attain good if we do not hear from qualified teachers? Those who want real benefit should be careful about their association. Do not bring about your ruination by hearing *hari-kathā* from so-called sadhus.

If out of good fortune and by the Lord's mercy we attain the association of a real devotee, we should hear from him submissively and with faith. It is our duty to engage every moment of our lives in the worship of Hari without wasting even a second on other activities. We should be anxious to associate with sadhus. We can carry on the mundane duties of life in any form of life, but to worship Kṛṣṇa in the association of a bona fide spiritual master is possible only in the human form.

5. How can we go back to Godhead?

Lord Śrī Hari is the transcendental Absolute Truth situated beyond the material creation. There is no way to meet with that transcendental object or Supreme Lord other than to hear about Him. Discussions about Vaikuṇṭha, emanating from the lotus mouths of devotees, have extraordinary potency. When these transcendental sound vibrations enter our ears, our consciousness is awakened and we become Kṛṣṇa conscious. This is because these vibrations descend from Vaikuṇṭha into this world help us go back to Godhead. Discussions about this world only help us go to hell. Śrī Caitanyacandra came to this world to tell us about Vaikuṇṭha, but due to our own misfortune, the teachings of this most merciful personality do not enter our ears. Only the fortunate can understand Mahāprabhu's teachings. If we want to become fortunate, we must develop the propensity to serve. Then Vaikuṇṭha topics and teachings will enter our ears and we will understand them.

We must try to make spiritual advancement from our present position, and this includes hearing enlivening discourses from living sources, bona fide Vaiṣṇavas. The moment we stop hearing *hari-kathā* from and serving real devotees, Maya will swallow us. Thus it is our duty to give attention to wherever actual *hari-kathā* is being discussed. Our constitutional propensity will be revived if we hear *hari-kathā* from a living source through service-inclined ears. Then we will be able to realize or see the Supreme Lord in our purified hearts. We can realize the Supreme Lord only by aural reception. Apart from hearing, there is no way to go back to Godhead.

6. How is it possible to know the transcendental Absolute Truth?

Lord Śrī Hari is the transcendental Absolute Truth. We can know Him only by hearing with service-inclined ears from the mouth of the spiritual master and the saintly persons. Whenever we hear something, we try to analyze it with the help of our other senses in order to find out whether or not it is true. But we have no power to understand whatever the spiritual master or the śastras explain without the help of ears tuned to Kṛṣṇa consciousness. It is useless and foolish to try to understand the Absolute Truth through the blunt material senses because the Absolute Truth is transcendental. We will never succeed in understanding Him through dry argumentation. Therefore if we are fortunate enough to hear discussions about transcendental subject matter from the lotus mouth of our guru, we should try to understand what he says by practicing surrender, honest inquiry, and developing a service attitude.

7. Please instruct us: What are we supposed to do?

We request everyone, for the time being, to stop and lend your submissive and regardful ears. Put your imagination and experience aside and hear a little bit of Vedic knowledge. I am in favor of transcendental sound. If you walk with the heavy burden of the rubbish you have accumulated balanced on your head, you will not be able to move an inch toward Vraja or the Lord. Those who are established as intellectual giants should suspend their philosophy for some time and hear transcendental sound. Empiricism must never be the medium for understanding. Devotional service is not supposition nor is it haphazard. Rather, it is scientific. The concept of subordinating ourselves to the personal Godhead is called devotional service.

8. How should we live in this world?

Go on hearing *hari-kathā* from the pure devotees and seeing this material world from the vantage point of the Lord's servant. Then you will have nothing to lament. Please concentrate your mind on subject matters related to Kṛṣṇa. Hear attentively what the Supreme Lord instructs. What does He instruct? He says, "O living entities! Although you have been averse to Me from time immemorial, you were originally God conscious. You could have served Me, but instead you have been demanding service from Me. You are trying to become masters by forgetting Me. But know for certain that you are never masters but are always My servants."

Lord Hari alone is everyone's master; we are all His servants. Therefore, our engagement in this world is to hear *hari-kathā*. Those who glorify Hari are spiritual masters, and those who hear from spiritual masters are disciples. Listeners must be submissive and eager. That day is inauspicious when we fail to discuss *hari-kathā*.

You should hear *Śrīmad-Bhāgavatam* every day. *Śrīmad-Bhāgavatam* tells us that we have attained the human form of life after many births; a human birth is extremely rare. Although it is rare, however, it awards us spiritual perfection. By sincerely worshiping Hari with full surrender while renouncing our false independence, we can attain the Supreme Lord in this lifetime. Therefore a sober person will try to attain the ultimate goal of life, working at learning to surrender until he leaves his body. He will not waste a moment. Eating, sleeping, mating, and defending are available in any form of life, but spiritual life is available only to humans. We can find sense gratification in any species. We should not use the human form of life to cultivate sense gratification but Kṛṣṇa consciousness, which is the ultimate goal of human life. Service to the Lord is the supreme destination for the living entities.

And we should know what service is. Pleasing the object of our service is called devotion. Lord Hari is the origin, Lord, master, and object of everyone's service. We are all His servants. Attaining Him and His devotional service is our only duty, nature, and engagement.

The Supreme Lord is the complete whole and the worshipable Lord of the living entities. In order to achieve His service, we must take shelter of His representative, the spiritual master. We must serve the spiritual master, for he gives us information about the Lord. The spiritual master is our only selfless friend and relative in this world. We can achieve perfection if we treat him as our best well-wisher. By serving him with love and devotion, we will awaken our identity as the Lord's servant and develop love for guru and Govinda.

9. From whom should we hear kṛṣṇa-kathā if we wish to attain ultimate benefit?

The one who serves Kṛṣṇa twenty-four hours a day can show us Kṛṣṇa. We must hear kṛṣṇa-kathā from such a devotee or guru. Then our propensity to serve the Lord will be awakened. The maṭhas or temples teach service to the Lord because such places are centers for the Lord's service. What makes a temple or maṭha attractive is that its atmosphere is surcharged with *hari-kathā*. If we hear the *hari-kathā* spoken by a bona fide spiritual master to devotees who are dear to Caitanya Mahprabhu with surrender, honest inquiry, and a service attitude, our perfection is guaranteed. We will certainly become fully Kṛṣṇa conscious.

The Lord's devotees see Śyamasundara in their hearts with eyes anointed with devotion. If such a devotee favors us, we will also come to see the Lord in our hearts. We cannot see the Lord with our present blunt, material eyes. We can only see the Lord through devotion-filled eyes. Our eternal perfection lies in worshiping Kṛṣṇa. The moment we realize that we are Kṛṣṇa's servant and Kṛṣṇa is our master, the door to auspiciousness opens. We should know for certain that there is no object of worship in this world other than Śrī Hari.

10. Can't we hear without having "service-inclined ears"?

The Hare Kṛṣṇa maha-mantra is the predominating agent, and our ears are the predominated agent. This means that the Hare Kṛṣṇa maha-mantra is the regulator, the Lord, and the ears are regulated or subordinate. Whenever the ears want to become the controller, we cannot engage in pure hearing and chanting about transcendence. Pure hearing and chanting about Hari are not possible with ears that want to hear glorification of Hari in an enjoying spirit. We must render service to the object of service through senses inclined to serve. To pretend to hear through ears that are fond of material enjoyment is an offense, not a service. Therefore Śrī Rūpa Gosvmī Prabhu states, ataḥśrī-kṛṣṇa-namadi, na bhaved grāhyam indriyaiḥ/ sevonmukhe hi jihvādau, svayam eva sphuraty adaḥ: "No one can understand the transcendental nature of the names, forms, qualities, and pastimes of Śrī Kṛṣṇa through his materially contaminated senses. Only when one becomes spiritually saturated by transcendental service to the Lord are the transcendental names, forms, qualities, and pastimes of the Lord revealed to him." (Bhakti Rasāmṛta Sindhu 1.2.234)

11. How can we become determined?

Hari-kathā should be heard from Hari's devotees. By constantly hearing the powerful topics about Hari from the lotus mouths of those who always serve the Lord, we will be able to understand the Lord's energies and glories. By faithfully and attentively hearing *hari-kathā* from a living source or a powerful saintly person, we will become determined. Gradually, as we attain faith, attachment, and love of God, we will achieve perfection. Then Maya's prowess cannot defeat us.

12. What should the aim of our endeavors be?

We say, "Always hear *hari-kathā*. Associate with devotees and divert your enjoyment-prone heart toward Kṛṣṇa's service. Then your perfection is guaranteed." Whatever karma you have will come automatically. You do not need to endeavor separately either to escape it or to bring it about. If you endeavor for anything, endeavor to worship Hari.

I am so engrossed in material enjoyment that I consider one who induces me to enjoy material happiness my best friend, although he is actually my worst enemy. Neither am I interested in hearing the good advice the selfless saints offer when they forbid me to indulge in sense gratification or to become attached to matter. My real friends seem to be enemies. How unfortunate I am!

13. Why don't you allow the singing of Lord's conjugal pastimes in the Maṭha?

We do not object to hearing and chanting about Kṛṣṇa's pastimes. In fact, the Lord's pastimes must be heard and chanted. Only then will the conditioned souls' natural taste or eagerness for hearing and chanting about their own heroic activities and other forms of idle talk be destroyed. There is no substitute for this. We should hear from devotees superior to ourselves. If we hear from others, we will gain nothing. We should hear glorification of the Lord only from a spiritual master or pure devotee. A real devotee thinks, "I will hear *hari-kathā* only from my spiritual master's mouth and hear and discuss the *Śrīmad-Bhāgavatam* Śrī Sukadeva Gosvamī spoke. I will hear glorification of the Lord as it was inaugurated by Caitanya Mahaprabhu, or discuss Lord Kṛṣṇa's names, forms, and qualities. I will discuss the Lord's pure devotees, who are fully dedicated to their spiritual master."

However, there is no difference between chanting about the Lord's pastimes and chanting about the mellows of the Lord's conjugal pastimes and we should therefore not think that one is higher and the other lower. Hearing about the conjugal pastimes requires qualification. Living entities with *anarthas* can hear and chant about the pastimes of Lord Gauraṅga and the childhood pastimes of Lord Kṛṣṇa. If people try to hear and chant about the confidential pastimes between Śrī Radha and Kṛṣṇa they will find misfortune rather than auspiciousness. Hearing and chanting about ŚrīŚrī Radha-Kṛṣṇa's confidential pastimes is certainly the best way to worship the Lord. It is, however, improper and even offensive to sing about such pastimes in public. A person wishing to attain auspiciousness must obey these words from the mahajanas, pana *bhajana* kathā na kahibe yatha tatha: "Do not disclose your confidential mode of worship to anyone and everyone." We should sing the holy name's glories, offer prayers to the Lord, and chant the glories of the Lord's service where people of different natures and statuses are assembled. If we are qualified, we can hear about the Lord's confidential pastimes only in the association of like-minded devotees, feeling our own mood according to our constitutional position. Otherwise we will receive an opposite result. If in order to maintain this standard singing the Lord's glories must be stopped altogether, let it be so. We are interested in benefiting the people. It is Kali who keeps alive the public singing of the Lord's confidential pastimes simply to accumulate money and enjoy sense gratification.

14. Why do I lack faith in spiritual life?

Because we don't hear topics about the Lord from the Lord's devotees, we lose faith in spiritual life. By hearing *hari-kathā* from a living source, we become faithful. But we will not become faithful if we listen with a challenging mood. The Bhagavad-gīta states that we must hear with complete surrender, honest inquiry, and a service attitude. Only then will we profit, develop faith in spiritual life, and receive the opportunity to actually lead a spiritual life.

15. What is the special nature of the ears?

In this world, it is possible to gain experience about the transcendental object only through the ears. No other sense, even the sense of sight, can help us. By manipulating the other four senses while keeping the ear holes blocked we find ourselves floating on previously acquired experience and we remain in the dark with our pride. Thus we drown further in the ocean of our own *anarthas*.

The materialists' conceptions can be regulated and even changed if they use their ears to hear Caitanya Mahaprabhu's teachings. If they manipulate any of their other senses, they will never be able to give up mental speculation. However, for hearing to be effective, the speaker must be transcendental, a pure devotee. The speaker of transcendental sound vibration must be *akiñcana* if he is to remove the sense of false proprietorship in the members of his audience.

16. Why do we not appear to be making advancement despite our repeatedly hearing kṛṣṇa-kathā?

How can we hear if we keep our ear holes blocked? Inattentive hearing yields no result. What to speak of inattention, we must not hear only with the mind, because the mind is restless. Hearing means following. What is the use of hearing if we do not follow what we have heard? That is why we must hear *hari-kathā* with our life. Then we will attain auspiciousness.

17. In what direction does our taste move when we are hearing?

Whatever we hear draws our taste. We do not develop a taste for new things without having heard about them. At present we are averse to the Supreme Lord, so we have no interest in *hari-kathā*. Rather, we are fond of worldly topics. Sense objects that reveal themselves in form, taste, smell, sound, and touch dominate our thinking and engage us in sense gratification. We want sense gratification. Therefore those who give us more sense gratification are dearer to us than others. We simply run after immediate material happiness and remain busy living our lives for sense pleasure. Consequently our intelligence gradually becomes degraded. At present our only aim or taste, our only endeavor, is to oppose God.

We tend to speak only about the mundane, about products of matter. Whatever devotees speak, however, is above mundane sound vibration. Such sounds are invested with extraordinary power. As soon as they enter human ears, they awaken people's spiritual consciousness. These sound vibrations can penetrate Brahmaloka, pass over the Viraj River, and enter Vaikuṇṭha. The same sound that appears in this world from Vaikuṇṭha takes us back to Vaikuṇṭha. The sound produced in the material sky stays in the material sky for some time, then finally dissolves in that sky. Such mundane sounds take us to hell. Since we are interested only in material topics, we are bound to suffer from restlessness. We will attain auspiciousness only when we develop a taste for topics about Vaikuṇṭha and not otherwise.

18. Why are we unable to follow despite hearing hari-kathā?

Only the fortunate adopt a lifestyle suitable to performing devotional service. Those who are unfortunate pretend to hear *hari-kathā*, but they are actually cheated because they do not hear with faith. If we are blessed enough to really desire to serve the Lord, we will be eager to hear *hari-kathā*. Not only that, we will understand it.

We have to make spiritual advancement from our present position. The Lord's illusory energy is trying to make us averse to the Lord at every moment. We are so foolish that we busily place Maya around our neck like a garland. Therefore I tell you, Do not be fools! Be conscious. Be intelligent. Associate with a living source. By associating with powerful devotees, all your obstacles will be destroyed and you will achieve spiritual strength.

The moment you are left without a master or protector, everything around you will become an enemy and attack you. As soon as you fail to hear about Kṛṣṇa from devotees, giving up your sincere service to guru and Vaiṣṇavas, by taking advantage of the situation, Maya will devour you. Therefore your duty is to find out where *hari-kathā* is being discussed and to pay attention to it. There are millions of people in this world who worry about various insignificant matters; they cannot understand the purport of transcendental sound vibration, which has descended from the spiritual sky. They cannot speak about Hari. Rather, they speak like gramophones. There is no use hearing their advice, because it will simply drown you in matter.

Chanting the Holy Name

1. What is the gravest offense in chanting the holy names?

To consider the spiritual master an ordinary human being is the gravest, most deadly offense one can commit when chanting the holy name. If we consider the spiritual master a mortal being, we will never profit from our practices. Rather, various obstacles and problems will surface and drown us in an ocean of material desire. No one other than the spiritual master is capable of protecting us from bad association. Because the living entities consider the spiritual master an ordinary human being, they are unable to surrender to his lotus feet.

2. Are we servants of the holy name?

As spirit souls, we are servants of Kṛṣṇa. Upon realizing this we will also realize that we have no other business than to serve Him. Kṛṣṇa's holy name is Kṛṣṇa Himself. Serving the holy name is the same as serving Kṛṣṇa.

As soon as we forget service to Kṛṣṇa or His names we forget our constitutional position and remain in an incompatible situation. We become conditioned by the Lord's illusory energy and suffer material misery. When by the spiritual master's mercy we gain knowledge about our relationship with the Lord, we remember that we are Kṛṣṇa's eternal servant and that everything in this material world is meant for His service.

Those who desire liberation from material existence and who wish to become eternally happy should always chant Kṛṣṇa's holy name. This is Mahāprabhu's order. Therefore the devotees consider themselves servants of the holy name, every living entity as meant for Kṛṣṇa's enjoyment, and every object as meant for His service.

Kṛṣṇa's holy name is the reservoir of all transcendental pleasure. The holy name of Kṛṣṇa is sat-cit-ānanda, eternal and full of knowledge and bliss. Kṛṣṇa's holy names are Śyāmsundara, Yaśodānandan, etc. Service to these names, which are the reservoir of transcendental pleasure, is direct service to Kṛṣṇa. That is why the devotees constantly serve Kṛṣṇa by chanting His holy names. Thus they please both the spiritual master and Kṛṣṇa.

3. How should we chant the Lord's holy names?

Pure devotees do not chant the Lord's names to counteract sinful reactions, accumulate piety, attain heavenly pleasures, to mitigate famine, devastating epidemics, social unrest, disease, civil strife, or to obtain wealth or an earthly kingdom. Since the Lord is the Supreme Personality of Godhead, to ask Him to fulfill our wishes is to treat Him as our servant. This is an offense. Therefore calling the Lord's names for any reason other than to attain His devotional service is useless. Jesus Christ told us not to take the Lord's name in vain.

However, this does not mean we do not need to always chant the Lord's names—while sleeping, awake, eating, or enjoying happiness. To chant the Lord's name, begging for His service, is not a useless activity. It is our only duty.

But to make a show of chanting for some other purpose—in other words, to fulfill our own desires—is useless. We should not take to the chanting of the Lord's names uselessly. We should not chant to attain religiosity, economic development, sense gratification, or liberation. Instead, we should always chant to attain the Lord's service.

4. Is chanting the best limb of devotional service?

Among all the limbs of devotional service, śrī-kṛṣṇa-*saṅkīrtana* is principal. If we perform śrī-kṛṣṇa-*saṅkīrtana* we will attain the qualification necessary to lead a perfect spiritual life. All energies, beauty, fulfillment, and the perfection of all our *sādhanas* are included in chanting Kṛṣṇa's holy name. All our activities, propensities, thoughts, and imaginings are regulated by the process of chanting Kṛṣṇa's holy names. If the holy name appears on the tip of the tongue, we can easily give up temporary material activities, the material sense of duty, the tendency to enjoy the perishable world, and all surrounding inconvenience. Chanting the holy name easily destroys all the impediments on our path. Chanting Kṛṣṇa's holy name is not only *sādhana* but sādhya, the goal of life.

However, we must chant the name repeatedly and under the guidance of a bona fide spiritual master. All perfection is achieved by chanting kṛṣṇa-nāma. The living entities will achieve all auspiciousness simply by serving the holy name. Only Kṛṣṇa's holy name can drown us in an ocean of eternal bliss. Kṛṣṇa's holy name is the reservoir of all transcendental pleasure.

Śrī Gaurasundara is the supreme object of worship. He is the ultimate object of everyone's worship. Although Śrī Gaurasundara is Kṛṣṇa Himself, He has preached *bhāgavata-dharma* to the entire world by following it Himself. Śrī-kṛṣṇa-*saṅkīrtana* is certainly the ultimate goal of *bhāgavata-dharma* and the highest form of meditation, sacrifice, and worship. Meditation on Kṛṣṇa, sacrifice centered on Kṛṣṇa, and worship of Kṛṣṇa are ordinary activities, but such activities become perfect when they are performed along with śrī-kṛṣṇa-*saṅkīrtana* .

5. What is the easiest way to control the mind?

The mind can only be controlled by chanting the holy names of Kṛṣṇa. Karma, *jñāna*, and yoga may temporarily check the mind, but they can also cause the mind to be drowned in an ocean of expanded restlessness.

6. How should we remove anarthas?

If the living entities do not worship Hari they will become *karmīs*, *jñānīs*, or sense enjoyers. That is why we should always loudly chant the Lord's holy names. By chanting a fixed number of rounds daily, our *anarthas* will be vanquished and our laziness destroyed. If we chant the holy name without offense, then all perfection is automatically achieved.

7. What does "lower than the straw in the street" mean?

Although the Vaiṣṇavas are topmost they consider themselves lower than the straw in the street. Actually, they are not fallen or low-class; they are very dear to the Lord and are fit to be worshiped. Everyone should show them respect.

To think, "I am a particle of dust at the lotus feet of my spiritual master," or, "I am the servant of guru and Kṛṣṇa," is what is meant by becoming lower than straw in the street. We should show compassion toward all living entities, develop a taste for chanting the Lord's names, and serve Vaiṣṇavas. These are Mahāprabhu's three principal instructions. If we think ourselves lower than straw in the street, we will not take shelter of duplicity while displaying only a pretense of humility. We will actually become humble and thereby eligible to chant. In other words, true humility means to develop a taste for chanting and to become a true servant of the holy name. Service to guru and the Vaiṣṇavas is the gateway through which we develop such taste.

Service to the spiritual master and the Vaiṣṇavas certainly amount to becoming lower than the straw in the street. This does not mean that we should become subordinate to nondevotees. Rather, it means to beg mercy from and show respect to devotees. The mahājanas instructed us not to display our humility before everyone. To show our humility toward hypocrites or envious atheists like Rāvaṇa is not what it means to think ourselves lower than straw in the street. If we break this instruction we will never become qualified to chant the holy name. Rather, our actions will amount to our becoming envious of others. Hanumān burnt Laṅkā for Rāma. That is an example of becoming lower than straw in the street.

8. When will we understand that Lord Kṛṣṇa is nondifferent from His holy names?

The Lord's holy names and the Lord Himself are nondifferent. We will realize this clearly when our *anarthas* are destroyed. If we chant Kṛṣṇa's names without offense, we will come to understand that by chanting the Lord's holy names we can achieve all perfection.

When *anarthas* are destroyed while chanting the Lord's names, then the Lord's form, qualities, and pastimes automatically manifest. We do not need to meditate artificially on these things. Chanting the holy names closes the distance between our gross and subtle bodies and our perfected self. As soon as we realize our constitutional position and begin to chant the Lord's pure name, we can see the transcendental form of the Lord face to face. The holy names of the Lord revive the living entity's constitutional position and attract him to Kṛṣṇa. The holy names actually revive the living entity's constitutional nature and attract him to Kṛṣṇa's transcendental nature. Likewise, the holy names revive the living entities' constitutional activities and attract them to Kṛṣṇa's pastimes.

All the required functions and activities of a chanter are included in his service to the holy name. We can achieve all perfection simply by chanting Kṛṣṇa's name. If we wish to develop a taste for chanting, we should hear and study scripture and cultivate Kṛṣṇa consciousness.

9. What will give us benefit?

I am confident that simply by calling out the Lord's names with full attention that you will attain all auspiciousness. The Supreme Lord is the only one capable of awarding you material advancement, prosperity, or calamity. We are meant to be maintained by Him. It is our duty to accept His arrangements for us without reservation.

10. What is hari-nāma?

The holy name of Hari is not a product of matter, something imaginary, or an object of this visible world. Rather, it is an incarnation of the Lord and as such is nondifferent from Him. Hari's name is Hari Himself. The holy name is fully transcendental. It is the complete whole. The holy name is the Supreme Personality of Godhead and is full of all energies. The transcendental holy name is directly the Lord Himself. The holy name can take initiative. There is no difference between the Lord and His names, forms, qualities, and pastimes. The transcendental name is the form, quality, and activity Himself. There is no difference between the Lord and His holy names.

The transcendental name is a transcendental sound vibration. Kṛṣṇa and His names are one. Kṛṣṇa has appeared in Kali-yuga in the form of His holy name. The supremely cognizant holy name can speak. One who chants the holy name is also cognizant. Such a person prays, "O holy name of Hari, I am your servant and I accept my subordination under You."

One who is inclined to chant the holy name is the holy name's servant. Kṛṣṇa has directly appeared in this form, so we should take full shelter of the name and not approach anyone else for protection.

11. Is chanting the Lord's name the best and easiest way to attain supreme auspiciousness?

There can be no better process than chanting the holy name. Only those who have no other business in this world can chant Hari's holy names. Chanting the holy name of Hari is the only way to be delivered. There is no other way to enter God's spiritual kingdom. Chanting the holy name is the only process by which we can attain the goal of life; there is no alternative to chanting. Love of God, which is attained by chanting the holy name, is the ultimate goal of life. The *śāstra* states, harer nāma harer nāma, harer nāmaiva kevalam/ kalau nāsty eva nāsty eva, nāsty eva gatir anyathā: "In this age of quarrel and hypocrisy the only means of deliverance is chanting the holy name of the Lord. There is no other way. There is no other way. There is no other way." (*Śrī Caitanya-caritāmṛta* Ādi 17.21) To give emphasis to the point the *śāstras* repeat the statement three times. Elsewhere in *śāstra* it states, kalau tu nāma mātrena, pujyate bhagawān hariḥ: "Lord Hari is worshiped in this age of Kali simply by chanting His holy names." (Nārāyaṇa-saṁhitā)

12. Why do mundane thoughts appear while chanting?

By chanting Kṛṣṇa's holy name under the spiritual master's guidance, we quickly attain good fortune. If material thoughts appear in the mind while chanting, do not lose interest or slow down the chanting. Such useless thoughts will gradually be destroyed by the chanting itself. Do not be in a hurry to achieve the goal; it is not possible to attain the result in the beginning.

If we develop love and devotion for Kṛṣṇa's holy name, the hankering for material thoughts will diminish. How can we hope to vanquish material thoughts unless we become extremely eager to chant? If we simply chant with body, mind, and speech, Śrī Nāma Prabhu will display His supremely auspicious form.

13. The Lord's holy names and the topics about Him are both from Vaikuṇṭha. How can we gain access to them from this world?

There is no difference between the Lord's holy name and the Lord Himself, but there is a difference between material names and the objects those names represent. The holy name of the Lord mercifully appears in this world from God's kingdom. The Lord's Deity form, His holy name, and the spiritual master bring topics about the Lord into this world. These three are nondifferent from one another. The Lord's Deity and holy name are worshipable God, whereas the spiritual master is worshiper God. By taking shelter of the spiritual master or an *ācārya* we can approach Kṛṣṇa, the worshipable Lord.

There is another consideration in this regard: Since Śrī Rādhā is the worshiper God, the name of Śrī Rādhā and Śrī Rādhās Deity form are both in the category of worshiper God.

14. Are Śrī Hari and His holy names one?

The holy name of Hari and Lord Hari Himself are not two separate objects but one. They are nondifferent. By the holy name's mercy, the Lord's form, qualities, characteristics, and pastimes manifest to a devotee engaged in chanting and allows him to be completely aloof from material experience. At such a stage, the conditioned soul is no longer disturbed by material thoughts or mental restlessness.

We should pray to the holy name in such a way that the holy name bestows its mercy upon us. It is not the business of those filled with *anarthas* to remember the aṣṭa-kāliya-līlā. When we learn to hear as we chant, the opportunity to remember will arise automatically. At that time, remembering the aṣṭa-kāliya-līlā will become possible. There is no need to try for it artificially.

15. What result can we expect from chanting the Lord's holy names?

While chanting Kṛṣṇa's holy name we cultivate Kṛṣṇa consciousness and thus find our desire to enjoy the fruits of our karma and our thirst for liberation vanquished. By the holy name's influence, all our *anarthas* are gradually destroyed. The holy name of Kṛṣṇa is Kṛṣṇa Himself. We cannot remove our misfortune if we do not chant. Happiness derived from chanting Kṛṣṇa's name protects us from the desire for material happiness or thoughts of material enjoyment. We are meant to be enjoyed by Kṛṣṇa. If Kṛṣṇa is pleased with my eternal form and attracts me, then I will become overwhelmed by the beauty of His eternal form.

16. Is it possible to find benefit if we don't chant Hari's holy names?

How is it possible to benefit without chanting? Chanting Hari's name is the yuga-dharma, the prescribed process for this age. How can people of this age attain auspiciousness without following the prescribed method for the particular age? How can we attain auspiciousness by following paths other than chanting? After all, the chanting was introduced by the all-auspicious Lord Himself.

To think there is an alternative to the process of chanting hari-nāma is mental speculation. In this material world, people spend their time imagining alternatives to hari-nāma. Avoiding hari-nāma is what this world is about. Those who think that hearing and chanting are not the only necessary process for spiritual fulfillment try to measure the transcendental Lord against themselves and thereby transgress His orders. Such people are nondevotee servants of Maya. It is not good to contradict the Lord, for by so doing our ruination is inevitable. The *śāstra* states, harer nāma harer nāma, harer nāmaiva kevalam/ kalau nāsty eva nāsty eva, nāsty eva gatir anyathā: "In this age of quarrel and hypocrisy the only means of deliverance is chanting the holy name of the Lord. There is no other way. There is no other way. There is no other way." (*Śrī Caitanya-caritāmṛta* Ādi 17.21)

17. Is chanting the Lord's holy names the principal form of bhajana?

According to the conclusion of Śrīman Mahāprabhu and the Gosvāmīs, congregational chanting of the Lord's name is certainly the principal form of *bhajana*. Among the limbs of devotional service, chanting Kṛṣṇa's holy name is the best. Activities such as hearing and chanting about the Lord's pastimes are subordinate to chanting of the holy name. Without the holy name's mercy, we cannot experience the Lord's pastimes. Trying to separately remember the Lord without chanting is nothing but an attempt to achieve mundane fame.

Chanting manmade kīrtana is not the same as actually chanting the Lord's name. Manmade kīrtana is an offense against the chanting because it is not aimed at gratifying Kṛṣṇa's senses. We do not worship the Lord with mundane sound.

Chanting the Lord's name as Śrī Caitanya Mahāprabhu taught us to do when He inaugurated the *saṅkīrtana* movement is the topmost form of *bhajana* because it is capable of awarding us the treasury of love of God. The Lord's self-manifest nectarean holy name first appears in one of our senses, and then by its own sweetness inundates all our other senses. Lord Śrī Gaurāṅgadeva concludes, bhajanera madhye śreṣṭha nava-vidhā *bhakti*, 'kṛṣṇa-prema', 'kṛṣṇa' dite dhare mahā-śakti/ tāra madhye sarva-śreṣṭha nāma-*saṅkīrtana* , niraparādhe nāma laile pāya prema-dhana: "Among the ways of executing devotional service, the nine prescribed methods are the best, for these processes have great potency to deliver Kṛṣṇa and ecstatic love for Him. Of the nine processes of devotional service, the most important is to always chant the holy name of the Lord. If one does so, avoiding the ten kinds of offenses, one very easily obtains the most valuable love of Godhead." (*Śrī Caitanya-caritāmṛta* Antya 4.70-71)

18. What result do we attain when we chant the holy names?

Chanting Kṛṣṇa's holy name means directly cultivating Kṛṣṇa consciousness. Chanting destroys *anarthas* such as material desire and the thirst for liberation. By the holy name's mercy all our *anarthas* are gradually destroyed. Kṛṣṇa's holy name is nondifferent from Himself. The holy name is unlimitedly powerful; nothing is impossible by His mercy. Therefore if we chant, our *anarthas* will be destroyed and we will quite easily attain the goal of life. That is, we will attain love of Kṛṣṇa. Thus, the Lord's holy name is the only shelter for all living entities. In Kali-yuga, the only way to realize God is to chant Kṛṣṇa's name. If we do not chant, we will neither find fortune nor remove misfortune.

19. Should the fire of Kṛṣṇa-saṅkīrtana burn continuously in the Maṭha?

The fire of śrī-kṛṣṇa-*saṅkīrtana* should burn constantly in every *Maṭha*. We must be especially attentive to ensure that it never goes out. There should be no tinge of lust or sense gratification in the *Maṭha*. The desire to gratify Śrī Rādhā-Govinda's senses should conquer everything else. Unless the blazing fire of *saṅkīrtana* , which cleanses the mirror of the heart, burns continuously, various *anarthas*, such as differences of opinion, faultfinding, deceit, envy, and hatred will pollute our hearts. As a result we will find the blazing fire of material existence progressively increasing.

Unless the fire of kṛṣṇa-*saṅkīrtana* burns continuously both in the *Maṭha* and the heart, we will neither be able to uproot material life nor achieve love of God. The fire of *saṅkīrtana* has the power to overcome the desire for material enjoyment and burn to ashes karma, *jñāna*, yoga, and material vratas and austerities. Only fools will accept these ulterior practices as the goal of life. Intelligent persons, however, will worship Mahāprabhu by performing the sacrifice of *saṅkīrtana* .

Simply by performing *saṅkīrtana* we can execute the meditation performed in Satya-yuga, the fire sacrifice performed in Tretā-yuga, and the Deity worship performed in Dvāpara-yuga. If we do not perform *saṅkīrtana* we will not be able to serve Śrī Gaurasundara, the combined form of Śrī Rādhā-Govinda. We cannot worship Śrī Rādhā-Govinda by performing only Deity worship; we must also perform *śrī-Kṛṣṇa-saṅkīrtana* . That is why the first *śloka* of *Śikṣāṣṭaka* states, *paraṁ vijayate śrī-kṛṣṇa-saṅkīrtana*: "All glories to *śrī-kṛṣṇa-saṅkīrtana*."

20. What is the yuga-dharma for Kali-yuga?

Kali-yuga's occupational duty is harināma-*saṅkīrtana* , congregational chanting of Hari's holy names. The following verse from Bṛhat Nāradīya *Purāṇa* provides proof of this fact:

harer nāma harer nāma, harer nāmaiva kevalam
kalau nāsty eva nāsty eva, nāsty eva gatir anyathā

In this age of quarrel and hypocrisy the only means of deliverance is chanting the holy name of the Lord. There is no other way. There is no other way. There is no other way.

Śāstra also states, *kaliyuga dharma kṛṣṇa nāma saṅkīrtana, niraparadhe nāma laile pāya prema dhana*: "Chanting the holy name of Kṛṣṇa is the dharma of Kali-yuga. If one chants the holy name offenselessly, he will attain the treasury of love of God." *Śrīmad-Bhāgavatam* 12.3.52 states, *kṛte yad dhyāyato viṣṇuṁ, tretāyāṁ yajato makhaiḥ/ dvāpare paricaryāyāṁ, kalau tad dhari-kīrtanāt*: "Whatever result was obtained in Satya-yuga by meditating on Viṣṇu, in Tretā-yuga by performing sacrifices, and in Dvāpara-yuga by serving the Lord's lotus feet, can be obtained in Kali-yuga simply by chanting the Hare Kṛṣṇa mahā-mantra."

If Lord Hari is glorified, then everything has been arranged. Meditation was prescribed for Satya-yuga, but in Kali-yuga, the mind is so disturbed that it is impossible to meditate on the Supreme Lord. That is why the great meditation prescribed for this age is harināma-*saṅkīrtana* . Also, the simple meditation process prescribed for Satya-yuga was insufficient to help one meet the most magnanimous personality, Śrī Gaurasundara. Therefore we call harināma-*saṅkīrtana* the "great meditation." Since the process of Satya-yuga, meditation, became contaminated over time, fire sacrifice became the yuga-dharma for Tretā-yuga. Similarly, the great *saṅkīrtana* sacrifice has been prescribed for Kali-yuga. Since fire sacrifice was contaminated over time, Deity worship was established in Dvapara-yuga. As a doctor after becoming baffled by his attempts to cure a dying patient prescribes him a poisonous tablet as a last resort because of its extreme potency, so the Lord prescribed the chanting of His holy name in this age of Kali after seeing our pathetic condition. The Lord's holy name is fully empowered, and in fact, all of the Lord's energies have been fully invested in His name.

Harināma-*saṅkīrtana* is the best form of meditation, the best form of fire sacrifice, and the best form of worship. Meditating on Kṛṣṇa, performing fire sacrifices for His pleasure, and worshiping Him are all part of the devotional process, but the complete perfection of the entire process comes when we follow the supreme process of Kṛṣṇa-kīrtana. We should not be inattentive while performing this best meditation. Only intelligent persons perform this best meditation, best fire sacrifice, and best worship, whereas fools follow other paths and do not gain anything.

Śrīmad-Bhāgavatam 11.5.32 states: *kṛṣṇa-varṇaṁ tviṣākṛṣṇaṁ, sāṅgopāṅgāstra-pārṣadam/ yajñaiḥ saṅkīrtana-prāyair, yajanti hi su-medhasaḥ:* "In the age of Kali, intelligent persons perform congregational chanting to worship the incarnation of Godhead who constantly sings the names of Kṛṣṇa. Although His complexion is not blackish, He is Kṛṣṇa Himself. He is accompanied by His associates, servants, weapons and confidential companions."

Śrī Caitanya-caritāmṛta states something similar: *saṅkīrtana-yajñe kalau kṛṣṇa-ārādhana, sei ta' sumedhā pāya kṛṣṇera caraṇa* "In this Age of Kali, the process of worshiping Kṛṣṇa is to perform sacrifice by chanting the holy name of the Lord. One who does so is certainly very intelligent, and he attains shelter at the lotus feet of Kṛṣṇa." (Antya 20.9)

21. What are the special characteristics of the holy names of Kṛṣṇa and Gaura?

We cannot chant Kṛṣṇa's transcendental holy name when we are full of *anarthas* because while chanting it is possible to commit offenses. There is no such consideration of offenses while chanting Śrī Gaura-Nityānanda's names. If a living entity sincerely chants the names of Gaura-Nityānanda, considering these personalities Supreme, all his *anarthas* will be destroyed even if he is full of *anarthas*. *Śrī Caitanya-caritāmṛta* states:

kṛṣṇa-nāma' kare aparādhera vicāra,
kṛṣṇa balile aparādhīra nā haya vikāra

"There are offenses to be considered while chanting the Hare Kṛṣṇa mantra. Therefore, simply by chanting Hare Kṛṣṇa, one does not become ecstatic." (Ādi 8.24)

caitanya-nityānande nāhi esaba vicāra,
nāma laite prema dena, vahe aśrudhāra
svatantra īśvara prabhu atyanta udāra,
tāṅre nā bhajile kabhu nā haya nistāra

"But if one only chants, with some slight faith, the holy names of Lord Caitanya and Nityānanda very quickly, he is cleansed of all offenses. Thus, as soon as he chants the Hare Kṛṣṇa mahā-mantra, he feels the ecstasy of love for God. Śrī Caitanya Mahāprabhu, the independent Supreme Personality of Godhead, is greatly magnanimous. Unless one worships Him, one can never be liberated." (Ādi 8.31-32)

22. Who is qualified to glorify Hari?

Only a person who thinks himself lower than straw in the street, who is more tolerant than a tree, who does not demand respect for himself, and who is always ready to give respect to others is qualified to glorify Hari. Although a devotee is the best of all, he considers himself humbler than a blade of grass. Unless we are sincere, we cannot think ourselves lower than a blade of grass. Only those who are free of material desires can become sincere devotees. Persons who chant Kṛṣṇa's holy name are the most fortunate. The mahājanas and *śāstras* have declared that congregational chanting is both the ultimate goal of life and the means to attain it. Those who chant the holy name are free of pride and false ego. They are amāni, free from the desire to be respected by others. Such persons do not maintain mundane pride.

23. Is everyone eligible to perform śrī-kṛṣṇa-saṅkīrtana?

Everyone is eligible to perform śrī-kṛṣṇa-*saṅkīrtana* . As Kṛṣṇa is full of energies, so are His names. The idea that only men can worship Hari but women cannot, that only healthy people can worship Hari but the ill cannot, that only the strong can worship Hari but the weak cannot—these considerations do not apply to the performance of śrī nāma-*saṅkīrtana* . He is a child and I am an old man. Therefore I will not chant the name of Hari with him. I am a learned person and he is a fool. Therefore I will not worship Hari with him. I am a respected *brāhmaṇa* and he is from a low-class family. Therefore I will not worship Hari in his company. All these mental and bodily conceptions have no relevance in the performance of śrī-kṛṣṇa-*saṅkīrtana* . I cannot chant the name of Hari while passing stool or urine. I cannot chant the name of Hari with a sinful heart. Such considerations are also insignificant. We can chant the name of Hari while we are passing stool or urine, and even the most sinful can chant Hari's name. But those who are duplicitous, thinking they will counteract their sins by chanting, can never actually chant Hari's name. If we have the propensity to commit sinful activities on the strength of chanting, we will find that we cannot chant the holy name of Hari.

24. How will we develop a taste for chanting the holy names?

A practitioner who desires his own fortune should surrender himself at the lotus feet of Nāma Prabhu. He should be firmly convinced that congregational chanting of Kṛṣṇa's name is the infallible path to perfection. The day we achieve perfection in chanting the mahā-mantra, Hari's holy name will dance constantly on the tip of our tongue. There is no use in making a show of worshiping the Lord while remaining averse to serving the Vaiṣṇavas, who live in the *Maṭha* simply to glorify Kṛṣṇa. Simply by serving the *Maṭha*'s devotees with love and devotion, our taste for chanting the holy name will increase, and we will become qualified to chant the holy name.

Instead of doing that, however, we remain absorbed in serving our relatives. Therefore we cannot chant. If by associating with Vaiṣṇavas and practicing *bhajana* householder devotees become free from both attachment to household life and the idea that they are proprietors, and if they can accept their residence and their relatives as ingredients for Kṛṣṇa's service rather than for their own pleasure, they can attain their own fortune.

It is only possible to chant the Lord's name in the association of devotees. Hari's pure name does not appear in the association of nondevotees. If we are indifferent to *sādhu-saṅga*, *hari-kathā*, and service to guru, Kṛṣṇa, and the Vaiṣṇavas, we will not gain anything. Therefore whether we are householders or residing in the *Maṭha*, we must pay special attention to these three items. Then our success will be guaranteed and we will develop a taste for chanting, self-realization, and find ourselves reestablished in our constitutional position.

25. How will we know whether or not we are chanting purely?

If a person is able to utter the pure name, it means he cannot possibly have loose character, an evil cheating mentality while acting as guru, or desire material wealth. Neither women nor fame will be able to capture his heart. Simply by chanting the reflection of the name, sin, the desire to commit sin, and nescience are vanquished. If any of the above items is present in the heart, we can understand that we have never uttered the pure name. The holy name is directly the Lord Himself; it is transcendental sound vibration. We cannot control the Supreme Absolute Truth, the holy name; we are controlled and delivered by the holy name.

If by the mercy of guru and the Vaiṣṇavas we are fortunate enough to know that we are the servant of Nāma Prabhu, then our desire for material name, fame, wealth, and women will not disturb us. The pure name appears on the tongue only of those persons who are liberated from the clutches of gold, women, and fame. The pure name manifests in the pure existence of the soul. Kṛṣṇa's holy name is directly the transcendental Cupid. The transcendental Cupid and mundane lust cannot stay together.

26. What is pure chanting?

Our success at chanting depends on our willingness to hear. Whatever we are doing for our sense gratification is neither chanting nor devotional service. Real chanting, pure chanting, is done for God's pleasure. Śrī Caitanyadeva has said that the chanting of Śrī Hari is cent-percent education. In other words, it is the actual teachings. The more one hears *hari-kathā*, the more he will attain perfection of life.

27. Should chanting the holy names be definitelyperformed?

The ultimate goal of the Gauḍīya *Maṭha* is paraṁ vijayate śrī-kṛṣṇa-*saṅkīrtana* , glorifying śrī-kṛṣṇa-*saṅkīrtana* . We should know that chanting the holy name is devotional service. There is nothing more we should be doing. The Lord does not accept anything offered by those who do not chant one hundred thousand names a day. Every devotee of the Lord must chant one hundred thousand names a day. Otherwise, he will be unable to serve the Lord because he will be unable to free himself from sensual enjoyment. Everyone who lives in the Gauḍīya *Maṭha* should chant one hundred thousand names daily. We should also remember that we cannot possibly learn to chant if we do not offer sincere and loving service to our spiritual master, who is an *ācārya* of the holy name.

If one desires to chant without offense under the spiritual master's guidance, one must chant constantly. In this way, all offenses will be destroyed. If one does not chant the holy name, one will not find another way to remove misfortune. Those unfortunate people who pretend to perform other types of *bhajana* by becoming indifferent to kīrtana, which is fit to be called "the only process of *bhajana*," or who make a show of chanting or reciting literature like the *Śrīmad-Bhāgavatam* yet give up serving guru and the Vaiṣṇavas, never profit. They are too proud.

28. Is chanting Kṛṣṇa's holy names the only sādhana?

People cannot understand that they have no other duty but to worship Hari. Whether we are children, old men, young men, male or female, rich or poor, learned or foolish, sinful or pious—we have no other *sādhana* than to chant Kṛṣṇa's holy name.

29. Is chanting the Lord's name the crest jewel of sādhanas?

Chanting the holy name is certainly the topmost *sādhana* in this age of Kali. Actually, it is the only process of *sādhana* in this age. The chanting of the holy name awards all perfection. *Śrī Caitanya-caritāmṛta* Ādi 17.21-25) states:

harer nāma harer nāma, harer nāmaiva kevalam,
kalau nāsty eva nāsty eva, nāsty eva gatir anyathā
kali-kāle nāma-rūpe kṛṣṇa-avatāra,
nāma haite haya sarva-jagat-nistāra
dārḍhya lāgi' 'harer nāma'-ukti tina-vāra,
jaḍa loka bujhāite puna 'eva'-kāra
'kevala'-śabde punarapi niścaya-karaṇa,
jñāna-yoga-tapa-karma-ādi nivāraṇa
anyathā ye māne, tāra nāhika nistāra,
nāhi,nāhi, nāhi—e tina 'eva'-kāra

In this age of quarrel and hypocrisy the only means of deliverance is chanting the holy name of the Lord. There is no other way. There is no other way. There is no other way. In this Age of Kali, the holy name of the Lord, the Hare Kṛṣṇa mahā-mantra, is the incarnation of Lord Kṛṣṇa. Simply by chanting the holy name, one associates with the Lord directly. Anyone who does this is certainly delivered. This verse repeats the word "eva" ["certainly"] three times for emphasis, and it also three times repeats "harer nāma" ["the holy name of the Lord"], just to make common people understand. The use of the word "kevalam" ["only"] prohibits all other processes, such as the cultivation of knowledge, practice of mystic yoga, or performance of austerities and fruitive activities.

This verse clearly states that no one who accepts another path can be delivered. This is why "nothing else" is repeated three times: it emphasizes the real process for self-realization.

Elsewhere in *Śrī Caitanya-caritāmṛta* it is stated:

nāma vinu kali-kāle nāhi āra dharma,
sarva-mantra-sāra nāma, ei śāstra-marma

"In this Age of Kali there is no religious principle other than the chanting of the holy name, which is the essence of all Vedic hymns. This is the purport of all scriptures. "(Ādi 7.74)

bhajanera madhye śreṣṭha nava-vidhā bhakti,
'kṛṣṇa-prema', 'kṛṣṇa' dite dhare mahā-śakti
tāra madhye sarva-śreṣṭha nāma-saṅkīrtana,
niraparādhe nāma laile pāya prema-dhana

"Among the ways of executing devotional service, the nine prescribed methods are the best, for these processes have great potency to deliver Kṛṣṇa and ecstatic love for Him. Of the nine processes of devotional service, the most important is to always chant the holy name of the Lord. If one does so, avoiding the ten kinds of offenses, one very easily obtains the most valuable love of Godhead." (*Antya* 4.70-71)

Among the sixty-four limbs of devotional service, chanting is topmost. Simply by congregationally chanting the holy name, one achieves all perfection. The nine types of devotional service are included in chanting the holy name. Śrī Gaurāṅgadeva's internal mood teaches that chanting Kṛṣṇa's holy name is the only process for attaining the goal of life. One who chants the holy name attains all auspiciousness.

Who can chant the holy name? First one must hear about the name. Congregational chanting is the crest jewel of all *sādhanas*. By serving the name, a living entity attains perfection. Our only business is to chant the holy name in Vaiṣṇava association. Chanting the holy name is the ultimate goal enjoined by *Śrīmad-Bhāgavatam*. The liberated souls have no duty other than to chant the Lord's name. A chanter of the holy name completely surrenders himself at the feet of the name. The day a living entity attains perfection in chanting, the holy name begins to dance on the tip of his tongue.

30. How important is Vaiṣṇava sevā to those who wish to chant purely?

People should not make a show of worshiping the Lord while remaining averse to serving devotees living in the *Maṭha*. A *Maṭha* contains all the ingredients for the Lord's service. Simply by serving the *Maṭha*'s residents, we become qualified to chant the holy name. That is, our taste for chanting will increase. If instead we remain absorbed in serving materialistic relatives we will never learn to chant Hari's holy name. If we remain busy in the service of family members while remaining indifferent to serving Hari, guru, and the Vaiṣṇavas, we will never become inclined toward chanting. To induce us to chant Kṛṣṇa's name, Śrī Gaurāṅgadeva, the combined form of Śrī Rādhā-Kṛṣṇa, appeared in this world. If we show no interest in chanting and thereby disregard His teachings, we will never attain auspiciousness.

Chanting is the best form of kṛṣṇa-sevā. If other *sādhanas* help us develop our chanting, then they deserve to be called *sādhana*. Otherwise, they are simply impediments on the path of chanting. Congregational chanting of Kṛṣṇa's holy name is the king of *sādhanas*. It is the only infallible *sādhana* capable of bringing us to perfection. Śrī Mahāprabhu did not teach Deity worship in His *Śikṣāṣṭaka*; He simply taught us to chant.

In *Bhakti-sandarbha* (anuccheda 173) Śrī Jīva Gosvāmī Prabhu writes, *yadyapi anyā bhakti kalau kartavyā tadā kīrtanākhya bhakti saṁyogena eva kartavya*: "Although we should perform other limbs of *bhakti* in this age of Kali, they should be performed along with chanting the Lord's holy name." Kṛṣṇa's holy name and Kṛṣṇa Himself are not two separate entities. The holy name is Kṛṣṇa and Kṛṣṇa is His holy name. The holy name of Kṛṣṇa is the son of Nanda; He is Śyāmasundara. If we realize that our only duty is to chant those holy names congregationally, our perfection is guaranteed.

31. What is śrī-kṛṣṇa-saṅkīrtana?

Śrī Kṛṣṇa plus *saṅkīrtana* equals śrī-kṛṣṇa-*saṅkīrtana* . Śrī plus Kṛṣṇa equals Śrī Kṛṣṇa. Śrī refers to Lakṣmī, or Śrī Rādhikā, the origin of all Lakṣmīs. Therefore the words "Śrī Kṛṣṇa" refer to the son of Nanda Mahārāja with Śrī Rādhā.

When many people gather and perform kīrtana, it is called *saṅkīrtana* . Saṅkīrtana also means to offenselessly chant Kṛṣṇa's names, and to discuss His forms, qualities, associates, characteristics, and pastimes.

32. Can we actually meditate on Kṛṣṇa and His pastimes before we have achieved spontaneous devotion?

When we achieve the state of spontaneous remembrance by the influence of our chanting, we can worship the Lord in a solitary place. It is not possible to meditate with a disturbed mind. Trying to meditate artificially is simply another form of covered sense gratification. Meditation in the form of chanting the glories of the transcendental Absolute Truth is natural and genuine. The minute conscious living entities are related to the supremely conscious Lord in one of five *rasas* . The natural attraction between them, and the living entities' worship of the Lord based on that attraction, amounts to spontaneous meditation. There is no question of mental disturbance in such meditation and certainly no cheating. Kṛṣṇa's servants all engage in spontaneous meditation.

33. Should chanting Hari's holy names be performed constantly?

Glorifying Hari is the best form of relaxation. By this method, all our fatigue and distress are vanquished. A moment's diversion from glorification of Hari will leave us again feeling averse to the Lord. Great personalities and their followers always engage in glorifying Hari under all circumstances. They have no other business. Śrī Caitanyadeva ordered, kīrtanīya sadā hariḥ: "Always chant the holy name of Hari." The symptom of a living liberated soul is that he is always engaged in glorifying Hari with body, mind, and speech.

34. When we chant "Rāma" in the Hare Kṛṣṇa mantra, which Rāma is being referred to?

According to *aiśvarya-rasa* Rāma refers to Lord Rāmacandra, the son of Daśaratha. According to *mādhurya-rasa* Rāma refers to Kṛṣṇa, who enjoys Rādhās company. This Rāma is the son of Nanda Mahārāja. Whenever the name Rāma indicates service to Rādhā-Ramaṇa Kṛṣṇa, the word "Hare," which is the vocative form of Harā, refers to Śrī Rādhārāṇī, who is the origin of the spiritual energies.

Śrī Rādhā is known as Harā because She attracts Kṛṣṇa's mind. Harā means "attracter.""Hare" is also the vocative form for the word "Hari."

There are three Rāmas: Rāma, the husband of Sītā, Rāma (Balarāma), the husband of Revatī, and Rāma (Kṛṣṇa), the husband of Rādhā.

35. Is transcendental sound vibration eternal?

Transcendental sound vibration is certainly eternal. In this world of anxiety, there is a difference between sound and its source. Every sound in this material world is temporary. However, in Vaikuṇṭha the name and its owner are nondifferent. There is no difference between sound and its source in the spiritual world.

36. Is chanting Hari's holy names most auspicious?

There is danger at every step in the attempt to practice solitary *bhajana*. If we sing *hari-kathā*, however, others can also hear and be benefited. In kīrtana, service to Hari is rendered in three ways: Hari is served directly, He is served by our own hearing, and He is served by our giving others the opportunity to hear. Apart from this, kīrtana also allows us to remember the Lord. Therefore we are also able to serve Hari by remembering Him when we perform kīrtana.

37. Where is the Hare Kṛṣṇa mahā-mantra mentioned in the Vedas?

Hari's name is Hari Himself. The mahā-mantra was present before the *śāstras* appeared. The *Bhāgavatam*'s catuḥ-ṣloki verse, beginning with aham evasam evagre, offers proof of this. The supremely independent holy name is not under the *śāstras*' control. In fact, the *śāstras* have manifest by the holy name's supreme will. It is not a fact that the *śāstras* came first and the holy name followed. The *Brahma-saṁhitā* states that the holy name appeared first in Brahmās heart. The Rg Veda also mentions the holy name.

The mahā-mantra or the importance of the Lord's holy name is mentioned in various literature, such as *Kali-santaraṇa Upaniṣad* (from the Yajur Veda), *Bṛhat Nāradīya Purāṇa, Jñanāmṛta-sāra, Pippalāda-śākhā* (from the Atharva Veda), *Śrī Kṛṣṇa Caitanya-carita-mahakāvya, Śrī Caitanya-bhāgavata, Śrī Caitanya-maṅgala, Brahma-yāmala, Rādhā Tantra, Padma Purāṇa, Śrīmad-Bhāgavatam, Brahmaṇḍa Purāṇa, Sanat-kumāra Saṁhitā, Agni Purāna, Ananta-samhitā, Caitanya Upaniṣad* (from Atharva Veda), *Śrī Caitanya-caritāmṛta, Bṛhat-Bhāgavatāmṛta, Śrī Nāma Kaumudi*. We have also received instructions regarding the *mahā-mantra* from the Supreme Personality of Godhead, Śrī Gaurasundara.

38. What does "Hare" mean?

Some people conclude that the word "hare" in the Hare Kṛṣṇa mahā-mantra is an address to Hari. Those who are more attached to the āśraya-tattva rather than the *viṣaya-tattva*—that is, those whose service propensity is more awake—accept "hare" as a call to Harā, Rādhā. Since Rādhā attracts Kṛṣṇa's mind with Her love, she is known as Harā.

39. What does the word "Oṁ" mean?

Oṁ is the preliminary manifestation of the holy name, and "Kṛṣṇa" is the fully manifest holy name.

40. What is a mantra?

A mantra is a sound vibration that can deliver the mind from its enjoying spirit and relieve it of its concentration on sense gratification. When we attain perfection in chanting a mantra, we are given respite from mental speculation. Unless we renounce pride, we cannot serve guru and Kṛṣṇa. To become independent is a symptom of pride.

41. Should everyone be engaged in chanting?

Everyone must perform kīrtana. The eternal occupational duty of all living entities is to glorify Lord Hari's names and topics. Of course, before "everyone" can begin to hear and chant about Kṛṣṇa we ourselves will have to hear about and glorify Kṛṣṇa. Whether others agree with us or not we must personally follow this authorized method.

42. What is the difference between Deity worship and chanting?

When we engage in Deity worship only the worshiper is benefited. When we chant the holy name both chanter and hearer are benefited. Deity worship is performed personally—others cannot see it—but the sound of the chanting vibrates in other people's ears. The spiritual master will always help his disciples rectify their mistakes. Chanting the holy name is lively, dynamic, and most purifying.

43. When does pure chanting begin?

We will not be able to chant purely as long as we are absorbed in material thoughts. How can we chant Kṛṣṇa's name if we are not inclined to serve Him? A person interested in sense gratification, who is fond of cheating and who is a hypocrite, can never chant the holy name. Those who do not understand that the Lord's holy name and the Lord Himself are nondifferent will face obstacles in chanting. Chanting begins when we are inclined to serve the Lord. Unless we are convinced that the holy name is directly the Lord Himself, how will we chant? The Lord's sacred name does not manifest on the tongue if the heart is filled with the current of mundane thought. Therefore it is not possible to chant the holy name until the mind is spiritualized. Only a person whose material conception has been destroyed is able to chant Hari's name constantly.

We are suffering because we serve our material desires. If our material desires are strong we will become Maya's servants and may even take birth as ghosts or evil spirits. When by serving guru and Kṛṣṇa the heart becomes purified, the Lord's pure name will appear in the heart. Otherwise, we will continue to commit offenses against the holy name.

12. What is the [illegible] between Deity worship and [illegible]

[illegible]

Material and Spiritual Topics

1. What is the difference between soul, mind, and body?

The scriptures have analyzed the difference between soul, mind, and body—between spiritual spark, reflection of spirit, and matter. The spirit soul is the proprietor of both body and mind; body and mind are properties of the soul. The soul is the property of the Supersoul.

The spirit soul has two bodies or designations. One of them is the subtle designation in the form of the mind, and the other is the gross designation in the form of the body. The external body is made of five gross material elements, which are composed of atoms, and the internal or subtle body directs the external body. In the conditional state, the spirit soul is absorbed in foreign matters through its identification with the mind. Since the spirit soul is dormant at that time, it does not remember that it is meant to serve the Supersoul. Realizing that their master is dormant, the two subordinate servants, body and mind, become busy looking out for their selfish interests rather than for their master's interest.

The mind is changeable, but the soul is unchangeable and eternal. The mind's activities are to enjoy and renounce matter. The soul's activity is to serve the Supreme Lord. The mind is able to understand things up to the third dimension, but it has no ability to understand things of the fourth dimension (transcendental objects). It is impossible to understand the Absolute Truth, the transcendental Personality of Godhead, through either material experience or knowledge.

2. Does lack of faith in God cause distress?

Wherever there is an absence of complete faith in the most auspicious personality, there is bound to be inauspiciousness. Therefore, the ascending or unauthorized path should be totally rejected and the descending or authorized path of disciplic succession accepted. If we really want to benefit, we will have to offer everything we have accumulated since birth to the Lord's lotus feet without reservation and await His causeless mercy. Until we are favored by a glimmer of His causeless mercy, we will not be able to understand kṛṣṇa-kathā. If we do not have full faith that the Lord alone bestows all auspiciousness, we will not be able to give everything up without hesitation. We may think, "If I give everything to Kṛṣṇa, I may actually lose everything and find myself in trouble if Kṛṣṇa has nothing to give me." Such doubts are baseless. By maintaining such doubts, we simply invite inauspiciousness.

The Lord never refuses His surrendered devotee or leaves his desires unfulfilled. The Lord has the sole power to fulfill all our requirements and to give us full protection. If we can gain this conviction, we will become fearless. We will no longer feel anxiety. We will become happy. It is not possible to describe how much benefit the living entity receives by the Lord's causeless mercy.

When the Lord does bestow His mercy, it's not that we become satisfied even after serving Him constantly. Rather, we receive an invaluable wealth of transcendental longing for the Lord's service. We will not lament that we cultivated attraction to the Lord's name, form, qualities, and pastimes, and we will not think they are boring or that our future is dark with possible disappointment. We will never think we have been cheated by surrendering to His lotus feet.

Our most magnanimous, able, and grateful Lord will never throw us into the ocean of disappointment. We have an invaluable jewel called independence, but even in our independence we are dependent on the Lord. The moment we attempt to misuse our independence by opposing this understanding we will bring about our own ruination.

If we approach worldly people with high expectations, they can neither fulfill our ambitions nor solve our problems. That is why *Bhagavad-gītā* clearly instructs us to take complete shelter at Śrī Kṛṣṇa's lotus feet. He alone is the Absolute Truth, the Supreme Lord. To surrender to Him is the ultimate goal of our life. Simply by surrendering to Him, we perfect our life. We should discuss how to surrender completely despite our *anarthas* and impediments.

3. Why is it that those who live near devotees may not be as good as the devotees?

It is true that where there is light there is no darkness, but darkness is present immediately underneath light. Wherever there is light, there is darkness. Wherever there is piety, there has to be some nearby sin. The absence of darkness does not brighten the light. Because there is foolishness, we feel the strength of knowledge. Unless there is distress, we will not realize need.

4. What is illusion?

Illusion means to accept that which is not—a rope for a snake, for example. Śrī Caitanyadeva never claimed we were our bodies. Rather, He told us that to consider the body as the self was illusion.

There is a difference between the body and its owner. The soul is the proprietor and the body is the property. There are two bodies— the gross and subtle—and the soul owns both of them. The mind is the reflection of spirit, and the body is devoid of spirit. We think in terms of "I" and "mine" concerning these bodies, but this is simply illusion, misconception.

5. What is the difference between spirit and matter?

Matter is that which is devoid of consciousness or spirit. Material objects have no initiative. They have no power to know, will, or feel. Inanimate objects cannot respond to anything, but spirit can. Spirit is present within us, in animals, and proportionately less in plants.

6. Why do people visit holy places?

The places where the Lord and His devotees perform pastimes are called tīrthas, holy places. Pious people travel to holy places to associate with devotees and to serve them, thereby serving the Supreme Lord. Sinful people travel to holy places for a different reason. They want to accumulate mundane fame and temporarily wash off their sins. They make their journey, but maintain their sinful propensities. Kṛṣṇa's exalted devotees also enact the pastime of traveling to holy places, but they do so to transform these ordinary places into sacred tīrthas and to purify the contamination accumulated in such places. While there, they search after their worshipable Lord and remain absorbed in the mellows of separation from the Lord. Thus they are intoxicated in His service.

7. What is the difference between activities and pastimes?

This is the Gauḍīya Vaiṣṇava philosophy. The difference between karma (activities) and *līlā* (pastimes) is that karma is performed with the material senses and līlā is performed with the service-inclined spiritual senses. Karma lives in the material world and is based on gross and subtle designations. It is temporary. Lilā, however, is eternal. The conditioned souls enjoy and suffer the threefold miseries through karma. Lilā is the fully independent Supreme Personality of Godhead's enactment of blissful pastimes executed by His own sweet will. Līlā lives in Vaikuṇṭha or Goloka, which is situated beyond the fourteen worlds, the Virajā River, and Brahmaloka. Even though līlā manifests in this world by the desire of the Lord's internal potency, it is neither under the control of material nature nor influenced by matter. Rather, it is inconceivable and transcendental by nature.

8. What is devotional service and what is nondevotional service?

To retain sensual knowledge is called nondevotional service. Nondevotional service flows through three channels: sense gratification, fruitive activities, and the cultivation of impersonal knowledge. To work for our own benefit and for the benefit of others is called karma. To neither work for our own benefit nor for the benefit of others is called *jñāna*. Pleasing the senses of Śrī Hari, the transcendental Absolute Truth, by renouncing both the cultivation of sensual knowledge and impersonal knowledge is called *bhakti*. Bhakti does not begin until we are liberated from the hands of both material enjoyment and liberation.

9. Some people say that everyone is equal. Are they correct?

How can the honest and dishonest, devotee and nondevotee, pious and impious, literate and illiterate, demigod and Supreme Lord, chaste and unchaste, religious and irreligious, light and dark, constitutional and conditional, as well as devotional service and nondevotional service be equal? Everything seems easy to those who are unaware of internal objects or who cannot enter more subtle understandings of them. A foolish boy may claim that his illegible writing has meaning because the writing of an intelligent person has meaning. If illegible writing and meaningful writing are considered equal, foolish people will think that anyone trying to make a distinction between them is guilty of sectarianism or partiality. If we appeal to those who have no understanding of the Supreme Lord Hari to discuss topics about Hari and their conclusion, they will say that to reveal the conclusion would be sectarian. Then they would say that refuting an improper conclusion amounts to blasphemy. They think that because we don't know everything, better to balance the account by calling everything equal. In this way, everyone will be pleased and we will have created no enmity. But truth and falsehood, devotional and non-devotion, are never one. For those devoid of devotional sentiment, who feel no necessity to serve the Supreme Lord, who do not want actual benefit, and whose life's goal is material enjoyment and fame, devotional service and pseudo devotional service appear one.

10. What is the difference between Vaikuṇṭha and the material world?

The spiritual world is the Lord's supremely pleasant original abode, whereas the material world is the perverted reflection of the spiritual world. The difference between them is that in the spiritual world everything is fully transcendental and there is no question of mundane contamination. Even though spiritual qualities resemble material qualities, still, the material world is the perversely reflected shadow of the spiritual world. All objects in the material world are destined to be ruined in due course of time. Happiness in this world is temporary because all material things and conditions are subject to change according to time, place, and persons. The spiritual world is eternal, devoid of dead matter, all auspicious, and full of variegated happiness. It is adorned with all transcendental qualities and constantly bestows eternal happiness. In the material world, however, there are abominations, displeasures, and scarcities, which constantly create disturbance for the living entities. In our day-to-day life we all realize these facts.

11. What is the difference between a jñānīs acceptance of sannyāsa and a bhakta's acceptance of sannyāsa?

Complete *sannyāsa* means executing devotional service to the Lord. To the *jñānīs*, who preach ahaṁ brahmāsmi, "I am nondifferent from the Supreme Brahman," *sannyāsa* means to give up service to the Supreme Brahman. While accepting the renounced order of life, they renounce the Lord's service. They are so unfortunate that they cannot understand that actual *sannyāsa* means to constantly engage in worship of the Supreme Lord. Therefore the Māyāvādī sannyāsīs altogether renounce interest in Kṛṣṇa's holy names, forms, qualities, associates, and pastimes. The renunciation of bhaktas is different. Bhaktas renounce material enjoyment and the desire for liberation. The Māyāvādīs also renounce material enjoyment when they take *sannyāsa*, but they also take *sannyāsa* from devotional service. The bhaktas take shelter at the lotus feet of Śrī Bhakti-devī by renouncing material desires and their attachment to renunciation. The Lord's devotees do not renounce chanting the transcendental name of the Lord, the tip of whose lotus feet are adored by the personified Vedas. They have not considered the holy name a temporary, material manifestation. Because they come fully under the holy name's shelter and serve the holy name, they remain constantly eager to chant.

12. Who is a materialist?

A materialist is one who accumulates material objects for his own pleasure and who engages them as ingredients of his sense gratification. One who accumulates material objects for the Lord's service is not a materialist but a devotee. It is not possible to differentiate between a material enjoyer and a devotee on the basis of their respective activities, but it is possible to differentiate by studying the motivation of each. One who eats for personal sense gratification is a materialist; one who eats to maintain the body for Kṛṣṇa's service is a devotee. A devotee is neither a material enjoyer nor a dry renunciant but a servant of the Lord. A devotee engages wealth, material objects, and everything in this world in the Lord's service.

13. If we are faced with a calamity, how should we respond?

If we learn to see from the spiritual point of view, from Kṛṣṇa's point of view, then we will know that everything is all right. If we see only from the material point of view, everything will appear upside down during a calamity. To see from the spiritual point of view means to see through the deductive process under the disciplic succession. This is the proper way to see. To see from the material point of view means to use one's empiric reasoning, through the senses and with the pride of material knowledge, denying the Lord's supremacy. The result will be material distress.

14. What is the present condition of the living entities?

We spend our few days of life busily caring for our bodies, but we never think about what comes after death or what our duty is. The various religions that ordinary human beings meet and which form their current of material thought, are all cheating religions. *Śāstra* states, *pṛthivīte yāra kichu dharma-nāme cale, bhāgavata kahe tāhā paripūrṇa chale:* "Whatever is going on throughout the whole world as religion, the Bhāgavata condemns it as cheating." Someone should make a comparative study to decide whether human society is making progress or lagging behind. The mental speculators always move in the direction opposite to the Absolute Truth. Śrī Caitanyadeva taught everyone to advance on the path of the Absolute Truth. If they are to do that, it is necessary to deliver those who proudly say they will become one with Brahman from their path of illusion. Let people know something good before they die. Thousands of Indian philosophies can be reconciled if people are given the opportunity to associate with Śrī Caitanyadeva's devotees.

People bereft of foresight spend their days eating food mixed with cockroach stool, thinking there is nothing else to eat. Some of these people say there is no need to live in this world and think it better to finish their existence altogether. Their philosophy is more or less like the philosophy of Sākhya Siṁha. ŚrīŚaṅkarācārya has said that Brahman is factual while everything else is false. Moreover those who preach the philosophy of materialism are busy pursuing their altruistic ideas. They are eager to accumulate mundane knowledge. But the flow of thought should be directed toward the spirit.

An opposing force deludes humans. By discussing topics of the Supreme Lord, one can remain unaffected by it. If one sees the material world as an ingredient for the Lord's service, then there will be no more distress. All our miseries are because we do not cultivate Kṛṣṇa consciousness. Whatever Lord Kṛṣṇa said in *Bhagavad-gītā*, Mahāprabhu summarized in these words as follows:

jīvera 'svarūpa' haya—kṛṣṇera 'nitya-dāsa',
kṛṣṇera 'taṭasthā-śakti' 'bhedābheda-prakāśa'

It is the living entity's constitutional position to be an eternal servant of Kṛṣṇa because he is the marginal energy of Kṛṣṇa and a manifestation of simultaneously one with and different from the Lord. (*Śrī Caitanya-caritāmṛta* Madhya 20.118)

kṛṣṇa bhuli' sei jīva anādi-bahirmukha,
ataeva maya tāre deya saṁsāra-duḥkha

Forgetting Kṛṣṇa, the living entity has been attracted by the external feature from time immemorial. Therefore, the illusory energy [Maya] gives him all kinds of misery in his material existence. (*Śrī Caitanya-caritāmṛta* Madhya 20.117)

The Lord says, "O living entity! You have been averse to Me since time immemorial. You were also God conscious and could have served Me, but instead you demanded service from Me. Despite being manifest from the Absolute Truth, you have become materially conditioned, trying to enjoy independently. You are trying to be the master, but know for certain that you are always a servant."

We are the Supreme Lord's servants. If instead of serving the Lord we demand service from Him, we will never achieve auspiciousness. Lord Hari is everyone's master; everyone is His servant. It is everyone's duty, therefore, to hear *hari-kathā*. Material topics do not constitute *hari-kathā*. It is the spiritual master who speaks *hari-kathā* and the disciple who listens. A listener must be submissive. Those who are reluctant to hear will not find benefit when *hari-kathā* is spoken to them. A listener must be both eager to hear and inquisitive. If one wants to waste time he will allow himself to be influenced by the current of other thoughts. If he is fortunate, he will search only after pure *hari-kathā*. The *Śāstra* states, *tad-dinaṁ durdinam manye meghāchhanam na durdinam, yad-dinaṁ kṛṣṇa samlāpa kathā pīyuṣa varjitaṁ*: "A cloudy day is not inauspicious, but a day devoid of discussing kṛṣṇa-kathā is actually inauspicious."

15. Why are people, devoid of the desire to serve the Supreme Lord, as good as animals?

Serving the Lord is the living entity's only duty. Animals do not have this knowledge. The animals know only their own sense gratification and the sense gratification of their community. They do not know anything other than sense gratification. If human beings are similarly busy seeking their own happiness and sense gratification— if they simply spend their time eating, sleeping, mating, and defending like animals—and if they do not develop the propensity to serve and please the Supreme Lord, then what else can they be called but animals in a human form?

It is the occupational duty of the human being to desire Kṛṣṇa's pleasure and to render Him devotional service. Anyone who practices devotional service is eligible to be called human. *Śāstra* states, dharmena hīna paśubhiḥ samānaḥ: "Without religion, people are animals." Desiring one's sense gratification is the business of an animal, and desire to please Kṛṣṇa is the business of a human being.

16. Did humans create religion?

Śrīmad-Bhāgavatam (6.3.19) states:

dharmaṁ tu sākṣād bhagavat-praṇītaṁ,
na vai vidur ṛṣayo nāpi devā
na siddha-mukhyā asurā manuṣyāḥ,
kuto nu vidyādhara-cāraṇādaya

Real religious principles are enacted by the Supreme Personality of Godhead. Although fully situated in the mode of goodness, even the great ṛṣis, who occupy the topmost planets, cannot ascertain the real religious principles, nor can the demigods or the leaders of Siddhaloka, to say nothing of the asuras, ordinary human beings, Vidyādharas and Cāraṇas.

The supreme religious principles, *bhāgavata-dharma*, were not created by humans, nor were they created after the creation of human beings. They are eternal and will continue to be eternal, unchangeable, and uninterrupted. Devotional service to Lord Hari is the religious principle. Apart from *bhakti*, all other concocted religious systems that have been, are, and will be preached in this world, are manmade temporary religions,

religions opposed to the supreme religious principle. *Bhāgavata-dharma*, param-dharma, or ātmā-dharma cannot be merged with the religion of the body. Therefore Lord Śrī Kṛṣṇa instructs us in *Bhagavad-gītā* to give up all varieties of religion and surrender unto Him. *Bhagavad-gītā* (18.66) states: *sarva-dharmān parityajya, mām ekaṁśaraṇaṁ vraja/ ahaṁ tvāṁ sarva-pāpebhyo, mokṣayiṣyāmi māśucaḥ*: "Abandon all varieties of religion and just surrender unto Me. I shall deliver you from all sinful reactions. Do not fear."

Bhāgavata-dharma is the spirit soul's eternal propensity. The spirit soul was present even before the creation of human beings. Devotional service, which is the eternal propensity of the eternal spirit soul, is also eternal. The true religious process or *sādhana* is that which awakens the spirit soul's constitutional propensity.

It is the function of worldly moralities to transform animal-like humans into proper humans, but *bhāgavata-dharma* is above this. Cultivation of *bhāgavata-dharma* is eternally necessary to award the living entities the complete qualification to engage in the Supreme Lord's service. *Bhāgavata-dharma* makes no arrangement for sense gratification. It consists in cent-percent eternal service to the transcendental Lord. This is the only way to attain actual happiness, unlimited pleasure.

We should know that vox populi is not the same as vox dei, but the word of God should be the word of the people. Popular opinion is not the same as God's opinion, although the Supreme Lord's opinion should be the opinion of pious people. This is what the *mahājanas* instruct. People who mix spirit with matter say just the opposite. They say, *yata mata tata pata*: "As many opinions, as many ways." How amazing! The popular voice should be the voice of the Supreme Lord! People think that the process of attaining Him, where every popular opinion is given equal credence, should be as highly regarded as love and devotion to the Supreme Lord, even though in those processes devotion is totally absent. Wherever popular opinion is the criteria for ascertaining the Absolute Truth, non-duplicitous truth is far from being realized.

17. Whose offerings does the Supreme Lord accept?

The Lord eats the offerings from those who know how to invite and feed Him. Not everyone is able to call Him to eat. If they do not know, how will they feed Him? If a learned nondevotee offers food to the Lord with the proper recitation of mantras, the Lord does not accept His offering. Finely cooked rice mixed with ghee and various cooked vegetables offered by a nondevotee does not attract the Lord's attention. But anything offered by even a beggar inclined toward the Lord's service in any way attracts His attention and love.

18. What is the nature of love?

Love and hate are different. It is the spirit soul's nature to love God; it is the mental speculator's nature to hate Him. On the platform of love—the platform of devotional service, of supreme religious principles, and of service to the Lord—there is no conflict of interest,. There is only complete harmony. As soon as we fall down from the platform of cultivating love of God, however, we begin to see one another as objects of enjoyment. The entire human race is meant to serve Kṛṣṇa. When people realize this, they will no longer have problems. They will understand themselves as Vaiṣṇavas and there will be natural loving exchanges between themselves and other Vaiṣṇavas. There is no love in this material world, because everywhere here has a conflict of interest.

19. Manmade religion does not appear to be the eternal religion of the soul. What is your opinion in this regard?

Apart from the sanātana dharma described in *Śrīmad-Bhāgavatam* and the *bhāgavata dharma* preached by Śrī Caitanyadeva, every other religion born from human knowledge is filled with imagination and cheating. Bhāgavata dharma, the pure religion of the soul that Śrī Caitanyadeva preached, is the only religion free from cheating. It is therefore approved and practiced by nonenvious saintly persons. *Bhāgavata-dharma* is the eternal religious principle received through disciplic succession. Various current religious systems are manufactured religion; that is, mental speculation. They are not the soul's eternal religion. *Śrī Caitanya-caritāmṛta* states, caitanya-gosāñi yei kahe, sei mata sāra āra yata mata, sei saba chārakhāra: "Whatever meaning Śrī Caitanya Mahāprabhu gives is perfect. Any other interpretation is only a distortion." (Madhya 25.45)

As the soul is eternal, so our occupational duty is eternal. God enacts religious principles. No one other than the twelve mahājanas and their followers know about them. How, therefore, can religion be created by man?

20. Is a renunciant conditioned by matter?

Both bhogīs and tyāgīs are conditioned. Only the devotees are eternally engaged in Kṛṣṇa's service. The devotees are neither bhogīs nor tyāgīs. The devotees have no personal desire for sense gratification. Rather, they are engaged always in satisfying the Supreme Lord. But both bhogīs and tyāgīs desire material enjoyment and thus suffer material distress. The devotees have no material desire—they are completely free from material desire—so they are actually happy.

The occupational duty of the living entity is to serve the Supreme Lord. As soon as the living entity becomes indifferent to the Lord's service, the living entity desires to master the material world. If we are careful we will not face disturbance either in this world or the next, because we will engage in Kṛṣṇa's service.

21. What are the functions of the external and internal energies of the Lord?

The perishable material world was created by the Lord's external energy, in which the three modes of material nature are active. The eternal spiritual world was manifested by the Lord's internal energy, in which the three potencies, namely, hlādinī, sandhinī, and saṁvit are active. The world manifested by the internal energy and the world created by the external energy are different from one another. The living entity is constitutionally both one with and different from the Lord; he was created by the Lord's marginal energy. These three energies—the material, spiritual, and marginal—are eternal. As soon as the living entities, who belong to the Lord's marginal energy, desire to enjoy the temporary material world, they suffer various miseries. As soon as the godless living entities become averse to the Lord's service, they are attacked by the Lord's external energy, Maya. But when they are inclined toward the Lord's service the Lord's internal energy helps them serve the Lord.

22. Are sects such as the Āul and Bāul not Vaiṣṇava?

The Āuls and Bāuls are not Vaiṣṇavas. They artificially dress as renunciants, but keep women with them. Even though the activities of a devotee and the mischievousness of a pseudo devotee appear the same from the external viewpoint, there is a gulf of difference between them, just as there is a difference between milk and water mixed with limestone. The difference between them is like the difference between the sky and the earth. *Śāstra* states, asat-*saṅga*-tyāga,—ei vaiṣṇava-ācāra/ 'strī-saṅgī'—eka asādhu, '*kṛṣṇābhakta*' āra: "A Vaiṣṇava should always avoid the association of ordinary people. Common people are very much materially attached, especially to women. Vaiṣṇavas should also avoid the company of those who are not devotees of Lord Kṛṣṇa."

The Bābājīs who live in cottages are attached to women and are nondevotees. Their association should be firmly rejected. Otherwise it will be impossible to worship Hari. At the same time, it is always better not to criticize people. So we stay away from such bad association. Let the nondevotees think about sinful activities and the devotees think about the Supreme Lord. We will follow in the footsteps of the devotees.

23. What is the difference between impersonal monists and Vaiṣṇavas who follow Vedānta?

Impersonal monist or Māyāvādīs are partial to impersonalist philosophy, whereas Vaiṣṇavas who follow Vedānta believe in the philosophy of eternal personalism. Impersonalists are covered atheists, whereas Vaiṣṇavas are sincere theists. Impersonalists follow the ascending path, whereas Vaiṣṇavas follow the descending path. Impersonalists are opposed to surrendering to the Lord, whereas Vaiṣṇavas favor eternal, unalloyed surrender to the Lord.

24. What are the developmental stages of religion?

There are two paths of gradual development in the world of religion: the gradual development of sense gratification or material knowledge, and the gradual development of Kṛṣṇa's sense gratification or transcendental knowledge. The more one gradually develops sense gratification or material knowledge, the more one's sense of godlessness increases. The more one gradually develops Kṛṣṇa's sense gratification or transcendental knowledge, the more one's faith in God grows.

In the gradual development of sense gratification or material knowledge, the first stage is atheism, then skepticism, then agnosticism, then impersonalism, and finally voidism. In the gradual development of Kṛṣṇa's sense gratification or transcendental knowledge—that is, when the conception of spiritual variegatedness surpasses the stages of impersonal Brahman and Vāsudeva without His energies, the first stage is the worship of Lakṣmī-Nārāyana, the second is the worship of Sītā-Rāma, the third is the worship of Rukmiṇī-Dvārakādīśa, and the fourth is the worship of Rādhā-Govinda.

As human beings gradually develop sense gratification, Rādhā-Govinda's transcendental pastimes appear to them obscene, while the pastimes of Rukmiṇī-Dvārakādīśa appear a little bit better. Moreover, they consider the idea of Rāmacandra, who vowed to accept only one wife, as more ethical than the behavior of Dvārakādīśa Kṛṣṇa, who accepted many wives. They consider Lakṣmī-Nārāyana to be more pure than Rāmacandra. Moreover, they imagine that the conception of Vāsudeva without His śaktis to be more ethical than the conception of the Supreme in the form of male and female.

But to imagine Vāsudeva, who is full of spiritual energies, without His energies, is the first step toward atheism and impersonalism. In this way through the exercise of material knowledge, one ultimately ends up with impersonal Brahman. Impersonalism tries to perpetually separate the Absolute Truth from His eternal spiritual characteristics. In other words, it endeavors to destroy the existence of His transcendental personality. When this conception is further advanced, it embraces the philosophies of Jainism and Buddhism. Overly ethical Jainism and Buddhism transform the spiritual concept into a material concept, theism into atheism or voidism. Thus the gradual development of sense gratification distracts human intelligence from the idea of gratifying Kṛṣṇa's senses and sets a course toward the deep water of godlessness. The more the living entities advance on the path of their own sense gratification by being distracted from the concept of gratifying Kṛṣṇa's senses, the more they rush toward godlessness.

25. What is real danger according to a devotee?

Those who consider worldly scarcities, difficulties, and the threefold miseries of material existence to be dangerous end up aspiring for religiosity, economic development, sense gratification, and liberation. Both sense enjoyers and renunciants consider their failure to fulfill their respective self-interest as dangerous, whereas the Lord's devotees consider anything that hinders their endeavor to please the Lord's senses dangerous. Since the desire for religiosity, economic development, sense gratification, and liberation place obstacles on the path of gratifying Kṛṣṇa's senses, the devotees want freedom from those dangers. This means that the Lord's devotees desire to become liberated from material enjoyment and the desire for salvation.

26. What mentalities do the karmī, jñānī, and bhakta have?

Normally, human beings do not want to understand anything other than their own sense gratification. Karmīs want to be happy, even at the cost of hundreds of thousands of other people's inconvenience. Jñānīs want to renounce both the happiness and distress of this world and become impersonalists. Karmīs are busy trying to prove their superiority, while *jñānīs* heave a sigh of relief when they can establish that the all-powerful Supreme Lord is impotent. Since in both cases the Supreme Lord's energy is neither accepted nor glorified, persons who desire auspiciousness accept the path of *bhakti* rather than karma or *jñāna*. A devotee wants to fully depend on and give pleasure to the Lord. All their activities and knowledge are used simply to gratify Kṛṣṇa's senses. To offer everything to the Lord is called devotional service. Anything opposed to this conception is not devotion.

Bhaktas are free from material desire. They possess not even a tinge of the desire the *karmīs*, *jñānīs*, and yogīs have for sense gratification. Instead, they are always eager to please the Lord. They are humbler than a blade of grass. They have no thought or business other than to serve the Supreme Lord. Therefore they are fearless, free from anxiety, and happy. The *karmīs* and *jñānīs*, however, are restless and unhappy, driven as they are by their material desires. *Śrī Caitanya-caritāmṛta* states, *kṛṣṇa-bhak-*

ta—niṣkāma, ataeva 'śānta', bhukti-mukti-siddhi-kāmīsakali 'aśānta': "Because a devotee of Lord Kṛṣṇa is desireless, he is peaceful. Fruitive workers desire material enjoyment, *jñānīs* desire liberation, and yogīs desire material opulence; therefore, they are all lusty and cannot be peaceful."

27. Is it good to become a renunciant?

We will become neither sense enjoyers nor dry renunciants. Rather, we will become devotees, servants, of the Lord. Those who hanker after religiosity, economic development, and sense gratification are cheaters and are not devotees. Those renunciants who desire liberation also cheat; devotees want only to serve Kṛṣṇa.

The dry renunciants may appear to have been saved from the pain of material enjoyment, but their policy is like sleeping on the floor because the couch is broken. Their happiness or distress, depends only on them and has nothing to do with the Lord. The devotees give up material enjoyment and remain engaged in devotional service purely for Kṛṣṇa's pleasure. Hence they receive eternal benefit and become eternally happy.

Whatever inconvenience we may experience comes when we try to take advantage of the Supreme Lord. Some say they will become Kṛṣṇa and enjoy beautiful women, while others say they will become beautiful women and enjoy Kṛṣṇa. Both are full of material desires. Unless we see every object in relation to Kṛṣṇa, we will either indulge in sense gratification or dryly renounce it. Both karma (material enjoyment) and *jñāna* (renunciation) are opposed to devotional service because there they contain no *hari-kathā*. The root of both material enjoyment and renunciation is personal happiness. Bhakti, however, is rooted only in the desire to please the Supreme Lord.

28. What is an impure mind?

The heart that accepts and rejects things is the living entity's mind, and the heart that is constantly engaged in Kṛṣṇa's service by giving up both karma and *jñāna* is the pure mind. It is in the pure mind that the Supreme Lord finds enjoyment. Form, taste, smell, sound, and touch are called viṣaya, objects of sense gratification. The mind that proudly considers itself the enjoyer is materially absorbed and impure. One who has such a contaminated mind cannot realize the Supreme Personality of Godhead, Śrī Hari. Śrī Kṛṣṇa is realized in the heart purified by devotional service.

29. What is anartha?

Our self-interest is the Absolute Truth, Lord Hari. Anything opposed to that self-interest, such as desire for sense gratification, is anartha, the principal impediment on the path to the Lord's service. Anartha means Maya. Even though something in māyās realm appears real, it is illusory. Anarthas cause interruptions in one's remembrance of the Lord and thereby allow material thoughts to take over. Therefore, *anarthas* are obstacles on the path of self-interest and must be overcome.

30. What are worldly peace and worldly disturbance?

God is one, but the living entities are many. Since we have developed relationships with the many, our relationship with the one, God, has diminished. In the world of consciousness, everyone is engaged in the service of the One, God, and there is neither worldly happiness nor worldly distress in that world. Material happiness and distress are born of thirst for matter. When our enjoyment is temporarily absent, we experience distress, and when we temporarily achieve enjoyment, we call that happiness. We do not understand that temporary happiness is the primary stage of distress. Happiness and distress are both changeable. We are happy when our distress dissipates and in distress when our happiness lessens. Despite this knowledge, however, people sacrifice their lives simply to attain some temporary happiness and prosperity.

31. What are intolerance and impatience?

Intolerance and impatience create problems in life, so we should learn tolerance and patience. It is important to be tolerant during dangerous times. Examples of impatience are: to rush to a liquor shop upon finding one while walking down the street, to try to become rich on seeing a rich man's wealth, to rush to enjoy the beauty of a beautiful object, and to try to become wise upon seeing others' learning.

32. Are karma and jñāna the constitutional duty of the soul?

It is not the constitutional goal of the living entity to become either a *karmī* or a *jñānī*. Since the living entities are servants of the Supreme Lord, service to Kṛṣṇa is their eternal occupational duty. Both *karmīs* and *jñānīs* are selfish, busy for their own happiness. They are not bhaktas but abhaktas. Thus rather than becoming *karmīs* or *jñānīs*, pious persons traverse the path of devotional service by taking shelter of the Lord's lotus feet.

33. Who is considered a nondevotee?

Those who eternally serve Viṣṇu are called Vaiṣṇavas and those who do not, although they are supposed to, are called non-Vaiṣṇavas. Non-Vaiṣṇavas hear topics unrelated to Viṣṇu, contemplate subject matters unrelated to Viṣṇu, and consider eating, sleeping, mating, and defending as religious principles.

It is our eternal function to hear and speak kṛṣṇa-kathā and to follow in the footsteps of saintly persons. Remnants of Lord Viṣṇu's foodstuffs should form our regular meal. If we are bereft of these services, we are non-Vaiṣṇavas. As nondevotees, we will suffer from various forms of distress, but the cause of all our distress will be our aversion to serving the Lord. We suffer because we do everything but serve the Lord. Controlled by our own independence we have abandoned the Lord's service and instead have tried to get others to serve us. With such a mentality, we pose as the doer. Because we forget that we are meant to serve the Lord, misconceptions such as, "I am the enjoyer,""I am the proprietor,""I am the director," and, "I am the seer" swallow us. Only when we approach a saintly person can we know that we are not enjoyers or proprietors but simply servants of the Lord. Serving Him is our ultimate duty.

A fruitive worker traverses the path of karma. Often, such persons want to become famous by performing welfare activities. They want to attract the attention and sympathy of their relatives by serving them. However, karmic activities will give us neither benefit nor freedom from material existence. Therefore the devotees inform us that service to the Lord is our prime duty—and not only our duty as human beings, but the duty of the demigods, animals, and birds. Rather than heeding the devotees' words, people think that they have many duties to perform and many responsibilities to carry out. They think they have to be educated, civilized, to perform and rebuild society, and they hope to enjoy family life, mastership, ride in cars, and get their children married. These are all non-Vaiṣṇava, aversion to the Lord's service.

34. Who is qualified to recite Śrīmad-Bhāgavatam?

One whose life and activities are based on the teachings of *Śrīmad-Bhāgavatam* should serve Hari at every moment and with every breath of life. *Śrīmad-Bhāgavatam* is directly the Absolute Truth. One should not recite the *Bhāgavatam* as a business; the *Bhāgavatam* is worshipable. Therefore a professional reciter or contractor cannot describe *Śrīmad-Bhāgavatam*. Before hearing a *Bhāgavatam* recital, one should try to see whether the reciter is serving the Bhāgavata twenty-four hours a day or not. One reciting for a stipend or on contract cannot explain the Bhāgavata. Refrain from approaching professional priests. See first whether they devote themselves fully to the Bhāgavata.

Simply becoming an expert in the Purāṇas does not make one qualified to explain *Śrīmad-Bhāgavatam*. *Śāstra* establishes that *Śrīmad-Bhāgavatam* is not understood by those possessing only an academic knowledge of scripture. To understand it requires devotion. A person who explains *Śrīmad-Bhāgavatam* must himself be a bhāgavata. If one desires wealth or fame from his recitation of the *Śrīmad-Bhāgavatam*, then even though he becomes a renowned reciter, he will actually be far away from *Śrīmad-Bhāgavatam*. Hearing *Śrīmad-Bhāgavatam* from such a person, the people's hearts will not become attracted toward the Absolute, which is the goal of the *Bhāgavatam*.

Śrīmad-Bhāgavatam is not glorified when coming from the mouth of a person who is not a pure devotee and who does not base his life on the *Bhāgavatam*'s teachings. Such a person cheats himself and cheats others by making a show of his recitation.

The relationship between the *Śrīmad-Bhāgavatam* reciter and the audience is not like the relationship between a professor and his students. A professor who can nicely explain a lesson to his student is considered the best professor. It does not matter whether his lifestyle or character are exemplary. However, a *Bhāgavatam* reciter must follow the *Bhāgavatam*'s teachings before he will be able to preach. *Śrī Caitanya-caritāmṛta* states that unless one practices, he cannot teach religious principles to other.

One of loose character, who is lusty, full of material desires, and who wants wealth and fame can never explain *Śrīmad-Bhāgavatam*. Such a person simply gratifies his senses on the pretext of reciting *Śrīmad-Bhāgavatam*.

35. How do materialists and spiritualists see things differently?

Spiritual topics may often sound unpleasing, whereas discussions of sense gratification are always pleasing. The audience often wants a speaker to speak about what they like to hear, whereas a transcendentalist will want to hear impartial truth even if the message sounds bitter.

Materialists busily search out their own happiness, whereas transcendentalists eagerly seek Kṛṣṇa's happiness. Materialists do not follow Śrī Vyāsadeva, whereas transcendentalists follow the path traversed by the mahājanas. Transcendentalists want to follow the path shown by the great personalities; they follow the descending path of Vedic knowledge, whereas materialists follow the unauthorized, concocted, ascending path.

36. What are the various concepts of karmīs, jñānīs, and bhaktas?

A *karmī* is a sense enjoyer, a *jñānī* a renunciant or a covered sense enjoyer, and a devotee a servant of the Supreme Lord.

Dry renunciants think, "I will become one with the supreme Brahman and leave the ingredients for my sense gratification in this world." It is the habit of impersonalists to attack the Supreme Lord, the bhaktas, and the philosophy of *bhakti*. They think, "Whatever we do, even if we sit at Kāśī and play chess, we will become Lord Śiva as soon as we die."

Sinful people think, "We will enjoy everything by causing trouble to others." Pious fruitive workers think, "In order to accumulate piety, we will give charity, meditate, and serve saints. We will work hard, earn money, and save it for our relatives and descendants."

A bhakta thinks, "We will accumulate wealth only for the service of Hari, guru, and those Vaiṣṇavas who are worshiping the Lord at present and who will worship the Lord in future. Let all our wealth be spent for the worship of Hari."

37. What is the difference between the material and the spiritual worlds?

The material world is the perverted reflection of the eternal spiritual world and is full of imperfections. The variegatedness of this world includes temporality, imperfection, and perversion. In the spiritual world everything is spiritual. The place, time, and inhabitants are all transcendental and exist eternally there. There the object of service is one without a second. Since there are many servants, there is no lack of consistency. It is only when we consider the one object of service plural do we experience problem, although there is no fault in accepting variety in the Absolute Truth's energies.

38. Can there be one spiritual master for all religions?

Forget about many religions. There is only one real religion. Similarly, there is only one spiritual master. The one religion is the eternal religion of the soul. Everything else is either the religion of the body or mind. Regarding these religions there are various opinions and modes of worship. They have nothing to do with the religion of the soul. Religion of the soul is one without the second, and it contains no scarcity of variety. It is not boring but is the spontaneous propensity of the pure spirit souls, who are transcendental to all material contamination.

39. Is the phrase "As many opinions, as many paths" correct?

Opinion is born from mental speculation. As there are innumerable living entities, there are innumerable thoughts and tastes. The path that has been created, is being created, and will be created in the future by peoples' whims can never be the eternal occupational duty of the spirit soul (sanātana-dharma). Although there have been and will be innumerable opinions based on mental speculation, *Śrīmad-Bhāgavatam*, the king of all *śāstras*, declares, s*a vai puṁsāṁ paro dharmo, yato bhaktir adhokṣaja/ ahaituky* *apratihatā, yayātmā suprasīdati*: "The supreme occupation [dharma] for all humanity is that by which men can attain to loving devotional service unto the transcendent Lord. Such devotional service must be unmotivated and uninterrupted to completely satisfy the self." (*Śrīmad Bhāgavatam* 1.2.6)

The philosophy of "as many opinions, as many paths" found in this world is a path born from material knowledge; it is a path favorable to the material world. It is unmotivated, uninterrupted devotional service to Hari that is the supreme opinion for all humanity. The soul can be happy by no other means. Since other religious principles and processes award little pleasure to body or mind, gross materialists and mental speculators consider such religious principles and processes as their ultimate goal. Discussions of the Absolute Truth must be heard from the living source. Then the living entities can attain highest eternal benefit. Otherwise, there will be danger at every moment for those who are misguided.

40. What is Maya?

Maya means "that which is not." That which is not the Supreme Lord. The Lord is the positive and Maya is the negative idea devoid of God.

41. Do Vaiṣṇavas follow the ascending path or the descending path?

Although there are innumerable types of philosophical thought, they can be divided into two categories. One is the path of disciplic succession (the descending path) and the other is the path of mental speculation (mental experience or the ascending path). Moreover, many people advertise themselves as followers of the descending path who actually follow the ascending path. Mahāprabhu called them unauthorized followers of the disciplic succession. When Śrī Caitanyadeva referred to the Māyāvādīs in a conversation with Sārvabhauma Bhattācārya, a follower of the Vedānta school, he called Māyāvādīs covered atheists.

veda nā māniyā bauddha haya ta' nāstika,
vedāśraya nāstikya-vāda bauddhake adhika

The Buddhists do not recognize the authority of the Vedas; therefore they are considered agnostics. However, those who have taken shelter of the Vedic scriptures yet preach agnosticism in accordance with the Māyāvāda philosophy are certainly more dangerous than the Buddhists. (*Śrī Caitanya-caritāmṛta* Madhya-līla 6.168)

One cannot obtain spiritual knowledge through mental speculation. As the Ganges flows from the Himalayas through Gomukh, the flow of transcendental knowledge flows from the mouth of the spiritual master to the disciple. The spiritual master is the Supreme Lord's messenger. He carries the Lord's message to us from the transcendental world. The Vaikuṇṭha news that the spiritual master is carrying can only be accepted through service-inclined ears.

We have to hear about Calcutta from someone who has seen Calcutta. Instead of challenging such a person, we should submit ourselves and hear from him humbly. No one should decry the habit of honest, inquisitive hearing, as if it were less intelligent than presenting challenges. Therefore the *śāstras* declare that the spiritual master must be given the minimum period of one year to examine whether the disciple is approaching him with challenge or an honest inquisitiveness. We should approach a spiritual master and hear from him submissively, not challenge him. We must be careful about this. Hearing in this way means that we are receiving knowledge through the descending process, the path of disciplic succession.

42. Some people say "Time is money." Is that true?

The idea that "time is money" is not correct. Rather, that "time is precious" is a better motto. Instead of thinking that life or time is what gives us our temporary material benefits, we should spiritualize time by engaging whatever time we have in the Lord's service. Even while busy with our various worldly activities, we must pay attention to our spiritual advancement. If money is not spent properly, it will increase our *anarthas* and prolong our material existence. It takes intelligence to use wealth in the service of Nārāyaṇa, the Lord of wealth. Wealth is the father of all enjoyment. Therefore, it should be offered to Lord Mādhava for His service.

If we do not spend our hard-earned money for a spiritual cause, then that money will ruin us. We will become degraded and eventually meet death. It will make us forget God, because material enjoyment clears the path for destruction. Rich people often save their hard-earned money for their descendants. But their descendants in turn finish all their wealth in a moment by misusing it. In this, they go to hell and send their forefathers to hell as well.

43. Who is a devotee and who is a nondevotee?

Devotees serve Lord Hari and have no other duty. They treat the Lord's mission as their own. They know no one but the Lord. Pious persons practicing devotional service worship Lord Hari. People devoid of devotion are unconscious, inert, sense enjoyers. Karmīs, *jñānīs*, yogīs, and ascetics are all nondevotees. They are simply busy with their own self-interest.

The *śāstras* state, "A person who does not serve the Lord is dead though he is breathing." If we do not serve the Lord, then the tendency of enjoyment will overcome us and make us servants of Maya. Unless we are engaged in the Lord's service twenty-four hours a day, Maya will swallow us. Because we fail to see every object in relationship to Kṛṣṇa, we become misguided, considering ourselves enjoyers. The Lord's devotees are not sense enjoyers, fruitive workers, or mental speculators. They do not serve matter. Only nondevotees desire to master matter.

Devotional service is the devotees' treasury; it is their life and soul. It is their internal propensity to try to please Kṛṣṇa. The nondevotees are just the opposite: they are busy arranging for their own happiness.

44. What is the living entity's constitutional duty?

Religiosity, economic development, and sense gratification are considered categories of karma, while liberation is considered a category of *jñāna*. In order to deliver human society from the witches of material enjoyment and liberation, *bhāgavata-dharma* manifests in this world. Human society has decided that either material enjoyment or the freedom from material enjoyment is its only religion. But *bhāgavata-dharma* has created a revolution in the thoughts of the entire human society. The *Bhāgavatam* instructs: "The eternal occupational duty of all living entities is to engage in the service of the transcendental Personality of Godhead, after getting freedom from the desire for material enjoyment and liberation." If the integral parts, the living entities, want to fulfill their self-interest, independent of the Supreme Lord, their downfall is inevitable. A living entity's happiness lies in his endeavor to please the Supreme Lord. His distress comes when he tries to achieve personal happiness.

Religion is divided into two categories. One is the religion of measuring everything according to our sensual knowledge, and the other is the religion of worshiping transcendence. By following the former, one can never attain the Supreme Lord's association. Unrestricted material enjoyment, karma, *jñāna*, yoga, and observing vows, fall into this former category. Every other religion teaches the philosophy of enjoyment and renunciation, but *bhāgavata-dharma* teaches service to the transcendental Lord. Thus the philosophy of *Śrīmad-Bhāgavatam* is unique.

We should put the philosophy of sense gratification, karma, and *jñāna* on one side of the scale and the teachings of *Śrīmad-Bhāgavatam* on the other. Then we should make a comparative study to see which side of the scale is heavier. Put the pure worship of Viṣṇu on one side and the worship of Sūrya, Gaṇeśa, Durgā, and Śiva, along with hypocritical worship of Viṣṇu based on considering Him a demigod, on the other. Let the intelligent decide which side has undivided truth.

45. How can one actually observe an object?

We must find the link between whatever object we come across in our day-to-day life and Kṛṣṇa, because every object is an integral part of Kṛṣṇa. Therefore, to discover the factor that unites them is actual observation of an object.

46. Are devotional service and material enjoyment two separate things?

Devotional service and material enjoyment are not the same. Wherever there is devotional service there is no question of material enjoyment, and wherever there is material enjoyment there is no trace of devotional service. Material enjoyment comes into effect when one considers himself the enjoyer, and devotional service comes into effect when one identifies himself as the Supreme Lord's servant. Material enjoyment is like darkness and devotional service like illumination. Material enjoyment is based on personal sense gratification, and devotional service on giving happiness to Kṛṣṇa. When we walk the path of material enjoyment, we face lamentation, illusion, and fear. Thus the Lord makes us understand the consequences of becoming attached to matter. It is intelligent to worship the Lord with utmost care. Material enjoyment is nothing but a path of misery, but devotional service is the means to happiness.

47. Are sin and offense the same?

To transgress social etiquette is called sin. Deviation from and showing disrespect to Lord Viṣṇu and the Vaiṣṇavas is called an offense. Offenses are millions of times more serious than sins. Sins can be nullified by atonement, but not so with offenses. However, by chanting the most auspicious names of Śrī Gaura-Nityānanda, the deliverers of fallen souls, all offenses run away.

48. Are the family lives of devotees and conditioned souls the same?

Conditioned souls are those who desire wealth, women, and fame. Materialists and nondevotees are synonymous. By accepting three types of enjoyment, materialists become averse to the Lord's service. The Lord's devotees never taste wealth, women, and fame as sense gratification. Rather, they engage them in the Lord's service. If we change our material consciousness to spiritual consciousness—if instead of trying for our own happiness we try to please the Lord and His devotees—then we can become devotees and attain pure devotional service. We must give up attachment to material life. Devotees and conditioned souls do not have the same sense about family life. An *akiñcana* devotee may remain in any varṇa or *āśrama* yet remain aloof from the influence of his varṇa and *āśra-*

ma, because he remains engaged in Hari's service twenty-four hours a day. This is not true of the conditioned soul.

48. Is there respect for genuine devotees in this world?

Pure items are rare. Because they are not easily attainable, there is less demand for them. People tend not to respect them. Pure devotees are rare. Therefore, there is no appreciation, demand, or respect for those who do not misguide people but are busy trying to attract them toward the Lord by introducing them to *saṅkīrtana* and *hari-kathā*. At present, it is fashionable to be cheated by those who, in the name of religion, misguide people. Real devotees do not speak to please their audiences. They don't cheat people. Rather, pure devotees expose the defects of cheaters who love to compromise. Only those who are fortunate learn to be cautious after hearing the saints' words. Although the words of real devotees may appear to contradict our present taste and experience, they are nevertheless most auspicious for us.

Demand for pure things is less and demand for the impure is high. Wine is sold on every street corner, whereas cow milk is sold only in select places. Impurity is in abundance, but purity is rare.

49. What is the difference between weakness and cheating?

Cheating and weakness are two separate things. Persons devoid of a cheating propensity achieve perfection in life, but a cheater is never successful. Vaiṣṇavism is another name for simplicity. Cheaters are nondevotees. Sincere persons can be weak, but they are not cheaters. Cheaters say something and do something else. Weak people are embarrassed by their defects, whereas cheaters are maddened by their achievements.

"I will cheat the *ācārya* ,""I will deceive the doctor,""I will nourish the poisonous snake of my sinful propensity with banana and milk, hiding him in the hole of my cheating propensity," and, "I will demand name and fame from the people while posing as a saint": these are not symptoms of weakness but of utter deceitfulness. Such cheaters will never achieve any good.

By hearing humbly from saints with a sincere attitude, however, one will gradually attain auspiciousness. After accepting tridaṇḍi-*sannyāsa*, if one remains busy with worldly activities, thinking that family life is more important than spiritual life or maintaining the sinful mentality of kidnapping Sītā from Rāma as Rāvaṇa did even while dressed as a devotee, then one is a self-killer. We are far from the worship of Hari. Even if we have weakness and have enough *anarthas* to last us for millions of years, we are not as misfortunate as if we possessed a cheating propensity. It is better to take birth as animals or birds than to take shelter of cheating.

50. Who is learned?

A devotee of the Lord whose intelligence is illuminated with Vedic knowledge is actually learned. The *śāstra* states, paṇḍito bandha-mokṣa-vit, mūrkho dehādy-ahaṁ-buddhiḥ: "A wise man is one who knows the process of freedom from bondage, and a fool is one who identifies with his material body and mind." (*Śrīmad-Bhāgavatam* 11.19.41-42). One who considers the material body the self is certainly a fool, even though he may be certified educated.

Mundane scholars are aware only of mundane sound vibration. Since they are conditioned by Maya and consider the body the self, they are unable to realize the scriptures' actual purport. Because *Śrīmad-Bhāgavatam* and other Vedic literatures are nondifferent from the Supreme Lord, they are understood and realized only by devotion.

Since the proud mundane scholars are devoid of devotional service to the Lord, they are intoxicated by false ego. Therefore how will such proud people understand the confidential purport of theśāstras headed by the *Śrīmad-Bhāgavatam*, which are nondifferent from the Lord? Can an idol-maker see the Lord's Deity form?

If wealth, beauty, high birth, and learning are not attributed to proper candidates, they cause ruination. For nondevotees they are as good as death. They give anxiety, cause material existence, and enhance the false ego. For devotees, however, they are ornaments and do not produce *anarthas*.

The meaning of the *śāstra* and the meaning of material sound vibration is not the same. The *śāstras* appear to contain mundane words, but they are full of transcendental sound vibration. They are the incarnation of the Supreme Lord. Therefore, the mahājanas said that transcendental subject matter is inconceivable The *śāstras* can be realized only by a devotee practicing devotional service and not by worldly academic learning.

51. Is it good to live a long life?

It is good to live a long life if one worships Hari, but for those who do not worship Hari, it is better to die young than live long enough to do much nonsense. If human beings and demigods do not worship Hari, they disturb their respective societies.

52. Should people worship both Kṛṣṇa and the demigods?

Kṛṣṇa, who is the worshipable Lord of the demigods, is also the worshipable Lord of the human beings. Humans should therefore worship Kṛṣṇa, the Lord of all, rather than worshiping the demigods. In this way, one automatically worships everyone.

53. Why does one fall down?

As soon as we become proud, we find ourselves unable to follow the spiritual master's orders. As a result, we are bound to fall down. Before a living entity falls down, however, he develops a feeling called faithlessness. If we keep our faith at the lotus feet of the spiritual master and Vaiṣṇavas intact, then our perfection is guaranteed; otherwise, we will be doomed and our desire for matter will simply increase.

To challenge the Supreme Lord is a symptom of sinful mentality, pride, and the desire for material enjoyment. "The Lord is always seeing me": this is the proper way to understand things. Therefore one should see the Lord through one's ears. In order to attain the Lord's mercy and to please Him, one should approach Him with humility and eagerness.

To lose faith in material enjoyment and dry renunciation means to develop faith in the Supreme Lord. If we are faithful to the living entities in this world, it is a symptom that we want material enjoyment. "Let me enjoy this world to my heart's content": we develop this mentality because we lack spiritual initiation or transcendental knowledge.

If we cannot consider who we are and what is our relationship with the Lord, then how is it possible to surrender or develop faith? Unless one develops faith, one can see neither a pure devotee nor the Supreme Lord but will simply indulge in envious, violent, or blasphemous activities.

54. How can we vanquish our previous material experiences?

Whatever we have learned since childhood is mundane education. Such education simply taught us how to live in this world. When spiritual knowledge is established in the heart, we easily realize the insignificance of the above-mentioned education. "I am a servant of the Lord and not the object of service. To render service to the Lord is my only duty. I will not do anything other than serve the Lord": when these pious mentalities capture my heart, all my sinful mentalities and whatever I have learned from my worldly father, mother, relatives, and teachers will be removed. As soon as I forget that Kṛṣṇa is the only enjoyer, I will fall into the ocean of material existence.

The conditioned life of those inclined to the Lord's service is exhausted, and the conditioned life of those averse to the Lord's service is enhanced. Those who are attached to this world do not like to serve, hear about, or have time for the Lord. Even if they make a show of hearing about the Lord, they immediately reject the teachings if they are not to their liking. They give no importance to *hari-kathā*. They prefer to pay attention only to needs of the today.

If we want to know God, we must approach God's devotees. There is no other way to know Him.

55. Why aren't we interested in God?

How can anyone be interested in the Supreme Lord if he has no good fortune or piety? Does everyone like working in an office, doing business, or studying mathematics? Those who have a natural tendency for karma-yoga love to engage in karma-yoga, and those who have a natural tendency for *bhakti*-yoga love to engage in *bhakti*-yoga. Lacking faith in devotional service is a symptom of misfortune. The Supreme Lord is the ultimate object of worship and the transcendental Absolute Truth. He cannot be understood by the material senses. Rather, He reveals Himself to a service-inclined devotee. By following the ascending path no one can achieve His mercy.

56. Why can't everyone understand the glories of devotional service?

How will one understand the glories of devotional service unless he has extraordinary merit? With ordinary merit, one can understand the glories of material enjoyment and liberation.

57. What is direct, indirect, beyond direct and indirect, and transcendental perception?

Direct perception refers to what is perceived with the senses. Indirect perception refers to placing faith in objects seen by others through their senses. Beyond direct and indirect perception refers to perception that is neither direct nor indirect and which is sometimes called tabula *rasa* , absolute, or Brahman. The impersonalist philosophy is the ultimate conclusion of this type of perception. But our concept of the absolute is completely different from that of these types of perceivers. Our absolute is Śyāmasundara, the son of Nanda who plays a flute. *Śrīmad-Bhāgavatam* has called this absolute adhokṣaja, transcendental. One has to transcend the platforms of direct, indirect, and beyond direct and indirect perception, and come to the platform of transcendental perception in order to engage in the service of the Personality of Godhead. Śyāmasundara is the supreme worshipable Lord. He is supremely independent and the highest authority. Adhokṣaja can take initiative. One cannot approach Adhokṣaja with a businessman's mentality and it is impossible to cheat Him; He is the omniscient Supersoul. He does not come into the range of mundane vision.

58. What is devotional service and what is nondevotional service?

Devotional service means *sādhana-bhakti*, bhāva-*bhakti*, and prema-*bhakti*. Nondevotional service means anyābhilāṣa, karma, *jñāna*, yoga, and the innumerable other ways to turn away from Hari created by the mixture of these items.

Dependence and Independence

1. Does the Supreme Lord interfere with the living entity's independence?

The living entities are fragmental parts and parcels of the supreme conscious Lord. The qualities found in the vast ocean are also found in a single drop of ocean water, but in minute quantity. Thus the Lord is supremely independent and the minute spirit souls possess minute independence.

The living entities are not created but are eternal. The living entities are not products of matter but are spiritual. The living entities' independence is not imposed upon them but is their natural constitution. It is by the misuse of this constitutional independence that the living entities suffer. The Supreme Lord does not interfere with any entity's independence because He does not kill the living entities' spiritual characteristics. The Lord is an ocean of mercy. That is why He informs the living entities how to properly use or to misuse their independence. Only those who hear His instructions from the scriptures and worship Him, thus properly using their independence, attain perfection.

2. Should independence be renounced?

Those who are independent are proud, and those willing to subordinate themselves are humble. If after taking shelter of devotional service we become proud, and if after worshiping the Lord we neglect to serve His devotees and thus commit offenses at their feet, we will find ourselves facing inconveniences and then becoming detached from the Lord's service. This human form of life is not meant for misfortune. Rather, it is meant to attain auspiciousness. Why do we always forget this? Why do I forget that I am the most useless, insignificant wretch? To be tempted by Maya to become great or to enjoy is an insignificant and unnecessary occupation. If we really want to become humble, thus decreasing our hankering for greatness, then we should follow and associate with the Lord's humble devotees, who are servants of the great.

3. What is actual independence?

To try to become God is nondevotional. The desire to become independent in this world means to become the servant of others. Material independence is simply a covered form of dependence. Complete independence is obtained by becoming dependent on the Lord, who is full of eternality, knowledge, and bliss, and desiring only to serve Him. As long as the living entities hold the rope of Lord's mercy they are known as His servants. Those who think themselves self-dependent or independent should know that they are actually dependent on others. Only those who depend on the Supreme Lord are truly independent.

When we attain actual independence then the conception that we are eternally dependent on Śrī Hari becomes prominent. Any object that is a complete whole is transcendental. Service to or dependence on that transcendental Absolute Truth, Śrī Hari, is actual, joyful independence. Otherwise, the show of independence while identifying oneself as the doer or master brings only distress. It is nothing but subordination under Maya.

4. Why are we not able to depend fully on the Supreme Lord?

We are infinitesimal spirit souls, and it is our nature to remain surrendered and to take shelter of the infinite Soul. Because we listen with so much dependence to mundane discussions and solutions in the external world, we are unable to depend on the Supreme Lord. Only a person who desires nothing from this world, who is *akiñcana*, and does not depend on objects visible in this world, can faithfully depend on the Lord. By hearing enlightening *hari-kathā* from the mouths of the ever-lively saintly persons and the scriptures, we can come to completely depend on the Supreme Lord.

5. Do the living entities have independent will?

The living entity is infinitesimal and can therefore be covered by powerful Maya. When the living entities fall under Maya's control, they become averse or indifferent to the Lord's service. The living entities are minutely independent. With their independent will, they can either remain devotees or become nondevotees. Non-devotional existence is called the conditional state, and is based on aversion to the Lord's service. Such entities who choose this path develop the desire to become God; an uncontrollable endeavor to become the master of Maya is found in such entities. Only by the pure devotee's mercy does the propensity for serving the Lord awaken in the living entities, and thus they regain their original position. Properly situated, they no longer remain conditioned.

Trying to subdue the living entities' independence results in the development of mundane qualities. Consciousness and unconsciousness are not synonymous. Desire for material enjoyment covers the spiritual consciousness of the living entities and throws them into the material atmosphere. By the devotees' mercy the living entities' conditioned state based on their independent will is easily destroyed. Subordination to the devotees is the proper utilization of independence, and desire for sense gratification is its misuse.

6. Is it essential to become subordinate?

An independent person cannot worship Hari or become a devotee. One's benefit lies in following in the footsteps of one's *ācārya* . People with independent natures maintain different opinions. If millions of gopīs have millions of opinions, then there will certainly be disturbances in their discharge of service to Kṛṣṇa. No one has the power to please Śrī Mādhava without subordinating themselves to the daughter of Vṛṣabhānu. The spiritual master is nondifferent from and an intimate associate of the daughter of Vṛṣabhānu. That is why it is important for a person desiring auspiciousness to take shelter of a bona fide spiritual master. There is no other way to achieve auspiciousness.

7. How did the dependent independent souls receive their independence?

We are part and parcels of the fully independent Personality of Godhead, and therefore God's qualities are present in us in minute quantity. Kṛṣṇa is fully independent. Therefore we also possess minute independence.

In our independence, there are two kinds of aversion to the Lord, aversion in the form of desire for material enjoyment, and aversion in the form of renunciation of material enjoyment. For the independent souls, there are only two ways open; to walk the path of material enjoyment or to walk the path of devotional service. No one can remain neutral; everyone must choose one of these two paths.

By constantly worshiping the Lord with love and devotion, one is not covered and thrown by the Lord's illusory energy. But worship should be constant. If there is even a slight interruption in our attention, Maya will take advantage of the situation and cause us trouble.

8. Is the proper use or misuse of the living entities' independence inspired by the Lord?

If the Lord was inspiring the misuse of our independence, then the result would be service to the Lord, not forgetfulness of Him.

9. What is the fruit of service?

It is one thing to sincerely take shelter of the Supreme Lord, and another to lead a whimsical life in the name of serving the Lord. Independence is not subordination, and subordination is not independence. Those who follow the path of śreyaḥ believe in subordinating themselves to the Lord, and those who follow the path of preyaḥ believe in their own independence. We can judge the value of a path by its result. The fruit of devotional service is progressive advancement on the path of devotion and the development of an intense desire for more and more service. Anything opposite to this is advancement toward material enjoyment.

10. Why do we lack the tendency to chant God's name? Why do we wish to remain fallen in the well of material existence?

We are spirit souls and as such have the freedom to choose whether to serve the Lord or remain averse. If we do not choose correctly, we will have to suffer the consequences. If we chant the Lord's holy name with heart and soul, we will certainly attain His mercy.

Spirit or consciousness can take initiative, but matter has no independence. The Lord is the proprietor of both matter and spirit. The spirit soul owns an invaluable jewel called independence, but there is a difference between the living entity's independence and the independence of the Supreme Lord. The Supreme Lord is fully independent, while the living entity's independence always depends on His will. The living entities can either use their independence properly or they can misuse it. If the Lord forced the living entities to act against their own free will, then their spiritual nature would be destroyed. That is why the Lord never interferes with their independence but rather tries to revive their natural propensities toward service.

The spirit souls were not created; they are eternal. The Lord appears in this world in the form of His devotees, the spiritual master, and the *śāstra* to help the living entities awaken their pure, spiritual characteristics. This material world is not our eternal residence. *Śrī Caitanya-caritāmṛta* states:

sādhu-śāstra-kṛpāya yadi kṛṣṇonmukha haya
sei jīva nistare, māyā tāhāre chāḍaya

If the conditioned soul becomes Kṛṣṇa conscious by the mercy of saintly persons who voluntarily preach scriptural injunctions and help him to become Kṛṣṇa conscious, the conditioned soul is liberated from the clutches of Maya, who gives him up. (*Madhya* 20.120)

māyā-mugdha jīvera nāhi svataḥ kṛṣṇa-jñāna
jīvere kṛpāya kailā kṛṣṇa veda-purāṇa
'śāstra-guru-ātma rūpe āpanāre jānāna
'kṛṣṇa mora prabhu, trātā jīvera haya jñāna

The conditioned soul cannot revive his Kṛṣṇa consciousness by his own effort. But out of causeless mercy, Lord Kṛṣṇa compiled the Vedic literature and its supplements, the Purāṇas. The forgetful conditioned soul is educated by Kṛṣṇa through the Vedic literatures, the realized spiritual master, and the Supersoul. Through these, he can understand the Supreme Personality of Godhead as He is, and he can understand that Lord Kṛṣṇa is his eternal master and deliverer from the clutches of Maya. In this way, one can acquire real knowledge of his conditioned life and can come to understand how to attain liberation. (*Madhya* 20.122-123)

'nitya-bandha kṛṣṇa haite nitya-bahirmukha
'nitya-saṁsāra' bhuñje narakādi duḥkha
sei doṣe māyā-piśācī daṇḍa kare tāre
ādhyātmikādi tāpa-traya tāre jāri' māre
kāma-krodhera dāsa haṣā tāra lāthi khāya
bhramite bhramite yadi sādhu-vaidya pāya
tāṅra upadeśa-mantre piśācī palāya
kṛṣṇa-bhakti pāya tabe kṛṣṇa-nikaṭa yāya

Apart from the ever-liberated devotees, there are the conditioned souls, who always turn away from the service of the Lord. They are perpetually conditioned in this material world, and are subjected to the material tribulations brought about by different bodily forms in hellish conditions.

Due to his being opposed to Kṛṣṇa consciousness, the conditioned soul is punished by the witch of the external energy, Maya. He is thus ready to suffer the threefold misery—miseries brought about by the body and mind, the inimical behavior of other living entities, and natural disturbances caused by the demigods.

In this way the conditioned soul becomes the servant of lusty desires, and when these are not fulfilled, he becomes the servant of anger, and continues to be kicked by the external energy, Maya. Wandering

and wandering throughout the universe, he may by chance get the association of a devotee physician, whose instructions and hymns make the witch of the external energy flee. The conditioned soul thus gets in touch with devotional service to Lord Kṛṣṇa, and in this way he can approach nearer and nearer to the Lord. (*Madhya* 22.12-15)

'kṛṣṇa-nitya-dāsa jīva tāhā bhuli' gela
ei doṣe māyā tāra galāya bāndhila
tāte kṛṣṇa bhaje, kare gurura sevana
māyā-jāla chuṭe, pāya kṛṣṇera caraṇa

The living entity is bound around the neck by the chain of Maya, because he has forgotten that he is eternally a servant of Kṛṣṇa. If the conditioned soul engages in the service of the Lord and simultaneously carries out the orders of his spiritual master and serves him, he can get out of the clutches of Maya, and become eligible for shelter at Kṛṣṇa's lotus feet. (*Madhya* 22.24-25)

Material Life

1. What is material desire?

"I will simply enjoy sense gratification as long as I live in this world." To maintain such a mentality is called material desire.

2. Is this material world a prison house for conditioned souls?

Those *akiñcana* devotees who want nothing from this world understand that there is nothing in this world that can give us eternal happiness. There is no eternal happiness in this world. The material world is a prison house for conditioned souls. We are imprisoned here because we are averse to Kṛṣṇa. This is the result of our unlimited miseries and distresses. According to the dictation of the mind, which is compared to the superintendent of a prison house, we think our lesser miseries happiness and our bigger miseries great suffering. Fools who run after material happiness find themselves simply entangled in Maya's network.

Attached householders think, "Becoming householders will make us happy. We will find ourselves some servants and will understand everything we want to know through the manipulation of our senses." To desire to become politicians, literateurs, scholars, aristocrats, philanthropists, national leaders, and good workers is simply an attempt to master the illusory energy. But Prahlāda Mahārāja warned us not to engage our senses in external activity or to aspire for selfish interest.

We think we have become masters in this world because we have become attached to family life and accepted the body as the self. We think the material world and everything in it is for our enjoyment. Earth, water, fire, air, ether, sun, moon, planets, stars, animals, birds, trees, and creepers—all have been placed here for us to enjoy. Along with that idea, we think everyone and everything here has been designed to serve us. We never think about the actual purpose of this material world: it is an ingredient for the Supreme Lord's worship. If we are not worshiping Hari, we have no right to take even a blade of grass from this world.

3. Why is this material world full of miseries?

The Lord says, "I have arranged all these miseries and dangers not to give you trouble but to teach you that such miseries are unnecessary and that you should search after eternally desirable eternal happiness."

4. What is Maya?

Maya mean "that which is not." Maya is that which we can measure. All temporary perishable objects are Maya. That which is not the Supreme Lord is Maya. The Supreme Lord is Maya's controller and no one can measure Him. According to the Christians, Godhead is separate from Satan, but the Maya described in *Śrīmad-Bhāgavatam* is not like that. According to the Bhāgavata school Maya is present in the Supreme Lord, although she is ashamed of her role, to rectify the living entities who are averse to Kṛṣṇa by punishing them.

5. What is the ascending path?

The ascending path can be compared to Rāvaṇa's attempt to build a staircase to heaven. Such uphill work is a most puzzling task. *Śrīmad-Bhāgavatam* has instructed us to reject uphill work, or Rāvaṇa's policy of building a staircase to heaven.

There are two ways to look at things. One can try to forcibly see the sun at night with the help of a lamp, or one can wait until sunrise and see the sun with the help of the sunshine itself. If one wants material prosperity, one is bound to adopt the ascending path. If one wants to tread the path of jñāna, karma, or yoga, he must make endeavor. But the ascending path will always remain incomplete. A twenty-year civilization or experience will prove faulty and incomplete before a one hundred-year civilization or experience. Two hundred years of experience may seem silly in the eyes of a thousand years of experience. Intelligent persons do not follow the ascending path but the descending path, which is based on real experience.

6. Does anyone in this world respect a real devotee?

In a world full of cheaters, cheaters are respected. Pure devotees who do not misguide people are not respected in this world. It has become fashionable to be cheated by those who misguide people in the name of *hari-kathā*. Genuine devotees and those who expose nondevotees are often mistaken for ordinary people because nondevotees and cheaters mislead ordinary people by calling these devotees thieves. In this way they try to sustain their own cheating. The illusory energy does not allow the living entities to become sincere at any cost. Therefore she arranges various tricks to keep people away from the association of real devotees.

7. What kind of people find fault with Vaiṣṇavas?

Only those averse to Lord Hari and whose only assets are their defective material senses find fault with Vaiṣṇavas. In *Bhagavad-gītā* Lord Kṛṣṇa states that His devotees never perish. Can those who worship the Lord without deviation ever fall down? They certainly achieve perfection. Since our vision is polluted we find fault with others and thereby ruin ourselves. When we thus become materialists we become bereft of service to guru and Kṛṣṇa. We think of the trouble of others because we ourselves are in trouble. Because we are full of faults we find fault with others. If we can correct ourselves, we will find that we have no time to find fault with others.

8. Can you define our disease?

Our main disease is that we wish to accumulate material enjoyment, things unrelated to Kṛṣṇa, simply for sense gratification. We get pleasure from sense gratification, but we do not find pleasure in chanting and serving the Supreme Lord, who is the ultimate object of all enjoyment. This is our misfortune. Just as a jaundice patient does not relish sugar candy, we who are attached to sense gratification do not relish the sweet holy names or the Lord's service. When the body is poisoned, even honey tastes bitter.

Still, sugar candy is the only medicine for jaundice. As one applies the cure, the sugar candy gradually begins to taste sweet. Similarly, our aversion to the Lord and our attachment to sense gratification will gradually diminish if we willingly or even unwillingly chant the holy name and serve the Supreme Lord. As we are cured, we will taste the sweetness of the Lord's service and the sweet holy name will automatically engage our spiritual senses in the service of the transcendental Lord.

9. What is our primary mistake and how have we tried to rectify it?

We all want to be happy, but we have mistaken distress for happiness. We often call a doctor to treat our illness, but if instead of following his prescription we advise him to prescribe a cure of our choice, how will we be cured? Similarly, after accepting a spiritual master, if rather than following his instruction we act whimsically, how will we find benefit? That is why a flatterer cannot be a doctor. If a flatterer, instead of prescribing suitable medicine and diet, prescribes according to the patient's taste only to collect his fee, then although the patient may gain temporary relief, his disease will not be cured.

10. Why can't everyone understand transcendental subject matter?

How can they if they are unfortunate? There must be purity. Those who are fortunate hear transcendental topics with faith and by the Lord's mercy understand them, and those who make hasty conclusions cannot understand the Absolute Truth. Such persons cannot even spend time cultivating complete transcendental knowledge. Our society is so engrossed in materialism that people are unable to spend even a moment to discuss eternal life. We are busy in worldly activities twenty-four hours a day. We don't even bother to know who we are. But human beings should spend twenty-four hours a day on spiritual cultivation. It is not the duty of intelligent persons to waste their valuable lives gratifying their senses.

We should search out our self-interest. Most of us are engaged in pursuing selfishness. The children play, the young maintain family life, and the old endeavor to protect their lives and their property. Consequently, they are indifferent to their own self-interest. In order to focus on worldly self-interest, materialists sacrifice eternal self-interest. What a pity!

Some people say one need not worry about the soul's welfare at present. Why think about the future? All that's necessary at present is to work. But this is not right, because if one fails to get an education in childhood, he will suffer inconvenience as an adult. A person desiring social welfare necessarily also desires welfare for himself. Such a person should endeavor to see that devotional service, which is the characteristic of the spirit, is not impeded by sense gratification.

Many people may think it is enough to give up sinful activities and accumulate piety, but this is not the ultimate goal. Those who are actually intelligent consider the relationship between their present activities and their eternal existence at every stage of life. If one fails to think about this, he will find himself in trouble. Work done at the proper time reaps proper fruits in the future. If one does not use his time properly he will face difficulty. People who desire to discuss spiritual topics in old age will find themselves unable to do so because they will remain preoccupied with and disturbed by family life.

11. Is human birth superior to birth as a demigod?

Human birth is better than birth as a demigod, and that is why the demigods aspire for human birth. The demigods are so intoxicated with material enjoyment that they cannot think of how much distress awaits them. They are fully absorbed in the intoxication of temporary happiness. A demigod's life is also temporary. *Bhagavad-gītā* (9.21) states:

te taṁ bhuktvā svarga-lokaṁ viśālaṁ,
kṣīṇe puṇye martya-lokaṁ viŚanti
evaṁ trayī-dharmam anuprapannā,
gatāgataṁ kāma-kāmā labhante

"When they have thus enjoyed vast heavenly sense pleasure, and the results of their pious activities are exhausted, they return to this mortal planet again. Thus those who seek sense enjoyment by adhering to the principles of the three Vedas achieve only repeated birth and death."

Human beings are more concerned about the future than the inferior living entities. The demigods live happier and more prosperous

Also, the miseries we experience in the human form of life constantly remind us of the temporality and insignificance of material existence. In the relatively superior life of the demigods this realization is not easily achieved. In the human form of life, therefore, we have received the opportunity to become truly fortunate, to know what is beneficial and not beneficial for us.

12. What is the difference between the weak-hearted and the offenders?

The weak-hearted and the offenders are not in the same class. Although weak-heartedness may eventually become offense, it contains a hatred for sinful activities and offense. While the weak-hearted know that committing sinful activities and offenses is unlawful, they are unable to give them up. Offenders never consider such activities unlawful. They think whatever they do or understand is good and whatever the saints say is wrong. Weak-hearted people should give up material desires by condemning them, not embracing them with love and taste. Then they will certainly attain Kṛṣṇa's mercy. Otherwise they will be deprived of Kṛṣṇa's mercy.

13. Is there any happiness in this material world?

There is no happiness in the material world. Rather, the world is full of danger, which disturbs us. Conditions may sometimes appear pleasant, but ultimately they end in misery of one type or another. That is why the *Śrīmad-Bhāgavatam* verse beginning tat te anukampām was spoken. There is no waywardness in Goloka. In this world, there is no alternative but to tolerate inconvenience at any particular time or in any circumstance.

14. What is the fate of the atheist?

We believe that the Supreme Lord always makes arrangement for our benefit. Atheists can never attain good standing in this world. They jump around for a few days and are ultimately subdued by providence. Because they are envious of Vaiṣṇavas, atheists attain inauspiciousness both in this world and the next.

15. Does a doubtful soul find fortune?

A doubtful person is bound to fall down and his destruction is inevitable. Every object in this world is directly and indirectly related to Kṛṣṇa and is meant for His enjoyment. Unfortunate persons who maintain a contrary conception are doubtful. They lack surrender, honest inquiry, and a service attitude.

16. What does it mean to be an attached householder?

One who proudly considers himself either the enjoyer or the enjoyed is an attached householder. The attached householders are greedy for gold, women, and fame. Those who have the propensity to enjoy wealth, women, and fame, are materialists, and such people want only to freely enjoy sense gratification surrounded by servants.

We become materialists because we accept the body as the self. We have become so-called masters of the world. But we get into trouble when we see the material world with an enjoying spirit. Our mentality as gross materialists will not be removed unless we develop the good intelligence that everything in the world is meant for the Lord's service. Those who try to either enjoy the material world or reject it as worthless are ruined and can never realize the Supreme Lord.

By depending on this temporary material world we will gain only distress and death. To lead a godless family life means to fall into the trap of death, first suffering the threefold miseries. All activities and thoughts in this material world bring us closer to death. The attached materialists are not concerned that day by day they are going to hell while suffering the pangs of material misery.

17. What is the mentality of a fruitive worker?

An altruistic fruitive worker wants to save the shoes and shirt of a drowning man. In the religion of the Western countries, to do good for the external dress of a human being is considered laudable. Many people consider welfare to mean taking care of a person's clothing. Two bodies cover the spirit soul, a gross body made of the five material elements and a subtle body made of mind, intelligence, and false ego. Most people consider offering service to those two temporary bodies the best form of welfare work. Therefore one of our German devotees said, "If a man is drowning, let him drown. If a person is being degraded, let him be degraded, but the so-called altruistic fruitive workers consider that to save the shoes and shirt of such drowning or degraded people is real welfare activity. How sad!"

18. What is anartha?

That which is not artha, which is devoid of spiritual significance, is called anartha. Material enjoyment, desire for religiosity, economic development, sense gratification, liberation, and the desire for wealth, women, and fame are *anarthas*. When one chants the holy name of Hari, all *anarthas* are destroyed. Anartha in this context refers to the desire for sense gratification. Desire for sense gratification is the principal impediment on the devotional path. Material desires interrupt one's attempt to constantly remember the Lord and direct one's attention to things unrelated to Kṛṣṇa.

19. Why are we unable to maintain faith in transcendental objects?

The most sinful cannot maintain faith in transcendental objects. Hearts that are contaminated with sinful reactions cannot repose faith in pure spiritual objects. Therefore both the Mahābhārata and the Skanda *Purāṇa* state:

mahā-prasāde govinde, nāma-brahmaṇi vaiṣṇave
svalpa-puṇya-vatāṁ rājan, viśvāso naiva jāyate

Persons who are not very highly elevated in pious activities cannot believe in the remnants of food [prasādam] of the Supreme Personality of Godhead, or in Govinda, the holy name of the Lord, nor in the Vaiṣṇavas

At present we have lost faith in these four spiritual objects and we have therefore been swallowed by various *anarthas*. Mahāprasādam, Govinda, the holy name, and the spiritual master are all nondifferent from Lord Viṣṇu, but since we have come in contact with this material world we have lost faith in that truth. The word Maya means "that which is not" or "that which one can measure." These four items cannot be measured. Śrī Govinda is the self-effulgent Absolute Truth; we do not need another light to help us see Him. The word Govinda means "protector of the cows." The transcendental personality Govinda is not a concoction of the human mind. No one has imagined or created Śrī Govinda; He is the supreme transcendental Absolute Truth and is beyond the reach of material perception. The spiritual master, the highest benefactor, the giver of transcendental knowledge, and the king of Vaiṣṇavas, reveals to us this most confidential understanding about Śrī Govinda. Śrī Govinda is the personification of unalloyed supreme bliss. That which temporarily appears as truth according to our mundane knowledge is only apparent truth, local truth. It cannot be positive or absolute truth. Nothing has ever existed before Śrī Govinda. This material world has been created for those who are averse to serving Him.

20. Who is not eager for the Lord's service?

Those whose hearts hanker for objects other than service to the lotus feet of Kṛṣṇa are not praiseworthy. They suffer from the poisonous fruit of their own misfortune. Those less intelligent people who are not yet qualified to attain perfection do not become eager to serve the Lord. Rather, they become attached to sense enjoyment and thus increase their attachment for material existence. Do not bother with such people. Sva karma phala bhuk pumān: every living entity must enjoy the fruits of their own karma.

21. What is karma?

Work done for one's own happiness and the happiness of others is called karma. There is nothing about trying to please Kṛṣṇa in the performance of karma. The goal of karma is to search after one's own happiness and the happiness of others, whereas searching for Kṛṣṇa's pleasure is called devotional service.

This material world is the field of karma for ordinary people, but for the devotees the material world is a place in which to cultivate devotional service. Whatever is performed in this world with the prideful thought, "I am the doer," is called karma, whereas whatever is done for the Lord's pleasure, induced by the Lord, with the idea, "I am Kṛṣṇa's servant," is called devotional service.

22. How long should we engage in karma?

The *Bhāgavatam* (11.20.9) states:

tāvat karmāṇi kurvīta, na nirvidyeta yāvatā
mat-kathā-śravaṇādau vā, śraddhā yāvan na jāyate

One should continue to perform the Vedic ritualistic activities until one actually becomes detached from material sense gratification and develops faith for hearing and chanting about Me.

One who does not manifest either of these symptoms must engage in karma. The root of devotional service is taste for and faith in *hari-kathā*. Hari-kathā hy kevalam paramam śreyaḥ: discussing topics of Hari is the supremely beneficial activity. Possessing firm faith in *hari-kathā* is a symptom of one's developing taste for *hari-kathā*.

Those who have faith in and taste for some activity find the activity their principal engagement. If we wish to develop faith in *hari-kathā* we must associate with strong devotees. There is no other way to develop the inclination to serve the Lord and to give up the inclination for karma and sense gratification. Without becoming disappointed or restless, therefore, one should hear enlivening *hari-kathā* from a living source and try to practically apply them in his or her life. This is the symptom of intelligence. *Śrīmad-Bhāgavatam* (11.26.26) states:

tato duḥsaṅgam utsṛjya, satsu sajjeta buddhimān
santa evāsya chindanti, mano-vyāsaṅgam uktibhiḥ

An intelligent person should therefore reject all bad association and instead take up the association of saintly devotees, whose words cut off the excessive attachment of one's mind.

Śrī Caitanya-caritāmṛta (Madhya-līla 24.97) states:

sādhu-saṅga-kṛpā kimvā kṛṣṇera kṛpāya
kāmādi 'duḥsaṅga' chāḍi' śuddha-bhakti pāya

One is elevated to the platform of devotional life by the mercy of a Vaiṣṇava, the bona fide spiritual master, and by the special mercy of Kṛṣṇa. On that platform, one gives up all material desires and the association of unwanted people. Thus one is elevated to the platform of pure devotional service.

23. Does one need to check one's material propensity?

If the propensity to enjoy material life is not checked, then one will continue in the cycle of repeated birth and death. It is important to stop acting for sense gratification. Unless one stops acting for sense gratification, the propensity for material life—and the suffering that comes from material distress—will not be destroyed. It is essential to cultivate Kṛṣṇa consciousness. Spiritual cultivation removes the desire for material life, destroys the desire to try for artha, kāma, dharma, and mokṣa, and gives one supreme fortune. All the material desires in the heart of a person in which Lord Kṛṣṇa has manifest are automatically destroyed, because Kṛṣṇa is the transcendental Cupid and all desires serve Him and no one else. One who has captured Kṛṣṇa in his heart has no desire for sense gratification.

Whenever we do not follow the Vaiṣṇava lifestyle, our senses will become misguided and fall prey to material objects. We will forget that Lord Kṛṣṇa is the proprietor of our senses. We have been given this human form of life to worship Hari. Guided by the sailor in the form of guru, we can cross the ocean of material existence on the boat of the human body and attain Śrī Kṛṣṇa's lotus feet. Why, then, should we prefer to drown in the ocean of material existence?

24. Does a proud person achieve any benefit?

Those who engage in karmic activities are known as proud materialists. The path of karma is inauspicious, and there is no benefit or devotion on this path. We run toward misfortune when we accept the path of karma. By executing pious activities we try to become popular. By performing our family duties we try to attract our relatives' appreciation. These things will not give us peace of mind, nor will they deliver us from material bondage. Therefore the Lord's devotees have mercifully instructed us to serve the Supreme Lord as our only duty. Devotional service is the duty of everyone, including the demigods, animals, birds, and human beings. Instead of paying attention to the devotees' words, however, we think we have become fathers and must now dutifully serve our sons and daughters. When we are small, we think it is our duty to serve our parents. In this way various propositions and dispositions appear constantly in the heart. Answering those propositions and dispositions is what it means to be averse to the Supreme Lord and to serve Maya.

25. Why do the animals become human beings?

Animals become human beings in order to worship Lord Hari. This is not only true of the animals but even the demigods desire birth in the human form so they can worship Hari. If we simply remain busy eating, sleeping, mating, and defending like animals, even after attaining this most rare human form—if we remain intoxicated by material life and do not worship Hari—our lives are useless. We will have failed to take advantage of the human body. What, then, is the point in remaining alive? Life devoid of devotion to Hari is useless. All we will have is a life of material misery.

26. Is life devoid of hari-bhajana useless?

If we do not worship Kṛṣṇa, what is the point of eating and drinking? Even after having received this rarely attained human body, if we do not worship Kṛṣṇa we will have to suffer birth after birth. We came to the material world only to serve Kṛṣṇa, but due to Maya's conditioning, we have become entangled in the material complexities.

27. Is this material world meant for our enjoyment?

This material world is an ingredient of the Supreme Lord's service. If one sees this world as here for one's own enjoyment, he commits an offense and suffers the pangs of material existence. As soon as we forget our constitutional position and try to enjoy this material world, conditioned by Maya, we think of enjoying the material world with our gross material senses. We should know that the material world is not here for our enjoyment. If we try to enjoy matter, we are usurping things that are meant for Kṛṣṇa's enjoyment.

28. Does the mind cheat?

If my mind gets an opportunity it will ruin me. This stupid mind has a tendency to serve lust, anger, and other material propensities. In order to engage everyone in Maya's service—the service of lust and anger—this wicked mind takes the position of instructor. A materialistic mind is always ready to envy Hari, guru, and the Vaiṣṇavas. Therefore rather than listening to its dictations, one should hear from the guru, *sādhus*, and *śāstras*.

29. What is karma-kāṇḍa? What is jñāna-kāṇḍa?

To enjoy the fruits of one's karma is called *karma-kāṇḍa*, and to deprive both oneself and the Lord of the fruits of one's karma is called *jñāna-kāṇḍa*.

30. What is materialism?

Those whose only assets are their material senses, who hoist the flag of self by bragging even though they are covered with illusory sensual knowledge, who sew a network of arguments while maintaining themselves as sense gratifiers, and who try to imagine the transcendental object from the mundane platform are gross materialists.

There are two paths, the path of aural reception and the path of argument. The path of aural reception is also called the descending path, and the path of argument is called the ascending path. On the descending path one renders service to the transcendental Lord by hearing, whereas on the ascending path one manipulates his senses to gain expertise in material science.

When the sun's rays enter our eyes, we are accepting the sun's help to see the sun. We are seeing the sun by the descending process. When we renounce the sun's help and try to see the sun by some independent means—perhaps taking the help of an artificial light— we fail to see the sun. This is the ascending method. Rāvaṇa adopted this process, as do other godless people. Materialists tend to be casual and covered logicians. Simply by taking shelter of Śrī Kṛṣṇa's lotus feet with sincerity and renouncing the material concept of life we will be able to understand Kṛṣṇa's life and will personally practice devotional service by guru and Kṛṣṇa's mercy.

31. What is a mental speculator?

Mental speculators are those who dare to attack the Absolute Truth in a challenging mood. Mental speculation, the path of argument, is the opposite to what is taught in *Bhagavad-gītā* (4.34).

There are two kinds of people, those who want to become inclined toward Kṛṣṇa by hearing from a bona fide spiritual master who glorifies the Absolute Truth, and those who want to challenge the transcendental Absolute Truth on the strength of the knowledge they have gained through their senses. The former is the authorized descending path of disciplic succession, and the latter is the path of argumentation. Whatever is accepted directly is the path of disciplic succession, and whatever is accepted indirectly is the path of argumentation. The five types of philosophical work (darśanas) are based on argument. Only the Vedānta *darśana* has accepted the authorized path of disciplic succession. In order to bewilder ordinary people, Saṅkarācārya has mixed argument into the Vedānta *darśana* and confused it with the descending path. One becomes a mental speculator when he enhances his material knowledge, even while apparently pursuing spiritual understanding.

Vaiṣṇavas do not concoct or speak from their imagination. Rather, they lead people to the guru's lotus feet. There are not five or ten spiritual masters; guru is one. And the Absolute Truth requires no challenge from anyone.

32. Why have the living entities become conditioned?

The living entities have become conditioned because they misused their free will.

33. What does the Bhagavad-gītā verse beginning īśvara sarva-bhūtānām (18.61) mean?

This verse confirms that Lord Viṣṇu alone is the controller and director of all living entities. The Supreme Lord rewards everyone according to their respective karma. The living entities are the cause of their own activities, and the Supreme Lord is the director. As the director, the Supreme Lord is not responsible directly or indirectly for the karmic activities the living entities perform or the fruits they then become eligible to enjoy. The Supreme Lord gives the fruits of karma and the living entities enjoy them.

34. Why are we busy with activities other than devotional service?

We are unfortunate, and so we have become busy in activities other than the Lord's service. Somehow or other we are not able to understand that our only duty is to serve the Lord. Therefore we give more importance to other activities than to the Lord's service. Even though we repeatedly associate with devotees, we are unable to remove this misconception. Since we are averse to the Lord, our tendency is to become conditioned by Maya, to fall for Maya's temptations, and to work like asses to accumulate wealth to gratify the senses of our wife, children, and relatives whom we will never meet again. We plant mango trees, we buy movable and immovable assets, but people we will never meet will enjoy the fruits of these purchases. We work so hard to earn money, but someone else will spend it indiscriminately. What an illusion!

35. Don't the smārthas worship Lord Viṣṇu?

The smārthas' worship of Viṣṇu is part of their worship of demigods such as Ganeśa, Sūrya, Dūrga, etc; and does not amount to worship of the Supreme Personality of Godhead. Worshiping Viṣṇu as if He were one of the five demigods means one considers Him one of the demigods. Such worship is both offensive and atheistic. *Śāstra* states:

yas tu nārāyaṇaṁ devaṁ, brahma-rudrādi-daivataiḥ
samatvenaiva vīkṣeta, sa pāṣaṇḍī bhaved dhruvam

One who considers Lord Viṣṇu to be in the same category with the demigods like Lord Brahmā or Lord Śiva, or who thinks Lord Brahmā and Śiva to be equal to Lord Viṣṇu, is to be considered a pāṣaṇḍī, a faithless nonbeliever. (*Śrī Caitanya-caritāmṛta* Madhya 15.117)

Atheistic Hindus do not consider Kṛṣṇa's holy name both the ultimate goal of life and the perfect means to achieve it. They consider Kṛṣṇa equal to the demigods, and Kṛṣṇa's holy name equal to fruitive activities such as yajña, tapasya, yoga, meditation, and observing vows. Mahāprabhu said:

koṭi aśvamedha eka kṛṣṇa nāma sama
yei kahe, se pāṣaṇḍī, daṇḍe tāre yama

One who says that ten million aśvamedha sacrifices are equal to the chanting of the holy name of Lord Kṛṣṇa is undoubtedly an atheist. He is sure to be punished by Yamarāja. (*Śrī Caitanya-caritāmṛta* Ādi 3.79)

Worship of Viṣṇu in the course of worshiping the five gods does not please Lord Viṣṇu. It is simply demigod worship and therefore improper.

36. Why do some people instruct us to increase the mode of passion?

"The mode of passion should be increased": this is what unfortunate people say. Still, people in the world marketplace accept such a foolish and unreasonable statement as if it represented great charity toward human society. *Śrīmad-Bhāgavatam* states: "One should destroy the mode of ignorance with the help of the mode of passion, the mode of passion with the help of the mode of goodness, and the mode of mixed goodness with the help of pure goodness." Those who favor increasing the mode of passion either think the mode of pure goodness to be the mode of ignorance or some temporary material mode. Thus they consider impersonalism transcendental to the material modes. At present people in this world are busy pursuing childish religions. People with animalistic propensities do not understand anything other than their own sense gratification. The thirst for sense gratification appears in four forms, religiosity, economic development, sense gratification, and liberation. These are not limbs of devotional service. Among them, the first three fall into the category of bhukti, material enjoyment, and the last is the fiercest form of sense gratification, mukti, liberation. Liberation in the form of attaining complete freedom from all types of material misery is nothing but a thirst for happiness or sense gratification.

37. What is the fate of a person who instead of utilizing his wealth for the Lord's service uses it for his children and grandchildren?

If we do not properly use the wealth God gives us, it means we have failed to understand a simple truth. How unfortunate we are! Those who whimsically spend their wealth on various sinful activities will certainly end up in hell.

38. When a living entity who is averse to the Lord falls down, in what species does he first take birth?

The living entity averse to the Lord first becomes Brahmā and then a human being. The fallen soul first becomes Brahmā. In order to enjoy Maya, many living entities took birth as Brahmās sons. Among them a number were entrusted with the responsibility to create progeny. As soon as the living entity proudly considers himself an enjoyer he becomes conditioned by Maya. While trying to become the Lord of Maya in the material kingdom he ends up as her servant.

39. Why do we like material existence?

We are bound to suffer if we cause anxiety to the spiritual master and the Vaiṣṇavas, who are not ordinary like us. The spiritual master and the Vaiṣṇava are by nature harder than a thunderbolt and softer than a flower. We must take utmost care when dealing with Viṣṇu's devotees. We must not play any trick on the spiritual master or the Vaiṣṇavas. Such behavior would be most dangerous.

Unless one gladly follows the spiritual master's orders one cannot call himself a disciple. If one gives up the lifestyle and rules and regulations of the *Maṭha*, one is bound to become a materialist. If one does not realize the importance of living in the *Maṭha*, serving the *Maṭha*, and fulfilling the spiritual master's mission, one will certainly become a materialist. A *Maṭha* is nondifferent from Vaikuṇṭha, and this material world is just like a gateway to hell. As soon as a living entity turns his face away from the Lord's mercy, he falls down to material existence. *Śrīmad-Bhāgavatam* (3.9.10) states:

ahny āpṛtārta-karaṇā niśi niḥśayānā
nānā-manoratha-dhiyā kṣaṇa-bhagna-nidrāḥ
daivāhatārtha-racanāṛṣayo 'pi deva
yuṣmat-prasaṅga-vimukhā iha saṁsaranti

Such nondevotees engage their senses in very troublesome and extensive work, and they suffer insomnia at night because their intelligence constantly breaks their sleep with various mental speculations. They are frustrated in all their various plans by supernatural power. Even great sages, if they are against Your transcendental topics, must rotate in this material world.

Constant endeavor to please Kṛṣṇa is called devotional service. Actually, we have no duty other than to please Kṛṣṇa at all times. All perfection is achieved simply by chanting the Lord's holy name. We cannot serve the Lord without serving the holy name. If we can become servants of Kṛṣṇa we will attain the ultimate goal of life, but if we serve Maya no one can protect us from misfortune.

40. Why does a person who was once properly motivated develop material attachment after some time?

This person must not have heard *hari-kathā*, due to inattention while hearing. He has not tried at all to refrain from seeking immediate happiness. Rather, he is maddened for sense gratification on the advice of sinful people. The most important thing is to take shelter of the Supreme Lord. It does not matter whether we are educated or uneducated, powerful or weak. The living entities are transcendental by nature, but when they think they belong to this world, consisting of the three material modes, they become attached to this world.

41. Are woman and wealth obstacles on the devotional path?

Wealth, women, and fame are each bait for the senses. The conditioned souls are attracted to material enjoyment at every moment because Maya is constantly piercing us by showing us the bait. Tempting us with a woman's association, Maya entangles us in this material world, just as a hunter captures a wild male elephant by luring him with a female elephant.

The living entities wander throughout the universe seeing illusory objects as real and miserable existence as happy. Maya has arranged for some momentary happiness in this world in order to deceive the living entities. Whatever we see in this world that tempt us for sense gratification are all Maya's baits. Anyone who tries to enjoy them will be deceived, will be pierced. "Eat, drink, be merry, and go to hell." This mentality has swallowed human society. What a shame!

42. Please explain how one gradually becomes degraded.

When one falls down from the position of Kṛṣṇa's devotee, he becomes a devotee of Viṣṇu. When he falls down further he becomes an impersonalist. Still further he becomes a fruitive worker, and finally an unrestricted sense enjoyer.

43. Is it bad to read newspapers?

All newspapers are full of worldly topics. We should not read anything that deals with Maya's message. Reading such topics is synonymous with accepting bad association.

44. What is a sinful mentality?

"I am the enjoyer of this material world": this is a sinful mentality. This mentality brings about one's ruination. That one is a servant of the Supreme Lord is the proper mentality.

45. Why do the living entities, who are meant to serve the Supreme Lord, proudly think themselves doers?

It is a fact that the living entity is neither the master nor the enjoyer, but because he has forgotten Kṛṣṇa, his false ego has become prominent and thus he thinks himself the master. The living entities are by nature the Lord's servants. As soon as they forget this, Maya captures and devours them. Unless one sees all objects in relation to the Lord, one cannot help but be misguided by the conception that he is the master. Then he suffers miseries as he busily serves matter. Devotee always serves the Supreme Lord. Their conviction that they are the Lord's servant is prominent in their consciousness. Nondevotees pretending to be masters of the material energy suffer only anxiety. Only those whose knowledge of transcendence has not been awakened accept service as masters. Glorious are those who, rather than becoming masters, serve the Lord's devotees.

46. How should we live in this world?

As one who is tied up and beaten feels pain even though he does not want to, we should accept our place in this material world, while condemning it.

47. Is indulging in worldly talks inauspicious?

Indulgence in worldly topics or the topics of material enjoyment increases our material existence, while indulgence in spiritual topics or topics related to Kṛṣṇa's enjoyment awards us devotional service. If we are not thinking about Hari, we are certainly thinking about material enjoyment. People in this world are always and will always indulge in worldly topics. Instead we should chant Hari's name while remaining indifferent to such topics. Otherwise we will become just like the materialists. Mahāprabhu has warned us not to speak about or hear worldly topics.

48. Why have we come here?

We have come here because we have forgotten Kṛṣṇa. This planet suits our purposes. It is just the right distance from the sun; if we were not this exact distance, we would be burnt to death. But we are part and parcel of Kṛṣṇa. To help us, the Lord mercifully assumes a form measuring three and half hands [one hand is equal to the measurement from the tip of the finger to the elbow] of His own hands so that we may approach Him. We have to adjust ourselves to His desires. Otherwise, if we try to become God ourselves we will never find fortune. If instead of disturbing the Lord we can properly adjust ourselves to Him and favorably cultivate Kṛṣṇa consciousness, then we will be able to attain His mercy.

Karmīs and jñānīs have a strong attachment to intellectualism. They think karma and jñāna are prominent, but the Lord has a different perspective. *Śrī Caitanya-caritāmṛta* (Madhya-lila 20.117) states:

kṛṣṇa bhuli' sei jīva anādi-bahirmukha
ataeva māyā tāre deya saṁsāra-duḥkha

Forgetting Kṛṣṇa, the living entity has been attracted by the external feature from time immemorial. Therefore, the illusory energy [Maya] gives him all kinds of misery in his material existence.

49. Are fruitive activities and the cultivation of knowledge constitutional duties of the spirit soul?

Both karma and jñāna are the activities of conditioned souls. Karma awards temporary results; and jñāna allows one to become proud of his dry renunciation and invites one to experience self-destruction by cultivating meditation on the impersonal Brahman under the shelter of monism. Both sense enjoyers and dry renunciants are mistaken and misguided. Both are cheaters. One should free oneself from the influence of these two paths.

Spiritual Life

1. What is sannyāsa?

Constant worship of Hari is actual *sannyāsa*. The Lord's devotees take *sannyāsa* from material enjoyment and liberation and take shelter at the lotus feet of Bhaktī-devī.

2. Who should be given charity?

If one wants to give charity or do a favor for someone, he should give only to the spiritual master and the Vaiṣṇavas. All credit is due only to those who love God. One should trust and serve those who are engaged twenty-four hours a day in the Lord's service. One need not give anything to or trust those who do not serve the Lord but who accept service for themselves.

3. Do Vaiṣṇavas ever become ritually contaminated?

Whether a Vaiṣṇava is a householder or a renunciant he is not impure or contaminated. Performance of funeral rites and the offering of oblations to forefathers are automatically taken care of simply by serving Hari. Devotees do not have to perform these activities separately. But to maintain worldly etiquette, householder devotees become purified by chanting Hari's holy names and on the eleventh day after a death, or on any other day, perform the *śrāddha* ceremony by offering mahāprasāda to the forefathers. This is Vaiṣṇava *śrāddha*.

4. Is it beneficial to give charity to build a temple?

Instead of spending lavishly to build an opulent house, if one uses his hard-earned money for the Lord's service, the service of the spiritual master and the Vaiṣṇavas, and to help build the Lord's temples, he will attain immense benefit. Such activities are praiseworthy, and their result cannot be described. Those who build temples for Lord Viṣṇu do not go to Yamarāja's abode. Rather, they are taken to Vaikuṇṭha by the Viṣṇudūtas. Yamarāja and his order carriers are servants of the Lord's servants.

5. What is the difference between following and imitating?

Just as subordination and flattery are not synonymous, similarly following and imitating are not synonymous. Many people think imitation means following. Playing the role of Nārada in a drama is called imitating, while following the path of devotional service Nārada taught is following. To copy something artificially is imitating, but to follow in the footsteps of the great mahājanas is following.

We often think we are following when we are actually imitating. Following depends on one's own behavior, and it cannot be done while imitating. Imitation is a behavior based on a perverted reflection of an action. From the external point of view, both imitating and following appear similar, just as fool's gold and pure gold look similar. Imitation means posing. We have the propensity to cheat others. In order to accumulate name and fame, we often pose or imitate. If we only imitate the Vedic path we will not gain the same result we would attain if we followed properly. Imitation actually has no value.

6. The living entities belong to the Lord's marginal potency and therefore can serve either the Lord or Maya. The seed of enjoyment is present in them in an unmanifest form. Do the living entities carry the seed of enjoyment even after they have attained perfection?

Śrī Caitanya-caritāmṛta (Ādī 7.27) states:

jagat ḍubila, jīvera haila bīja nāśa
tāhā dekhi' pāñca janera parama ullāsa

When the five members of the Pañca-tattva saw the entire world drowned in love of Godhead, and the seed of material enjoyment in the living entities completely destroyed, they all became exceedingly happy.

In the Supreme Lord's marginal potency, the seed of material enjoyment in the form of aversion to Kṛṣṇa is indistinctly present along with the propensity to offer service. Because that seed is watered, the seed of material enjoyment, dropped from the tree of material existence, causes the conditioned souls to suffer the threefold miseries day and night. It binds them with the ropes of material enjoyment. As there is no possibility of a seed fructifying if it is fully submerged, similarly if the seed of material enjoyment, which is not related to Kṛṣṇa, is submerged in the vast ocean of devotional service to the Lord, there is no possibility of its fructifying.

7. What is the proper use of wealth?

We are not performers of pious or sinful activities, nor are we mental speculators or fools. We are the shoe-carriers of the non-duplicitous devotees of Hari and are initiated into the mantra, kīrtanīya sadā hariḥ, "Always chant the holy names of Hari." The proper use of wealth is to spend it to publish Vaiṣṇava literature, to preach the topics of Hari, and to serve Śrī Hari, guru, and the Vaiṣṇavas. Using wealth in this way awards one inexhaustible piety.

8. Is it condemned to blaspheme others?

No one should blaspheme or glorify others' natures or activities. *Śrīmad-Bhāgavatam* confirms this instruction. The *Caitanya-Bhāgavata* states, *para carcakera gati nāhi kona kale*: a blasphemer never attains benefit. Blasphemers go to hell. Instead of blaspheming others, one should rectify himself. The spiritual master's chastisement is beneficial for ordinary persons. We should not get involved in such matters by judging them one way or another.

9. What is a Vaiṣṇava's duty?

Regarding the behavior of a Vaiṣṇava, Śrīman Mahāprabhu has said that a householder should maintain his livelihood by accumulating as much material enjoyment as he requires and a renunciant should maintain himself by begging alms. Both should cultivate Kṛṣṇa consciousness. Whether they manage to obtain food and clothing is dependent on the Lord's mercy. Everyone must depend completely on the Supreme Lord.

10. In the Śrāddha ceremony, should the forefathers be offered mahā-prasādam?

In the *śrāddha* ceremony, the departed souls who were inclined to chant Hari's holy name may be offered mahā-prasādam. It is not intelligent to offer oblations to the forefathers other than mahā-prasādam. Fruitive activities invite enjoyment of their fruits. Those who chant Hari's holy names have no desire to enjoy the fruits of their karma, and the *śrāddha* ceremony is a fruitive activity. Still, it is the duty of relatives to help departed souls achieve auspiciousness by offering them some of the Lord's remnants in the Lord's ceremony. The devotees should be satisfied by offering mahāprasādam followed by congregational chanting of Hari's holy names.

11. Should we study Vedānta?

We should discuss Vedānta, but we should not discuss ŚrīŚaṅkarācārya's commentary on it. We will be greatly profited if we study Vedānta with the help of Śrībhāsya or Govindabhāsya. *Śrīmad-Bhāgavatam* is the natural commentary on Vedānta-sūtra. We should study Vedānta under the *Śrīmad-Bhāgavatam*'s guidance. The Vedānta discusses topics about chanting the Lord's holy name. We should study Vedānta and also chant Hari's holy names.

12. Do rich householder devotees and Maṭha residents commit offenses if they do not use their wealth to serve the Lord?

In his *Bhakti-sandarbha*, *jagad-guru* Śrīla Jīva Gosvāmī Prabhu states, ye tu sampattimanto gṛhastās tesām tu arcana mārga eva mukhyaḥ: "The rich householders must use their wealth in the worship of the Deity form of the Lord."*Śrīmad-Bhāgavatam* (10.84.37) states:

ayaṁ svasty-ayanaḥ panthā
dvi-jāter gṛha-medhinaḥ
yac chraddhayāpta-vittena
śuklenejyeta pūruṣaḥ

This is the most auspicious path for a religious householder of the twice-born orders: to selflessly worship the Personality of Godhead with wealth honestly obtained.

If instead of doing so, rich householder devotees engage in hearing, chanting, and remembering the Supreme Lord like the *akiñcana* devotees, they commit the offense known as vitta-śathya, or miserliness. Therefore despite following the processes of hearing, chanting, and remembering, householder devotees and *Maṭha* residents should renounce miserly and cheating propensities and use all their wealth to serve Hari, guru, and the Vaiṣṇavas. Lord Śrī Hari becomes displeased when He sees the propensity to cheat or be miserly. These things are *anarthas* on the devotional path.

Regarding the duty of householders Lord Śrī Gaurāṅgadeva instructed the residents of Kulīna-grāma:

prabhu kahena, 'kṛṣṇa-sevā' vaiṣṇava-sevana'
'nirantara kara kṛṣṇa-nāma-saṅkīrtana'

Śrī Caitanya Mahāprabhu replied, "Without cessation continue chanting the holy name of Lord Kṛṣṇa. Whenever possible, serve Him and His devotees, the Vaiṣṇavas."
(*Śrī Caitanya-caritāmṛta* Madhya-līla 15.104)

13. What do we mean by the phrase, "the favorable cultivation of Kṛṣṇa consciousness"?

Our only duty is to cultivate Kṛṣṇa consciousness. The daughter of Vṛṣabhānu is most favorable to Kṛṣṇa. Another name for Vṛṣabhānu's daughter is Anukulā, "most favorable" or "most intimate." The dear devotees of Śrī Rādhā are all spiritual masters. The Gauḍīya Vaiṣṇavas worship Anukulās Kṛṣṇa, Śrī Rādhās Kṛṣṇa. They are more partial to the daughter of Vṛṣabhānu than to Kṛṣṇa. Favorable cultivation of Kṛṣṇa is possible under the favorable guidance of the most favorable devotee of Kṛṣṇa. We must cultivate this mentality in relation to Kṛṣṇa alone. But alas! Instead of making Kṛṣṇa the center note of our household chord, we have made ourselves the center note and thus we have become attached materialists.

14. What do devotees do when they meet danger?

Sometimes, in order to test us, the Lord places us into difficulty. Those who are real servants of the Lord will not become disturbed in any condition of life. Instead, they will always engage in the Lord's service with body, mind, and speech. Material enjoyment cannot influence such persons because they are always situated in devotional service. Such persons know that serving the Lord is their life and soul, their very existence, their only duty. Apart from the Lord's service, everything leads simply toward death or material existence.

15. What is the difference between sādhana-bhakti and sādhana-kriyā?

Sādhana-kriyā, ritualistic regulative practices, is not performed by the soul but on the platform of the mind, which is the reflection of the soul. There is a difference between eternal *sādhana-bhakti* (pure devotional service) and the ritualistic pious activities one performs (*sādhana*-kriyā). These ritualistic activities may destroy aversion to Hari under the control of time, and among the activities of *sādhana*-kriyā are the limbs of *bhakti* that when performed, attempt to destroy *anarthas*. When *anarthas* are completely destroyed, pure devotional service, *sādhana bhakti*, automatically manifests.

Sādhana kriyā is not effective in terms of the soul, whereas *sādhana-bhakti* is eternally effective in the pure state. The constitutional propensity of the soul is to perform devotional service. Sādhana is meant to help one control the mind. When the mind's material propensities are checked, the soul's propensities can properly manifest. When *sādhana-bhakti* manifests in a soul, that soul gradually surpasses the platform of bhāva and ultimately attains prema. Bhāva-*bhakti* and prema-*bhakti* are the progressively matured platforms of *sādhana-bhakti*, like when a mango goes through the three stages of unripeness, half-ripeness, to full ripeness. *Sādhana-kriyā* is something different. Because people don't understand the difference between *sādhana-bhakti* and *sādhana*-kriyā, there are various disturbances in the world.

16. Is the whole family benefited if a devotee takes birth in it?

One hundred generations forwards and one hundred generations backwards of a family in which a mahābhāgavata appears are automatically delivered. Fourteen generations forwards and fourteen generations backwards of a family in which a madhyama-adhikārī appears are automatically delivered. Three generations forwards and three generations backwards of a family in which a kaniṣṭhā-adhikārī appears are delivered.

17. Is that place a dhāma where the glorification of Hari takes place?

I cannot think of those places where the devotees of the Lord constantly glorify and discuss *hari-kathā* as other than a holy place. Such places are expansions of the eternal abode. We should also know that Lord Viṣṇu exists in the hearts of all living entities and within every atom. Thus every place is holy. When one receives the mercy of his spiritual master he understands this fact.

18. Why aren't we making progress on the path of worshipping the Lord?

How can we make progress? We are busy with external objects and engrossed in the material concept of life. If we want to make progress we need to give up external conceptions and become introspective. We should become eager to serve the Lord of our heart. But we don't feel that eagerness. How then can we hope to spiritual progress? How is it possible to make spiritual advancement if we are busy enhancing our own happiness and prosperity? How will we become enthusiastic to serve our eternal well-wishers, guru and Kṛṣṇa, if we are enthusiastically and busily making our relatives, who are simply plunderers, happy? If we walk toward the west, we cannot expect to arrive in the east. We have explained these things so many times, but still illusion is not destroyed. This means that we are destined to suffer. What can we do?

19. Should a devotee continue to worship the Lord, even when the devotee is ill?

One should not become detached from serving the Lord when one is not physically well. I will never refrain from engaging in the Lord's service. If I am physically unable to serve, my worship will turn to remembrance of the Lord.

20. Should one consider a nondevotee guru a devotee, even if he presents himself as such?

The spiritual master is an *ācārya* and chanter of the holy name. Those who offend the feet of the holy name cannot be guru. A bona fide spiritual master does not encourage anyone to seek sense gratification, nor does he flatter people. Those interested in material enjoyment do not like the devotees' instructions, because the devotees are interested only in spiritual life. Such persons look for people who speak according to their own taste and thus they deprive themselves of any real benefit.

To consider a nondevotee a devotee and nondevotional activities devotional is simply self-deception. Until one is fortunate enough to serve and respect devotees, one will continue to mistake nondevotees for devotees. Can a crow become a peacock simply by wearing peacock feathers? Can a blue fox become the king of animals? How long can cheating remain covered? Truth will certainly prevail. Those who serve Kṛṣṇa are not weak but are strong and determined. Service to Kṛṣṇa is the most important factor. Devotees of Kṛṣṇa are glorious. Only fortunate persons understand this. If out of aversion to the Lord's service one glorifies himself for his insignificant possessions—wealth, education, beauty—then he will find himself in trouble and remain indifferent to the service of Kṛṣṇa and His devotees.

21. Is it good to become over-intelligent?

Disobeying the spiritual master and desiring fame bring ruination. We should not be proud of our wealth or that we are intelligent. This kind of pride is not helpful to a devotee. Rather, it causes difficulties, because it causes one to transgress the spiritual master's order. Please bless me so that my heart never runs towards over-intelligence. I apologize to all those to whom I have spoken rudely or harshly because I considered them my relatives. Instead of understanding my intentions, however, they misunderstood me, and that has made me sad.

22. How should an initiated devotee perform the śrāddha ceremony?

An initiated devotee who has taken shelter of the holy name should offer oblations of mahā-prasāda to his forefathers on the eleventh day after his forefather's death. Thereafter, he should feed the brāhmaṇas with mahā-prasāda. This is best done in the *Maṭha*. Those who are not initiated devotees, who do not chant Hari's holy name, and who are unable to tolerate the arrowlike words of society, can offer oblations to their forefathers according to the prescribed method of the smārtas. They should eat only boiled food once a day for a month and wear a loincloth. Devotees who chant the holy name should honor mahā-prasāda every day. They need not worry about the smārtas' prescribed methods. Please rid yourself of the superstition that a Vaiṣṇava becomes a ghost after death and that his *śrāddha* should be performed with foodstuff that is not first offered to the Lord. The *śāstras* do not approve of this idea. The arrangements provided in the smārta system are based on one's position in society. And the smārtas say that performing the *śrāddha* ceremony according to their system exempts one from entering the womb of another mother. The Lord's devotees, however, never accept such statements. Since the smārtas' consideration is opposed to *śāstra*, the devotees do not accept their process. At the same time, the smārtas find the considerations of liberated souls incomprehensible.

23. Is simplicity essential?

Simplicity means we have to become sincere. We have to give up the cheating propensity, crookedness, and blaspheming others at all costs. One cannot pass foolishness or crookedness off as sincerity. True sincerity and apparent sincerity, true punctuality and apparent punctuality—none of these are the same. What a devotee thinks and what a nondevotee thinks are not the same. If one is not engaged in hari-*bhajana* twenty-four hours a day, he will have to bid goodbye to worshiping Hari.

24. Who can understand a devotee's activities?

Only those who follow and cultivate the teachings and behavior of the Lord's devotees can understand the activities of devotees, whose characteristics are incomprehensible. Ordinary people never understand a devotee's dealings; Vaiṣṇava characteristics cannot be understood by mundane knowledge. Devotees are often not even recognized by examining their external behavior. If by good fortune we get the opportunity to see a devotee and his or her Vaiṣṇava characteristics with a service attitude, we will be blessed. But to try to measure transcendental objects with our sensual knowledge will only cause us problems.

25. Who is a brāhmaṇa?

A *brāhmaṇa* is one who searches after Brahman. A *brāhmaṇa* is one who is neither in the bodily concept of life nor a mental speculator. A *brāhmaṇa* is one who knows the Supreme Brahman.

26. Is it most important to worship Hari?

Without wasting more time, one should try to achieve Kṛṣṇa's mercy. This applies to everyone—child, old man, young man, or woman. There is no guarantee that we will live for any particular amount of time; life could end at any moment. Therefore we should immediately begin to worship Lord Hari.

Some people say, "Let's enjoy life now and worship Hari at the end of life." But this is not a reasonable idea. Time is life. At every moment our duration of life is being reduced. Time lost can never be regained. Considering this, one should not waste time in pursuits other than hari-*bhajana*. One of the mahājanas sings:

jīvana samāpti kāle kariba bhajana
ebe kari griha sukha
kakhana e kathā nāhi bale vijñājana
e deha patan unmukha

"Let me enjoy family life now. I will worship the Lord when I an old": A learned person never speaks like this because he knows that death is inevitable."

If we lose the golden opportunity we have at present to worship Lord Hari, we will be forced to suffer the threefold miseries of materiel existence. We must associate with *sādhus* to help. Only in the association of saintly persons will we become fortunate enough to understand that worship of Kṛṣṇa is life's aim. When we finally understand this point, we will give up both material enjoyment and dry renunciation and engage eagerly in His service. Thus we will attain self-realization. When we engage in the Lord's service under the spiritual master's guidance, reactions to our previous misdeeds will gradually be destroyed and we will attain perfection.

27. How does one's propensity for material enjoyment diminish?

Material existence is like a well covered by grass. It is difficult to get out of such a well if one should fall into it. No one can deliver himself from material existence without the Lord's mercy. As soon as we forget that we are Kṛṣṇa's servants, we begin to serve Maya. Service to Kṛṣṇa is called devotional service, and the desire for material enjoyment is called nondevotional service. The only way to give up nondevotional desires is to hear kṛṣṇa-kathā from the spiritual master and the Vaiṣṇavas with surrender, honest inquiry, and a service attitude. Thus one's material propensities will be destroyed and one will begin to taste Kṛṣṇa's name.

28. Is it necessary to worship Hari after having taken birth in a human body?

By good fortune and the Lord's mercy we have been given a human birth. The human form of life is extremely rare, and there is no guarantee that in our next life we will again become humans. By some misfortune we might become a ghost, witch, hobgoblin, animal, bird, or insect. It is not possible to worship Hari in those species. Therefore we should not use whatever time we have left in our present body for pointless activities.

Life is temporary. Still, human life can award spiritual salvation. Therefore as long as we are alive, we should quickly earn our spiritual perfection. Human beings proudly consider themselves brāhmaṇas, kṣatriyas, vaiśyas, or śūdras, *brahmacārīs*, gṛhasthas, vānaprasthas, or sannyāsīs. Those who are intelligent, however, should not claim these false identities. We are simply the Lord's servants. We are not products of this world. To consider the body the self is an illusion. Śrī Mahāprabhu said:

jīvera svabhāva, kṛṣṇa-'dāsa'-abhimāna
dehe ātma-jñāne ācchādita sei 'jñāna'

The original nature of every living entity is to consider himself the eternal servant of Kṛṣṇa. But under the influence of Maya he thinks himself to be the body, and thus his original consciousness is covered. (*Śrī Caitanya-caritāmṛta* Madhya 24.201)

Hari's holy name does not appear on the tongues of persons puffed up with the false ego of material proprietorship. We are eternally conditioned souls. Due to our forgetfulness of Kṛṣṇa we have fallen into illusion. Now we have no alternative but to give up our false ego and take complete shelter at the lotus feet of guru and Kṛṣṇa. Elephants think themselves elephants and dogs dogs, but humans should not think like this. Rather, they should be proud of their real identity. Śrī Mahāprabhu said, jīvera 'svarūpa' haya kṛṣṇera 'nitya-dāsa': "It is the living entity's constitutional position to be an eternal servant of Kṛṣṇa" (*Śrī Caitanya-caritāmṛta* Madhya 20.108)

Lord Hari is situated in every atom, and He attracts fools and the learned alike. Only those who have no desire for material enjoyment, for becoming the master, no desire to command respect as *sādhus*, are qualified to hear His instructions. Those who are attached to something so insignificant as their own pride, however, will not hear the Lord's call.

Still, such persons should know that death is inevitable. adya vābda śatānte vā mṛtyur vai prāninām dhruvaḥ: either today or in a hundred years every living entity must die. We are cognizant, but if despite our cognizance we did not approach the Lord's devotees and hear their instructions attentively, ruination is inevitable.

There is no chance to worship Hari in any form of life other than the human form. Therefore we should engage in hari-*bhajana* until we die by giving up all other engagements. That's the only way we can attain the ultimate goal of life.

Everyone in this world is ready to ruin us. In this land of no-friendship, our so-called relatives are unfavorable for our devotional service. We therefore have no alternative but to take shelter of Vaiṣṇavas. Vaiṣṇavas are our actual relatives. We do not need to do anything for anyone. Just serve the Lord's devotees along with others. Let everyone serve the Lord with his or her knowledge, intelligence, academic qualification, physical strength, wealth, and expertise. The more we delay doing so, the more trouble we will find ourselves in.

People who follow non-Vaiṣṇava religious principle cannot attain auspiciousness. All auspiciousness is held in the hand of those who take shelter at the lotus feet of a Vaiṣṇava. The non-Vaiṣṇavas are decorated only with the garlands of birth and death. Persons attached to hari-*bhajana* no longer enter the wombs of mothers. What to speak of Vaiṣṇavas, even those who have the opportunity to see the lotus feet of an extraordinary Vaiṣṇava will not take birth again.

29. What is the difference between the words of a sādhaka and the words of a person who has achieved perfection?

To express one's own realization or distress is easier than pleading the realization or distress of others. A person who can plead his own case can speak without duplicity, whereas those who are advocating on behalf of someone else may not have the same power. That is the difference between a sādhaka and a siddha.

30. Is it proper to touch a sannyāsīs feet?

One should not touch the lotus feet of,a saintly person or *sannyāsī* with his enjoyment-prone body or sinful body. If the saintly person becomes displeased as a result of our touching his lotus feet, then it will certainly create inauspiciousness for us. Sannyāsī devotees do not like people touching their feet. It is currently become a fashion— a disease—to touch the lotus feet of guru and *sādhu*. We should pay close attention to whether the spiritual master and Kṛṣṇa are being pleased by each one of our actions. If we do not do so, then we will dig our own grave.

Let me tell those who, under the control of their emotions, attempt to touch the feet of a *sannyāsī* like me. In the language of my spiritual master, "Why should they dare to stretch their hands to take dust from the feet of the saintly persons? Is such boldness proper? What qualification do they have? What right? An attached householder, who has no real interest in serving the saint, is certainly unjustified in touching his lotus feet. Better that we offer one another obeisances from a distance. If an attached householder forcibly tries to touch the saint's feet, it means his mind is attracted to gross matter. That will cause him more harm than good. Those who desire fortune should carefully refrain from committing such offensive activities.

31. How should we see sense gratification?

We should accept as much sense gratification as is necessary to keep body and soul together. We should not live in luxury. At the same time, we should not unnecessarily trouble the body so that it dies. We should lead our lives in a way that is favorable for cultivating Kṛṣṇa consciousness. There is no way to attain perfection if we don't serve the transcendental sound vibration. Therefore the Vedānta-sūtra states: anāvṛttiḥ sabdāt, one becomes liberated by sound.

Simply by glorifying the Lord He is satisfied. The mass of people cannot find their real welfare either collectively or individually by satisfying their senses. The body should be maintained only for the Lord's service. What is the use of maintaining a body simply to gratify its senses? This will result only in one's going to hell. Maintaining the body means accepting as much material enjoyment as necessary to be able to serve Lord Hari. We should take neither more nor less than that.

32. How should one show others respect?

A devotee is not in favor of giving respect to others unless they are directly or indirectly related to Kṛṣṇa. However, knowing that Kṛṣṇa is situated in the hearts of all living entities as the Supersoul, devotees give respect to all living entities, including the demigods and humans, as servants of the Supreme Lord. Śrī Mahāprabhu states (*Śrī Caitanya-caritāmṛta* Antya 20.25):

uttama hañā vaiṣṇava habe nirabhimāna
jīve sammāna dibe jāni' 'kṛṣṇa'-adhiṣṭhāna

Although a Vaiṣṇava is the most exalted person, he is prideless, and gives all respect to everyone, knowing everyone to be the resting place of Kṛṣṇa.

33. Can one be attached to sense gratification even after taking initiation?

The process of attaining transcendental knowledge is called initiation. We should know that the Supreme Lord is the transcendental Absolute Truth, we are His eternal servants, and we have no duty other than to serve Him. Knowing this is actual initiation. The absence of this understanding is ignorance. At present, there is a controversy about the word "initiation". People proudly claim that they have taken initiation from a bona fide spiritual master, but how can they maintain material attachment even after taking initiation? How can they desire to make advancement in material life? If they don't learn about their relationship with the Lord, independent and proud people uselessly brag about their initiations. Rather than treating their spiritual master as if he were as good as God, they treat him as their disciple, fit to be their order-supplier. Considering the guru an ordinary mortal being, these persons become offenders at his lotus feet.

The spiritual master is worshipable. There is no one more worshipable to us than guru. Serving the guru is superior to serving the Lord. There is no greater religious principle than serving the spiritual master. Even though we repeatedly hear this, due to our strong attachment for body and house, we forget it and think that serving our family members and ourselves is more important. Our position is similar to that of the boy who forgets his duty and absorbs himself in play rather than study.

If after accepting initiation we do not awaken our propensity to serve the Lord, then we must be cultivating a desire for fame, wealth, and serving our family members. It is only by good fortune that one receives the opportunity to serve the Lord, but we foolishly waste that opportunity. The results of our folly are so poisonous that we are left only with disappointment. Do not doubt my words. If we do not follow the guru and the Vaiṣṇavas' orders, what can they do to help us?

34. What is the object of our meditation?

There is nothing in this material world that attracts us. Lord Kṛṣṇa is the actual truth, the Absolute Truth. That Lord Kṛṣṇa, along with His associates, is the focus of our thoughts.

35. How will we realize the Supreme Lord?

Śrīman Mahāprabhu said that serving Kṛṣṇa and the devotees and congregationally chanting the holy name are the living entity's three duties. Kṛṣṇa is the object of service, and one who serves Him is His servant. The propensity to engage in that service is called *bhakti*. The object of service, the servant, and the propensity to serve are eternal and are not subject to the material time factor. They are not created or destroyed as are the conditioned souls. Only those who sincerely endeavor to serve the Lord can realize this fact. The Absolute Truth is not understood by adulterated endeavor.

If we do not follow the spiritual path and do not become eager to always serve the Supreme Lord, we will go to hell, praising the path of material enjoyment. We cheat people when we tell them that we worship Viṣṇu or serve Kṛṣṇa when we are actually serving our senses. We serve our wives, children, and other relatives, enjoy our senses, and are good for nothing. Until a living entity develops the pure and unadulterated propensity to serve the Supreme Lord, he is still in ignorance. Our present pathetic condition is because Śrī Gaurasundara's teachings have not yet entered our hearts.

Until we realize that service to Kṛṣṇa and His devotees is our prime duty, we will continue to be cheated by Maya. We can get freedom from our sinful mentality only when we sincerely take shelter at the lotus feet of Kṛṣṇa's devotees. If we serve those who constantly worship the Supreme Lord, then by their mercy we can go back to Godhead. However, if we think the Nārada in the drama party to be the real Nārada, and if we think a mixture of water and chalk to be milk, we are deceived. Only service to a great personality who is always engaged in the service of the Lord and nothing else can award us realization of the Supreme Lord.

As long as people who are fond of sense gratification remain captivated by mental speculation and covered by the *rasa* of sense objects, they cannot realize the Supreme Lord. Kṛṣṇa is the devotees' property, and only a devotee can give Kṛṣṇa to us. We cannot understand Kṛṣṇa if our heart is full of material desire. We can understand Him only if our hearts are inclined to service. Spiritual realization is attained when we constantly serve the Supreme Lord while thinking ourselves His servants. Meeting Kṛṣṇa is possible only through the devotional process and in no other way.

36. What is the meaning of Kṛṣṇa's appearance?

The complete manifestation of the Super Consciousness within the pure hearts of all living entities is known as the appearance of Kṛṣṇa, the birth of Lord Kṛṣṇa. At present we are absorbed in mundane subject matters. If we can somehow reduce that absorption, we will get a respite from material existence or the mundane conception.

37. Is a devotee's body the Lord's temple?

The living entity's body is the temple and residence of the Lord. The Lord's various Deity forms are installed in temples built of bricks, wood, and stone, but the Lord resides eternally in the temple of the devotee's spiritualized body. When devotees honor mahā-prasāda, they are attempting to protect the Lord's temple.

38. Who will attain success in spiritual life?

The Supreme Lord is one without a second. Those who think there is something beyond the Lord suffer from an incomplete and defective conception. The Supreme Lord is ekam eva advitīyam, one without a second. He is not five or ten. Those who think the Absolute Truth can be successfully challenged cannot attain success. We worship the personal Godhead and are not impersonalists, and therefore our success is inevitable provided we surrender. Worshipers of the Supreme Personality of Godhead Viṣṇu can capture Nanda Mahārāja's son, who is the ultimate object of service, within the core of their hearts. The second verse of *Śrīmad-Bhāgavatam* proves this.

Those who take shelter of the Lord attain liberation. Such persons can walk over the head of unlimited dangers and attain success simply with guru and Kṛṣṇa's blessings. Devotees who have taken complete shelter of the spiritual master, Kṛṣṇa's topmost devotee, will never fail.

The community of nondevotees will collapse in due course of time, but devotees never fall down. The nondevotees fall down. Hypocrites who make a show of performing devotional service also fall down. Mental speculation will be vanquished.

39. Why are we bereft of Kṛṣṇa's darśana?

Without approaching the lotus feet of a bona fide spiritual master one cannot approach Kṛṣṇa or His service. Because we do not hear properly from the mouth of the spiritual master we are unable to see Kṛṣṇa. If we hear properly, then we will chant properly. If we chant properly, then we will remember Kṛṣṇa properly and thus realize Him. We must surrender everything at the spiritual master's lotus feet, because Kṛṣṇa Himself appears before the fortunate souls in the form of guru. He does not appear before unfortunate souls at all. The first order is to take shelter of a spiritual master. That requires humility. Actually, humility and taking shelter are synonymous. If we do not take shelter, who can help us?

One attains a spiritual master by the Lord's grace. Everything becomes possible by Kṛṣṇa's mercy. If we fail to attain His mercy, then we will achieve nothing, even if we try forever. His mercy is most important. If we are sincere at heart and are eager to attain His lotus feet, he will certainly bestow His mercy on us. If out of good fortune we receive a bona fide spiritual master, we must observe carefully how he serves Kṛṣṇa constantly with all his senses. Unless we hear from the spiritual master and apply his instructions in our lives, how can we give up material enjoyment? One cannot hear properly if he is too attached to worldly matters. If hearing is not done properly, one will be far from achieving auspiciousness.

40. What is the duty of a householder?

To please the Supreme Lord, the householder devotees should associate with and serve the spiritual master and saints with love and devotion. This will enable them to become spiritual householders. If householders do not associate, serve, and discuss about both the book Bhāgavata and the devotee Bhāgavata, they cannot attain auspiciousness. They should live at home with the resolution, "I will serve Kṛṣṇa with all respect." Otherwise their household life, devoid of Hari's service, will lead them to hell.

If family life is favorable to the cultivation of Kṛṣṇa consciousness, then it is acceptable and praiseworthy. If it unfavorable, then family life, which is compared to a dark well, should be rejected. There is no difference between devotees living at home or at the *Maṭha*, because in either case they are constantly engaged in the Lord's service.

But one should not confuse the life of an attached householder with the life of a a devotee who lives at home. By serving and associating with pure devotees who have made guru and Kṛṣṇa their life and soul, attachment for family life and material existence is destroyed. There is no way to become free of family attachment without sincerely serving the spiritual master.

One should live at home only to serve Kṛṣṇa under the guru's guidance. The householders should refrain from eating too much or accumulating more than he needs. He should not over-endeavor, gossip, become overly attached to following the rules and regulations, associate with nondevotees, or be greedy. He must also maintain his enthusiasm, confidence, determination, patience, taste for hearing and chanting Hari's holy name, and firmness in service to guru and Kṛṣṇa.

A householder has no business indulging in illicit sex, in becoming overly attached to his wife, or in becoming henpecked. He should give up bad association and tolerate the urges of speech, mind, anger, tongue, belly, and genitals. A householder should not only refrain from sinful activities but should also avoid the pious activities that are unfavorable to devotional service. By engaging in sinful activities he will definitely not be able to serve Hari. The desire to accumulate piety will also block his worship. A householder devotee must not become indifferent to the service of Hari, guru, and the Vaiṣṇavas on the pretext of chanting the holy name. This is nothing but cheating, and it will lead to greater feelings of family attachment rather than devotion. Unless the living entity serves guru and Kṛṣṇa, he or she cannot develop love of God. A householder should always try to assist those devotees who are constantly engaged in Kṛṣṇa's service.

41. O Master,will you go to Guṇḍicā?

Guṇḍicā is the heart of the human being. When the mirror of one's heart is cleansed, it becomes a suitable place for the Lord's residence. I have no intention to visit the Gundicā of your consideration, because I could not clean the temple of my own heart. I am proud of my position as enjoyer and master. I am gradually becoming disappointed, and my hope in life is fading. I am forced to associate with insincere people; I always meet them. I have no intention to come in contact with Śrī Rūpa and Sanātana. I gladly invite my own danger.

Anyway, as long as we have this material body we are in an ocean of discomfort. Therefore we prefer to be absorbed in Cārvākism. We do not understand that these discomforts are Kṛṣṇa's mercy, so we leave spiritual life and go home. We do not remember that Kṛṣṇa's lotus feet are our eternal home and that our soul's eternal health lies at Kṛṣṇa's lotus feet.

42. From whom should we take guidance?

No one who places obstacles in the path of Kṛṣṇa's sense gratification is allowed to enter Kṛṣṇa's kingdom. Thus we should not follow such people. We will not allow anyone to lord it over or subdue us. Only Lord Viṣṇu and His servants can establish their undisputed domain over us. Apart from Lord Viṣṇu and the Vaiṣṇavas, if we allow others to lord it over us on the pretext of being magnanimous, or if we compare guru and Kṛṣṇa with these others, then we should know that Maya has certainly spread her mastery over us. We should kick out the idea of so-called impersonal liberation. Liberation in the form of merging into the Brahman is the topmost offense. Māyāvādis are offenders at the Lord's feet. They cannot chant Kṛṣṇa's holy name. Their pretension of chanting pierces Lord Kṛṣṇa's body like a thunderbolt. We will not resolve that mental speculation or dry arguments alone are our destination. We will not reach any conclusion on the strength of argumentation. Argument does not allow us to realize subject matter that is beyond the reach of argument. Therefore in order to know Lord Hari, one must give up the path of argument and take shelter of the Lord's devotees. We should neither become materialists nor follow in the footsteps of materialists.

43. What is the difference between Bhagavad-gītā and Śrīmad-Bhāgavatam?

Śrīmad-Bhāgavatam preaches the impartial Absolute Truth. It is the most desirable object for the nonenvious devotee. *Bhagavad-gītā* is the curriculum of the infant class, whereas *Śrīmad-Bhāgavatam* is the curriculum of the postgraduate class. In order to qualify for the postgraduate class, those who do not know anything about spiritual life use *Bhaga-*

vad-gītā as the entrance exam. *Bhagavad-gītā* awards them the necessary knowledge. Those who want to pick up a masters or doctorate degree in spiritual subject matter are required to study further.

However, impartial devotees do not discriminate between *Bhagavad-gītā* and *Śrīmad-Bhāgavatam*. The variety of adjectives and grammatical explanations found in this world only increase the beauty of the lotus feet of *Śrīmad-Bhāgavatam*. *Śrīmad-Bhāgavatam* explains the spirit souls' constitutional duty. *Śrīmad-Bhāgavatam* is directly the Lord's incarnation. No one can shake *Śrīmad-Bhāgavatam* from its unique position even by an inch.

Bhagavad-gītā is recommended for the infant class in the spiritual school as well as for those new students who desire to enter the spiritual kingdom. Those who have finished studying *Bhagavad-gītā* and who wish to attain higher spiritual knowledge can gain immense profit by properly hearing and studying *Śrīmad-Bhāgavatam* from a pure devotee.

Śrīmad-Bhāgavatam is directly the incarnation of the Supreme Lord, the Absolute Truth. He cannot be measured by our blunt material senses. That which is rare and confidential is more protected. *Śrīmad-Bhāgavatam* does not reveal itself before the godless people.

44. How does Vaiṣṇava dharma benefit the whole world?

Even a one-millionth portion of the great favor attributed to the people of this world by Vaiṣṇava dharma cannot be attributed by thousands of yugas of political maneuvering. We do not instruct people to become narrow-minded and sectarian like politicians.

45. How many persons know about Vaiṣṇava dharma?

How many people can study at the postgraduate level? How many people can become Newtons? Is it reasonable to stop discussing science because there are no Jagdish Chandra Basus?

46. Some people may personally benefit by following Vaiṣṇava dharma, but how is the whole world benefited?

Only a neophyte will think like this. Those who are advanced in spiritual activities and who engage in glorifying the Lord would not agree. Those who worship the Deity think only of their own benefit, but those who chant the Lord's glories benefit everyone in the world, including the beasts, birds, demigods, demons, and even the trees, creepers, and stones.

47. Is Vaiṣṇava dharma meant to be accepted by all?

Vaiṣṇava dharma is the only propensity for all living entities. It is their eternal occupational duty. There is no need to become a Muslim, Christian, or Hindu, or an animal, bird, demigod, demon, or human being. All that is required is to become a Vaiṣṇava. In other words, simply take to the soul's eternal occupational duty. This is exactly what Śrī Mahāprabhu did when He traveled to south India, where He loudly chanted the Lord's glories while traveling. His chanting created many Vaiṣṇavas. By His mercy even the birds, animals, trees, and creepers became Vaiṣṇavas as He walked through the Jhārikhaṇḍa forest. Worshipers of Śiva and Durgā, the atheists, Hindus, Muslims, Buddhists, impersonalists, materialists, mental speculators, yogīs, ascetics, learned, foolish, sick, and healthy all became Vaiṣṇavas. Mahāprabhu's only weapon was the chanting of Kṛṣṇa's holy names. Those who became Vaiṣṇavas in turn made others Vaiṣṇavas by acting as spiritual masters under Mahāprabhu's order.

48. Although demigod worship is unauthorized, doesn't it amount to worship of Kṛṣṇa in the end?

Worship with true understanding and by following the proper rules and regulations bears fruit. Unauthorized worship is useless. Lord Kṛṣṇa is the undisputed emperor of the entire universe and of Vaikuṇṭha, which is beyond the material universe. Therefore no one can challenge Him or place obstacles on the path of His enjoyment. In fact, everyone worships Him. Some worship with understanding and some worship without understanding. Those who worship without understanding accomplish nothing. Those who worship Gaṇeśa, Sūrya, or Durgā, worship Kṛṣṇa's shadow potency, because no one has an existence of Kṛṣṇa. But since they are worshiping Kṛṣṇa's shadow potency, they do not attain self-realization or knowledge of their relationship with the Lord. When they attain self-realization, they will understand that Kṛṣṇa alone is their supreme master and that all living entities are His eternal servants. They will know that service to Kṛṣṇa is their eternal occupational duty.

Worship of Kṛṣṇa, the Lord of all, is the living entity's eternal duty. All the demigods are Lord Viṣṇu's servants. Therefore it is their duty to follow the Lord's order. Those who instead of recognizing the demigods as Lord Viṣṇu's servants imagine them to be as good as or superior to Lord Viṣṇu never become liberated.

49. Is Vaiṣṇava dharma the original religious principle?

Vaiṣṇava dharma is the supreme religious principle, the ultimate occupational duty of all living entities. All other forms of religious systems are either supports of Vaiṣṇava dharma or perversions of it. When they are supportive, particular classes of transcendentalists will accept them, and when they are perverted, they are completely rejected.

50. How do the five-god worshipers worship Viṣṇu?

Devotees are firmly fixed in devotional service. Wherever there is an absence of fixity, there is a lack of unalloyed attention. There is certainly such a thing as adulterous or pseudo devotional service. The five-god worshipers are like that. They are not devotees of the Supreme Lord but nondevotees.

Lord Viṣṇu is the transcendental Cupid and the supreme controller of all the universes. He is eternally worshipable for all living entities, including human beings and demigods. The demigods act simply as coverings of Lord Viṣṇu's. They serve as universal order-suppliers. When the five-god worshipers worship Viṣṇu in order to fulfill their material desires or attain liberation, they categorize Lord Viṣṇu as a demigod. Thus Lord Viṣṇu's actual identity remains covered.

51. What is the most essential activity for living entities?

Our most desirable object is remembrance of Hari. Our ability to remember Him will depend on our hearing and chanting. If we hear, we can chant. Remembrance will come automatically.

"We are in trouble": this mentality often produces taste for hearing *hari-kathā*. While hearing *hari-kathā*, chanting and remembering occur naturally. Whenever we glorify Hari, we remember Him.

To develop a natural taste for the Lord is called total surrender.

arādhanānāṁ sarveṣāṁ, viṣṇor ārādhanaṁ param
tasmāt parataraṁ devī, tadīyānāṁ samarcanam

My dear Devī, although the Vedas recommend worship of demigods, the worship of Lord Viṣṇu is topmost. However, above the worship of Lord Viṣṇu is the rendering of service to Vaiṣṇavas, who are related to Lord Viṣṇu. (*Padma Purāṇa*)

When we realize the import of this verse, our lives will be successful. We associate with many sinful people every day, and this certainly increases our troubles. We must renounce bad association and thrive on good association.

Engaging in public service by giving up Kṛṣṇa's service will only yield temporary results. Mundane welfare work does not award actual peace or even help the mind's restlessness to subside. If the Lord favors us, then only will we receive the association of the most sanctified devotees. We are constantly attracted to sense objects based on form, taste, smell, sound, and touch. We must learn how to remain in the Lord's association.

We have rendered public service for many births. Animals also work hard for their fellow animals. As human beings, don't we deserve a promotion? Everything in this world is temporary and perishable. Have we ever discussed eternal objects? The special characteristic of the human form of life is that we can discuss life after death and eternal life. Hearing and chanting *hari-kathā* is possible only in the human form of life, and such hearing and chanting is the only way to remember the Lord. We have no duty other than glorifying Hari. While we are alive and after death we must sing Hari's glories. Intelligent persons chant kṛṣṇa-kathā and fools engage in sense gratification, karma, or *jñāna*. The daughter of Vṛṣabhānu always chants Kṛṣṇa's name even though She is nondifferent from Kṛṣṇa. The daughter of Vṛṣabhānu is the crest jewel among the intelligent. Similarly, Śrī Gaurasundara is the original personality among intelligent persons.

52. What is renunciation?

Vairāgya means to not become attached to objects unrelated to the Lord but to simply cultivate Kṛṣṇa consciousness. If instead of this we become pseudo renunciants, we will find ourselves cheated, just as by cheating a blacksmith of iron we cheats ourselves. Therefore I advise you: whether you live at home or in the forest, simply cultivate Kṛṣṇa consciousness. If you discuss *hari-kathā*, your attachment for material objects will vanish automatically.

53. What is our topmost duty?

We have many duties. Which is most important among them? Lord Śiva states: "Among the various duties of the living entities worship of Viṣṇu is the most essential. Still more essential is the worship of the spiritual master and the Vaiṣṇavas." Lord Hari is the supreme Absolute Truth. He is the transcendental personality of Godhead. We are also eternally individual persons. Therefore we need to worship the eternally transcendental personality of Godhead. A relationship between persons is natural and opens the scope for service. If we need to reestablish our relationship with the Absolute Truth, then it is reasonable that all our activities be performed for the sake of that Absolute Truth.

54. What does it mean to limit the Supreme Lord?

Measuring things means to enjoy them. In order to attain real liberation, we must give up the tendency to measure things with our senses.

55. Who is a tridaṇḍī sannyāsī?

The topmost desire in human life is to become a tridandī. The word tridandī refers to a devotee who chants Hari's holy name while offering respects to others and without expecting respect for himself. Such a devotee is also tolerant. Vaiṣṇavas are godly, but they never proudly consider themselves godly. Rather, they remain humbler than a blade of grass. It is the duty of those who possess brahminical qualification to accept tridaṇḍī *sannyāsa*. Such acceptance means to engage the body, mind, and speech in the Lord's service Lord and to not use them in any other activity.

56. What is jñāna and what is vijñāna?

Jñāna refers to information about the Supreme Lord, and vijñāna refers to knowledge about the Supreme Lord along with His associates and characteristics.

57. Is it prohibited to look at women?

Looking at women is prohibited for sannyāsīs and *brahmacārīs*, but this does not mean that we should consider women bad. That would not be intelligent. Looking at a woman with the spirit of enjoyment is prohibited and condemnable. In this case, there is no fault in the object, only in how we are approaching it. The variety in this world is not bad or faulty, but to misuse it is condemned. What we see is good and acceptable only if it is engaged in the Lord's service.

Prayer

1. To whose prayer does Lord Kṛṣṇa listen?

"O Kṛṣṇa! I do not want from You any happiness for myself. Whatever You want from me, I will obey without fail. Even if I have to suffer in doing Your will, that suffering will be my pleasure. You are the all-auspicious Lord, and as such Your arrangements can never be inauspicious." If a servant of Kṛṣṇa prays to Him with such faith and feelings, the Lord will certainly accept his offering. Without these feelings and faith, the Lord does not.

2. How should a devotee pray?

A devotee prays, "O Rādhā-Ramaṇa, enjoyer of Rādhā, please protect me. May I not bring about my own ruination by ever leaving Your service." Those who have entered family life should pray, "O Lord! May I not become overly attached to family life. May my desire for material life be exhausted. May my attention remain always fixed on Your service. Please protect me."

3. How should we call the Supreme Lord?

Śrī Gaurasundara taught us that in order to chant the Lord's holy names, we must become lower than the straw in the street. Unless we consider ourselves insignificant, we cannot call upon another for help. Only when we pray for another's help do we consider ourselves helpless. In such a state of mind we think that without another's help we will be unable to do anything. We will feel it impossible to do that thing alone which is meant to be done by five people.

Śrī Gaurasundara has instructed us to chant the Lord's names. We get this information from our spiritual master. To chant the Lord's names means to take His help. But while chanting, if we consider Him our servant or expect Him to do our work, then there is no question of our living in the conception, "I am lower than the straw in the street."

An external display of humility is not necessarily genuine humility but cheating. Our call will not reach the Lord if we call Him as a master calls his servants. He is supremely independent and not under anyone's control. Unless we transform our false ego and become sincerely humble, our prayers will not reach the supreme, independent Lord.

One more point: We have to remember that while humbly chanting the Lord's name, if we do not become tolerant, our chanting will remain imperfect. If we display our intolerance by being greedy for particular objects, then we are opposing the principle of humility. If we have complete faith that the Supreme Lord is the Absolute Truth and by chanting His names we will not experience poverty, we will have no lack of tolerance. As soon as we become greedy and try to exhibit our impatience or our own skill, we cannot call the Supreme Lord properly.

We often think we are doing the Lord a favor by offering Him prayers—that we could have engaged in some other activity than chanting the Lord's name. Such a mentality is an example of a lack of tolerance. We need someone to protect us from such a mentality, someone to help us become lower than the straw in the street. We certainly need to take shelter of a person who will deliver us from sinful motives. Śrīla Narottama Ṭhākura says, "Lord Kṛṣṇa does not reject those who worship Him under the shelter of the spiritual master. Others simply die uselessly."

4. What should be the object of our prayer?

The object of our constant prayer should be to beg the Lord for His causeless mercy. The final goal of every living entity is to attain kṛṣṇa-prema.

Deity

1. Is the Lord's Deity form directly the Lord Himself?

Kṛṣṇa's Deity form is directly Kṛṣṇa Himself. It is said, "You are not an idol but directly the son of Vraja's king." The Deity is the form of the Lord that accepts His devotees' worship. The Lord of our heart appears before us in the form of a Deity.

2. What is the Lord's Deity form?

The Lord's Deity form is His direct manifestation to accept His devotees' offerings. *Śrī Caitanya-caritāmṛta* states, "You are not an idol; You are directly the son of the king of Vraja." We should not look upon the Deity as if He were an idol. Unlike the conditioned souls, there is no difference between the Deity's body and self. The Deity is sat-cit-ānanda, most merciful, and an incarnation of the Supreme Lord.

3. Is Deity worship idolatry?

The godless atheists say there is no need to worship the Lord's Deity. In their opinion, Deity worship is against Vedic injunction. They say the Vaiṣṇavas' Deity worship is like the Buddhist philosophy—unauthorized. If they are fortunate, they will one day understand that to bestow mercy on the living entities the Supreme Lord has appeared in this world in His Deity.

The proxy or replica of the spiritual subject matter, which is not perceived through the material senses, appears before us in the form of the Deity, holy name, pictures, and so on. The Lord's holy name is the Lord

Himself. To think there is a difference between the Lord and His name, form, qualities, or pastimes is to oppose the conception of advaya-jñana. Therefore my spiritual master used to warn us that we should never consider the Lord's Deity a material object meant for our enjoyment. To do so is to commit an offense leading to hell. Due to ignorance of our relationship with Kṛṣṇa we consider the Lord's Deity separate from the Lord. This mentality is most unfortunate. The Supreme Personality of Godhead, Śrī Gaurāṅgadeva, says in *Śrī Caitanya-caritāmṛta* Madhya-līla 6.166-167):

īśvarera śrī-vigraha sac-cid-ānandākāra,
se-vigrahe kaha sattva-guṇera vikāra
śrī-vigraha ye nā māne, sei ta' pāṣaṇḍī,
adṛśya aspṛśya, sei haya yama-daṇḍī

The transcendental form of the Supreme Personality of Godhead is complete in eternity, cognizance and bliss. However, you describe this transcendental form as a product of material goodness. One who does not accept the transcendental form of the Lord is certainly an agnostic. Such a person should be neither seen nor touched. Indeed, he is subject to be punished by Yamarāja.

Idol worshipers are degraded because they consider the Lord's Deity form stone. They think śalagrāma-śilās and gaṇḍakī-śilas are nothing but ordinary stone. They also think the spiritual master an ordinary human being. This is hellish mentality. The Vaiṣṇavas are not idol worshippers. They do not consider the worshipable Deity stone. They do not begin to worship before they have purified themselves thoroughly. They do not worship with their material senses by which external objects related to form, taste, and smell are accepted. By serving the Supreme Lord, who is eternal and full of knowledge and bliss, with their spiritual senses, they give pleasure to their worshipable Lord.

Śrī Caitanyadeva has displayed the pastime of seeing Śrī Jagannāthadeva as nondifferent from Kṛṣṇa, the son of Nanda. He did not worship with the same conception of the idol worshipers— that the Lord had manifested within the nīm wood. Rather, He said, "You are not an idol. You are directly the son of Nanda Mahārāja."

4. Some people say that Deity worship is a means to an end. Is this correct?

It is a huge blasphemy to say that Deity worship is a means to an end. Śrīman Mahāprabhu states:

prākṛta kariyā māne viṣṇu-kalevara,
viśṇu-nindāāra nāhi ihāra upara

One who considers the transcendental body of Lord Viṣṇu to be made of material nature is the greatest offender at the lotus feet of the Lord. There is no greater blasphemy against the Supreme Personality of Godhead. (*Śrī Caitanya-caritāmṛta* Ādi 7.115)

And:

īśvarera śrī-vigraha sac-cid-ānandākāra,
se-vigrahe kaha sattva-guṇera vikāra
śrī-vigraha ye nā māne, sei ta' pāṣaṇḍī,
adṛśya aspṛśya, sei haya yama-daṇḍī

The transcendental form of the Supreme Personality of Godhead is complete in eternity, cognizance, and bliss. However, you describe this transcendental form as a product of material goodness. One who does not accept the transcendental form of the Lord is certainly an agnostic. Such a person should be neither seen nor touched. Indeed, he is subject to be punished by Yamarāja. (*Śrī Caitanya-caritāmṛta* Madhya 6.166-67)

Lord Viṣṇu's Deity form is fully spiritual. He is not a manmade God like the ordinary demigods. *Śrī Caitanya-caritāmṛta* states, 'nāma', 'vigraha', 'svarūpa'—tina eka-rūpa, tine 'bheda' nāhi,—tina 'cid-ānanda-rūpa: "The Lord's holy name, His form, and His personality are all one and the same. There is no difference between them. Since all of them are absolute, they are all transcendentally blissful." (*Śrī Caitanya-caritāmṛta* Madhya 17.131) Kṛṣṇa's Deity form is directly Kṛṣṇa. The Deity is an incarnation of the Supreme Lord. The worshipable Lord of our heart mercifully manifests Himself externally in the form of a Deity.

5. What two representatives of the Supreme Lord exist in this world?

There are two representatives of the Supreme Lord in this world, the transcendental sound vibration of the Lord's holy name and the Lord's Deity, who enjoys eternal spiritual pastimes. We cannot see with our eyes; smell with our nose, taste with our tongue, or touch with our body that object that is at present far from us, just as we cannot touch London with any of our senses from this place. None of the above four senses can touch an object situated at such a distance. All we can do is use our sense of hearing to gather knowledge about that object. We can learn about London even while sitting here by hearing about it, perhaps over the telephone. Reading is considered an extension of hearing because printed words are simply visualized sounds.

The scripture is revealed transcendental sound that has been visualized in the form of writing. We can hear the transcendental sound vibrations through writings, vibrations that were made by *sādhus* thousands of years ago. Therefore the *śāstra*, the work of saintly persons, is the Deity form of transcendental sound vibration.

Mundane sound does not work in the same way. With mundane sound, there is a difference between the name of an object and the object itself. For example, the sound "London" is different from the place London. The sound "water" is different from the substance that is water. In the spiritual world there is no difference between an objects name and the object iself. In Vaikuṇṭha, the sound and the object are synonymous. A name is nondifferent from the person who is called by that name.

The Lord's holy names are not products of matter but have incarnated from Vaikuṇṭha. Maya has no jurisdiction over the transcendental sound vibrations that have descended into this world. Such transcendental sound is directly the Supreme Brahman, who is full of spiritual variegatedness. Therefore those who constantly hear transcendental sound are constantly in touch with the Supreme Brahman.

Just as a person who lives at a distance from an object gathers information about that object with the help of transcendental sound, and upon meeting the object offers prayers, praise, and adoration, thereby attaining proper realization of the object, similarly in the spiritual sense, it is vital to hear transcendental sound vibration if one wishes to understand the Supreme Object. This is true both for the sādhaka and the siddha. Jagad-guru Śrī Caitanyadeva, crest jewel among *ācāryas* , glorified the process of hearing transcendental sound and taught us to engage in the congregational chanting of the Lord's holy name as both our *sādhana* and our *śādhya*.

Chanting becomes useless when the Supreme Lord is not the beneficiary of the chanting but we use it to fulfill some temporary self-interest. If a servant calls the master to eat, or the master's wife and children call him to give him pleasure, would we consider such calling in vain? Rather, to refrain from calling is useless. Devotees chant Kṛṣṇa's holy name simply to give Him pleasure, to serve Him, and not to fulfill their own sense gratification.

We do not care about those who consider the Deity an idol. The Lord's Deity form is His merciful incarnation, who enjoys eternal pastimes in Vaikuṇṭha as well as in the material world. The Deity is a direct manifestation of the Lord's personal form and as such is nondifferent from the Supreme Personality of Godhead. The Deity is supremely worshipable. Lord Caitanya said about the Deity that He was not an idol but directly the son of Nanda Mahārāja.

Vaiṣṇavas are not idol worshipers who simply imagine that the Lord has a material form. Nor do they deny that the Lord has any form at all. Such thoughts are for those endowed with material conceptions. To them, any form reflected in the heart must be an idol. Impersonalists worship matter as the Supreme Lord and they are therefore idol worshipers under the shelter of imaginary formlessness.

We see the Lord's spiritual form as sat-cid-ānanda and not as lumps of matter. Thus we worship Him with the proper recitation of mantras and devotion-filled hearts. It is only possible to communicate with the Lord when we are living our spiritual propensity. Only those whose intelligence and current of thoughts have been materially influenced, who have no information about spiritual propensities, consider the Deity an idol. The Lord's Deity form is worshiped by chanting His holy name. Spirit is served only by spirit.

6. Is seeing the Lord's Deity the same as seeing the Lord Himself?

There is no difference between the Lord and His body. To award me the opportunity to serve Him the Lord of my heart has appeared in this world. As long as one thinks the Deity nothing but an idol or piece of stone, one cannot understand the Lord's transcendental nature. If one does not see the Deity as directly the Lord Himself, then what is the question of one's finding fortune? Śrī Caitanyadeva saw Śrī Jagannāthadeva as Śyāmasundara, player of the flute. He saw Him as neither an idol nor a concocted image, but as the Supreme Personality of Godhead.

7. Are all devotees qualified to offer food to the Lord in the temple?

An initiated kaniṣṭha-adhikārī, under his spiritual master's guidance, offers food to the Deity while chanting the proper mantras. Liberated souls also offer food to the Lord, but they offer with love and devotion. A madhyama-adhikārī, instead of offering food directly to the Deity sometimes offers it to the worshipable Lord in his heart. Then he takes the Lord's remnants. A mahābhāgavata thinks, "Whatever I have received has been sent by the Lord as His remnants." Such a soul sees the Lord's presence in each and every object. After hearing this, no one should think that mahābhāgavatas never offer food to the Lord in the temple. Śrī Rāghava Paṇḍita, Śrī Gaurīdāsa Paṇḍita, Śrī Raghunandana Ṭhākura, Śrī Mādhavendra Purī, and many other exalted devotees have fed the Lord in the temple by offering Him food with love.

The Deity of the Lord does not speak with me because I am full of *anarthas*. But He certainly speaks with His devotees and eats the food they offer Him.

Krishna's Servant

1. How will our pride in being doers be destroyed?

Become lower than the straw in the street. Think yourself the Supreme Lord's servant. Then your prideful thinking that you are the doer will go away. In such a state of mind, you can chant the holy name of Hari happily.

2. How can one attain Kṛṣṇa's service?

Until one is liberated one is not qualified to serve Kṛṣṇa. One who gives everything to Kṛṣṇa is a liberated soul. Conditioned life means to be miserly; you do not want to give Kṛṣṇa everything. The liberated souls serve Kṛṣṇa with everything they possess. All their endeavors are meant to please Kṛṣṇa.

Without the spiritual master's mercy one cannot give everything to Kṛṣṇa. That is, one cannot becomes liberated. Lord Kṛṣṇa is the spiritual master's possession. Without guru's grace no one can achieve Kṛṣṇa or become qualified to serve Him.

We have to serve Kṛṣṇa through the spiritual master. Then only will we attain Kṛṣṇa's service. Service to Kṛṣṇa is impossible if subordination and service to the spiritual master is absent.

3. Are there no duties for the living entities other than serving Kṛṣṇa?

The living entities are Kṛṣṇa's eternal servants. They have no duty other than to render Him service. But this truth is manifest only in the hearts of those who have unshakable faith in the Supreme Personality of

Godhead and the spiritual master. The day we realize that the spiritual master, who personifies service, is nondifferent from Śrī Caitanyadeva, that is the day we will attain Śrī Gaurasundara's service; on that day we will attain the good fortune of being allowed the confidential service of ŚrīŚrī Rādhā-Govinda. When we understand that the spiritual master is Śrī Kṛṣṇa Caitanyadeva's intimate associate, then Śrī Rādhā-Govinda's pastimes will manifest in our pure, uncontaminated heart.

4. Who does Lord Kṛṣṇa attract?

Kṛṣṇa attracts the three worlds. The Absolute Truth is all-attractive. But magnets attract iron, not wood, and the worshipable Lord attracts His servants and those inclined toward His service by the sweetness of His service and not others. If at some point those inclined to service become attracted to something other than Kṛṣṇa, they fall away from the main attraction. On the one side there is attraction to material existence, the source of material bondage, and on the other side, attraction to all-auspicious Kṛṣṇa. The objects of material attraction—form, taste, smell, touch, and sound—are near to us. Because we are so weak, it is easy for us to become attracted by them. Realizing our danger, we should constantly hear *hari-kathā* from guru and the Vaiṣṇavas. Only that will relieve us of our enemies. If we are not attracted to Kṛṣṇa's lotus feet, we will become attracted to Maya. If we can become attracted to Kṛṣṇa's name, form, pastimes, and qualities, we will find respite from the present trouble caused by our enjoying spirit. The more we discuss Kṛṣṇa, the more our pride as enjoyers is destroyed and the more Kṛṣṇa will attract us.

5. Who is the director of the living entities?

Lord Viṣṇu alone directs and controls all living entities. The Supreme Lord awards the fruits of our karma according to what we deserve. The living entities develop particular propensities according to their previous karma. These propensities become effective when inspired by the Supreme Lord. Therefore the Supreme Lord is the cause and the living entities are the effect; the Supreme Lord is the controller and the living entities are the controlled. Whatever karmic reactions the living entities are enjoying in the present, and whatever reactions they will enjoy in the future, the Supreme Lord is responsible as the director and bestowal of those reactions. But the Lord directs the various types of living entities differently. He personally directs the surrendered devotees, whereas He allows His illusory energy Maya to direct the godless living entities on His behalf.

6. Is the performance of varṇāśrama-dharma one of the soul's constitutional duties?

The sages have instructed us to become fixed in the practice of *varṇāśrama*-dharma. It is certainly important to follow *varṇāśrama*-dharma, but Śrī Gaurāṅgadeva questioned its necessity. Varṇāśrama-dharma is not our eternal dharma. It is not the constitutional propensity of the soul and therefore not our constitutional duty. Rather, it speaks to certain material propensities that lead toward self-realization even while we remain in the conditioned state. Varṇāśrama-dharma is based on trying to worship Lord Viṣṇu from a particular position. It is not unmotivated, uninterrupted, pure devotional service to Kṛṣṇa. Service to Kṛṣṇa is not rendered from the platform of *varṇāśrama*. Varṇāśrama only admits a little Viṣṇu worship. Therefore Śrī Caitanya Mahāprabhu said that we should first ascertain who we are. To decide that we are brāhmaṇas, kṣatriyas, vaiśyas, or śūdras, sannyāsīs, gṛhastas, vānaprasthas, or *brahmacārīs* is all right, but these are temporary designations of conditioned living entities. They are not our eternal constitutional position. We are eternal servants of Kṛṣṇa. A spirit soul is a servant of the Supersoul. Serving the Supersoul is a living entity's duty.

7. How should we think of ourselves?

Although I am Kṛṣṇa's servant, at present I am not completely eligible to remain in His service. At present I am unable to attain His association, unable to understand *hari-kathā*. Therefore my first duty is to try my best to understand that I am Kṛṣṇa's eternal servant. Unless I associate with *sādhus* and take shelter at Kṛṣṇa's lotus feet, I will not be able to understand who I am—I will certainly not attain self-realization by my own endeavor.

8. Are the designations expressed in varṇāśrama-dharma eternal?

Every living entity considers his body the self, but the living entities should learn to think as follows: "I am the Lord's eternal servant and it is my eternal constitutional duty to serve Him. I belong neither to the four varṇas nor the four āśramas." If this is true, how can *varṇāśrama* dharma be an eternal dharma? By properly following the practices of *varṇāśrama* dharma, one receives an immense advantage both in this life and the next. One can follow the *varṇāśrama* system as long as one has a material body. It is appropriate when one is trying to make material advancement. It is good to follow this system as long as one wanders throughout the fourteen worlds. But it has no use in the spiritual world. Śrī Caitanya Mahāprabhu states:

nāhaṁ vipro na ca nara-patir nāpi vaiśyo na śūdro
nāhaṁ varṇī na ca gṛha-patir no vanastho yatir vā

kintu prodyan nikhila-paramānanda-pūrṇāmṛtābdher
gopī-bhartu pada-kamalayor dāsa-dāsānudāsaḥ

I am not a brāhmaṇa, kṣatriya, vaiśya, or śūdra. I am not a brahmacārī, gṛhastha, vānaprastha, or sannyāsī. What am I? I am the eternal servant of the servant of the servant of Lord Krishna" (*Padyāvalī* 63)

The Supreme Lord is cognizant, as are the living entities, because they are part and parcel of the Supreme Lord and share His qualities. But the living entities are not super-cognizant; they are only minutely cognizant. Therefore the living entities are subordinate to the Supreme Lord. Because they have misused their independence, the living entities have been degraded. As soon as they fall down from the Lord's service, they begin to suffer material miseries. Once they again engage in His service, they attain auspiciousness.

9. Who are the harijanas?

The word harijana is currently being misused. Harijana actually refers to the transcendental devotees who have attained self-realization. Those who are unalloyed servants of Hari, having taken shelter of a bona fide spiritual master, are harijanas. It does not matter whether they were born in one family or another; they are harijanas as long as they have no other ambition than to serve Hari.

It is both improper and unauthorized to call nondevotees who have not attained self-realization harijanas. Although everyone by nature is an eternal harijana, as long as they are materially conditioned they cannot bear the name harijana. We will not hesitate to call them harijanas if they begin to engage in Hari's service and attain self-realization. Paddy is nothing but rice, yet it cannot be used in place of rice. When the paddy's husks are removed, then we call the paddy rice. Similarly, although all living entities are servants of Hari, only when they engage in Hari's service do we call them harijanas.

10. What is the duty of all living entities?

Kṛṣṇa, the son of Nanda Mahārāja, is the supreme enjoyer and the eternal object of everyone's service. The jīvas' eternal constitutional duty is to serve Him. Forgetting that service, the living entities sometimes become impersonalists and consider themselves God. At other times, they become busy following the *varṇāśrama* principles in the guise of material enjoyers. Sometimes they care only to please their wives. Therefore I say, O living entities! Give up your false pride, self-adoration, and subordination to your wives. Please serve the Supreme Lord under the direction of Śrīmatī Rādhārāṇī and Śrī Rūpa-mañjarī. Please constantly engage in Kṛṣṇa's service under the guidance of the gopīs of Vraja.

11. What is the science of living entities?

The word jīva means "living entity" or "one who has life." The Supreme Lord has three principal energies, the internal energy, the external energy, and the marginal energy. The jīvas belong to the Lord's marginal energy. The jīvas are factual, not false like flowers in the sky. The jīvas are unborn. They are not created but are eternally present. Even though the living entities are conscious, they have only a minute amount of consciousness. The Supreme Lord is super-conscious. Therefore there is a gulf of difference between the jīvas and the Supreme Lord. Śrī Mahāprabhu explains that the Lord and the jīvas are different in that the Lord controls Maya while the jīvas are controlled by Maya.

The Lord is the Supreme Personality of Godhead, the Absolute Truth, whereas the jīvas are insignificant parts of the Lord. The Lord controls Maya whereas the jīvas live under Maya's control. The living entities are by nature Kṛṣṇa's eternal servants, and Kṛṣṇa is their eternal master, controller, protector, and object of service.

It is the eternal function of the jīvas to serve Kṛṣṇa. *Śrī Caitanya-caritāmṛta* states:

jīvera 'svarūpa' haya——kṛṣṇera 'nitya-dāsa'
kṛṣṇera 'taṭasthā-śakti' 'bhedābheda-prakāśa'

It is the living entity's constitutional position to be an eternal servant of Kṛṣṇa, because he is the marginal energy of Kṛṣṇa, and a manifestation of simultaneously one with and different from the Lord. (*Madhya* 20.108)

kṛṣṇa bhuli' sei jīva anādi-bahirmukha
ataeva māyā tāre deya saṁsāra-duḥkha

Forgetting Kṛṣṇa, the living entity has been attracted by the external feature from time immemorial. Therefore, the illusory energy [Maya] gives him all kinds of misery in his material existence. (*Madhya* 20.117)

sādhu-śāstra-kṛpāya yadi kṛṣṇonmukha haya
sei jīva nistare, māyā tāhāre chāḍaya

If the conditioned soul becomes Kṛṣṇa conscious by the mercy of saintly persons, who voluntarily preach scriptural injunctions and

help him to become Krishna conscious, the conditioned soul is liberated from the clutches of Maya, who gives him up. (*Madhya* 20.120, 122)

tāte kṛṣṇa bhaje, kare gurura sevana
māyā-jāla chuṭe, pāya kṛṣṇera caraṇa

In the Kṛishna conscious state, the living entity engages in devotional service under the direction of the spiritual master. In this way he gets out of the clutches of Maya and takes shelter under the lotus feet of Lord Krishna. (Madhya 22.25).

We are spirit souls, not these bodies and minds. The spirit soul is the body's proprietor. When an embodied soul gives up his body, the body remains behind. The jīva is fully spiritual. The mind is the reflection of spirit, and the body a product of dead matter. The mind is part of the subtle body; it is the reflection of animation meddling with the world. The mind is not synonymous with the spirit soul. The mind always wanders about in the external world and can both accept or reject the gross objects in this world as well as provide information about the Absolute Truth. It can tell us that we are spirit, and that we are neither body or mind. We are separate from the body, just as a house and its proprietor are two separate items. The jīva is the proprietor of his or her gross and subtle bodies. It is only out of ignorance that the jīvas consider their body to be the self. Śrī Mahāprabhu states:

jīvera svabhāva kṛṣṇa-'dāsa' abhimāna
dehe ātma-jñāne ācchādita sei 'jñāna'

The original nature of every living entity is to consider himself the eternal servant of Kṛṣṇa. But under the influence of Maya he thinks himself to be the body, and thus his original consciousness is covered. (*Śrī Caitanya-caritāmṛta* Madhya 24.201)

vastuta pariṇāma-vāda sei se pramāṇa
dehe ātma-buddhi ei vivartera sthāna

Transformation of energy is a proven fact. It is the false bodily conception of the self that is an illusion. (*Śrī Caitanya-caritāmṛta* Ādi 7.123)

The living entity is eternal, not temporary like the gross and subtle bodies. The jīvas' miserable condition is due to their forgetfulness of Kṛṣṇa. Kṛṣṇa consciousness is the healthy condition for jīvas. To consider themselves Kṛṣṇa's eternal servants is their constitutional position. Considering themselves enjoyers, the jīvas are diseased. Turning toward Kṛṣṇa is the only effective medicine. To help the godless living entities turn toward Kṛṣṇa is real compassion and is the highest type of welfare work. Kṛṣṇa's living entities are suffering because they have forgotten Him. If the *sādhus* can influence them to dovetail all their activities with Kṛṣṇa's service, they will become eternally happy.

12. Is it possible to make someone a Vaiṣṇava?

It is not possible to either become a Vaiṣṇava or make someone else a Vaiṣṇava. Everyone in this world is already by nature a Vaiṣṇava. In other words, everyone is Lord Viṣṇu's servant. One can understand this fact when one associates with devotees.

13. Who are the devotees?

The Vedas say that one who is situated in his constitutional position is a devotee. It is the living entity's nature to serve Lord Kṛṣṇa, so a person engaged in Kṛṣṇa's service is a devotee. Devotees of Kṛṣṇa are certainly saintly, because devotional service qualifies them as such. Those who have no devotion for Kṛṣṇa cannot be called *sādhus*. Nondevotees are not saintly. *Śrī Caitanya-caritāmṛta* states:

asat-saṅga-tyāga ei vaiṣṇava-ācāra
'strī-saṅgī eka asādhu, 'kṛṣṇābhakta' āra

A Vaiṣṇava should always avoid the association of ordinary people. Common people are very much materially attached, especially to women. Vaiṣṇavas should also avoid the company of those who are not devotees of Lord Kṛṣṇa. (*Madhya* 22.87)

kṛṣṇa-bhakta niṣkāma, ataeva 'śānta'
bhukti-mukti-siddhi-kāmī sakali 'aśānta'

Because a devotee of Lord Kṛṣṇa is desireless, he is peaceful. Fruitive workers desire material enjoyment, *jñānīs* desire liberation, and yogīs desire material opulence; therefore, they are all lusty and cannot be peaceful. (*Madhya* 19.148)

14. How can we destroy our desire for material enjoyment?

Only when we realize, by the mercy of guru and *sādhu*, that we are servants of the Supreme Lord will we attain auspiciousness. As soon as we receive transcendental knowledge our propensity to enjoy matter will be destroyed. Until we understand the principle that we are servants of the

Lord and devotees of Viṣṇu we will continue to see the material world as meant for our enjoyment. We will not be able to see this world in the mood of īśāvāsyam.

We try to lord it over material nature. The only hope we have of spiritual survival is to seek the association of a pure devotee. Those who desire their ultimate benefit should not approach preachers who are puffed up with lust, anger, greed, ego, or envy. If they do, they will never attain transcendental knowledge. Unless we associate with great personalities who are free from material desire, our own desire for material enjoyment will not be destroyed. We will not realize ourselves as the Lord's servants. The *Śrī Caitanya-caritāmṛta* states:

mahat-kṛpā vinā kona karme 'bhakti' naya
kṛṣṇa-bhakti dūre rahu, saṁsāra nahe kṣaya

Unless one is favored by a pure devotee, one cannot attain the platform of devotional service. To say nothing of *kṛṣṇa-bhakti*, one cannot even be relieved from the bondage of material existence. (*Madhya* 24.97)

sādhu-saṅga-kṛpā kimvā kṛṣṇera kṛpāya
kāmādi 'duḥsaṅga' chāḍi' śuddha-bhakti pāya

One is elevated to the platform of devotional life by the mercy of a Vaiṣṇava, the bona fide spiritual master, and by the special mercy of Kṛṣṇa. On that platform, one gives up all material desires and the association of unwanted people. Thus, one is elevated to the platform of pure devotional service. (*Madhya* 22.51)

15. What is transcendental knowledge?

That we are the object of worship, the proprietors, and the enjoyers are material concepts born of ignorance. We are meant to be entirely enjoyed by the Lord. We are His servants and He is the only enjoyer. Such realization constitutes transcendental knowledge.

17. Who is our master?

Lord Kṛṣṇa is the master of all and the only object of service. I always remember that I am Kṛṣṇa's servant. There is no question of our well-being until we are liberated from the mentality of wanting everyone to serve us. Every devotee should consider himself the most fallen and should engage in the service of other devotees in the *Maṭha*. Do not forget that service to Kṛṣṇa is our eternal duty. Service to the spiritual master and the Vaiṣṇavas is even more essential than service to Kṛṣṇa.

18. Are the Vaiṣṇavas akiñcanā?

The Vaiṣṇavas are under the Supreme Lord's shelter and are His servants. Their only pride is to be His servants. And they are akiṅcana, without material possessions, because they want nothing from this world. Nothing in this world tempts them. There is nothing in this world or the next that is more desirable than the beauty of Kṛṣṇa's toenails. Whenever we are not attracted to serving Kṛṣṇa purely, it must be understood that we are suffering from illusion and have been attacked by the many faces of Maya.

19. What is the difference between the Supreme Lord and the living entities?

The difference between the Supreme Lord and the living entities is that the Supreme Lord is the object of worship and the living entities are His worshipers. The living entities are meant to serve and the Lord is meant to accept service. The Lord is complete, perfect, and infinite, and the living entities are the most insignificant. The Supreme Lord is the supreme spirit, and the living entities are the supreme spirit's parts and parcels. The Lord controls Maya and the living entities are controlled by Maya. *Śrī Caitanya-caritāmṛta* confirms:

māyādhīśa' 'māyā-vaśa' īśvare-jīve bheda
hena-jīve īśvara-saha kaha ta' abheda

The Lord is the master of the potencies, and the living entity is the servant of them. That is the difference between the Lord and the living entity. However, you declare that the Lord and the living entities are one and the same. (*Madhya* 6.162)

20. Is the living entity the puruṣa ?

The living entity is neither male, female, nor neuter. The designations of male and female relate only to the body. The living entity is not the body but the soul, the body's owner. The soul serves the Supersoul. The living entity is not matter but cognizant spirit. Therefore the soul is qualified to see and speak with the Supersoul.

The living entities develop their spiritual bodies based on their particular moods. Those who worship Kṛṣṇa in the mellow of conjugal love develop female bodies to serve as Kṛṣṇa's lovers, whereas those who serve the Lord as servants of the Lord's friends attain male bodies. In the eternally pure spiritual body there is no difference between male and female. The maleness or femaleness of the body simply reflects a devotee's internal mood.

21. Who can actually worship Kṛṣṇa?

Until one is fixed in the conviction that, "I belong to Kṛṣṇa and Kṛṣṇa is mine," one cannot worship Kṛṣṇa. One who has unflinching devotion at Kṛṣṇa's lotus feet and who considers himself Kṛṣṇa's servant is capable of worshiping Kṛṣṇa. A devotee thinks, "Kṛṣṇa is my only self-interest. I belong to Kṛṣṇa. Apart from Him I have no interest in anything unrelated to Kṛṣṇa." One who completely surrenders to Kṛṣṇa can attain His complete mercy. Those who have other interests cannot attain Him or even understand what He is. Certainly they cannot understand what it means to love Kṛṣṇa. Such persons are simply entangled in their various obligations, such as duty to country, fellow citizens, and relatives. Because of that entanglement they become bereft of the guru's service and lose track of their real self-interest. It takes intelligence to act on one's self-interest and to serve the spiritual master and Kṛṣṇa.

22. Why do we act as doers?

Acting as the doer is a symptom of our unfortunate state. The living entities are not God, and therefore cannot become either master or enjoyer. Kṛṣṇa alone is the supreme enjoyer. We are all His eternal servants. But we try to become local leaders, heads of villages, kings of countries, and lords of the whole world, while forgetting this simple truth. Such is our misfortune!

Krishna, the Supreme Lord

1. What is the difference between Kṛṣṇa and Viśṇu?

In truth Kṛṣṇa and Viśṇu are one. Both are the Absolute Truth, complete, and full of energies. Kṛṣṇa, who is the personification of sweetness, is Viśṇu or Narayaṇa in His opulent feature. Kṛṣṇa has two arms and He plays the flute, and Viśṇu has four arms and carries a conch, disc, club, and lotus. Lord Viśṇu is full in sixty qualities and Lord Kṛṣṇa is full in sixty-four. Kṛṣṇa can attract Lakśmī, but Nārāyaṇa cannot attract the minds of the Vraja gopīs, who are Kṛṣṇa's beloved devotees. Lord Viśṇu is served in two and a half *rasas* , or namely, Śānta, dāsya, and gaurava-sakhya (friendship with awe and reverence), but Lord Kṛṣṇa is served in all five *rasas* (śānta, dāsya, viśrambha-sakhya [friendship with love], vātsalya, and *mādhurya*).

Śrī Kṛṣṇa is the Supreme Personality of Godhead. He is the original lamp from which innumerable lamps or Viśṇu-tattva forms have been ignited. Kṛṣṇa personifies sweetness and Viśṇu personifies opulence. Even though Kṛṣṇa is the Supreme Lord, He does not consider Himself as such. Rather, He considers Himself Nanda's son and the beloved of Rādhā. Viśṇu is proud of being the Supreme Controller. Kṛṣṇa is served on the rāga-mārga and Viśṇu is served on the vaidhi-mārga. Since Viśṇu's worship includes the mood of awe and reverence, the devotees always feel hesitant to approach Him, but the Vrajavāsīs serve Kṛṣṇa without hesitation.

2. Is the Supreme Lord controlled by the devotees?

Lord Govinda is controlled by His devotees. Although the devotees are energies of the Lord and are therefore normally thought of as subordinate, according to the service consideration the Lord's energies are superior to Him. If they were not superior, how could they serve the Lord? Even though the Lord is supremely independent, He becomes dependent on the service of His devotees. He states in the Ninth Canto of *Śrīmad-Bhāgavatam*:

ahaṁ bhakta-parādhīno, hy asvatantra iva dvija
sādhubhir grasta-hṛdayo, bhaktair bhakta-jana-priya

The Supreme Personality of Godhead said to the *brāhmaṇa*: I am completely under the control of My devotees. Indeed, I am not at all independent. Because My devotees are completely devoid of material desires, I sit only within the cores of their hearts. What to speak of My devotee, even those who are devotees of My devotee are very dear to Me.

Actually, one cannot properly serve the object of service unless he knows that object's value and glories. A perfect servant sometimes waits for his master's order and sometimes serves his worshipable master according to his master's internal mood. As the Lord resides in the devotee's heart, so the devotee resides in the Lord's heart. The devotee is the supersoul of the Supersoul.

3. Who is the ultimate object of worship?

Lord Kṛṣṇa is the only object of service and the master of all. He is the only friend of the jīvas, the only son of all parents, and the only lover of all women. A person who has accepted Kṛṣṇa as the object of his service does not serve anyone else. Lord Kṛṣṇa is the cause of all causes, and He is the cause of Brahman, Paramātmā, and all the Viśṇu-tattva forms.

4. Is material nature, Maya, the original cause of material creation?

The three modes of material nature Maya represents are not the primary cause of the material world. When Maya is empowered by the Lord's glance, on the strength of the Lord's energy she becomes the secondary cause of material creation, just as when iron is placed in a fire it acquires the power to burn.

But even for the indirect or secondary cause Lord Kṛṣṇa remains the ultimate cause. Nārāyaṇa is the direct cause. In the making of a pot, there is the direct cause, the potter, and the indirect cause, the wheel and a stick. Maya is the wheel and the stick. As no pots can be made without a potter, so creation cannot take place without Kṛṣṇa.

Kāraṇadaksāyī Viśṇu's glance towards Maya works in two ways. First, it injects her with unlimited living entities, each a spiritual spark, and second, it creates unlimited universes by the reflection of His touch. That His touch is a reflection means there is no direct bodily contact between Viśṇu and Maya. Therefore it should not be thought that the Supreme Lord appeared by Maya's help in each universe. Kṛṣṇa alone entered each universe as His Puruśa incarnation. Again, Kṛṣṇa is the original cause of material creation. *Śrī Caitanya-caritāmṛta* Ādi 5.60 states:

kṛṣṇa-śaktye prakṛti haya gauṇa kāraṇa
agni-śaktye lauha yaiche karaye jāraṇa

Thus prakṛti, by the energy of Lord Kṛṣṇa, becomes the secondary cause, just as iron becomes red-hot by the energy of fire.

Outside the spiritual sky is the effulgent abode of Brahman, and outside the abode of Brahman is the Causal Ocean. The spiritual abode is devoid of cause, but Maya is illusion, and in the place between the material world and the abode of Brahman is an ocean of spiritual water called the Causal Ocean. Lord Viśṇu lies in this Causal Ocean. The glance He cast on Maya, who is situated outside the Causal Ocean, agitates her to create. Maya herself cannot touch the Causal Ocean.

5. Whom does the Supreme Lord attract?

Kṛṣṇa, the son of Nanda Mahārāja, is the Supreme Personality of Godhead. This Kṛṣṇa attracts the three worlds. The spiritual master, who is dear to Kṛṣṇa, represents Kṛṣṇa's power of attraction. The Absolute Truth is all-attractive. Whom does He attract? As a magnet attracts iron and not wood, so the worshipable Lord attracts those inclined to serve Him. Through His inconceivable potency the Lord attracts both His own servants and those inclined to become His servants by His affection, mercy, and sweetness.

But if those who are attracted become absorbed in some irrelevant object on the way to their Lord, they fall down from their original attraction. The living entities therefore face two types of attraction, the bondage or artificial attraction of material existence, and attraction to Kṛṣṇa. Sense objects that have form, taste, sound, and touch are always nearby. Because we are weak, we are attracted to them. Therefore we should absorb ourselves in hearing *hari-kathā* from living sources, powerful devotees. If we continue to hear such kathā from guru and *sādhu*, we will be protected from the enemies that drag our senses away. Until we are fully attracted to Kṛṣṇa, Maya will always attract us.

6. What is the difference between God, Allah, and Kṛṣṇa?

The word "God" speaks of a limited idea. We find the perfect and highest conception of theism only in "Kṛṣṇa.""Allah" means "the greatest" and suggests that God possesses a particular quality. It is an objective. But Krishna is the source of all power. He is the proper noun.

7. How does the Absolute Truth manifest?

The Absolute Truth manifests in five ways: as parā tattva, vyūha, vaibhava, antaryāmī, and arcā. Each of these is the worshipable Lord. Apart from these manifestations, everything and everyone else is in the servant category. The Lord accepts offerings from His servants, and each of these five manifestations of the Lord reciprocates with His own servants. There is no meaning to being dominant if there is no servant to dominate. Therefore each manifestation of the Absolute Truth has His own servants.

When one begins Deity worship, one uses particular ingredients. Then one worships the Supersoul in the mind. Then, one worships the Lord's vaibhava incarnations. For example, one may worship Lord Rāma. Śrī Rāma appeared with His servants, especially Hanumān and Sugriva. One should worship the vaibhava incarnations only as They appear before Their servants. After worshiping the vaibhava manifestation, one worships the vyūhas. There are four vyūhas, namely Vāsudeva, Saṅkarśaṇa, Pradyumna, and Aniruddha. Ultimately one comes to the worship of the parā-tattva, Kṛṣṇa. To climb from the bottom of a hill to the top, we must go uphill step by step. In our journey toward parā-tattva Kṛṣṇa, we will find that worshiping the arcā will help us. Therefore *śāstra* states:

yena janma-śataiḥ pūrvaṁ,vāsudevaḥ samārcita
tan-mukhe hari-nāmāni, sadā tiśṭhanti bhārata

O descendant of Bharata, the holy names of Lord Viśṇu are always vibrating in the mouth of one who has previously worshiped Vāsudeva perfectly for hundreds of lifetimes.

Immanent, pure, unalloyed conscience is called antaryāmī or *caitya-guru*, the Supersoul. The antaryāmī is an internal entity. Because we have forgotten Kṛṣṇa, we have come to this material world, far from our eternal home. We are meant to return. The first aid on our journey is Deity worship, then awareness of and focus on the antaryāmī, then worship of the vaibhava incarnations, then worship of the vyūha forms, and finally, full consciousness of the parā-tattva.

Even after worshiping the Supreme Lord for many births a materialist cannot make the kind of advancement made by those who associate directly with guru and the Vaiśṇavas, hearing *hari-kathā* from them. The fortune we receive by faithfully hearing about Kṛṣṇa from the most merciful spiritual master and the Vaiśṇavas cannot be achieved even if the Deity form mercifully reveals Himself to us.

The Supersoul does not always speak to us directly. *Śāstra* states:

śikṣā-guruke ta' jāni kṛṣṇera svarūpa,
antaryāmī, bhakta-śreṣṭha ei dui rūpa

One should know the instructing spiritual master to be the Personality of Kṛṣṇa. Lord Kṛṣṇa manifests Himself as the Supersoul and as the greatest devotee of the Lord. (*Śrī Caitanya-caritāmṛta* Ādi 1.47)

jīve sākśāt nāhi tāte guru caitya-rūpe,
śikśā-guru haya kṛṣṇa-mahānta-svarūpe

Since one cannot visually experience the presence of the Supersoul, He appears before us as a liberated devotee. Such a spiritual master is none other than Kṛṣṇa Himself. (*Śrī Caitanya-caritāmṛta* Ādi 1.58)

antaryāmīīśvarera ei rīti haye,
bāhire nā kahe, vastu prakāśe hṛdaye

The Supersoul within everyone's heart speaks not externally but from within. He instructs the devotees in all respects, and that is His way of instruction. (*Śrī Caitanya-caritāmṛta* Madhya 6.83)

The vaibhava incarnations like Śrī Rāma speak with, instruct, and guide the jīvas, ascertaining what is for their benefit and what is not. The vyūhas' activities are of a different nature.

The supreme Absolute Truth, parā-tattva, manifests in four ways, but one can only understand this science by the Lord's mercy. *Śāstra* states:

īśvarera kṛpā-leśa haya ta' yāhāre
sei ta' īśvara-tattva jānibāre pare

If one receives but a tiny bit of the Lord's favor by dint of devotional service, he can understand the nature of the Supreme Personality of Godhead. (*Śrī Caitanya-caritāmṛta* Madhya 6.83)

We think that the Lord's Deity is inanimate; but He is not a product of matter. He is sat-cit-ānanda. Śrī Gaurāṅgadeva said:

īśvarera śrī-vigraha sac-cid-ānandākāra,
se-vigrahe kaha sattva-guṇera vikāra

The transcendental form of the Supreme Personality of Godhead is complete in eternity, cognizance, and bliss. However, you describe this transcendental form as a product of material goodness. (*Śrī Caitanya-caritāmṛta* Madhya 6.166)

śrī-vigraha ye nā māne, sei ta' pāśaṇḍī,
adāśya aspāśya, sei haya yama-daṇḍī

One who does not accept the transcendental form of the Lord is certainly an agnostic. Such a person should be neither seen nor touched. Indeed, he is subject to be punished by Yamarāja. (*Śrī Caitanya-caritāmṛta* Madhya 6.167)

Elsewhere in *Śāstra* it is stated:

pratimā naha tumi sākśāt vrajendra-nandana
vipra lāgi' kara tumi akārya-karaṇa

My dear Lord, You are not a statue; You are directly the son of Mahārāja Nanda. Now, for the sake of the old *brāhmaṇa*, You can do something You have never done before. (*Śrī Caitanya-caritāmṛta* Madhya 5.96)

The spiritual master helps us as the intermediary so that there will be a guide between the Deity, the worship, and the worshiper. Otherwise, if the worshiper is not self-realized or if he lacks knowledge of the Deity form, his worship will turn into the idol worship of children. We do not need idol worship; we have a great need to worship the Lord.

The Deity is defined as that form that is offered worship. The Deity is nondifferent from the Lord. For our benefit the Supreme Lord manifests in the Deity. Ordinary people think the Deity only an idol because He cannot walk and cannot take initiative. This is their illusion. If they learn to associate with pure devotees, their illusion can be removed.

Cultivation of the Absolute Truth depends heavily on hearing and chanting. That is why the *śāstra* states:

brahmāṇḍa bhramite kona bhāgyavān jīva,
guru-kṛṣṇa-prasāde pāya bhakti-latā-bīja
mālī hañā kare sei bīja āropaṇa,
śravaṇa-kīrtana-jale karaye secana

Out of many millions of wandering living entities, one who is very fortunate gets an opportunity to associate with a bona fide spiritual master by the grace of Kṛṣṇa. By the mercy of both Kṛṣṇa and the spiritual master, such a person receives the seed of the creeper of devotional service.

When a person receives the seed of devotional service, he should take care of it by becoming a gardener and sowing the seed in his heart. If he waters the seed gradually by the process of śravaṇa and kīrtana [hearing and chanting], the seed will begin to sprout. (*Śrī Caitanya-caritāmṛta* Madhya 19.151-152)

It used to be that when the spiritual master glorified Kṛṣṇa everyone listened. Nowadays it is just the opposite. Professional reciters sit on their guru's āsanas to glorify Kṛṣṇa without ever having become disciples. A real disciple should first learn what understanding his spiritual has and how he worships Kṛṣṇa. It is stated:

oṁ ajñāna-timirāndhasya, jñānāñjana-śalākayā
cakśur unmīlitaṁ yenam tasmai śrī-gurave namaḥ

I was born in the darkest ignorance, and my spiritual master opened my eyes with the torch of knowledge. I offer my respectful obeisances unto him.

When the cataract of our material eyes is removed, we are free from foreign conception. Don't think that pretense when approaching a spiritual master will give you perfection. It would be foolish to think that you have gained a coconut just because you are standing under a coconut tree. You have to climb the tree, pick the coconut from the treetop, and break its shell. Then only can you take advantage of the coconut and drink its water.

You should also not think that performing *bhajana* under the guidance of guru and the Vaiśṇavas and practicing mystic yoga are synonymous. If devotion is absent from a process, it is useless. If we simply live comfortably while studying Vedānta and logic, we will not make advancement. Even if we become geniuses in logic and Vedānta, we will not go to Vaikuṇṭha. The only path to spiritual fortune is to perform hari-*bhajana* while in the shelter of a bona fide guru's lotus feet.

8. How can we attain Kṛṣṇa's service?

Śrī Kṛṣṇacandra, Lord of Vṛndāvana, is the eternal son of Nanda and Yaśodā, who are eternally perfect residents of Vraja. He is no one else's son. Nanda and Yaśodā rendered unlimited amounts of service, and therefore they were given the gift of having the Supreme Personality of Godhead as their son. This Śyāmasundara, who is Yaśodās son, is our worshipable Lord. In the *śloka* beginning ārādhya bhagavān vrajeśa tanaya, Devakīs son has not been described as the worshipable Lord but the son of Yaśodā. Vasudeva and Devakī were not as qualified as Nanda and Yaśodā in terms of their service.

Worship of Nandanandana is the highest of all. Better than that, however, is the worship of Nanda, who by his service pleases Kṛṣṇa so much. If we receive Nanda's mercy, we will certainly receive the blessings to serve his beloved son.

Nandanandana lives in Vṛndāvana, and He lives in the pure soul's heart, which is compared to Vṛndāvana. Unless our heart is completely purified by serving the guru, Nanda, we will not be able to find the Lord in our heart.

The residents of Vraja want Kṛṣṇa simply so they can serve Him. They are extremely anxious to see Him. Their happiness lies only in making Kṛṣṇa happy. They do not trade favors with Kṛṣṇa but are selfless and devoid of the desire for personal happiness. They have natural attraction for Him. If we can follow in their footsteps, we will attain the good fortune of attaining Kṛṣṇa's service.

9. Are the scriptures nondifferent from the Lord?

Śāstra is directly Kṛṣṇa. It is His incarnation. Lord Kṛṣṇa has personally manifest in this world in the form of *śāstra* to provide us with something we need. Gaurāṅgadeva said:

śāstra-guru-ātma'-rūpe āpanāre jānāna
kṛṣṇa mora prabhu, trātā jīvera haya jñāna

The forgetful conditioned soul is educated by Kṛṣṇa through the Vedic literatures, the realized spiritual master, and the Supersoul. Through these, he can understand the Supreme Personality of Godhead as He is, and he can understand that Lord Kṛṣṇa is his eternal master and deliverer from the clutches of Maya. In this way, one can acquire real knowledge of his conditioned life and can come to understand how to attain liberation. (*Śrī Caitanya-caritāmṛta* Madhya 20.123)

If we try to study *śāstra* while in lost in mental speculation, we will be cheated. *Śāstra* reveals its treasures only to surrendered souls. If we have the same unalloyed devotion for the spiritual master as we have for Supreme Lord, the purports of all the scriptures will reveal themselves to us automatically. People proud of their knowledge cannot understand the true purport of *śāstra*. If we hear from the *sādhus* while surrendering body, mind, and speech, only then will we be able to realize the confidential purport of the *śāstras*.

10. What is God?

The Lord is sat-cit–ānanda, full of eternity, knowledge, and bliss. He is not formless, even though He does not have a material body like ours. There is no difference between His body and His self, His name, form, or qualities.

The Supreme Lord is fully independent and infinite. He does not require help from any living being. He may descend into any situation He pleases and is not dependent on anyone's help. He is impartial and self-manifest. His eyes, ears, and other senses are not material but are fully transcendental.

11. Is the Supreme Lord inconceivable?

Lord Kṛṣṇa is indeed inconceivable; He is not only inconceivable but conceivable for the service-inclined hearts. He is simultaneously the reservoir of all transcendental qualities and devoid of qualities. All qualities are found in Him. He is the source of the universe. This world is not His form, but He is present in every universe.

Anything that is perceived through the material senses is an object of sense gratification. The Supreme Lord is not the universe but the basis of the universe, and therefore we are not perceiving Him when we perceive the universe. Unless I give up my false ego, I cannot approach Him. Lord Hari is the Supreme Brahman, the Personality of Godhead. He is not limited by anything. It is impossible to measure or enjoy Him.

12. Why do some people consider the Supreme Lord formless?

This is their mistake. The Absolute Truth is not impersonal but full of spiritual variegatedness. He possesses transcendental forms, qualities, and pastimes. He has the ability to take initiative. He is fully independent. He is the Supreme Personality of Godhead and the director of His three principal energies.

Kṛṣṇa has the ability to know, feel, and will, just as we have those capabilities, but His ability is complete. As soon as we forget that Kṛṣṇa is the fountainhead of everything, we are attacked by His illusory energy. It is Maya who forces us to commit mistakes, become illusioned, and lose our power of discrimination.

The Absolute Truth manifests in the state of pure goodness. The heart of one favored by Kṛṣṇa becomes completely purified by His mercy. Whatever realization takes place in such a heart is true realization, the realization of eternity, knowledge, and bliss.

13. Who is God?

God is the transcendental Absolute Truth. The word "transcendental" means that object which is beyond the reach of sense perception. Godhead is He who has reserved the absolute right of not being exposed to our human senses. God is He who never comes under the control of the living entity's material senses. He alone reserves this right.

14. What is the transcendental object?

The transcendental object is that which is beyond the reach of our material senses, or that which cannot be measured by our material senses. Adhokśaja means "that which is beyond sense perception, transcendental." The transcendental object becomes the subject of our realization only when He appears to our service-inclined senses by His own sweet will. Otherwise, the science of Kṛṣṇa cannot be understood even partially by the best *sādhana* methods, studies, use of intelligence, or worldly ability to discriminate. Yet many people dare to discuss the science of the Absolute Truth by considering the scripture an ordinary literature or the philosophy mundane. The transcendental Absolute Truth never reveals Himself to such people. Transcendental subject matter belongs to the fourth dimension. Therefore being unable to realize Him, we try to compromise by calling Him impersonal. But the fully transcendental Absolute Truth is never impersonal.

The Absolute Truth is supremely independent. He has not been invented by the limited conceptions of jīvas. Anything invented or imagined is an idol. All such objects created by the power of discrimination and imagined to be either personal or impersonal are idols. The transcendental Absolute Truth, the Supreme Brahman, Kṛṣṇa, is not impersonal, not personal, not possessing form, and not formless like an idol. He is of the fourth dimension—beyond the reach of our senses.

Do not try to approach the Absolute Truth in a challenging mood. That is the path of argumentation. Better to approach Him with utmost humility. Kṛṣṇa Himself will take the initiative. We can make thousands of exertions and never find Him.

15. What is the ultimate object of worship?

Śrī Rādhā and Kṛṣṇa are the ultimate object of worship. The Vedic literature declares that Śrī Rādhā is the wife of the immortal. This immortal supreme being is Śrī Kṛṣṇa, who is the reservoir of all transcendental pleasure. Śrī Rādhā is His beloved. The Atharva-veda states: rādhe viśākhe saha bhānu rādhā: "Rādhā, the daughter of Vṛśabhānu, along with Viśākhā, worships the Lord." The service Vṛśabhānu's daughter offers to Kṛṣṇa is unique. She alone is capable of giving Kṛṣṇa complete happiness.

16. What is the complete whole?

The Supreme Lord is the complete whole. It is essential for everyone to strive toward meeting that complete whole. If we spend our lives trying to attain incomplete objects we will certainly attain them and nothing else.

Preaching

1. Should we live exemplary lives?

We should always be careful that other people do not get the wrong impression of our ideal character. Neophytes experience danger at every step because they are not introspective. They draw conclusions based only on external appearances.

2. What is the duty of the devotees?

It is the devotees' duty to destroy the conditioned soul's sinful propensities. A devotee stands with the chopper of sharp instruction in his hand before the wooden framework used for sacrificing animals. Then he kills the conditioned souls' material animal-like desires. The devotees flatter no one. If a devotee flatters me, he is my enemy.

The Vaiṣṇavas do not associate with nondevotees, but to benefit them, they destroy the nondevotees' sinful propensities with the weapon of their instructions and thus award them the opportunity to associate with devotees. If we sincerely take shelter at our guru's lotus feet, we will see the Supreme Lord in one lifetime.

3. Who is the most beneficial friend?

There are no real friends or well-wishers in this world except those who attract the living entities to chant Kṛṣṇa's holy names. The charity given by millions of magnanimous donors is insignificant compared to the magnanimous nature of the preachers of the holy names.

4. How should we preach to ordinary people?

Human beings carry a variety of diseases and each needs to be treated individually. Unless the disease is properly diagnosed, proper treatment cannot be administered and the ailment will not be cured. A platform speaker cannot do much for most sick people. He can give only token relief. I have not found anyone sincerely interested in Kṛṣṇa consciousness for forty years. Now whomever comes to me is not interested in hearing *hari-kathā*. They are not ready to give up their dependence on their own education and intelligence. In this world people like to become popular; they do not like to inquire about the Absolute Truth. Those who claim to be religious preachers are busy trying to protect their own existence by flattering others. By speaking and hearing the truth, one's popularity is unlikely to be enhanced. Therefore, we are not interested in the sympathy or support of ordinary people who are averse to the Lord.

5. Should we boldly speak the truth?

Without cheating anyone we should boldly speak the truth to everyone. If the truth is bitter or unpopular but bestows blessings on the living entities, we must speak it. This will not ultimately cause them anxiety.

We ourselves should inquire about the Absolute Truth, and then we should try to understand how to help everyone else. Giving Kṛṣṇa consciousness to others requires firm determination. Do not think of saving only the people of the present age. Think of the people in all ages and all times. Teach about the most pleasant kingdom of Vaikuṇṭha, the place from which no one ever returns to this material world. If you want to preach transcendence, it is vital that you yourself have taken shelter at the lotus feet of your spiritual master.

Always serve the spiritual master who imparts to you transcendental knowledge. Even if you live at home instead of in the *Maṭha*, we should all serve him together. We should also maintain the Lord and His devotees in opulent houses with comfortable atmospheres, and we ourselves should live in ordinary cottages. If we feed Kṛṣṇa nicely rather than enjoying things for ourselves, we will attain His mercy. Always remember that everything belongs to Kṛṣṇa. Our lives will become successful only when we use everything in this world in His service. However, before preaching these instructions we must live them.

Unless we speak the truth boldly we cannot please guru and Gaurāṅga. The more determined one is in devotional service, the bolder and more courageous he will be as a preacher.

If I fail to speak the impartial truth because I might become unpopular, I have certainly abandoned the path of my disciplic succession and accepted an unauthorized path. In the end I will either find myself cheated or will become an atheist.

6. Why were the Maṭhas established?

The Maṭhas were not established to favor ordinary people but to help pure devotees advance in spiritual life. We serve Lord Gaurāṅga simply by performing śrī-kṛṣṇa-*saṅkīrtana* . The *Bhāgavatam* verse, yajnaiḥ *saṅkīrtana* prāyair yajanti hi sumedhasaḥ, supports this idea. The example set by Śrī Kṛṣṇa's Gaura pastimes is the only auspicious way to perfection for the jīvas.

The Maṭhas have not been established to please bhogīs or tyāgīs. They have been established to preach pure devotional service. We receive blessings as we serve Hari by establishing Maṭhas.

Our intention is not to collect one or two rupees to benefit the *Maṭha*. We should not be eager to take help from unscrupulous people. Rather, if we can benefit anyone by speaking the bold truth, then the *Maṭha*'s purpose is served.

People will often play tricks on us. We should consider such tricks the Lord's test. It is difficult to cross beyond insurmountable Maya unless we are greatly fortunate. Māyāvādīs and bhogīs are both conditioned souls. By the mercy of Kṛṣṇa's devotees, persons who surrender to Hari can discriminate between good and bad, right and wrong. Know for certain that being drawn by the enjoying spirit, many people cannot realize the Absolute Truth.

7. Who can give us Kṛṣṇa?

Kṛṣṇa is not a product of this world but the Supreme Personality of Godhead. He is the primeval Lord, the Absolute Truth, the supreme worshipable Lord, the supreme enjoyer and the ultimate object of service. No one in this world can give us Kṛṣṇa, the controller of Maya. Yet Kṛṣṇa is the property of His devotees, because Kṛṣṇa appears in their pure, service-inclined hearts. Therefore the devotees can give us Kṛṣṇa.

Kṛṣṇa's devotees distribute Kṛṣṇa door to door. Such is their mercy! Out of compassion for the living entities, the devotees go door to door and distribute the holy name, which is Kṛṣṇa Himself. The most merciful Śrī Gaurāṅga Mahāprabhu also distributed the Lord's holy name, the ultimate object of worship for everyone. If by good fortune we can take shelter of Kṛṣṇa's devotee and sincerely surrender ourselves at his or her lotus feet, then that devotee will certainly give us Kṛṣṇa.

8. Should we glorify Hari constantly?

Mahāprabhu taught kīrtanīya sadā hariḥ, that we should always chant the holy name of Hari. The word "sadā" leaves room for no interruption. Human beings have no work or duty other than to glorify Hari. Hari should be glorified even before birds and animals. We do not care if the ignorant call us mad or fools. We will constantly propagate *hari-kathā* under the order and guidance of our spiritual master and Lord Gaurāṅga.

In order to hear mundane topics, people read daily newspapers and remain ever absorbed in worldly matters. Our proposition is to let everyone hear about Caitanya Mahāprabhu every day. Let them discuss Caitanya whenever they meet one another, and let them survive on the strength of these topics. Let there be nothing else discussed in this world. In order to keep the cultivation of Caitanya and His instructions alive forever, we ourselves have to remain absorbed in caitanya-kathā. At present, despite impediments put forth by materialists, we are spending large amounts of money to arrange for the constant glorification of Hari.

This world's senseless people suffer from a variety of *anarthas* and are intoxicated by material life. They are so intoxicated that they will do anything but try to remedy their suffering. Instead, they use their time, money, and intelligence to hear mundane topics, thereby inviting their own ruination by worsening their diseased condition. It is as if they are eating improper food instead of healthy food. Finally, they will go to hell. But still they will not hear about Śrī Caitanya even a little. It is as if they have taken a vow to avoid the proper remedy. Nevertheless, despite the obstacles, Śrī Caitanya's devotees regularly propagate the message of Śrī Caitanya throughout the world.

9. What is our principal duty?

Our principal duty is to first follow Śrīman Mahāprabhu's instructions and then to preach them everywhere. That will benefit us and help others as well. We are poor living entities, but we are never daridra-nārāyaṇas. Still, because we are poor we should accumulate wealth to ease our poverty. That wealth is love of Kṛṣṇa. Without the treasury of love of God our lives are useless and impoverished. Pray to the Lord to accept you as His servant and pay you with love of Himself as your salary.

Śrī Mahāprabhu has said, "In every town and village, the chanting of My name will be heard." Mundane sound vibration has filled the entire world. We should replace it with transcendental sound vibration. The Lord's temple should be established according to the pāñcarātrika system to aid this process. Worship the Lord with love and devotion and benefit the whole world. Those who are of a higher class should preach. It was Mahāprabhu's desire that we each propagate the transcendental sound vibration, so we should engage in nāma-*saṅkīrtana* everywhere. For this, we need to print many pamphlets to help us in our broad-scale preaching work.

Rich and educated people wander about desiring money and women. Even though we make our throats sore by screaming before them, they never pay attention to our words. Don't waste time on them. I repeat: We must print plenty of pamphlets so we can preach widely. Let them see the philosophy in the scriptures and the importance of the subject matter about which we are trying to speak.

Those who are proud cannot preach. Those who are proud only consider themselves great when they speak about Kṛṣṇa to others. The Absolute Truth does not reveal Himself to such persons. Thus it is impossible for them to preach and therefore to help others. Mahāprabhu instructed us to chant the holy name while remaining lower than the straw in the street and ready to offer all respect to others.

Don't gossip. Gossip benefits no one. Understand carefully what is good for you. And don't blaspheme. The mahājanas have said that blasphemers never achieve anything good. Let the materialists engage in whatever activities they choose—we need not bother about them. But think about yourself. We often say that while others are bad, we are worse. It is imperative that we keep our sinful minds engaged constantly in worshiping the Lord. To spend time attacking others, trying to dissuade them from this or that, is not the preacher's course but the act of a cheater. We have become busy in various activities and have forgotten our original constitutional duty. Make a sincere endeavor to clean out the filth accumulated in your heart. Although this appears to be self-interest, it is essential and should be done immediately, because preaching without following has no value. Unless one constantly engages in hari-*bhajana*, it will be impossible for him to induce others to worship Hari.

It is vital to take shelter of the spiritual master, who is nondifferent from Śrī Nityānanda. The spiritual master, who is Kṛṣṇa's energy, is the principal preacher, and we should all preach under his guidance. Otherwise, we will not be successful. *Śrī Caitanya-caritāmṛta* Antya-līla 7.11 states:

kali-kālera dharma kṛṣṇa-nāma-saṅkīrtana
kṛṣṇa-śakti vinā nahe tāra pravartana.

The fundamental religious system in the age of Kali is the chanting of the holy name of Kṛṣṇa. Unless empowered by Kṛṣṇa, one cannot propagate the saṅkīrtana movement.

The six Gosvāmīs, headed by Śrī Rūpa and Sanātana, are our gurus. Follow in their footsteps. We cannot advance in spiritual life without the guidance of Śrī Rūpa. Let the dust from the lotus feet of our guru, who is nondifferent from Śrī Rūpa, become our only asset. Then we will attain our fortune.

In the kingdom of devotional service, the idea that we are servants is prominent. The mood of servitorship is found in all the *rasas* , including sakhya, vātsalya, and *mādhurya*. The *Caitanya-caritāmṛta Ādi* 6.82 contains this verse:

pitā-mātā-guru-sakhā-bhāva kene naya
kṛṣṇa-premera svabhāve dāsya-bhāva se karaya

All the emotions, whether those of father, mother, teacher, or friend, are full of sentiments of servitude. That is the nature of love of Kṛṣṇa.

10. What is your mission's aim?

There was no need at all for us to form a mission, but people were walking in the wrong way and we wanted to deliver them. Serving the Supreme Lord is our mission. Even if we were offered the position of world emperor for millions of lifetimes, it would be easy to reject the proposal. Such things are just like stool and urine. Our insignificant endeavor is to deliver humankind from its wrong direction and to establish all living entities as servants at the lotus feet of Śrī Gaurasundara. Whether one is Brahmā, Śiva, Vāyu, or Varuṇa, whether one is a great religious preacher or religious leader, if he deviates even an inch from Śrī Caitanyadeva's teachings, he will find himself in trouble. Śrī Caitanyadeva's servants worship the supreme Absolute Truth. Śrī Caitanyadeva's servants are neither attracted to nor afraid of those who preach this world's religious principles because they have found immense beauty at Śrī Gaurāṅga's lotus feet. For the devotees of Gaura, the poisonous tooth of the snake-like sense objects is broken. No amount of this world's deceit can cheat those who have heard Śrī Gaurasundara's teachings.

Neither the yoga system propounded by Patañjali, which teaches one artificial self-control, nor association with woman such as Menakā and Urvaśī, can attract the Lord's devotees. Even the Vaiṣṇava's shoe-carriers are liberated from the clutches of those who pessimistically think that to become free from distress is a great achievement. The Lord's devotees do not think that being deprived of the necessities of life is great. They do not need to practice renunciation of the external world and so stuff their ears with cotton like the cloth weavers. They are not interested in their own happiness. They know that the attempt to enjoy material life will lead them to hell. They consider themselves ailing animals. No one can take shelter of Śrī Gaurasundara's lotus feet with their worldly acquisitions. They must become servants of His lotus feet.

Another type of cheating: I will sit in a solitary place and chant the names of Gaura-Nitāi. This is simply selfish. The senses are our enemies.

These senses have filled the path of devotional service, our eternal occupational duty and the path preached by Śrī Caitanyadeva, with thorns. Therefore people mistakenly identify pseudo devotional service, such as karma, *jñāna*, and yoga for *bhakti*.

But I will serve the transcendental Personality of Godhead. I will not become a sweeper by directly or indirectly serving my doglike senses. I will not become a washerman by serving my ass. I will not become an engineer of bricks and stone. Those who possess these mentalities can please Mahāprabhu only by taking shelter of devotional service. Śrī Gaurasundara is not a mundane object like a wall. By His mercy only can we be liberated from the aversion to the Lord we have developed since time immemorial. There is no alternative to submitting ourselves before His mercy. If others come forward to make a show of bestowing mercy, we will consider them cheaters. Those who do not constantly glorify Gaura's holy names and do not sing about His pastimes, cannot act as *ācāryas* . Those who are attached to the insignificant objects of this world can act as teachers only of the mundane school but never as spiritual masters. *Śrī Caitanya-caritāmṛta Madhya-līla* 8.128 states:

kibā vipra, kibā nyāsī, śūdra kene naya
yei kṛṣṇa-tattva-vettā, sei 'guru' haya

It does not matter whether a person is a vipra [learned scholar in Vedic wisdom] or is born in a lower family, or is in the renounced order of life—if he is master in the science of Kṛṣṇa he is the perfect and bona fide spiritual master.

Such a great soul can deliver me by hitting me in the core of my heart and by cutting the knots there. He will bestow his nonduplicitous mercy and he will not flatter me.

11. What does the Gauḍīya Maṭha teach?

The message of the Gauḍīya *Maṭha* is let's go back home, back to Godhead. The Gauḍīya *Maṭha* was inaugurated in order to preach about pure devotional service and to present Mahāprabhu's teachings to the world. Mahāprabhu's invaluable instructions and teachings are the object of the Gauḍīya *Maṭha*'s preaching. And the devotees at the Gauḍīya *Maṭha* preach *Śrīmad-Bhāgavatam* by personally

12. What is the devotees' opinion?

Hari's devotees say, "O living entity! You are a servant of the Supreme Lord and have no relationship with the material world. Since you are Hari's servant, your only business is to serve Him. As soon as you give up Hari's service and engage in some other activity, you will lose your peace of mind."

O living entity! Do not gratify your senses in the name of serving Hari. Remember, service means to gratify Kṛṣṇa's senses. To act in a way that pleases your own senses and the senses of your relatives is not service. If you think it service, you will be cheated. Do not wrongly identify service to family with service to the Lord. Do not waste time serving Maya after taking shelter of the Supreme Lord. If you do, how will you gain? You will simply become more attached to family life and ultimately fail to attain the Supreme. Be eager to serve the Lord if you wish to attain Him. Be intelligent and serve Kṛṣṇa at any cost. Then the spiritual master and Gaurāṅga will certainly be pleased with you.

13. Why do surrendered devotees beg alms?

Surrendered devotees do whatever the Lord dictates. By Śrī Gaurasundara's order, and to benefit others, the devotees go door to door and beg alms to engage others in devotional service. In order to distribute the contents of their topmost treasury, and to invite people to participate in the festival of Kṛṣṇa's service, they go door to door to beg. They do not go anywhere influenced of an enjoying spirit. The devotees' compassion is incomparable. They want only to induce everyone to become Kṛṣṇa conscious.

14. Can one do more for people by giving them personal instruction?

One who gives personal instruction to each and everyone does more for others than the platform speakers do. Generally, whatever platform speakers say cannot solve the problems of everyone in the audience, nor can it always benefit every individual. A person's defects are better rectified in a private tutorial class or private coaching than in hearing lectures in a school or college. Therefore those who instruct particular persons separately can award them something more permanent.

15. What is actual welfare?

Being averse to Lord Viṣṇu, innumerable living entities have come to Mahāmāyās prison house so they can envy Lord Viṣṇu unlimitedly. If you can deliver even one of these people and make him or her a devotee of Kṛṣṇa, then this is a much more important form of welfare than building hospitals or schools.

We hear, "I am a resident of India. Therefore it is my duty to see to India's interest according to the temporary situation. If I were born in foreign country and was living in India, then even though it would be against India, I would be concerned about that foreign interest."Śrī Caitanyadeva and His devotees are not so involved in insignificant sectarianism born of matter and based on time, place, and person. The welfare activities they perform and the example of patriotism they set do not temporarily benefit one group while harming another. The fruit of their welfare activities and patriotism can be had by all people at all time all over the world. This is not my imagination; it is fact.

Don't flatter when you preach. Those who flatter are not teachers or spiritual masters, and they are certainly not real preachers. In order to be popular or to accomplish their ends, those who wander about flattering people and thus supplying them with fuel to increase their sense gratification do not actually wish the people well. One need not hear from them, and if one does, it will cause ruination.

16. Why do so few people like to hear the truth?

It is a fact that many people are not interested in the Absolute Truth or even the spiritual path. This is because the supreme truth is not a path of sense gratification but of renunciation. Some people have spoiled the brains of the young Bengalis by encouraging them to become great religionists and fruitive workers. That is why we have to spend hundreds of gallons of blood to preach. Even so, few people are able to understand the actual truth. Unless one is fortunate and pious, one does not develop the desire to hear genuine truth or kṛṣṇa-kathā.

Human beings are entangled in either material enjoyment or renunciation, but the intelligent and fortunate scrutinize the paths of preyas and śreyas and conclude that the former is a path of bondage and the latter a path of liberation. Only sober persons give up preyas for śreyas. The less intelligent, who do not know how to discriminate, pray for preyas, hoping always to gain what they lack and preserve what they have. The Śāstras assure us that it will be difficult to find people interested in spiritual advancement, and even if we find such people, we can expect them to be unable to understand its importance. An expert speaker who knows the science of śreyas is extremely rare. Moreover, even if such a rare speaker is found, it is difficult to find a receptive and submissive audience to hear him.

Millions of flattering speakers will go to hell, but someday, someone will realize the confidential truth spoken boldly and be saved. It may take hundreds of lifetimes or hundreds of yugas before someone can hear properly, but it is not possible to make a person understand the truth unless one is prepared to spend hundreds of gallons of vital blood.

17. Is it our business to build a Maṭha and live there?

It is more intelligent to create a living *Maṭha* rather than to build a *Maṭha* for comfortable living. Creating a living *Maṭha* means to attract faithful persons to surrender at the lotus feet of the spiritual master. The highest welfare activity is to attract living entities to serve the spiritual master's lotus feet by describing to them the spiritual master's glories and service. For this we spend gallons of blood. Such preaching will please both guru and Kṛṣṇa. Therefore to dedicate body, mind, and speech to such philanthropic activities is the perfection of life.

A *Maṭha* surcharged with talk of Kṛṣṇa's glories and service is nondifferent from Vaikuṇṭha. Thus living in a *Maṭha* is just like living in a dhāma. Hari-kathā must be prominent in the *Maṭha*. There is no use in building a *Maṭha* simply to facilitate eating and sleeping. Maṭhas should be built only to spread *hari-kathā*. This will benefit ourselves and others.

Devotees who are fully dedicated to their spiritual master are the living source, and we are to hear from such living sources so that we too can become dedicated devotees. People devoid and bereft of service to the spiritual master are dead even as they breathe. Do not not associate with such nondevotees if you do not want to harm your spiritual progress.

18. What is the highest blessing one can give others?

The most auspicious blessing one can shower on the people, "May you all be Kṛṣṇa conscious." To divert the jīvas' attention toward Kṛṣṇa is the best thing you can do for them. It is an act of highest altruism to award Kṛṣṇa's devotional service to others. In their hearts, devotees are always eager to perform such an act of welfare.

Supreme knowledge is to know the Supreme Lord. *Śāstra* declares, vidyā bhāgavatābadhi, the limit of knowledge is to understand Kṛṣṇa. *Śrī Caitanya-caritāmṛta* Madhya 8.245 states:

prabhu kahe — "kon vidyā vidyā-madhye sāra?"
rāya kahe — "kṛṣṇa-bhakti vinā vidyā nāhi āra"

On one occasion the Lord inquired, "Of all types of education, which is the most important?" Rāmānanda Rāya replied, "No education is important other than the transcendental devotional service of Kṛṣṇa."

The godless education currently being propagated has not and will not benefit humankind but will further degrade it. The highest gift the devotees can give to the entire human race is the Śrī Caitanyadeva's mercy.

19. Who is qualified to preach?

The self-realized souls, who see the Supreme Lord face to face, are qualified to preach the Lord's glories. They are the principal preachers. Innumerable other preachers can preach under their guidance. After seeing the Supreme Lord face to face, Śrī Vyāsadeva preached *Śrīmad-Bhāgavatam* with a peaceful mind. The self-sufficient Śukadeva and great personalities such as the Nava-yogendras preached about the soul's eternal duty while wandering as mendicants. Only the liberated souls wander and preach about Hari. Śrīman Mahāprabhu and His associates preached everywhere.

Thousands of questions arise, but proper answers to all these questions can be found when one hears *hari-kathā* properly. Do not be impatient.

20. Who is an ācārya?

A devotee who practices what he preaches is an *ācārya* . An *ācārya* is impartial and liberated and can induce others to give up bad association by boldly and impartially instructing them about the imminent danger of such association while personally setting an ideal example of complete renunciation of bad association and constant cultivation of Kṛṣṇa consciousness. Unless one dedicates one's life completely, one cannot preach. An *ācārya* is a preacher.

21. Isn't giving people food and clothing compassionate?

If some persons believe in God or worship Hari, we will certainly help them with food and clothing. We have to feed the poor to make them worship Hari. We have to give them some tangible help. But to maintain a poisonous snake by feeding it milk and bananas is not compassionate. Mundane welfare work is like that; it leads people to godlessness by tempting them with sense objects.

Real compassion is to make the living entities who are averse to Kṛṣṇa inclined toward His service. The living entities are suffering in this world in so many ways because they have forgotten their service to Kṛṣṇa. By awakening their Kṛṣṇa consciousness in the association of devotees, they can become free of their suffering and become happy. Śrī Caitanyadeva displayed this kind of compassion. If we make a comparative study between Lord Caitanya's compassion and the so-called insignificant and incomplete compassion of mundane philanthropists, we will see that the compassion displayed by Mahāprabhu is complete and eternal, whereas the compassion displayed by others is limited and artificial.

22. Do devotees speculate?

As our guru's servants we speak only what we have been taught and do not put forth new proposals. At the same time, we do not miss any opportunity to speak the truth for the people's benefit. So far, whatever I have explained to you does not go to my credit. I have no personal qualification. As a disciple, I simply repeat my spiritual master's words. I preach about the Absolute Truth as the information has come down to me from my spiritual master in disciplic succession. I speak only what he has mercifully revealed to me or inspired me to speak. Apart from this, I have no qualification.

23. Why do devotees appear in this world?

The Lord's devotees come to this world in order to favor the living entities. They are not duty-bound to come here, and certainly they have no personal need. But to change the living entities' adverse taste for devotion to something favorable is their only compassionate duty. They want to spark interest in the people in this world in engaging in *bhakti*. If we miss their thrust and remain averse to the Supreme Lord and indifferent to *saṅkīrtana* , the yuga-dharma of the age, then whatever other welfare activities we do, such as feeding the poor or educating the foolish, is a complete waste of time and energy.

24. Is the preaching of contemporary devotees powerful?

Just as an arrow's power is calculated by the prowess of an archer, similarly the power and effect of one's preaching depends on how much devotional strength one possesses. Therefore there is a gulf of difference between the preaching of ordinary devotees and the preaching of a powerful devotee. Such powerful devotees are referred to as "the living source." Those who experience such persons in their own lives are certainly fortunate.

Śrī Caitanyadeva

1. Is the favor given by Mahāprabhu the highest favor?

There has never been nor will there ever be better benefactors than Mahāprabhu and His devotees. No other type of human welfare work can compare; all those others simply perform a great disservice to humanity. The favor offered by Mahāprabhu and His devotees is the supreme favor. This favor is eternal, not a temporary five or ten day promise. Mundane benefits tend to ultimately do harm, but Mahāprabhu's favor will never harm others.

For example, what is good for our country will certainly be harmful to another country. It is the nature of temporary happiness to cause distress to others. If I am happy to ride in a horse-pulled cart, the horse will be inconvenienced by my pleasure. Mahāprabhu and His devotees never deceive people by preaching about temporary favors. Their favor and charities are suitable for all people at all times and under all circumstances. Their gifts are good for the entire universe. Mahāprabhu and His devotees never offer gifts related to narrow or sectarian views.

Mahāprabhu's compassion is considered harmless compassion. Thus we say that He and His devotees are the most magnanimous. I am not speaking flowery language or myth but topmost truth when I say these things.

Mahāprabhu's compassion is complete, while all other forms of compassion are limited and deceptive. Matsya, Kūrma, Varāhadeva, Rāmacandra, and even Kṛṣṇa distributed mercy only to Their devotees and annihilated those who opposed Them. Mahāprabhu displayed compassion to everyone. He did not even hesitate to show His harmless mercy to the

Kazi and the Buddhists, and He converted the worshipers of Rāmacandra, known as the Rāmānandīs, into pure Vaiṣṇavas.

2. Is everything that happens Kṛṣṇa's mercy?

Everything that happens is an example of the Lord's compassion, for He is full of compassion. Śrī Gaurasundara tests us by putting us into various difficulties and inconveniences. Our success at passing those tests depends on our good fortune.

As the Supersoul, Śrī Gaurahari mercifully reveals eternal truth to sincere persons. Those who take full shelter at Hari's lotus feet and the feet of guru and the Vaiṣṇavas never repose their faith in the illusory words of misguided people. Only unfortunate people are cheated by deceitful words. Our only hope at avoiding such misfortune is to remain firmly fixed at the lotus feet of Śrīman Mahāprabhu.

Always study *Śrī Caitanya-caritāmṛta* and hear it explained by persons conversant with its actual purport. Chant Kṛṣṇa's holy names offenselessly in the association of devotees. And continue to read— *Śrī Caitanya-caritāmṛta*, Prārthanā, and Śaraṇāgati especially—and you will find fortune. If you chant in the association of devotees, Gaurahari will bestow His mercy on you.

3. What has Śrī Caitanyadeva done?

Śrī Caitanyadeva has instructed everyone to engage everything they have in Kṛṣṇa's service. Although Śrī Caitanya Mahāprabhu is Kṛṣṇa, He appeared in the mood of a devotee and revealed Kṛṣṇa to the world. He taught everyone to serve Kṛṣṇa by His own example. Śrī Rūpa Gosvāmī Prabhu, who was an associate of Śrī Kṛṣṇa Caitanya, glorified Mahāprabhu as follows:

namo mahā-vadānyāya, kṛṣṇa-prema-pradāya te
kṛṣṇaya kṛṣṇa-caitanya-nāmne gaura-tviṣe namaḥ

O most munificent incarnation! You are Kṛṣṇa Himself appearing as Śrī Kṛṣṇa Caitanya Mahāprabhu. You have assumed the golden color of Śrīmatī Rādhārāṇī, and You are widely distributing pure love of Kṛṣṇa. We offer our respectful obeisances unto You. (*Śrī Caitanya-caritāmṛta* Madhya 19.54)

O Śrī Kṛṣṇa Caitanya! You are most magnanimous! You have not established so-called schools and orphanages, nor have You spent your time digging wells, building hospitals, or performing other social welfare activities. Rather, You have established spiritual institutions to educate the people. You are therefore the ultimate shelter of all orphans. You have revealed the nectarean ocean of the mellows of devotional service. You have built Gauḍīya hospitals, centers where the root cause of material disease can be treated. Your mercy is causeless and yields no inauspicious results. The so-called mercy seen in this world always creates inauspiciousness in the end. But Your mercy on the living entities creates all auspiciousness for them. Therefore You are considered the most magnanimous personality and He who bestows love of Kṛṣṇa.

You are the object of the living entities' spontaneous propensity to render You service. You are most attractive and have appeared to manifest the most magnanimous pastimes in order to awaken our Kṛṣṇa consciousness.

O Śrī Kṛṣṇa Caitanya! You are the Supreme Personality of Godhead! You have an eternal spiritual body, a body full of knowledge and bliss. Your names, forms, qualities, and pastimes are all eternal. You are the energetic Lord Kṛṣṇa. Your energy, by whose influence the entire material world is bewildered, is known as Mahāmāyā. Lord Kṛṣṇa is the proprietor of this energy. The exquisitely beautiful Śrī Rādhikā, who enchants the entire universe, also enchants Mahāmayā. O Lord! You are fully absorbed in the mood and complexion of Śrī Rādhikā. Kṛṣṇa's mood as the enjoyer of Rādhā is not present in Your magnanimous pastimes. Śrī Rādhā is the personification of Kṛṣṇa's service, and Your heart is fully absorbed in Śrī Rādhās mood. Since You have awarded kṛṣṇa-prema to everyone, You are the most magnanimous and are the personification of love of God. You have incarnated to distribute love of God and are nondifferent from Kṛṣṇa.

4. Who is Śrī Caitanyadeva?

Śrī Caitanyadeva is not a personality two thousand or ten thousand years old; He is eternal. He is the Supreme Personality of Godhead. He is beginningless, the origin of all, and the cause of all causes. He is not born under the influence of time. Rather, past, present, and future originate in Him. He is eternal and almighty. He is not a physical body of flesh and bones but the primeval Lord. He is the supreme enjoyer and proprietor of everything. He is the Supersoul situated in the heart of all living entities. He is the supreme Brahman and the Supreme Lord. He is directly Kṛṣṇa and the fountainhead of all incarnations. He is full of all opulence and is the supreme Absolute Truth.

Śrī Caitanyadeva is the ocean of mercy. No one else can bestow as much mercy as He can. No other incarnation of the Lord has ever distributed so much causeless mercy. His mercy is distributed to worthless persons to make them qualified. His mercy is eternal. He is so merciful that He gives Himself to His devotees. Such compassion has never before been seen.

Karmīs, *jñānīs*, and yogīs are unable to see the beauty of His distribution of love of God, but any fortunate soul can attain it. Therefore I say, give up all your considerations and spend time hearing about Śrī Caitanyadeva. If we hear about such a personality, who is far superior to ordinary human beings, we can find enough qualification to engage in kṛṣṇa-*bhajana*, the actual path of peace. Then we will develop the propensity to love the Lord as our son. If we can replace the conception that the perception of human life or peace is attained by the marriage between a mundane man and a mundane woman, then a mother will no longer consider her son as hers own. Our success lies in reestablishing our relationship with the Supreme Lord. The five types of *rasas* such as śānta, dāsya, sakhya, vātsalya, and *mādhurya* are present in the Supreme Lord in full form. Since we have established our relationship with temporary objects rather than Him, we are unable to understand all these things.

The Absolute Truth is full of knowledge and bliss. We run here and there to try to know Him; but the Lord of Goloka has appeared in human form among us as Gaurāṅga to give us instruction. If we do not follow His instructions, how will we be benefited?

5. Why did Lord Caitanya reject the most important instruction of Bhagavad-gītā, the sarva-dharman parityaja verse, as "external"?

Mahāprabhu spoke these words to Śrī Ramānanda Rāya. Because devotional service is the constitutional propensity of the soul, there is no need for the Lord to encourage people to become devotees by establishing terms. Actually, the devotees are eager to please the Supreme Lord out of their own spontaneous love.

If a father has to work hard to make his son devoted to him, then where is the glory or credit to the son? Shouldn't the devotees serve the Lord out of their own accord? At present we have not only forgotten the Supreme Lord but forgotten our selves, our eternal constitutional position, and our eternal existence. We have become masters of temporary objects and also engaged in their service. Therefore Mahāprabhu has rejected such an important instruction in *Bhagavad-gītā* by calling it "external." Instead, He taught the people of the entire world pure devotional service and that the topmost form of worship emulates the mood of the Vrajavāsīs.

6. What does the phrase, "Compassion toward all living entities" mean?

By instructing that we should show compassion to all living entities, Śrī Caitanyadeva has induced us all to engage in the service of Lord Viṣṇu and the Vaiṣṇavas. This is the special nature of Śrī Caitanyadeva's mercy.

7. Is Śrī Gaurāṅgadeva Kṛṣṇa Himself?

Since Śrī Gaurasundara is nondifferent from Kṛṣṇa, He is the sole object of the twelve *rasas* . The only difference between Śrī Caitanya Mahāprabhu and Lord Kṛṣṇa is that Kṛṣṇa is the personification of enjoyment and Śrī Gaurasundara is in the mood of separation. Lord Kṛṣṇa personifies the āśraya and Śrī Gaurāṅgadeva plays the role of Kṛṣṇa's servant. The most magnanimous son of Nanda Mahārāja when combined with Śrī Rādhā is none other than Śrī Kṛṣṇa Caitanya. Śrī Gadhādhara is His most intimate energy. When we accept Śrī Gaurasundara as the predominating half and transcendental entity, we also accept His energy Gadhādhara as the predominated transcendental entity.

8. I have received great benefit from your instructions. Could you please explain more about Śrī Caitanya Mahāprabhu?

The type of *bhakti* Śrī Gaurasundara preached is the highest service. Glorification of the Lord such as it was inaugurated by Śrī Gaura is the remedy to cure our diseased condition and awaken our propensity for loving service to the Lord. It is our duty to faithfully accept this remedy. Then we will be peaceful. Chanting Kṛṣṇa's holy name is that infallible remedy. Thus we should glorify Hari all the time. The Lord has invested His holy name with all His energies, and He has included the crest jewel of all objectives in the chanting. It is the duty of those devotees who have taken complete shelter at the Śrī Caitanya's lotus feet to cultivate the conclusion of *Śrīmad-Bhāgavatam* while following in His footsteps.

Forgetting our service to Kṛṣṇa, we have become masters. We wanted to become masters, and this material world provided us with the opportunity. This world is perfectly arranged for that purpose. But mastership is not our constitutional position. Rather, it is the tendency of conditioned souls. There is no peace in following one's conditioning. Peace can only be attained by practicing devotional service, by considering oneself a servant of Kṛṣṇa.

We have become degraded because we have forgotten who we are. We are Kṛṣṇa's servants. The spiritual master, who is dear to Kṛṣṇa, imparts to us this transcendental knowledge. This process is called initiation. Simply by serving the spiritual master the desire to engage in devotional service is awakened. If we can sincerely approach Kṛṣṇa's devotees and hear from them submissively, we will certainly benefit both in this life and the next. Our lives will become fully successful when we begin to engage everything in the Lord's service.

You all are learned. I do not consider you nondevotees. Because you are devotees I fall at your feet and beg you to please give me these alms: forget that you are important persons in this world. Give up everything and become attached to the lotus feet of Śrī Caitanyacandra. If you are even a little attracted to the Lord, you can immediately understand that there is no inconvenience in practicing His teachings. Whoever hears His instructions will certainly begin to chant Hari's holy name. O my brothers! Why are you traveling the path of inauspiciousness? What do you gain by discussing worldly topics? Always hear kṛṣṇa-kathā and engage in Kṛṣṇa's service.

At present, the soul is sleeping peacefully after entrusting all its responsibilities to the mind. Break the soul's sleep, because the mind is the greatest enemy and extremely unreliable. The mind will lead you only deep into the ocean of distress. You must keep the mind under control.

It does not matter what our situation, if we forget the Lord we will find only trouble. Our fortune lies in taking shelter at Kṛṣṇa's lotus feet. If we give up Lord Hari, we will suffer material misery after falling into darkness. We have attained this human form of life by good fortune, not to become foolish or ignorant. Engage in your normal human condition as servants of the Lord. *Śrī Caitanya-caritāmṛta* Madhya-līla 22.33 states:

kṛṣṇa, tomāra haṅa' yadi bale eka-bāra
māyā-bandha haite kṛṣṇa tāre kare pāra

One is immediately freed from the clutches of Maya if he seriously and sincerely says, 'My dear Lord Kṛṣṇa, although I have forgotten You for so many long years in the material world, today I am surrendering unto You. I am Your sincere and serious servant. Please engage me in Your service."

9. How does the Supreme Lord perform His appearance pastimes?

Since mother Śacī and Jagannāth Misra are eternally perfect devotees, their hearts and bodies consist of pure goodness. They are never to be considered ordinary jīvas. Pure goodness is also called vasudeva. Lord Vāsudeva, who enjoys transcendental pastimes, appears only in pure goodness, or vasudeva.

Mother Śacīs pregnancy did not occur through lusty association with her husband, as if they were a mundane male and female interested only in sense gratification, whose bodies were made of flesh, bones, and blood. Even to think of them in this way is an offense. If one considers her pregnancy with a service-inclined heart, one will realize how glorious Mother śacīs transcendental pregnancy was, and how it personified pure goodness.

In his commentary on *Śrīmad-Bhāgavatam* (10.2.16) Śrīdhara Svamīpāda wrote that the Supreme Lord appears in a devotee's heart that is in the mode of pure goodness. He does not take birth like an ordinary human being. Śrī Rūpa Gosvāmī wrote in Laghu-bhāgavatāmṛta that Lord

Kṛṣṇa first manifests in the heart of Vasudeva, then from Vasudeva's heart He manifests in the heart of Devakī.

Śrī Caitanya-caritāmṛta, Ādi 13.84-85 states:

jagannātha miśra kahe svapna ye dekhila
jyotirmaya-dhāma mora hṛdaye paśila

Jagannātha Miśra then replied, "In a dream I saw the effulgent abode of the Lord enter my heart."

āmāra hṛdaya haite gelā tomāra hṛdaye
hena bujhi, janmibena kona mahāśaye

"From my heart it entered your heart. I therefore understand that a great personality will soon take birth."

10. Is Śrī Caitanyadeva the Supreme Personality of Godhead Himself?

Śrī Caitanyadeva is directly the Supreme Personality of Godhead. Śrī Gaurāṅga Mahāprabhu is the supreme Absolute Truth, and the supreme consciousness. He is the Supreme Lord Himself and the controller of all other controllers. The Lord's eternally perfect associate, Śrī Narottama dāsa Ṭhākura sings:

vrajendranandana yei śacīsuta haila sei
balarāma haila nitāi

The son of Nanda Mahārāja has appeared as the son of Śacī, and Balarāma has appeared as Nityānanda

Śrī Caitanya-caritāmṛta states:

svayaṁ bhagavān kṛṣṇa, viṣṇu-paratattva,
pūrṇa-jñāna pūrṇānanda parama mahattva
'nanda-suta' bali' yāṅre bhāgavate gāi,
sei kṛṣṇa avatīrṇa caitanya-gosāñi

Kṛṣṇa, the original form of the Personality of Godhead, is the summum bonum of the all-pervading Viṣṇu. He is all-perfect knowledge and all-perfect bliss. He is the Supreme Transcendence. He whom *Śrīmad-Bhāgavatam* describes as the son of Nanda Mahārāja has descended to earth as Lord Caitanya.

parama īśvara kṛṣṇa svayaṁ bhagavān,
sarva-avatārī, sarva-kāraṇa-pradhāna

Kṛṣṇa is the Supreme Personality of Godhead. He is personally the original Godhead, the source of all incarnations and the cause of all causes. (*Madhya* 8.134)

sei kṛṣṇa avatārī vrajendra-kumāra,
āpane caitanya-rūpe kaila avatāra

That same Lord Kṛṣṇa, the fountainhead of all incarnations, is known as the son of the King of Vraja. He has descended personally as Lord Śrī Caitanya Mahāprabhu. (*Ādi* 2.109)

We are servants of the Supreme Lord and serving Him is our eternal duty. Lord Śrī Kṛṣṇa appeared as Lord Gaurāṅga in Kali-yuga. Therefore Lord Gaurāṅga is the eternal worshipable Lord of persons like us who live in Kali-yuga. Anyone who does not worship Caitanyacandra is unconscious. Those who do not worship the most merciful Śrī Caitanyacandra are unable even to become conscious.

Śrī Caitanyacandra is the supreme Absolute Truth, full of sixteen transcendental characteristics. Therefore if His enlivening kathā enters our hearts, it will certainly attract us to His lotus feet. Those who hear about Him partially will surrender to Him partially. Until the living entities become constantly intoxicated by serving Śrī Caitanyacandra, offering body, mind, and words, house, children, and wife, at His lotus feet, it is to be understood that they have not heard about Śrī Caitanyacandra completely.

Śrī Gaurasundara is the eternal Absolute Truth. He existed in the past, exists at present, and will continue to exist in future. Śrī Gaurāṅgadeva is the combined form of Śrī Rādhā-Govinda. Although He is directly Kṛṣṇa Himself, He performs pastimes as Kṛṣṇa's servant to benefit the jīvas. He is fully absorbed in Śrī Rādhās mood. Because they are foolish, some people consider Him simply a great personality or a mere religious preacher. But He is neither. He is directly Kṛṣṇa, the son of Nanda. As Śrī Gaurāṅgadeva Kṛṣṇa appeared as the son of Śrī Jagannāth Miśra; Śrī Jagannāth Miśra was the Lord's servant.

11. What is Śrī Gaurāṅgadeva's compassion?

Śrī Gaurasundara said that *saṅkīrtana* is the only duty of humankind. This is proof of His magnanimous nature. Human beings can attain what it is impossible even for the best of the demigods to attain. Śrī Gaurāṅgadeva does not cheat and does not mix material enjoyment with spiritual understanding. He has preached what is most beneficial to all living beings. If one hears His teachings he will understand that all other teachings in this world are incomplete and weak. Śrī Gaurasundara has not descended to cheat people as the mental speculators cheat people by presenting their insignificant *sādhanas*. By preaching *Śrīmad-Bhāgavatam* Śrī Gaurasundara has proved that the *sādhanas* put forth by so-called sampradāyas are simply ineffective. He has also demonstrated that the congregational chanting of Kṛṣṇa's name is the only way to attain auspiciousness.

But the *saṅkīrtana* must be for Kṛṣṇa. Any kīrtana performed for one's own happiness or the happiness of others is not kṛṣṇa-kīrtana. The holy name of Kṛṣṇa is directly Kṛṣṇa Himself. The letters K-ṛ-ṣ-ṇ-a are nondifferent from Kṛṣṇa. By performing kṛṣṇa-kīrtana the sinful mentality of impersonalists and atheists is destroyed and they become eligible for ultimate liberation. Māyāvādī Prakāśānanda is the prime example of this fact.

Even people who are too attached to material enjoyment can attain ultimate liberation by performing kṛṣṇa-kīrtana. Pratāparudra, the king of Utkala, is the prime example of this fact. All jīvas, including men, women, animals, birds, trees, and even the dead stones can be liberated by the performance of kṛṣṇa-kīrtana. The animals, birds, trees, and creepers of Jhārikhaṇḍa forest are prime examples of this fact.

The living entities are not becoming liberated simply because they do not engage in kṛṣṇa-kīrtana. Śrī Gaurasundara incarnated in this world to benefit all living entities. Our only welfare lies in performing kṛṣṇa-kīrtana. There is no other way to attain the ultimate goal of education, knowledge, and life itself.

Actual kṛṣṇa-kīrtana is that kīrtana by which Kṛṣṇa is pleased. The show of performing kīrtana for one's own pleasure or the pleasure of others is not kṛṣṇa-kīrtana but māyā-kīrtana. As actions are judged by their results, so one can judge whether one is chanting the holy name by the results. If while chanting Hari's name one's propensity or attachment for material life increases, one can know that Hari is not the object of one's chanting. Hari-nāma-*saṅkīrtana* should destroy attachment for material life, not increase it. While chanting one will realize the insignificance and temporality of material life, and will no longer relish it. Then all one's *anarthas* will be destroyed, one's heart will be purified and become steady, one's material restlessness and misery will be destroyed, and one will attain love of God.

If these stages do not occur, one can only imagine what one must be doing other than kṛṣṇa-kīrtana.

śrī-kṛṣṇa-caitanya-dayā karaha vicāra,
vicāra karite citte pābe camatkāra

If you are indeed interested in logic and argument, kindly apply it to the mercy of Śrī Caitanya Mahāprabhu. If you do so, you will find it to be strikingly wonderful. (*Śrī Caitanya-caritāmṛta* Ādi 8.14)

'eka' kṛṣṇa-nāme kare sarva-pāpa nāśa,
premera kāraṇa bhakti karena prakāśa

Simply chanting the Hare Kṛṣṇa mahā-mantra without offenses vanquishes all sinful activities. Thus pure devotional service, which is the cause of love of Godhead, becomes manifest. (*Śrī Caitanya-caritāmṛta* Ādi 8.26)

anāyāse bhava-kṣaya, kṛṣṇera sevana,
eka kṛṣṇa-nāmera phale pāi eta dhana

As a result of chanting the Hare Kṛṣṇa mahā-mantra, one makes such great advancement in spiritual life that simultaneously his material existence terminates, and he receives love of Godhead. The holy name of Kṛṣṇa is so powerful that by chanting even one name, one very easily achieves these transcendental riches. (*Śrī Caitanya-caritāmṛta* Ādi 8.28)

harṣe prabhu kahena, "śuna svarūpa-rāma-rāya,
nāma-saṅkīrtana kalau parama upāya
saṅkīrtana-yajñe kalau kṛṣṇa-ārādhana,
sei ta' sumedhā pāya kṛṣṇera caraṇa

In great jubilation, Śrī Caitanya Mahāprabhu said, "My dear Svarū pa Dāmodara and Rāmānanda Rāya, know from Me that chanting the holy names is the most feasible means of salvation in this Age of Kali. "In this Age of Kali, the process of worshiping Kṛṣṇa is to perform sacrifice by chanting the holy name of the Lord. One who does so is certainly very intelligent, and he attains shelter at the lotus feet of Kṛṣṇa. (*Śrī Caitanya-caritāmṛta* Antya 20.8-9)

nāma-saṅkīrtana haite sarvānartha-nāśa,
sarva-śubhodaya, kṛṣṇa-premera ullāsa

"Simply by chanting the holy name of Lord Kṛṣṇa, one can be freed from all undesirable habits. This is the means of awakening all good fortune, and initiating the flow of waves of love for Kṛṣṇa. (*Śrī Caitanya-caritāmṛta* Antya 20.11)

saṅkīrtana haite pāpa-saṁsāra-nāśana,
citta-śuddhi, sarva-bhakti-sādhana-udgama
kṛṣṇa-premodgama, premāmṛta-āsvādana,
kṛṣṇa-prāpti, sevāmṛta-samudre majjana

"By performing congregational chanting of the Hare Kṛṣṇa mantra, one **can destroy the sinful condition of material existence, purify the unclean heart, and awaken all varieties of devotional service. The result of chanting is that one awakens his love for Kṛṣṇa, and tastes transcendental bliss. Ultimately, one attains the association of Kṛṣṇa, and engages in His devotional service, as if immersing himself in a great ocean of love."** (*Śrī Caitanya-caritāmṛta* Antya 20.13-14)

12. Can one worship Lord Gaurāṅga as one's husband?

The Supreme Personality of Godhead Kṛṣṇa is the only enjoyer and everyone is enjoyed by Him. Although Śrī Gaurasundara is the object of worship, Kṛṣṇa, He is absorbed in the mood of a devotee. Although He is Kṛṣṇa Himself, He is searching after Kṛṣṇa. Śrī Kṛṣṇa is the personification of sweetness, and Śrī Gaurāṅgadeva is the personification of magnanimity. As soon as one proudly considers himself the enjoyer, he falls into material existence. Thus one becomes degraded. It is important to understand that although Śrī Gaurasundara is the supreme enjoyer, the āśraya, He is playing the pastimes of being a devotee. Therefore Śrī Lakṣmiprīyā and Śrī Viṣṇuprīyā are His legitimate wives, and all others subordinate to them are maidservants on the platform of pure servitorship. One cannot use words relating to the conjugal mellows when referring to Caitanya Mahāprabhu's devotees. Wherever the word "husband" is used to indicate Śrī Gaurasundara in *mādhurya-rati*, it refers to the Kṛṣṇa form of Śrī Gaurasundara. Those who call Śrī Gaura nāgara, or "enjoyer of a damsel," are ignorant offenders and unauthorized. Gaura-nāgarīvāda is certainly not scripturally based. Therefore Śrī Vṛndāvana dāsa Ṭhākura writes in his Śrī Caitanya-bhāgavata, *ataeva yata mahā-mahima sakale, 'gaurāṅga-nāgara' hena stava nāhi bale*: "Therefore great personalities do not offer prayers addressing Lord Gaurāṅga as Gaurāṅga-nāgara, the enjoyer of damsels." [*CB Ādi-khaṇḍa* 15.30-32]

13. Who is Śrī Gaurasundara?

Lord Kṛṣṇa, the son of Vraja's king, has appeared in this world as Lord Gaurāṅga. Śrī Gaurasundara is the eternal Absolute Truth. He is the son of Jagannāth Misra. Although appearing as the Lord's father, Jagannāth Miśra is actually His servant. Śrī Gaurāṅgadeva is the Supreme Personality of Godhead and is fully transcendental. No one is equal to or greater than Him. He is a unique personality. Although superiors, His parents are also His servants.

Śrī Gaurasundara is eternally situated with His servants, subordinates, and energies, as the non-dual substance. He is eternal, and His servants, subordinates, and energies are also eternal. By servants we mean those who render service to Him. Those who have been counted as His subordinates serve Him with love and affection. They are His sons and He is their father.

Caitanyadeva distributes love of God in the form of chanting the holy name by appearing in the pure heart of His subordinates. They are His descendants, and they have maintained and are maintaining the flow of propagating Kṛṣṇa consciousness by distributing love of God and the holy name all over the world.

Śrī Gaurasundara is directly Nanda-suta Kṛṣṇa. According to vaidhi consideration, Śrī Lakṣmī and Śrī Viṣṇuprīyā were His wives, and according to *bhajana* consideration, intimate devotees such as Śrī Svarūpa Dāmodara, Śrī Gadhādhara Pandita, and Śrī Rāya Rāmānanda were His eternal consorts situated on the highest platform of *mādhurya-rasa* .

Although Śrī Gaurasundara is nondifferent from the son of Nanda Mahārāja, He is an incarnation of the mood of separation. Lord Kṛṣṇa is the personification of enjoyment, and Lord Gaurāṅga is the personification of the mellow of separation.

14. How does one worship Śrī Gaura?

To follow Śrī Gaurasundara's orders is to worship Śrī Gaura. It is said, dāsya *rasa* parākāsṭhā gaurāṅga *bhajana*, "In the worship of Gaurāṅga, the mood of servitorship is prominent." Elsewhere it is said, madhura rasete gaura yugala ākāra, "In madhurya-*rasa* , Śrī Gaurāṅga is Śrī Rādhā Kṛṣṇa."

People who are full of *anarthas* cannot go to Kṛṣṇa, but the most magnanimous personality, Śrī Gaurasundara, delivered materialists like Sārvabhauma Bhattācārya and sinners like Jagāi and Mādhāi from their respective *anarthas*, qualifying them to engage in worship of Kṛṣṇa.

Fortunate persons worship Gaurāṅga and Kṛṣṇa under the shelter of the spiritual master. The spiritual master is nondifferent from Śrī Gaura, because he is the manifestation of Śrī Gaura. He is servitor God. Although the spiritual master is as good as God, he is most dear to God. It is an offense to consider the spiritual master the supreme enjoyer or the object of service.

15. Why did Mahāprabhu chant "gopī, gopī"?

The materialist cannot understand why Mahāprabhu, who is the supreme teacher of all living entities, chanted "gopī, gopī." In order to teach people that without glorifying the devotees one cannot glorify Kṛṣṇa, and without engaging in the spiritual master's service one cannot engage in Kṛṣṇa's service, Mahāprabhu enacted this pastime. Śrīla Bhaktivinoda Ṭhākura sings, rādhā bhajane yadi mati nāhi bhelā kṛṣṇa *bhajana* tava akārana gelā: if one is not inclined toward the worship of Rādhā, his worship of Kṛṣṇa is useless.

16. Is Śrī Caitanyadeva only the Lord of the Bengalis?

Śrī Caitanyadeva is the Supreme Personality of Godhead, the supreme controller, the Absolute Truth, and the son of Nanda. In order to benefit everyone in the universe, Lord Kṛṣṇa appeared as Śrī Caitanyadeva. Needless to say He is worshipable by all and is the object of everyone's service. Therefore we say that Caitanya Mahāprabhu is not only the Lord of the Bengalis but of all humankind and all jīvas, including the demigods headed by Brahmā and Śiva. He is the Supreme Lord.

17. Is Śrī Caitanya-caritāmṛta simply a book of the Lord's pastimes?

Śrī Caitanya-caritāmṛta is not simply a book containing Śrī Caitanyadeva's pastimes. It is a wonderful philosophical work. It contains plenty of philosophical explanations. Śrī Kṛṣṇa's second pastimes are the pastimes of Śrī Caitanya, and Śrī Caitanya's second pastimes are the pastimes of Śrī Kṛṣṇa. Śrīla Kṛṣṇadāsa Kavirāja Gosvāmī Prabhu has written this book by taking guidance from *Śrīmad-Bhāgavatam*.

18. Can you please tell us Śrī Caitanyadeva's philosophy in brief?

We find Śrī Caitanyadeva's philosophy summarized in one ancient verse:

ārādhyo bhagavān vrajeśa-tanayas tad-dhāma vṛndāvanaṁ
ramya kācid upāsana vraja-vadhū-vargeṇā va kalpitā
śrīmad bhāgavataṁ pramāṇam amalaṁ premā pum-artho mahān
śrī-caitanya mahāprabhor matam idaṁ tatrādarāḥ na paraḥ

The Supreme Personality of Godhead, the son of Nanda Mahārāja, is to be worshiped along with His transcendental abode, Vṛndāvana. The most pleasing form of worship for the Lord is that which was performed by the gopīs of Vṛndāvana. Śrīmad-Bhāgavatam is the spotless authority on everything, and pure love of God is the ultimate goal of life for all men. These statements, for which we have the highest regard, are the opinion of Śrī Caitanya Mahāprabhu. (*Caitanya-mañjuṣa*, a commentary on *Śrīmad Bhāgavatam*)

Kṛṣṇa, the son of Nanda, is the complete manifestation of the Supreme Personality of Godhead. Lord Kṛṣṇa manifests Himself in three features before His devotees according to their respective qualifications. All of these features are complete. They are not partial or indirect manifestations of Kṛṣṇa the way His manifestations as Paramātma and Brahman are partial. These three features are complete, more complete, and most complete and are situated in Dvārakā, Maṭhurā, and Vṛndāvana. In Dvārakā Kṛṣṇa's manifestation is complete, in Maṭhurā, He is more complete, and in Vraja, He is most complete.

We live on earth, which is situated somewhere in the fourteen planetary systems. These fourteen planetary systems consist of seven upper planets, beginning from earth, and seven planets below the earth. Among the seven upper planets the first three are Bhū, Bhūva, and Svaḥ. These are the residence of the pious, ambitious materialists. The rest, beginning with Mahar, Jana, Tapa, and Satya are the destination of those who practice renunciation. Among them those brahmacāris who live at the gurukula for a fixed period of time and then return home after offering *dakṣiṇā* to their guru, attain the planet called Maharloka. Those *brahmacārīs* who remain in their guru's *āśrama* for their entire lives and who practice strict celibacy attain Janaloka. The destination of the vānaprasthas is Tapaloka, and sannyāsīs to Satyaloka. But devotees who have no desire either to enjoy in the material world or to merge into Brahman attain the most rare Vaikuṇṭhaloka.

Above Vaikuṇṭha is Dvārakā, above Dvārkā is Maṭhurā, and above Maṭhurā is Goloka Vṛndāvana. Those spiritual abodes, which are eternally present in the spiritual sky, are also manifest in this world. Whatever is absent in the spiritual world cannot appear in this one. As lotus flowers grow in the water but are not touched by the water, so Vṛndāvana-dhāma is in this world but untouched by matter. Those whose hearts are not inclined to serve the Lord cannot realize the transcendental nature of the Lord's abode as it appears in this world.

Holy places like Ayodhyā, Dvārakā, and Purī are particular provinces of Vaikuṇṭha. The happiness one feels in Ayodhyā is superior to the happiness one feels in Vaikuṇṭha; the happiness one feels in Dvārakā is superior to the happiness one feels in Ayodhyā; and the happiness experienced by the residents of Goloka Vṛndāvana is the crest jewel of all happiness.

The reason the happiness felt in one dhāma is superior to the happiness felt in another is based on the intensity of the *rasas* expressed in the particular dhāmas. The distress the devotees feel in Goloka dances on the head of all happiness. Distress in the spiritual world nourishes supreme happiness.

Śrī Caitanyadeva established the supremacy of serving the Lord of Vṛndāvana or Gokula. Kṛṣṇa is the fountainhead of all the Viṣṇu incarnations; He is the son of Nanda and the beloved child of Yaśodā. He is also the beloved Lord of Rādhā. This Supreme Personality of Godhead Kṛṣṇa alone is the eternally worshipable Lord of the Gauḍīyas, the followers of

Śrī Rūpa like ourselves. Śrī Caitanyadeva has instructed everyone to worship Kṛṣṇa, the Lord of Gokula.

19. Are Śrī Gaurāṅga's instructions the topmost teachings?

There is no truth superior to the truth preached by Śrī Gaurasundara. It is possible to attain to the highest kingdom of *bhajana* only by the Lord's holy name.

Surrender

1. It appears to us that our only asset is our worldly experience, so how can we renounce that to surrender to a transcendental object?

Do not be afraid, thinking surrender is too hard. In order to know the Absolute Truth one needs a strong heart. To learn to swim one must not be afraid of water. Surrender is not difficult but easy and natural for the spirit soul. Anything opposed to surrender is miserable and unnatural.

2. Are surrender and determination essential?

One must have full confidence in the Lord. One must also have firm determination to worship Hari: "I must receive His grace. I must not go astray. I must always go on chanting His name. God will undoubtedly help me if I am true." If we are completely surrendered to our spiritual master's lotus feet, we will certainly attain all perfection. May the mercy of the spiritual master, who is nondifferent from Śrī Rūpa, be our only asset! Then success is certain.

3. Can one totally renounce the empirical path?

As long as we tend to rely on our own strength, pride, and experience, we cannot fully surrender at the Supreme Lord's lotus feet. As long as we do not adopt the process of surrender, we glorify the ascending or empirical process of approaching God. When we understand the futility of borrowed strength, the insignificance of our pride, and how futile our endeavors, we will surrender to the Lord and accept the teachings of the disciplic succession.

To illustrate this point the *Bhāgavatam* tells the story of Gajendra, king of the elephants. Once when Gajendra, who was intoxicated, was enjoying the association of female elephants in a lake, the aquatics became disturbed. Because of Gajendra's careless behavior and their fear of him, the lake's inhabitants were on the verge of death. But after some time by the arrangement of providence, a powerful crocodile arrived and bit Gajendra's leg. A fierce battle between them ensued and continued for one thousand years, both trying to establish superiority over the other. Meanwhile, Gajendra found his strength gradually diminishing along with his pride in his own skill and expertise. When Gajendra was weakened to the point that he was about to lose the battle to the crocodile, he realized that the only way to survive was to take shelter at the lotus feet of the Supreme Lord.

As long as the living entities consider their insignificant false ego to be as great as that of the maddened Gajendra, they will continue to reach for God by their own endeavor. When the glories of taking shelter at the Lord's lotus feet are awakened in their hearts, however, they will face the choice between continuing the endeavor or simply making a complete surrender. The saints always glorify surrender and never encourage anyone to approach God by their own endeavor. However great we may be, if we think the ascending path beneficial, our downfall is guaranteed.

Kṛṣṇa is everyone's shelter. Taking shelter of others can never protect us. *Bhagavad-gītā* 13.28 states:

prakṛte kriyamāṇāni, guṇaiḥ karmāṇi sarvaśaḥ
ahaṅkāra-vimūḍhātmā, kartāham iti manyate

The spirit soul bewildered by the influence of false ego thinks himself the doer of activities that are in actuality carried out by the three modes of material nature.

People who are bewildered by false ego think that they are the doers and tend to follow the ascending path. Impersonalists desire liberation, which they try to attain by their own work, and yogīs especially want to ascend by their own endeavor. *Śrī Caitanya-caritāmṛta* states: "The *jñānīs* consider themselves as liberated souls while still living." The *jñānīs* want to become one with Brahman. The thirst for the insignificant to become great is what the philosophy of ascending knowledge is based on. The yogīs want to ascend a few feet and to attain mystic perfections or even oneness with the Lord. These are all examples of the goals of the ascending path.

From whatever our current position if we surrender body, mind, and speech to the *sādhus*, hearing submissively from them without the desire of maintaining the evil motive of *karmīs*, *jñānīs*, and yogīs, and without being driven by material temptations or the desire for liberation, then we will conquer the unconquerable Supreme Lord. It does not matter how learned or foolish we may be—or wherever else we are: simply hear about Vaikuṇṭha from the lotus mouth of the saints. We are presently in an incompatible situation in this world of anxiety.

If we study the scriptures under the guidance of our own minds we will be cheated. To think we can discuss the scriptures by interpreting them according to our own urges for material enjoyment or liberation means we think we can control the scriptures. But the scriptures are directly Lord Kṛṣṇa's incarnation. *Bhagavad-gītā* (4.34) states:

tad viddhi praṇipātena, paripraśnena sevayā
upadekṣyanti te jñānaṁ, jñāninas tattva-darśinaḥ

Just try to learn the truth by approaching a spiritual master. Inquire from him submissively and render service unto him. The self-realized souls can impart knowledge unto you because they have seen the truth.

Those who wish to become masters of the material energy practice karma-kāṇḍa. By making a show of accepting instructions while maintaining the desire to become the master, they deceive themselves. The *śāstras* do not reveal themselves to them. The *śāstras* are revealed only to surrendered souls. The Vedas state:

yasya deve parā bhaktir, yathā deve tathā gurau
tasyaite kathitā hy arthāḥ, prakāśante mahātmana

Only unto those great souls who have implicit faith in both the Lord and the spiritual master are all the imports of Vedic knowledge automatically revealed. (Svetāśvatara Upaniṣad 6.23)

Śrī Caitanya Mahāprabhu instructs:

tṛṇād api sunīcena, taror api sahiṣṇunā
amāninā mānadena, kīrtanīya sadā hari

One who thinks himself lower than the grass, who is more tolerant than a tree, and who does not expect personal honor yet is always prepared to give all respect to others can very easily chant the holy name of the Lord. (*Śrī Caitanya-caritāmṛta* Ādi 17.31)

So long as we see ourselves as humbler than a blade of grass, we can chant Hari's holy names. As soon as we try to become even a little higher, we will have to take leave from our chanting.

4. What should a devotee facing material distress do?

Everything that happens is the Lord's supreme will. Therefore there is nothing we can do but wait patiently for the Lord's mercy whenever we experience distress. Śrī Nṛsiṁhadeva always protects His devotees from all inauspiciousness. If we are fixed in devotional service we need not worry about our protection or maintenance. All material inauspiciousness will be destroyed simply by our surrendering to the Supreme Lord.

5. Is our fortune guaranteed by fully surrendering to the Supreme Lord?

The spiritual master knows perfectly how foolish, incompetent, evil, and unsteady we are. Thus he makes suitable arrangements for us to cure all our material diseases. A bona fide spiritual master is one who teaches us what we need to know and hear. If we surrender one hundred percent at the lotus feet of such a personality, in whose hands the most auspicious Supreme Lord has entrusted our well-being, then he will award us complete fortune. But if we take shelter of duplicity, follow a double standard, pretend to be devotees, and make only a show of executing devotional service, he will deceive us. He will say, "You have not become disciples. You do not follow the rules and regulations and still maintain material or sinful desires in your heart. Since you love to hear what the cheaters have to say and have not yet developed proper ears to hear my instructions; you are cheated." It is our duty to gladly obey the instructions our spiritual master mercifully and sincerely imparts. Such willingness to hear is a symptom of a surrendered soul.

6. What does the word namaḥ means as we find it in the mantras?

The word namaḥ means to surrender before the Lord by giving up false ego or independence. "O my spiritual master! O Lord Kṛṣṇa! From today onwards I am Your servant and a soul surrendered unto you. Please direct me and engage me in Your service. From today onwards I have given up false ego or my sense of being the doer. Now my only prayer is that let Your orders and instructions be the polestar director of my life."

To give up material pride based on being the enjoyer, doer, seer, or maintainer is the purport of offering obeisances. When by the guru's mercy one give up the mentality of being the doer, one can attain transcendental knowledge and actually become initiated. It is a symptom of intelligence that one works for perfection by faithfully serving his spiritual master, who is dear to Kṛṣṇa, as long as he is present in this world. But if we cannot attain such perfection because we are not respectful toward our immortal spiritual master, if we cannot serve selflessly even after knowing him to be the lord of our heart, then we are deceived. Unfortunately, we will have lost our best friend, well-wisher, protector, and deliverer despite having received his association. I am such an unlucky person! After approaching the Ganges I run toward the desert to accumulate water! After finding a mine of jewels I am attracted to pieces of glass in a shop! Those who are intelligent should sincerely renounce material desire and subordinate themselves at the lotus feet of the spiritual master with firm determination. Otherwise, they will be deceived.

7. Is it possible to achieve fortune without surrendering?

Without complete surrender to Kṛṣṇa the living entities do not attain complete fortune. If Kṛṣṇa is not in our remembrance at every step, at every movement, and at during every activity, we will certainly be misguided. If we maintain the conception of "I and mine" on the strength of the knowledge we have gained through our senses, we will be baffled in the end. If we are covered by the misconception that we are enjoyers and this material world is meant for our enjoyment, then we will certainly become degraded.

We are souls and this material world is dead matter. "Matter" is that which we can enjoy. Forgetting our constitutional position we are controlled by false ego, imagining ourselves enjoyers and all matter meant for our enjoyment. When false ego peaks, then the sinful conception, "I am almighty God" ruins us. If we are bewildered by our own apparent greatness, then we should know that our advancement has been totally obstructed.

8. Is a surrendered soul sure to achieve perfection?

The moment we surrender to the Supreme Lord, life's perfection comes within our grasp. By depending on the Lord who is the proprietor of everything, we can easily attain auspiciousness. We will achieve perfection in proportion to our surrender to the Lord. Kṛṣṇa did not send us to this world to give us trouble. We misused our independence and have ourselves invited trouble. By maintaining faith in the auspicious words of the Supreme Lord our pride doers will be vanquished forever. Then we will stop running to become expert fruitive workers and will surrender instead at Kṛṣṇa's lotus feet.

9. What is the symptom of a surrendered soul?

To renounce the mentality that "I am the doer" and to accept Kṛṣṇa as one's sole maintainer are the symptoms of a surrendered soul. Surrendered souls do not need to think themselves in charge. If we become dependent on the daughter of Vṛṣabhānu, then no insignificant pride in the activities of this world will capture our hearts. Unless we develop the pride that we are Kṛṣṇa's servants, we cannot fully surrender or take complete shelter.

Without complete surrender, we will naturally become proud to be called "father" or "doer."

10. How can we recognize a devotee?

We often try to measure devotees. Not understanding their devotional activities, we reject them as if we were their examiners. With what machine do we try to observe the devotees? Give up your false ego and approach the devotees with humility and eagerness. By fully surrendering at their lotus feet, you will learn by their mercy to recognize what is a devotee. It is not possible to understand them otherwise. But by sincerely hearing about Hari from the devotees, all obstacles will be vanquished and our hearts filled with immense strength. In *Bhagavad-gītā* (4.34), Lord Kṛṣṇa states:

tad viddhi praṇipātena, paripraśnena sevayā
upadekṣyanti te jñānaṁ, jñāninas tattva-darśina

Just try to learn the truth by approaching a spiritual master. Inquire from him submissively and render service unto him. The self-realized souls can impart knowledge unto you because they have seen the truth.

Pranipāt means "unconditional surrender," paripraśna means "honest inquiry," and seva means "serving temperament." If we approach a spiritual master with these three attitudes in tact, we will certainly gain knowledge about the Absolute Truth and become successful.

11. What is surrender?

Kṛṣṇa's will is supreme in all matters. Even if I think I will do something, I will not have the power to do that thing if the Lord does not sanction it. To dovetail our will with the Lord's will is called śaraṇāgati, surrender. Surrender means peaceful life. All material objects are favorable for Kṛṣṇa's pastimes, but if instead of offering material objects to Him we use them to seek our own happiness in this world, we will forget Him. Hence the merciful Lord has created this material world to test us. If we live here seeking material happiness, we will certainly forget Kṛṣṇa. That the material world is meant for our testing is proof of the Lord's compassion.

One cannot approach the land of Vraja by one's own will. Only by the grace and blessings of ŚrīŚrī Rādhā-Kṛṣṇa is one able to reside in Vraja. Our independent will to reside in Vraja is detrimental to the cultivation of Kṛṣṇa consciousness.

Although I had a strong desire to go to Mathurā in April, Kṛṣṇa had some other plan and I could not go. Now I desire to go to Mathurā in October, but if Kṛṣṇa thinks otherwise, there will be nothing I can do. If I try to do something against His will, I will become culpable.

By worshiping Hari one's body, mind, and self remain healthy. If one is averse to His worship, then all these three will become unfavorable.

12. How will we be protected?

The only way to be protected is to take shelter at the lotus feet of those great personalities who constantly speak about the Supreme Lord and who are fully dependent on Him. Such persons deliver the fallen souls and befriend the poor. If we sincerely take shelter of them, they will protect us.

13. How can we realize the Absolute Truth?

Transcendental subject matter never reveals itself to people who are enriched with material knowledge. The real nature of the transcendental Absolute Truth will be realized simply by surrendering unto those who have fully realized the Absolute Truth. Therefore the Vedas state:

tad-vijñānārthaṁ sa gurum evābhigacchet
samit-pāṇiḥśrotriyaṁ brahma-niṣṭham

To understand these things properly, one must humbly approach, with firewood in hand, a spiritual master who is learned in the Vedas and firmly devoted to the Absolute Truth.

Bhagavad-gītā 4.34 also states:

tad viddhi praṇipātena, paripraśnena sevayā
upadekṣyanti te jñānaṁ, jñāninas tattva-darśinaḥ

Just try to learn the truth by approaching a spiritual master. Inquire from him submissively and render service unto him. The self-realized souls can impart knowledge unto you because they have seen the truth.

The transcendental Absolute Truth, or the spiritual subject matter, is omniscient. Every sober person is naturally eager to serve that omniscient and independent Lord. Only those who are averse to such service suffer material distress by being thrown into this material prison house. In order to deliver the fallen souls, divert their attention, and purify their consciousness, the merciful Absolute Truth sends His liberated representatives to this world.

14. How can one surrender before realizing the truth?

Unless we surrender, we cannot realize the truth. As long as we remain unsurrendered, we will continue to rush on the path of ruination, doubtful and bewildered about religious principles. Therefore Arjuna told Kṛṣṇa, *śiṣyas te aham śadhi mām tvām prapannam*: "I surrender to You and become Your disciple."

If the person of whom I am taking shelter is a mortal, he cannot be called guru. A mortal being under the jurisdiction of sense perception can never be guru. Surrendering to such a spiritual master can never take us to the Absolute Truth. The spiritual master is Kṛṣṇa's energy. He is fully conversant with the science of Kṛṣṇa. He is nondifferent from Kṛṣṇa and is a manifestation of Him.

15. Why are we unable to depend on God?

As long as we depend on our own strength, pride, and experience, we cannot surrender at the Supreme Lord's lotus feet. Until we develop the mentality of surrender, we will continue to glorify the empirical path. When we finally understand the insignificance of our borrowed strength, pride, and the uselessness of our own endeavor, then we will learn to surrender to Kṛṣṇa and accept the knowledge coming through disciplic succession. When our hearts are filled with the glories of surrender to the Lord, our hearts will rush toward the Vaiṣṇavas who are glorifying Him. We should hear about Vaikuṇṭha from such persons while remaining in our present situation. Everything else will be maintained and we can simply repose our faith in the Supreme Lord.

16. How does one surrender to the Supreme Lord?

Subordination to Maya and subordination to the Lord are not synonymous. It is not possible to take shelter of both of them at the same time. Either we are under Maya's shelter or we are under Kṛṣṇa's shelter. If we are subordinate to Maya, it means we are attached to family life or to material life in general. Being subordinate to Kṛṣṇa means we are attached to Kṛṣṇa and His service. Therefore Prahlāda Mahārāja says, "Give up the dark well of family life and take shelter of the Lord by approaching the saintly persons." If due to weakness we are unable to leave home, then at least become detached from family life and worship the Lord in the association of devotees. This will certainly bring you ultimate fortune. If you make a show of serving the Lord while remaining attached to home and family life, then you will not awaken the propensity to serve the Lord. Instead you will remain forever drowned in the ocean of material existence.

After taking shelter of the Lord, if we remain attached to household duties and decide that serving and pleasing one's wife and children is the aim of life, if we remain ever indifferent to serving the Lord, giving more importance to our family life, then what is the use of taking shelter of the Lord? By serving the Lord we must become convinced that we are His eternal servants. Is that happening? We can judge by the fruit. The fruit of service is to want more service and to progressively increase in that way. We should analyze carefully what we are doing. Where is our shelter? In what direction does our mind rush? Don't let yourself be cheated.

A woman leaves her father's house and takes shelter of her husband's house. As a result, her surname is changed. She no longer remains attached to her father's house. It is natural to develop love for those whom we serve. Serve Kṛṣṇa and you will become attached to Him.

17. Who will be delivered from the material world?

If a person surrenders one hundred percent, the Lord will certainly deliver him. Unless one makes serving the spiritual master and the Vaiṣṇavas his life and soul, he will not learn to surrender completely. Moreover, until he gives fully he will not be rewarded fully. The Lord is the supreme Absolute Truth. He demands full surrender and will not settle for anything less. "As you sow, so will you reap."

Mercy

1. Is material distress an example of the Lord's mercy?

The Supreme Lord is full of mercy. Whatever He does is beneficial for the living entities. It is all for the best. People should live happily wherever they are situated by the merciful Lord and gladly accept His reward and punishment. All the Lord's rewards and punishments are awarded for the living entity's benefit. We love the rewards awarded by Maya and hate the punishments because they cause pain. But Maya's punishments are awarded to make us eligible for the Lord's mercy. That is why devotees gladly accept Maya's punishments with a smile; they understand that all suffering is the Lord's mercy. Those who cannot understand that mundane calamities are the Lord's mercy end up disappointed even as they seek material happiness and prosperity again and again.

2. Are the tests the Lord presents the living entities manifestations of His mercy?

Teachers mercifully arrange for examinations in order to take students to a higher class. For attentive, intelligent students, examinations are a source of happiness. Only the inattentive students are afraid of or dislike examinations.

Those who glorify material enjoyment and who speak accordingly to their audience's taste do not face danger, inconvenience, or obstacles in their preaching, but those who preach about devotional service and the soul's eternal propensity face many difficulties. These inconveniences come and try to cause discouragement. But those who have taken shelter of devotional service should definitely know that these obstacles have come to test our love of and determination for the Lord's service; they are actually assisting us in our progressive advancement on the devotional path.

We should remain firmly fixed in devotional service while accepting the ideal examples of nāmācārya Haridāsa Ṭhākura and the topmost devotee, Prahlāda Mahārāja. Both of them exhibited a wonderful service attitude and a high degree of tolerance. Simply to achieve something temporary, human beings are baffled for hundreds of lifetimes. If in spite of seeing thousands of examples of failure, such people will even dare to give up their lives to attain insignificant enjoyment, then can't intelligent and fortunate devotees dedicate their temporary lives to understand the Supreme Lord, who is the Absolute Truth for all time?

3. Is everything the Supreme Lord does beneficial?

Everything about the Lord is merciful. There is no inauspiciousness in the Lord's arrangements. Whatever He does is for the good of all living entities. Those conditioned souls who consider interference to their sense gratification inauspicious or as an example of the Lord's cruelty understand only one move of the chess game. They do not know what will happen four or five moves later.

The mercy of Śrī Caitanyadeva and His devotees is causeless and yields no negative results. When a doctor prescribes a bitter medicine, the patient thinks him cruel. When he becomes cured by taking that medicine, though, he understands how merciful the doctor really was.

4. Should we follow all the Lord's arrangements with happiness?

Everything takes place by the will of the Supreme Lord. Therefore if we suffer some inconvenience, there is nothing to do but wait patiently for the Lord's mercy. Due to our previous karma we sometimes become ill and sometimes remain healthy. When we think we are well, we become averse to Kṛṣṇa and consider ourselves superior to His devotees. Therefore according to our situation Kṛṣṇa places us in various types of distress, illness, or inconvenience. This forces devotees to try to understand the purport of the tat te 'nu kampām verse.

We should happily agree with whatever pleases Kṛṣṇa. If Kṛṣṇa is happy by turning us away, then we accept it. Śrī Bhaktivinoda Ṭhākura stated, "If I feel any distress while serving You, O Lord, I consider it a source of great pleasure." This is Vaiṣṇava realization, and one should try to follow it.

5. How is it possible to establish a relationship with Kṛṣṇa, who is transcendental to the three modes of material nature?

Although it seems impossible to establish our relationship with Kṛṣṇa, the most compassionate Kṛṣṇa mercifully agrees to come under our control. Although the sun is huge, yet it is possible to see the sun with our limited senses through the object we call the material sky. Similarly, the spiritual sky in the form of the devotees' devotional service is awarding us an opportunity to establish our relationship with Kṛṣṇa and to attain His association.

Although the sun is huge and far away from us, we can see it by the mercy of the sun's rays. Similarly, we can establish our relationship with Kṛṣṇa by the mercy of Kṛṣṇa's rays, His devotees. If we take shelter of the spiritual master, who is the personification of Kṛṣṇa's mercy, everything will become possible for us.

6. What is the mercy of the indwelling Supersoul?

The indwelling Supersoul awards us the strength to accept instructions from both the initiating and instructing spiritual masters. It is not possible to understand their words without His mercy, because without His mercy the heart remains contaminated and the teachings of the spiritual master do not take deep root. The indwelling Supersoul mercifully awards us the qualification to receive the mercy of the initiating and instructing spiritual masters. In the form of initiating spiritual master, Śrī Caitanyadeva personally bestows transcendental knowledge and pure devotional service. He also sends us spiritual masters to instruct us who are nondifferent from Himself. He protects devotional service and awards the qualification to those inclined to serve to receive initiation and instruction.

7. Are the mercy of the spiritual master and the mercy of the Supreme Lord one and the same?

The spiritual master's mercy and the Supreme Lord's mercy are not separate entities. The spiritual master has no engagement other than to worship Kṛṣṇa. Also, Kṛṣṇa does not accept service from anyone other than an intimate devotee. The spiritual master and Kṛṣṇa are attached to one another in love; and both treat one another as more dear to them than their own lives. They are one. The spiritual master is the personification of devotional service to Kṛṣṇa, and Kṛṣṇa is the personification of devotional service to the devotee.

Only the spiritual master offers our entire service to Kṛṣṇa. The spiritual master, who is to be served eternally, is not an ordinary human being from this world. In order to deliver the fallen conditioned souls he appears in this world by Kṛṣṇa's will and teaches the fortunate living entities devotional service. Through him only do we receive the mercy of Kṛṣṇa.

8. Why do devotees usually appear in lower families? Why do devotees appear like fools or as if they are diseased, even though they are not subject to enjoy the fruits of karma?

Devotees are never forced to enjoy the fruits of their karma. All their pastimes, such as taking birth, take place simply by the Lord's will. But it is often seen that devotees appear in low-class families or like fools to ordinary eyes, or afflicted with disease. There is a great purpose behind this. If people find that the Lord's devotees appear only in high-class families and that they are always strong, healthy, and highly learned according to material calculation, they will become discouraged. In order to display His causeless mercy and to benefit all living entities, therefore, the most merciful Lord induces His devotees to appear among various classes of men. It is to be understood that this is like sending a trained she-elephant into a kheda, an enclosure for catching wild elephants. Śrī Caitanya-bhāgavata states [*CB Ādi-khaṇḍa* 2.49]:

śocya-deśe śocya-kule āpana-samāna
janmāiyā vaiṣṇave sabāre kare trāṇa
yei deśe yāi kule vaiṣṇava 'avatāri'
tāṇhāra prabhāve lakṣa-yojana nistare
yata dekha vaiṣṇavera vyavahāra-duḥkhaḥ
niścaya jāniha sei parānanda-sukha
viṣaya-madāndha saba kichui nā jāne"vidyā-made,
dhana-made vaiṣṇava nā cine

The Lord had His devotees, who are equal to Him, appear at impious places and in impious families in order to deliver everyone.

In whatever place or family a Vaiṣṇava appears, people for hundreds of thousands of miles around are all delivered.

Know for certain that whatever worldly distress is seen in a Vaiṣṇava is actually spiritual happiness.

People blinded with pride over material enjoyment do not know anything. They cannot recognize a Vaiṣṇava due to pride born of education and wealth.

Just because devotees appear in low-class families does not mean that they are sinful or that they have appeared in such families as a result of karma. Rather, we should understand that they have appeared to purify those families. One who attains perfection by practicing the *sādhana* prescribed for the age of Kali is the best of all.

9. How can one attain the Lord's mercy?

If we do not transgress against the true servant of Hari who are constantly engaged in His service but follow in their footsteps, then we can attain the Lord's mercy. Only by the Vaiṣṇavas' mercy can one attain the mercy of Hari. If the Vaiṣṇavas are displeased, then no one can attain fortune. This is especially true of the spiritual master. Without pleasing the spiritual master one cannot attain the Lord's mercy.

11. Does Lord Govinda award us punishment?

The transcendental Personality of Godhead, Śrī Govinda, is our eternal master. The word prabhu refers to one who is able to both punish and bestow mercy. The Supreme Lord is capable of doing and undoing anything. It is not a fact that the Lord only displays compassion; but He can also punish. The Lord incarnates to rectify those proud people who are averse to Him by punishing them. It is the nature of the compassionate to both punish and show clemency accordingly. But punishment is a display of His indirect mercy, whereas clemency is a display of His direct mercy.

Conditioned living entities who are averse to the Lord or who act sinfully are fit objects for the Lord's punishment, and devotees inclined to Kṛṣṇa's service are qualified for His direct mercy. Even weak-hearted but simple-minded humble practitioners of devotional service are qualified for the Lord's compassion, whereas proud, crooked people are punishable because they cheat.

12. Are karmic fruits the Lord's mercy?

Considering the fruits of one's own karma the Lord's mercy, intelligent persons enjoy those fruits and surrender body, mind, and speech to the Lord's lotus feet. However great the danger, devotees accept it as karmic reaction. Therefore they do not attribute the Lord with any fault. Rather, accepting the reaction gladly as His mercy, they become more attached to Him. This is the attitude taught in the *Bhāgavatam*.

13. "Everything is done by the will and mercy of the Lord." Would you agree?

Śrīmad-Bhāgavatam 10.14.8 states:

tat te 'nukampāṁ su-samīkṣamāṇo
bhuñjāna evātma-kṛtaṁ vipākam
hṛd-vāg-vapurbhir vidadhan namas te
jīveta yo mukti-pade sa dāya-bhāk

My dear Lord, one who earnestly waits for You to bestow Your causeless mercy upon him, all the while patiently suffering the reactions of his past misdeeds and offering You respectful obeisances with his heart, words, and body, is surely eligible for liberation, for it has become his rightful claim.

Those who are qualified to go back to Godhead conclude: If I attribute fault to the most auspicious Supreme Lord, then due to my lack of desire to serve Him, I will never be able to be liberated. Those who are inclined to serve the Lord consider all inconveniences as His mercy and thus become more attracted to Him. They are actually qualified for liberation.

14. When we commit sinful activities, is that also some expression of the Lord's mercy?

No, it is not. We experience the desire to commit sins because we are being tested. Just as parents place money, rice, and a *Śrīmad-Bhāgavatam* before a newly crawling child in order to test that child's inclination, so the Supreme Lord, who is an ocean of mercy, does the same with us. Ignorant, godless people consider Him cruel, but whatever the Lord does only benefits others. Just as both a father's kissing and slapping of his son displays his mercy, so the Lord's activities are also His mercy. If the Lord's mercy is mistaken for punishment, then that means we lack the serving temperament or a developed attraction to God.

When a person desires to take shelter of the Lord, the Lord tests his sincerity by placing various obstacles before him, just as a doctor presents restrictions on the lifestyle of the patient in order to cure the disease. When a doctor is about to operate on a boil and picks up a knife, we would be foolish to consider him merciless. We should not be foolish enough to fail to recognize our well-wisher. Maya has arranged objects for our sense gratification to tempt us. Being attracted by these temptations we sometimes engage in unrestricted sense gratification, in welfare activities to benefit others, or begin to think the impersonal Brahman the goal of life. Similarly, sometimes we may become attracted to glorifying the philosophies propounded by Buddha and Śankarācārya. None of these activities benefit us. We should simply hear kṛṣṇa-kathā. There is no other way to attain our good fortune.

The Supreme Lord does not interfere with anyone's independence. He does not kill the living entity's spiritual propensities. If He interfered in our independence, we would have to consider Him merciless. Instead, He simply informs and warns the living entities about good and bad activities. In His form as Śrī Caitanyadeva, the Supreme Lord instructs us not to follow the doctrines propounded by Jaimini or Śankarācarya. Those doctrines do not teach us how best to use our minute independence. Rather, we should act only in ways that please the Supreme Lord.

15. Who is qualified to receive the Lord's mercy?

The Supreme Lord bestows mercy only on those sincere souls who fully surrender to Him. It is impossible to receive Him as long as one is puffed up with the conception of "I" and "mine".

16. Before whom does the Supreme Lord remains unmanifest?

The Lord is supremely cognizant and the living entities are minutely cognizant. If among the minutely cognizant living entities someone tries to cheat the Lord by hiding something from Him, the supremely cognizant Lord reserves the right of not showing himself to that cheater.

17. Can we see God with our present eyes?

The universe and the Lord of the universe are one. One cannot see the Lord of the universe until one gains transcendental knowledge or spiritual vision. At present I cannot see with my naked eyes, but I can see well with spectacles. Similarly, our present eyes are not capable of seeing the Lord of the universe. The Lord of the universe is seen only with the eyes of transcendental knowledge, devotional service given by the spiritual master. Our ability to see depends wholly on Kṛṣṇa's mercy. It is Kṛṣṇa's mercy that allows us to gain transcendental knowledge through aural reception, after which we can see Him.

18. Are we certain to receive Kṛṣṇa's mercy?

If we are sincerely eager at heart to attain Kṛṣṇa, we will certainly attain Him. Maintaining material desire spoils everything, because it makes us proud of high birth, opulence, knowledge, and so on.

By the grace of the Lord we are given a spiritual master. Our development depends on the Lord's mercy. Without His mercy all attempts are futile. His mercy is the root. However, we must learn how to sincerely beg for His mercy. Those who are sincere will certainly achieve His mercy. He cannot but bestow His mercy, because He is all-merciful.

If we wonder why we don't appear to be receiving His mercy, it's because we are not really sincere. The Lord helps those who surrender to Him completely.

Direct service to God awards us God. Without such service the soul cannot advance. Kṛṣṇa is our only worshipable Lord and we have no other duty but to serve Him. Devotional service is not sense gratification. Living only for sense gratification is simply selfishness.

Attaining Perfection

1. When does a living entity attain auspiciousness?

Only when one takes shelter at the lotus feet of the spiritual master and accepts Kṛṣṇa's service as one's life and soul does the Absolute Truth come within one's control.

2. How will one attain perfection in one lifetime?

One can certainly attain perfection in one lifetime by sincerely worshiping the Lord under the guru's guidance and giving up one's independence.

3. How can one know the Supreme Lord?

One should faithfully hear *hari-kathā* from the spiritual master's mouth. There is no way to understand God other than to fully surrender at the guru's lotus feet. Only those who fully surrender are able to know the Supreme Lord.

4. What current of thought allows one to attain auspiciousness?

If we see the material world as if we were the Lord's servants, we will no longer feel distress. By sincerely worshiping the Lord and by fully surrendering to Him while giving up our independence, we will certainly attain Him in this lifetime. We have to hear about the Lord from those persons who can introduce us to Him and who are engaged in His service twenty-four hours a day. Then our perfection is certain.

The Lord's devotees see through devotion-filled eyes the form of Śyāmasundara Kṛṣṇa in their hearts. If we associate with such devotees and receive their mercy, we will also come to see the Lord in our heart. We should not waste any more time, but should be constantly eager to serve the Lord in the association of devotees. If we remain ever in the association of the devotees, our propensity to serve the Lord will only increase.

The Supreme Lord fulfills all the desires of His surrendered devotees. He never disappoints them. It is said that Kṛṣṇa fulfills the desires of all those who beg for His service. We should also know that only the Supreme Lord is capable of protecting us by giving us shelter. No one else has that power. If we can learn to firmly believe this fact, we will find ourselves becoming fearless, anxiety-free, happy, and successful.

If we trust that the all-auspicious Lord Kṛṣṇa is our only benefactor, we will certainly achieve auspiciousness. It is impossible to express the incredible fortune given to those who fully surrender at the Lord's lotus feet.

5. How will we be liberated from material existence?

Without the Supreme Lord's mercy, no one can be delivered from material existence. The moment we forget that we are His eternal servants, we begin to serve Maya. The only way to become liberated from this formidable material existence is to approach the spiritual master and the Vaiṣṇavas, inquire from them submissively, and hear kṛṣṇa-kathā from them with a service attitude. By hearing kṛṣṇa-kathā with devotion, the propensities we have to enjoy matter will be destroyed.

6. How can we be benefited?

Kṛṣṇa is my eternal Lord and I am His eternal servant: if somehow or other this knowledge is attained, then all inauspiciousness is burnt to ashes and all auspiciousness captured.

7. What is the path of auspiciousness?

To surrender to the Supreme Lord in happiness and distress is the only path of auspiciousness. Kṛṣṇa will certainly protect us. If we give up this security and try to protect ourselves, we are doomed. Our fortune lies in fully depending on Kṛṣṇa. Otherwise, we will have to suffer misery birth after birth. The affectionate Lord takes all responsibility for His surrendered devotees.

8. What is the path of back to Godhead?

To simply depend on Kṛṣṇa's mercy while remaining inclined toward His service under the spiritual master's guidance is the path of back to

Godhead. The *Śrīmad-Bhāgavatam* verse that begins tat te 'nu kampām proves this. The path back to Godhead is made possible by serving the transparent spiritual master. The path of pure devotional service is the path back to Godhead.

9. Can one gain benefit by simply putting on a sannyāsīs dress?

One cannot gain anything simply by wearing the garb of a *sannyāsī*. One can become a real *sannyāsī* by becoming a staunch follower of his guru and by making the guru's service his life and soul. One should become such a Vaiṣṇava *sannyāsī* by becoming attached to both the spiritual master and the holy name. But those who indulge in bad association instead of serving Kṛṣṇa under the guru's guidance will certainly be ruined. They will never know the Supreme Personality of Godhead or attain His service. One can cheat people by dressing as a *sādhu*, but the omniscient Lord, who gives the fruit of karma, will never leave such cheaters alone. Those who engage in bad association while dressed as *sādhus* are chopping at their own legs with an ax.

10. How can we attain auspiciousness?

As long as we remain attached to family life or house, we are in trouble, but if we follow and serve the spiritual master, who constantly serves Kṛṣṇa, we will no longer have any problem. There is no way to make our lives auspicious except to follow the Lord's devotees. Service to the spiritual master, who is most dear to the Supreme Lord, is more beneficial than service to the Supreme Lord Himself. Our progress lies in serving the spiritual master, because by such service the fallen living entities are delivered. Those who want actual benefit must serve the spiritual master and the devotees with love and devotion.

What does it mean to serve them? Guru and the Vaiṣṇavas engage in no other activity but Kṛṣṇa's service. If we are to serve them, we should assist them in their service to the Supreme Lord and happily follow their orders without reservation.

Subordination to the spiritual master is required at all stages of life. To try to personally serve Kṛṣṇa with pride and without the guru's guidance simply causes disturbance. By denying or disobeying the spiritual master, one certainly brings about his own ruination. "I am serving Hariḥ.": to think this is a symptom of pride. False pride is the first and main cause of falldown. By finding fault with guru and the Vaiṣṇavas, one's ruination is inevitable. Without service to guru, the living entities cannot find benefit.

Becoming interested in one's own happiness brings misfortune on a living entity. Unless one is an unalloyed devotee he cannot serve Kṛṣṇa, and without serving guru one cannot become an unalloyed devotee. There is no other way for the conditioned souls to become delivered except to serve the spiritual master and the Vaiṣṇavas.

11. Why are we unable to realize the Supreme Lord?

How will the living entities, who are Kṛṣṇa's servants, realize the Lord unless they constantly serve and associate with the guru and the Vaiṣṇavas? If we are busy in worldly or family activities, how will we understand the Lord of the universe? Under the control of sinful desires, we have presently developed a bad mentality; we think we have great duties to perform in this world. This is because we are averse to the original fountainhead. Just as by stepping in quicksand one's legs are sucked down, so we have stepped into the quicksand of dependence on material phenomena and are being pulled down. Instead of becoming inclined to serve Kṛṣṇa, we spend our time influenced by sinful desires. Lord Viṣṇu's illusory energy has conditioned us to think that we are enjoyers and expert *karmīs*. Be careful. Accept guidance at every step. Be extremely careful. It is vital that we are controlled by the spiritual master at every step.

Serving the devotees is more beneficial to us than serving the Lord. The living entities can receive more mercy by associating with devotees than from trying to associate directly with the Lord. The place where the spiritual master or a devotee resides is more favorable for the pure worship of Hari than the place where the Supreme Lord resides. Understand the purport of the phrase, "Wherever there are Vaiṣṇavas, that is Vṛndāvana." If instead we are indifferent toward guru-sevā, it means we have failed to become servants. It means we are proud and entangled in material thought.

There is no greater topic of discussion in the theistic world than the topic of how to serve the lotus feet of Śrī Rādhā-Govinda. Always hear *hari-kathā*. Do not become materialists, bereft of the transcendental Lord's service. Pay close attention to the worship of Hari. We have already passed so many lifetimes engaged in other activities. Be always cautious to attain the goal of life. Always carefully serve the spiritual master and Kṛṣṇa with love and devotion and you will certainly realize the Supreme Lord.

12. How can we attain eternal benefit?

The auspicious desire of the Lord's devotees is that the living entities not always remain in a suffering condition. Let them achieve eternal fortune. To achieve that eternal fortune, they must take shelter of a bona fide spiritual master's lotus feet, a devotee most dear to Kṛṣṇa. They should serve that devotee with firm faith and devotion, because the spiritual master is nondifferent from Śrī Rūpa Gosvāmī. By taking shelter of the guru's lotus feet they will attain Nandanandana's service.

It is important that these people hear kṛṣṇa-kathā from the guru's lotus mouth. If they can make the dust from their spiritual master's lotus feet their only asset, they will attain pure devotional service to Kṛṣṇa, the enchanter of the whole world. Therefore the spiritual master's lotus feet are eternally worshipable.

The transcendental spiritual master is not of this world. He is not temporary, nor is he a lump of flesh and blood. He is eternal and full of knowledge and bliss like the Supreme Lord. The spiritual master is the Supreme Lord in human form. He is not an ordinary human being. Those who consider the spiritual master or Śrī Gaurāṅga material products simply prove the self-serving nature of their service. Such service is not unalloyed but a business exchange.

Until a living entity fully surrenders to the lotus feet of the most worshipable spiritual master, he cannot see the Supreme Lord. Those who are unaware that the spiritual master is fully transcendental, that he is as good as the Lord, and that he is dear to Kṛṣṇa are completely unqualified to enter the spiritual kingdom, the kingdom of service to Kṛṣṇa.

Only by the guru's mercy can we approach the transcendental Absolute Truth and attain the shelter and *darśana* of Śrī Caitanyadeva. Only then can we become glorious and successful. If we are attracted to material forms, we will not be able to attain the spiritual master's *darśana*. Simply by engaging in the worshipable guru's service, and thus the service of Śrī Kṛṣṇa, without duplicity, we will achieve good fortune.

We pray:

ādadānastrinaṁ dantair idaṁ yāce puna puna
śrīmad guru padāmbhoja dhuli syān janma janmani

"Holding a straw between my teeth, I repeatedly pray that I do not want anything else, I do not want religiosity, economic development, sense gratification, or liberation. I simply want to become a particle of dust at the lotus feet of my spiritual master. Under his guidance, I want to engage in the Lord's service in the same way he has constantly served the Supreme Lord. Kṛṣṇa belongs to me. If I do not serve him He will feel distressed."

If we develop such a mood we will certainly attain kṛṣṇa-prema. This good fortune is achieved only by lovingly serving the spiritual master.

13. What is the duty of a householder?

If we endeavor for personal happiness we will become attached to matter. By using all our energy for Kṛṣṇa's service, however, we will find fortune. Householder devotees should always be prepared to help or serve those who have come to worship Kṛṣṇa constantly, having given up wife, children, and relatives. Then only will such householders find benefit and their material attachments slackening. Householder Vaiṣṇavas should work hard to serve Hari, just as they work to satisfy their families. They should maintain their families as in service to the Lord. Vaiṣṇavas are not interested in feeding poisonous snakes with milk and bananas but in devotional service. Therefore they leave their families if they realize that family life has become unfavorable for their devotional service.

As soon as I want to enjoy or lord it over others, Maya controls me. The only auspicious activity for the present-day troublesome society is to liberate oneself from foolishness in the form of family life and to enter into Kṛṣṇa's family. Only by taking shelter of the guru's lotus feet without duplicity can one be delivered from material life. One cannot be delivered by any other means. Can the spiritual master, by whose mercy one can be delivered from material existence be merely a nondevotee, sense enjoyer, *karmī*, liar, covered atheist, impersonalist, or mystic yogī? Can any one become a real spiritual master unless he has devoted himself to the Supreme Personality of Godhead?

Whether one is a householder or a *sannyāsī*, it is his principal duty to serve the pure spiritual master. When the *hari-kathā* emanating from the lotus mouth of the spiritual master enters into the service-inclined ears, then the darkness of ignorance is vanquished. At that time one's eyes become purified, and through those purified eyes one is able to see Kṛṣṇa.

What has caused my ruination is my desire to become master. If I want to enjoy material life and I run after sense gratification, and if I become busy in family life, then the threefold miseries of material existence are inevitable. Therefore instead of listening to one's mind or the words of mental speculators, one should always hear the instructions of those who constantly serve the Supreme Lord.

14. Who is fortunate?

The fortunate among human beings are of two types, those with good fortune and those with bad fortune. Those with good fortune try to worship Hari and eventually attain His devotional service in this lifetime. Such persons do not need to wait for another birth. If one takes shelter of Śrī Caitanyadeva without deviation, he will attain all perfection in this lifetime. If in spite of attaining the path of auspiciousness, however, a person accepts bad association, he may fall down. Best to remain ever free from the attraction for wealth, women, and fame. By repeatedly hearing *hari-kathā*, all one's mundane thoughts will be vanquished. Śrī Caitanyadeva's topics, teachings, and instructions are so great and sublime that nothing can stand before them. The servants of Śrī Caitanyadeva's topics, which belittle religiosity, economic development, sense gratification, and liberation are actually the most magnanimous. One should at least impartially consider how intelligent, thoughtful, and helpful Gaura's devotees are! May Śrī Caitanyadeva's mercy protect us all from the evil motive that inspires us to lord it over others and allow them to serve us.

15. Who is qualified to return to the spiritual world?

Only those who sincerely follow in the footsteps of their spiritual master, who is nondifferent from Śrī Rūpa, will attain the Lord's mercy and come to love Kṛṣṇa.

16. What is the difference between attaining perfection in chanting mantras and attaining perfection in devotional service?

When one perfects his chanting of mantras he becomes liberated. From there, one can attain pure devotional service. Prior to attaining pure devotional service, however, one stands on the platform of either *sādhana*-kriyā or *bhajana*-kriyā. First one becomes liberated, and then his material bondage is destroyed. Then only is one qualified to become Kṛṣṇa's servant.

One who practices devotional service becomes liberated when he perfects his chanting of mantras. At that time, his mundane ego has no more influence, he becomes free of material desire, and he attains the good fortune of serving the Supreme Lord for His pleasure. That is called pure devotional service.

Perfection in mantra-chanting awards liberation, and perfection in devotional service awards one love of God. A devotee at prema is therefore obviously a perfected devotee, a *mahā-bhāgavata*.

It is important to note, however, that although perfection in chanting mantras awards liberation, one can attain liberation simply by chanting nāmābhāsa. Kṛṣṇa's holy names are the object worship for liberated persons. *Sri Caitanya-caritāmṛta* Ādi 7.73 states:

kṛṣṇa-mantra haite habe saṁsāra-mocana
kṛṣṇa-nāma haite pābe kṛṣṇera caraṇa

Simply by chanting the holy name of Kṛṣṇa one can obtain freedom from material existence. Indeed, simply by chanting the Hare Kṛṣṇa mantra, one will be able to see the lotus feet of the Lord.

17. Who will attain perfection?

Only those who follow the disciplic succession will attain perfection. Dry argument has no basis. Vedic knowledge received through aural reception is eternal and conclusive. Only those who glorify Hari and His qualities, names, and forms throughout the day and night can attain perfection.

18. What is our topmost duty?

This human form of life is temporary and rare, so one should give up everything, including atheism, offensiveness, and useless activity and engage his mind in worshiping Hari. We have received this human form of life after many lifetimes. This is why it is rare. Even though the human body, like any body, is temporary, it allows us to make spiritual advancement. Only the intelligent will give up all other activities and, without wasting a moment, try to achieve the ultimate goal of life as long as they have breath.

To achieve the ultimate goal of life one must take shelter at the lotus feet of a bona fide spiritual master. A bona fide spiritual master does not speak in favor of adverse tastes but about kṛṣṇa-*bhajana*, our only and most important duty.

Worldly people attract me by speaking about things for which I find taste. They appear to be my friends. However, only that person who does not wish to show me envy, who is honestly distressed upon seeing my distress, and who feels pain upon seeing my agony, is my well-wishing spiritual master. *Śrīmad-Bhāgavatam* has instructed us to take complete shelter of such a spiritual master.

19. How can we attain freedom?

There is no way to attain freedom or peace other than to take shelter at the Supreme Lord's lotus feet. Surrender, under the guru's guidance, is the proper use of our independence. Surrender is complete independence or real independence because it leaves us free to act according to our eternal constitutional position.

20. Is the path leading to the ultimate goal of life full of impediments?

Persons who want immediate happiness may seem to face no inconvenience at present, whereas persons who want ultimate fortune may face difficulties. Aspiring devotees should accept the difficulties. To accept such difficulties is called tolerance.

21. Please explain the Bhagavad-gītā verse that begins sarva dharmān parityajya.

Lord Kṛṣṇa said in *Bhagavad-gītā* that one should give up all varieties of religion and surrender unto Him. That same Lord also said that by giving up one's own occupational duty and taking up another's, one could not achieve benefit. It is better, He said, to die engaged in one's svadharma than to engage in the practices of another's dharma. Where is the consistency between these two statements?

Human beings cannot understand the Supreme Personality of Godhead by mundane knowledge or exercising their own intelligence or expertise. We can know Him only by His mercy. If we discuss Śrī Kṛṣṇa Caitanya Mahāprabhu's and pastimes we will be able to solve what appears to be a contradiction in Lord Kṛṣṇa's statements. Caitanyadeva appeared in this world to preach kṛṣṇa-kathā and to show the world Kṛṣṇa's magnanimous pastimes. He taught that we should hear His teachings with full attention. After accepting *sannyāsa* Mahāprabhu lived at the house of Chandraśekhara Ācārya in Kāśī. At that time Śrī Sanātana Prabhu, or Sākara Malik, the prime minister in the king of Bengal's royal assembly, was also present. He asked Mahāprabhu:

'ke āmi', 'kene āmāya jāre tāpa-traya'
ihā nāhi jāni 'kemane hita haya'

Who am I? Why do the threefold miseries always give me trouble? If I do not know this, how can I be benefited? (*Śrī Caitanya-caritāmṛta* Madhya 20.102)

Mahāprabhu replied:

jīvera 'svarūpa' haya kṛṣṇera 'nitya-dāsa',
kṛṣṇera 'tatasthā-śakti' 'bhedābheda-prakāśa'
sūryāṁśa-kiraṇa, yaiche agni-jvālā-caya
svābhāvika kṛṣṇera tina-prakāra 'śakti' haya

It is the living entity's constitutional position to be an eternal servant of Kṛṣṇa because he is the marginal energy of Kṛṣṇa and a manifestation simultaneously one with and different from the Lord, like a molecular particle of sunshine or fire. Kṛṣṇa has three varieties of energy. (*Śrī Caitanya-caritāmṛta* Madhya 20.108-109)

kṛṣṇa bhuli' sei jīva anādi-bahirmukha,
ataeva māyā tāre deya saṁsāra-duḥkha

Forgetting Kṛṣṇa, the living entity has been attracted by the external feature from time immemorial. Therefore, the illusory energy

[Maya] gives him all kinds of misery in his material existence. (*Śrī Caitanya-caritāmṛta* Madhya 20.117)

sādhu-śāstra-kṛpāya yadi kṛṣṇonmukha haya,
sei jīva nistare, māyā tāhāre chāḍaya

If the conditioned soul becomes Kṛṣṇa conscious by the mercy of saintly persons who voluntarily preach scriptural injunctions and help him to become Kṛṣṇa conscious, the conditioned soul is liberated from the clutches of Maya, who gives him up. (*Śrī Caitanya-caritāmṛta* Madhya 20.120)

tāte kṛṣṇa bhaje, kare gurura sevana,
māyā-jāla chuṭe, pāya kṛṣṇera caraṇa

If the conditioned soul engages in the service of the Lord and simultaneously carries out the orders of his spiritual master and serves him, he can get out of the clutches of Maya and become eligible for shelter at Kṛṣṇa's lotus feet. (*Śrī Caitanya-caritāmṛta* Madhya 22.25)

The living entities are Kṛṣṇa's eternal servants, and Kṛṣṇa is their eternal master. We are not these bodies but spirit souls, parts and parcels of Kṛṣṇa. This is the verdict of scripture. When we forget this, however, and consider the body and mind as the self, we suffer various inconveniences. We come to identify ourselves with the family and country in which we were born. We proudly consider ourselves brāhmaṇas, kṣatriyas, vaiśyas, or sudras, mlecchas, males, females, and so on. As our bodies grow, we also learn to consider ourselves children, adults, or old men. Accepting the body as the self, we proudly identify ourselves as Indian, Bengali, British, Hindu, Muslim, Marwari, Punjabi, or Bihari. We are proud to think of ourselves as brahmacāris, gṛhastas or sannyāsīs. These are the varieties of religion, and from there, we create or imagine religious principles.

Lord Kṛṣṇa speaks *Bhagavad-gītā*. In it He states that the spirit soul is eternal and unchangeable and that the material body is temporary and subject to change. Those who think the spirit soul changes when the material body undergoes change are fools. The phrase sarva dharmān refers to all the varieties of religions that come when one considers the material body the self, including the religion based on the four varṇas and āśramas. In fact, it refers to all kinds of religion within the fourteen worlds that are not related to serving Kṛṣṇa.

The merciful Lord instructs that we should give up the temporary physical and mental activities and completely forget about bodily concept of life. He wants us to serve the Supersoul. But the conditioned souls cannot accept this simple instruction. In the next line the Supreme Lord said, aham tvam sarva pāpebhyo mokṣayisyāmī: "I will deliver you from all sinful reactions." The living entities cannot imagine that giving up temporary religious principles does not incur sin. Alas! It is an offense not to follow eternal religious principles, but the conditioned souls who are indifferent to these principles consider not performing some temporary religious principles sinful— not only sinful but they imagine that by avoiding these temporary principles they will never find deliverance. Therefore the Lord said, māśucaḥ, "Do not worry."

Lord Śrī Kṛṣṇa personally came to give us instruction about how to serve Him. Are we following His instructions? Are we serious about His order? If we do not follow His orders or the orders contained in scripture, if we simply float along on our own imagination, consider prohibited activity as duty and neglecting the spiritual master's teachings, then who can be blamed for our failures?

22. How can one go back to Godhead?

Lord Hari is the only self-manifest object and an ocean of mercy. When we are inclined to serve Him, He mercifully reveals Himself to us—His name, form, qualities, and pastimes.

Material enjoyers are overwhelmed by the pride of considering themselves the cause of their own activities, but that pride blinds them from seeing the Supreme Lord. If one wishes to realize the Lord in his pure heart, he must hear about Kṛṣṇa attentively. Mundane experience cannot help one realize the supreme consciousness. Spirit is realized only through spiritual cultivation and seen only through spiritual eyes. Only servants can see the object of their service. The worshipable Lord mercifully manifests Himself before His worshiper. Therefore, first we practice introspection, then comes the external vision.

23. Should one act as one's own spiritual doctor?

Despite seeing the materialists undergo much distress, it is to be understood that those entering material life regardless must have strong desires for sense gratification. Otherwise they would not have taken the risk. Parents are available in every birth, but auspicious instruction may not. Instead of acting as one's own spiritual doctor, therefore, one should accept the treatment of an experienced devotee-physician.

24. How do we achieve auspiciousness?

It is our duty to seek the association of sincere devotees. If our hearts are filled with laziness, duplicity, or material desire, we will receive a spiritual master according to our interest in spiritual life. We can only attain the ultimate goal by taking shelter of a bona fide spiritual master who is dear to Kṛṣṇa and who chants Kṛṣṇa's holy names. If one is fortunate, then by Kṛṣṇa's mercy one will certainly meet such a bona fide spiritual master.

Those with no character can neither chant the holy name nor recite *Śrīmad-Bhāgavatam*. Only the Lord's devotees are qualified to recite scripture and chant the holy name. Hari's pure name does not emanate from people without good character, who are full of material desire and pride. Whatever those persons say is poisonous and illusioned. That is why it is improper to hear *hari-kathā* from just anybody. Hearing from improper persons will create inauspiciousness rather than auspiciousness. Therefore one should firmly abandon the association of those who have rejected their spiritual master and who are averse to their guru's service. By associating with such people one will certainly be ruined.

Hari-kathā should be heard from those devoted to their spiritual master. When we hear from the proper source, we ourselves will become fixed at guru and Kṛṣṇa's feet and in chanting the holy name. We will also find the determination and strength to surrender to the Lord. By hearing about Kṛṣṇa from *akiñcana* devotees, and under the influence of their association, we will realize that devotional service is our only shelter. At that time impersonalism, fruitive activities, mental speculation, and mystic perfection will all appear insignificant.

The ultimate fortune is to take shelter of Kṛṣṇa. Whether we are educated or uneducated, strong or weak, if we take shelter of the Supreme Lord we will attain the goal of our life.

The Lord's devotees appear in this world to benefit ordinary living entities. They are not bound by any mundane duties and are not compelled to appear in the material world. Yet they come. Their only business is to make everyone Kṛṣṇa conscious by diverting their godless propensities.

25. When can one take shelter of Vraja?

When one considers his spiritual master nondifferent from Gadādhara Paṇḍita, his journey to Vraja is confirmed. When one thinks otherwise he is in trouble. It is the duty of the intelligent to follow the mahājanas. To think one can attain perfection by one's own endeavor is a material conception. To think this leads only toward material existence and not to Vraja.

26. What is the most essential factor of the living entities?

Forgetting their original constitutional position, the people of this world consider religiosity, economic development, sense gratification, and liberation the ultimate goal of life. The fifth objective, however, kṛṣṇa-prema, dwarfs these other objectives. Śrī Gaurāṅgadeva distributed kṛṣṇa-prema. Although He is Kṛṣṇa Himself, it is He who gives kṛṣṇa-prema. There is no instructor superior to Śrī Gaurāṅgadeva.

27. Why do some people consider Kṛṣṇa's pastimes obscene?

One should hear, chant, and remember Kṛṣṇa's pastimes as they are discussed by the Lord's associates, the crest jewels among self-controlled personalities. If one does so, one will be liberated from sinful reactions and material existence, attain eternal peace, obtain love of God, and become free from material desire.

The insignificant brains of worldly moralists, however, cannot imagine how authentic and worshipable Kṛṣṇa's pastimes are for all their morality! The loving pastimes of Rādhā and Kṛṣṇa are not like the mundane lusty activities between Romeo and Juliet or any other hero and heroine in this world, even when those activities are exchanged between an ideal man and an ideal woman. In the mundane sphere, desire is manifest only in the form of a propensity, but in the transcendental kingdom it has form.

Desire for personal sense gratification is called lust, whereas the desire to please Kṛṣṇa is called love. Lust is darkness and love is as brilliant as the sun. Transcendental lust or love is a personification of the desire to fulfill Kṛṣṇa's wishes. It is not a product of the material senses. The material senses constantly agitate one to experience lust in this world, but in the transcendental abode the beauty of Kṛṣṇa's spiritual form induces Kṛṣṇa's lust.

The material senses drive worldly lust, but love is driven by Kṛṣṇa. It is an offense, therefore, to think Kṛṣṇa's pastimes are obscene. Kṛṣṇa alone is the supreme enjoyer, supreme Absolute Truth, and supreme spiritual despot.

28. Why are we unable to see God?

Since Kṛṣṇa is transcendental it is not possible to know or see Him with the knowledge we have gained through our senses. Kṛṣṇa is the supreme enjoyer, not an object for others' enjoyment. Everyone and everything is fit for Him to enjoy as He likes. That we think differently is because we are envious of Kṛṣṇa. It is this envy that stops us from seeing Kṛṣṇa.

The Lord's illusory energy has two functions, to prevent us from seeing Kṛṣṇa and to remove Kṛṣṇa from our line of vision. Only Kṛṣṇa's devotees are capable of removing these two influences.

In replying to the question of the residents of Kulīna-grāma, Śrīman Mahāprabhu said that the three principal duties of the human being are to serve Kṛṣṇa, to serve the devotees of Kṛṣṇa, and to chant Kṛṣṇa's holy name. Kṛṣṇa is the object of worship, the Lord's worshipers are the devotees, and the process of worship is devotional service. These three items are eternal. Unless one endeavors to serve the Lord with uninterrupted attention, one cannot realize this. It is not possible to realize the Supreme Lord with mixed endeavor.

We are pretentious when we call ourselves Vaiṣṇavas, because actually, we are servants of our own senses. Until the propensity to engage in pure devotional service is awakened in us, we should understand that we do not know much about Kṛṣṇa. That we are struggling with illusion is proof that we have not understood Śrī Gaurasundara's teachings. Until we realize that service to Kṛṣṇa and His devotees is our only duty, we will continue to be cheated. As soon as we sincerely take shelter of Kṛṣṇa's devotees, we will become free from such a sinful mentality.

We will see the Lord only when our eyes are opened by the lotus hands of those who worship the Lord constantly. Service to those personalities who do nothing other than serve the Lord with all their possessions is what gives us the opportunity to engage in Kṛṣṇa consciousness and to see Kṛṣṇa ourselves.

When by the mercy of our devotee-spiritual master we become fortunate enough to engage in glorifying Hari, then Lord Kṛṣṇa, the personification of *saṅkīrtana* , will mercifully remove all obstacles from the path of we, the most unqualified persons. He will protect us and give us His *darśana*. It is through the devotion-filled eyes of our spiritual master that we receive the Lord's *darśana*.

29. How can one attain eternal perfection?

Whenever we either indulge in sense gratification or remain aloof from it, we think we have gained something. But that gain is only temporary. Only service to the spiritual master and the Vaiṣṇavas is eternal and awards eternal benefit.

We render service to Viṣṇu by serving the spiritual master and the Vaiṣṇavas. Although due to my previous misdeeds I have become a sense enjoyer in this life, by my spiritual master's mercy I have come to understand the constitutional nature of the soul. They have freed me from the influence of mental speculation.

It is true that I am unqualified, but if I somehow engage in the service of guru and the Vaiṣṇavas, I can also become qualified. There is no other way to become qualified or to attain auspiciousness than to engage in this service. In the beginning we do not know how to serve Lord Viṣṇu. When we make a study, however, we realize that service to Viṣṇu's devotees is superior to service rendered directly to Viṣṇu. Although we may not get information about Lord Viṣṇu in this world, if we serve those who serve Viṣṇu we will also learn how to serve Him.

Don't be disappointed because you cannot understand Kṛṣṇa through your blunt material senses. The Supreme Lord is the transcendental Absolute Truth. Those who engage in His service are also transcendental. Service to the transcendental Lord is not incomprehensible or unattainable for them. Rather, such service is a direct exchange between these liberated souls and the Lord.

30. What is a devotee's most invaluable asset?

Śrī Gaurasundara's lotus feet are our most invaluable asset. Let topics of Mahāprabhu always be discussed throughout the world! Then all living entities will attain auspiciousness, realizing the transcendental subject matter. Everyone will understand the Absolute Truth and about Śrī Caitanyadeva. All other knowledge is inauspicious.

Lord Kṛṣṇa has given us various opportunities and assurances by telling us He will deliver us from all sinful reactions and that those who surrender unto Him can easily overcome His illusory energy. He said, "Just take shelter of Me and you will attain perfection." He has taken all responsibility for our deliverance. Still we have no faith in His words. Therefore He again appears before us as our spiritual master—in the form of His own servant. He also came as Gaurāṅga and said, "I am only a servant of Kṛṣṇa. If you want to follow My words, follow them and achieve perfection." Accepting the mood of a devotee, Lord Kṛṣṇa personally appeared in the world as Caitanyadeva and revealed that Kṛṣṇa is the Supreme Personality of Godhead and the supreme object of worship. Simply by taking shelter of His lotus feet and cultivating remembrance of His names, forms, qualities, and pastimes, we will attain ultimate fortune.

31. What is our duty?

We should give up false ego and take complete shelter at Kṛṣṇa's lotus feet if we wish to make our lives successful. When we engage in karma we see ourselves as the enjoyer of the fruits of our action. Thus we are recipients rather than givers. When we cultivate *jñāna* we are also recipient. But in devotional service, we make the transcendental Personality of Godhead the recipient. Follow the devotional path. Lord Kṛṣṇa is eager to mercifully reveal Himself to us at every moment. Accept His mercy gladly.

It is not necessarily our duty to make disciples. Better we become disciples ourselves. Vaiṣṇavas see their guru's presence in every object. If we treat others as disciples or servants, we will not be able to glorify Hari. Better we serve the spiritual master and the Vaiṣṇavas twenty-four hours a day, even if such service means giving up our service to Kṛṣṇa.

We should neither speak nor do anything under the influence of false ego. Doing so makes us culpable. Our only duty is to eternally glorify Hari. If we simply repeat *hari-kathā* as order-carrier servants of the Lord's beloved devotee, our guru, then we will bear no responsibility for the good or bad results that may ensue. Postmen deliver letters but are not responsible for the contents of the mail. Whether or not we are qualified, we are duty-bound to repeat the spiritual master's words with great faith. Why should this be a problem? As our guru's servants, we are confident that we will attain supreme fortune through our service.

Serving and associating with Maya leaves us feeling incomplete and unfortunate, while serving the Complete Whole leaves us satisfied. If we wish to become perfect we must serve the perfect. If we spend time on imperfect things, we will get imperfect results. As long as you live in this world, hear *hari-kathā* exclusively. Hearing is dependent on someone's chanting. If we are not fortunate enough to be able to hear in the association of *sādhus*, we should constantly hear and chant ourselves.

32. How can we see the Lord face to face?

Lord Kṛṣṇa is the devotee's personal property. Only the devotees can give or show Kṛṣṇa to others. Please the Lord and achieve all perfection. Meeting the object of service is possible only through service and in no other way.

33. Who is sure to attain Kṛṣṇa?

One who has firm faith that "Kṛṣṇa will certainly protect me" will surely attain perfection. To be qualified for such protection, we must take complete shelter at the lotus feet of those who are already fully dependent on the Lord and who constantly discuss kṛṣṇa-kathā. These souls deliver other souls. Simply by taking shelter of them, we will be delivered. Only the surrendered souls are saved, not those who maintain their independence, because full surrender attracts Kṛṣṇa's full mercy.

34. When does one achieve pure devotional service and see the Lord face-to-face?

When we realize that the spiritual master, who is the personification of the Lord's service, is nondifferent from Śrī Gaurāṅga Mahāprabhu, we will actually be allowed to serve the Lord. At that time religiosity, economic development, sense gratification, and liberation will appear insignificant. When we realize that guru is a most intimate associate of Śrī Gaurāṅgadeva, then Śrī Rādhā-Govinda's pastimes will manifest in our purified hearts and we will see the Lord face-to-face.

35. What is the path back to Godhead?

Śrīmad-Bhāgavatam (3.9.11) states:

tvaṁ bhakti-yoga-paribhāvita-hṛt-saroja
āsse śrutekṣita-patho nanu nātha puṁsām

yad-yad-dhiyā ta urugāya vibhāvayanti
tat-tad-vapu praṇayase sad-anugrahāya

O my Lord, Your devotees can see You through the ears by the process of bona fide hearing, and thus their hearts become cleansed, and You take Your seat there. You are so merciful to Your devotees that You manifest Yourself in the particular eternal form of transcendence in which they always think of You.

In his commentary on this verse Śrīla Śrīdhara Svāmī writes, śrutena śravaṇe ikṣitaḥ: one should see the Absolute Truth through the eyes of scripture. This is the path back to Godhead.

Similarly, in his commentary Śrī Visvanātha Cakravartī Ṭhākura writes that realization of the Lord is possible when one eagerly hears about Him with a pure heart. First one should hear from the spiritual master, and then one will be able to see the Lord. *Śrī Caitanya-caritāmṛta* Ādi 3.112 states: bhaktera icchāya kṛṣṇera sarva avatāra: "Lord Kṛṣṇa appears in all His innumerable eternal forms because of the desires of His pure devotees." In the same commentary Śrīdhara Svāmī explains, "The Lord manifests that particular form in the hearts of a devotee upon whom the devotee meditates."

36. What is the danger of cheating on the devotional path?

By sincerely worshiping the Lord while taking complete shelter of the spiritual master and Gaurāṅga, one will easily attain perfection. Cheaters never attain perfection. There is no place for cheating on the devotional path. The propensity to cheat is a grave impediment to devotional service. If while eating we duplicitously eat less for the sake of etiquette, we will not be satisfied and thus will have cheated ourselves. If we try to cheat a blacksmith by mixing the iron we give with some other metal, we ourselves will be cheated. One also cheats himself if he cheats while worshiping Hari. Serve the Lord with simplicity, and carefully follow spiritual master's orders.

37. What is the goal of life?

Lord Kṛṣṇa is the supreme Absolute Truth, the Supreme Personality of Godhead. He is the eternal object of everyone's service. We are all His servants. To serve and love Him is the goal of our life.

We have to serve Kṛṣṇa with our spiritual senses. We cannot attain Kṛṣṇa by mental speculation or through the imagination. We must know our relationship with Him with the help of our well-wishers, those devotees whose only aim is to serve Kṛṣṇa. As long as we consider our relatives our well-wishers, we cannot understand transcendental knowledge but will remain in ignorance even after initiation.

A Vaiṣṇava thinks that Lord Kṛṣṇa is his supreme well-wisher, worshipable Lord, and best friend. Do not look for material fame in the form of some type of sense gratification, and do not consider strangers your well-wisher. Serve Kṛṣṇa, not first with your flesh and bones, but with your spiritual consciousness through your service-inclined senses.

38. What does the Śrīmad-Bhāgavatam instruct us to do?

Śrīmad-Bhāgavatam does not teach karma-kāṇḍa but focuses on the importance of hearing *hari-kathā*. *Śrīmad-Bhāgavatam* describes pure devotional service and everything related to it. This *bhakti*-yoga is the supreme religious principle for the entire humanity.

Pure knowledge, pure renunciation, and pure devotional service are one and the same. *Śrīmad-Bhāgavatam* does not deal with any subject matter that enhances our sense gratification. It considers material happiness and distress two sides of the same coin—striving for material happiness inevitably brings distress. The *Bhāgavatam* reminds us that the karma-kāṇḍa path sometimes brings good results, but often brings bad ones. Karma-kāṇḍa is not the path of liberated souls

By reading literature other than the *Bhāgavatam* one is compelled to traverse the paths of karma and *jñāna* so one can enjoy happiness and distress and rotate in the cycle of birth and death. While on that path one may find religiosity, economic development, and sense gratification. When someone on the karma- or *jñāna*-kāṇḍa path finally desires liberation, he doesn't worship the Lord. Only Vaiṣṇavas serve the Lord.

The path of mystic yoga does not serve the Lord either. One can certainly work for and attain mystic perfections such as animā and laghimā by practicing yoga, but this has nothing to do with devotion. And forget about the salvationist serving the Lord. He wants nothing but respite from his distress.

Śrīmad-Bhāgavatam assures us that those who have accepted the paths of karma, *jñāna*, or yoga have accepted the wrong path. Bhakti is the correct path. While *karmīs* want to enjoy both in this life and the next, those who practice *bhakti* engage in their eternal function as pure souls. If we can simply regain our original soul understanding, we will have a chance at disassociating ourselves from this world. If we can only regain our spiritual health by becoming Kṛṣṇa conscious, we will go back to Godhead.

39. What does it mean to attain Kṛṣṇa?

To attain Kṛṣṇa means to completely disassociate ourselves from the material world. It means to see Kṛṣṇa in our heart after we are liberated. But without love we cannot attain the son of Nanda Mahārāja.

40. How can we maintain the fortune we have received?

Do not thirst for sense gratification. Do not desire to commit sinful activities. Rather, use your energy to engage in Lord Hari's service staying far away from the concerns of worldly morality. With such full surrender, you will achieve perfection. Jagāi and Mādhāi did not commit further sinful activities after taking shelter of Śrīmān Mahāprabhu, and we should not either.

Only those who understand that hari-*bhajana* is the ultimate goal can feel the distress of others. By worshiping Hari one achieves eternal life; those who worship Him do not die. While materialists engage constantly with the enemies of lust, anger, and greed, devotees have no such enemies. When one has the natural tendency to worship Hari, one need not control his senses by force. Rather, by sincerely engaging in the Lord's service, the poisonous teeth of the senses are easily uprooted by the Lord's mercy.

Even the most experienced conditioned souls are interested in sense gratification, even though in their pursuit of happiness they are forced to suffer distress. Devotees, however, do not meet the pendulum swing of happiness and distress in this world. Rather, this world is a place of complete happiness for them because they have no desires. They do not even desire to become an Indra, what to speak of a Brahmā, lord of all the demigods. A materialist would never choose to become an insect in this world, but a devotee would not mind such a birth as long as he could engage in hari-*bhajana*. Because of such an attitude, even the demigods are made fortunate by the mercy of Lord Caitanya's devotees.

It is important to become self-realized in this life. Otherwise, absorbed in matter at the time of death, we will be forced to take birth again in the material world. If we do not associate with the Lord's devotees during this life, we will end up forming narrow-minded groups and sects.

41. How will we become free of material existence?

At present we are fallen and in danger, and in such a condition we are always trying to gratify our senses. The final result of trying to achieve happiness through the material senses is death. If we want to be delivered from this condition, we must worship the Lord under the guidance and shelter of a spiritual master.

Taking shelter of the spiritual master and accepting initiation from him are gateways to devotional service. We will proceed on the path by following the mahājanas. As Bali Mahārāja served the Lord by surrendering everything at His lotus feet, we will also remain eternally surrendered by offering everything at the lotus feet of our spiritual master and Lord Gaurāṅga. By serving the spiritual master and the holy name with love and devotion as surrendered souls, we will easily become liberated from material existence.

tāte kṛṣṇa bhaje, kare gurura sevana
māyā-jāla chuṭe, pāya kṛṣṇera caraṇa

If the conditioned soul engages in the service of the Lord and simultaneously carries out the orders of his spiritual master and serves him, can he get out of the clutches of Maya and become eligible for shelter at Kṛṣṇa's lotus feet? (*Śrī Caitanya-caritāmṛta* Madhya 22.25)

prabhu kahe, "vaiṣṇava-sevā, nāma-saṅkīrtana
dui kara, śīghra pābe śrī-kṛṣṇa-caraṇa"

The Lord replied, "You should engage yourself in the service of the servants of Kṛṣṇa and always chant the holy name of Kṛṣṇa. If you do these two things, you will very soon attain shelter at Kṛṣṇa's lotus feet. (*Śrī Caitanya-caritāmṛta* Madhya 16.70)

sādhu-śāstra-kṛpāya yadi kṛṣṇonmukha haya
sei jīva nistare, māyā tāhāre chāḍaya

"If the conditioned soul becomes Kṛṣṇa conscious by the mercy of saintly persons who voluntarily preach scriptural injunctions and help him to become Kṛṣṇa conscious, the conditioned soul is liberated from the clutches of Maya, who gives him up." (*Śrī Caitanya-caritāmṛta* Madhya-līla 20.120)

42. Which path should be followed?

One should give up the path of argument and accept the path of aural reception or disciplic succession. Hear properly and do not try to see things on your own. Otherwise you will cheat yourself. Instead of following the mahājanas, if one tries to see their behavior, one will eventually risk imitating them and inevitably invite trouble. The path of depending on direct perception and material enjoyment lead to godlessness. Hence the need of the descending path.

43. How does one worship purely?

Perfection of life is attained by engaging in the service of Hari, Guru, and Vaiṣṇavas, while remaining in the association of saintly persons. To whimsically make a show of worshiping the Lord cannot be passed as the worship of the Lord. Pure form of worship is to serve the spiritual master and Kṛṣṇa under the instruction of the spiritual master for their pleasure.

44. How will we achieve complete benefit?

Lord Śrī Hari is complete. He is an ocean of mercy. Since He is complete, His mercy is also complete. The complete gives Himself to the incomplete so that the incomplete can achieve Him. Without approaching the complete, one cannot achieve complete benefit. Incomplete or limited happiness cannot satisfy us. Because the Lord is merciful, He has given us the opportunity to hear and chant about Him. Our hearts cannot be purified without hearing and chanting kṛṣṇa-kathā. Lord Kṛṣṇa is all attractive, and by hearing and chanting about the all-attractive Lord we can easily find ourselves attracted to Him by His mercy. That will give us complete benefit.

45. How can one attain the Supreme Lord?

When the Supreme Lord's mercy combines with the devotee's sincere eagerness to serve Him, the jīva easily attains Kṛṣṇa and ends his own material existence.

46. What has caused our degradation?

Who am I? Unless we try to answer this question we will remain drowned in an ocean of material temptation and misery. Taking advantage of our slightest carelessness, the witch Maya attacks and swallows us. Unless we hear daily about the Supreme Lord, there is no way to escape her clutches.

47. According to Mahāprabhu, what is a human being's most important duty?

First we have to know who we are. Then we will easily know what our duty is. Our duty is to worship the Supreme Lord and attain His mercy. This human form of life is the root of worship. Worship is not possible in other species of life. Whether or not one accepts the fact, we are all the Supreme Lord's servants and Kṛṣṇa is our eternal master. Service to Kṛṣṇa is our principal duty, our only duty. Forgetting the Lord, we become filled with false ego, identifying ourselves as enjoyers and masters. These designations are all mundane.

Our natural spiritual propensities can become maddened by the attempt to enjoy matter. Such is the definition of the mind. The mind is the perverted reflection of the soul, and as such, it is the enjoyer of matter.

Taking advantage of the soul's dormant condition, this mind acts as landlord of the body and continues to enjoy the body's senses.

The mind cheats the soul. Being controlled by pious and impious reactions, it sometimes enjoys heavenly pleasures and sometimes suffers in hell. Thus the mind is the main enemy of the soul and all scriptures recommend that we control the mind.

Śrī Caitanya Mahāprabhu instructs: We are devotees of Kṛṣṇa; we are Vaiṣṇavas and therefore related to Kṛṣṇa. We are neither Kṛṣṇa nor Viṣṇu. Viṣṇu is the manifestation of Kṛṣṇa's opulent form, and Kṛṣṇa is Viṣṇu's form of sweetness. Actually there is no difference between Kṛṣṇa and Viṣṇu. As Kṛṣṇa's servants we have no engagement other than to serve Him. As soon as we forget that, we fall into Maya. When by the mercy of the devotees the knowledge of our relationship with the Lord is awakened, we will understand that we are eternal servants of Kṛṣṇa and that all objects in this material world are meant for His service.

All of us will have to become liberated. The state of liberation is nothing but remaining situated in one's constitutional position and cultivating Kṛṣṇa consciousness favorably with all one's senses.

Śrī Caitanyadeva inaugurated the *saṅkīrtana* movement and delivered the fallen souls of this age. He is the most magnanimous personality. In the verse beginning tṛnād api, He taught that chanting Kṛṣṇa's holy name is our only duty. Those who desire liberation and eternal happiness, as well as those who desire the treasure of love of God, should always chant the Lord's holy name. The Lord's name is nondifferent from Him. It is capable of delivering us from material existence and awarding us with love of Kṛṣṇa.

One should chant the holy name of Kṛṣṇa in a humble state of mind, thinking oneself lower than the straw in the street. The attitude espoused in tṛnād api sunicena destroys the misconception that we are God. A chanter always thinks himself a servant of the holy name and considers every object in this world as meant for Kṛṣṇa's service and enjoyment.

Kṛṣṇa's holy names and Deity forms are nondifferent from Him. The holy name is sat-cit-ānanda, directly the son of Nanda Mahārāja and Yaśodā. The holy name can speak. The holy name is the Supersoul and omniscient. Kṛṣṇa in His holy name appears in a pure heart before spiritual eyes, on the service-inclined tongue, in the service-inclined ears, and in the senses engaged in satisfying His own senses.

We can achieve all perfection by performing *saṅkīrtana* . Even the reflection of the holy name destroys all sinful reactions and material bondage. At that point the living entity becomes liberated and becomes qualified to chant himself. Kṛṣṇa's holy name is the reservoir of all transcendental pleasure. The Lord's devotees serve Him by chanting that name.

Chanting destroys all misfortune and purifies our heart so that the Lord will appear there. The holy name of Kṛṣṇa is the Supreme Personality of Godhead. The holy name is the reservoir of transcendental pastimes. The holy name is the primeval Lord. The holy name is most independent, the supreme controller of the universes, and the maintainer of all planets. He is the protector of all living entities. The holy name is capable of destroying any amount of blockage. The holy name purifies all hearts no matter how contaminated and destroys all illusion. Our hearts have accumulated contamination from time immemorial, and therefore the Lord's pure name does not manifest in us, but by constant chanting that contamination is destroyed and the name full of transcendental energy and the source of all happiness will appear. The holy name is complete, perfect, and full of knowledge and bliss.

Kṛṣṇa's transcendental name appears only in a transcendental heart. Those hearts contaminated by the three modes of material nature cannot force the holy name to appear. Kṛṣṇa alone is our worshipable Lord. He is worshiped only by love and devotion and not by a show of opulence.

Kṛṣṇa's holy name, which is the reservoir of all transcendental pleasure, cannot be compared even with the holy name of Rāma. Rāma's holy name produces one-millionth of a portion of the mellow of nectarean love produced by Kṛṣṇa's holy name, because although Rāma's name is perfect, Kṛṣṇa's name is most perfect and complete. Rāma's name is a portion of Kṛṣṇa's name, and an incarnation.

The holy name of Kṛṣṇa is the source of all existence, knowledge, and bliss. It is the cause of all causes and it accepts the loving service of sincere servants.

48. How can one perceive the Absolute Truth?

We cannot meet the Absolute Truth here. It is impossible to approach the Absolute Truth with our present temporary senses. What is the alternative? If we are sincere about serving the Supreme Lord, then the Lord will mercifully appear before us and award us the qualification to serve Him by removing the aversion of our senses.

49. What is the path of auspiciousness?

Service to the Supreme Lord is the only path of auspiciousness. Our every step, breath, and activity should be performed in relation to Kṛṣṇa. We should always walk on the path of devotional service to Kṛṣṇa. May we never engage in any activity other than service to Hari, guru, and Vaiṣṇavas.

50. To which object is attachment auspicious?

Attachment for this world and its inhabitants causes our bondage and distress. Therefore we need to change the direction of our attachment. Instead we have to entangle ourselves with the most attractive personality. Then everything will be all right.

51. Why are we not inclined toward the Lord's service?

We have no inclination toward God and no inclination to remedy that situation. Therefore we need an expert doctor. Our inclination toward the Lord will arise if we associate with devotees. Just as a veterinary surgeon tactfully places medicine in an animal's mouth, similarly the spiritual master and the devotees, who are just like expert doctors, bestow mercy on us. Despite our reluctance they forcibly pour the mellows of devotional service into our mouths.

Final Instructions

I have caused a great deal of anxiety to many people. Since I was compelled to speak the truth, and since I had to instruct many people to sincerely worship Hari, perhaps many people have even considered me their enemy. I have caused anxiety to many people by instructing them to give up sense gratification and their cheating propensity and to thus become inclined to serve Kṛṣṇa. Someday they will certainly understand this simple truth.

All of you should enthusiastically preach the topics of Śrī Rūpa and Raghunātha together. Our ultimate goal of life is to become a particle of dust at the feet of the followers of Śrī Rūpa. All of you should stay together under the guidance of the original servitor to fulfill the desires of the Advaya-*jñāna* Kṛṣṇa. Simply for the sake of worshiping Hari somehow or other, maintain your life in this temporary material world. Do not give up the worship of Hari even if you face hundreds of obstacles and dangers. Do not be discouraged by seeing that most of the people in this world are not taking to Kṛṣṇa consciousness. Never give up the hearing and chanting kṛṣṇa-kathā, which is your ultimate goal of *bhajana*.

Always chant the holy name of Hari by becoming lower than the straw in the street and more tolerant than a tree. We should maintain the desire to sacrifice our useless lives in the fire of Śrī Kṛṣṇa Caitanya's *saṅkīrtana* movement. We do not want to become heroes. We do not want to become expert fruitive workers or religious reformers. Let the dust from the lotus feet of Śrī Rūpa Prabhu be our life and soul birth after birth. The flow of devotional service in the line of Śrī Bhaktivinoda Ṭhākura will never be checked. All of you should take stronger vows to preach Śrī Bhaktivinoda Ṭhākura's mission with more enthusiasm. Among you there are many qualified and experienced persons. We have no desire other than this ṛda dṛnas tṛnam dantair idaṁ yāce puna punaḥ/ srīmad rūpa padāmbhoja dhuli syāt janma janmani: "Holding a straw between our teeth we repeatedly pray to become a particle of dust at the lotus feet of Śrī Rūpa birth after birth."

There are many obstacles in this world, but it is not our goal to either become overwhelmed by them or to remove them. We should try to realize what is our goal of life and how we will attain eternal life—as long as we are present in this world. We should solve all our problems and dualities. The more we distance ourselves from Kṛṣṇa's lotus feet, the more we will be attracted by the action and counteraction of this world. By becoming attracted to Kṛṣṇa's transcendental name while remaining aloof from the attraction of this visible world, we can understand the mellows of Kṛṣṇa consciousness. The topics of Kṛṣṇa are so startling and perplexing that foreign matters place obstacles in the realization of our eternal goal of life. In order to eliminate this, human beings are more or less knowingly and unknowingly struggling. Our only goal of life is to become transcendental to this duality and enter into the kingdom of our eternal goal of life. We neither have any attachment nor any detachment for anyone in this world. All arrangements in this world are temporary. For every person, to attain the ultimate goal of life is inevitably necessary.

All of you live in complete harmony and attain the qualification to serve the original servitor. Let the current of thoughts of the followers of Śrī Rūpa be spread everywhere. May we never at any stage show indifference to śrī-kṛṣṇa-*saṅkīrtana* -yajña. We will attain all perfection if we simply increase our attachment for this. All of you should boldly and enthusiastically preach the teachings of Śrī Rūpa and Raghunātha under the guidance of the followers of Śrī Rūpa.

Appendix

The following is a lecture given by Śrīla Bhaktisiddhanta Sarasvatī Gosvāmī Prabhupāda on the bank of Śrī Rādhā Kunda during his Vraja-maṇḍala Parikrama on Sunday afternoon, October 16, 1932.

The eighth instruction of Śrīla Rūpa Prabhu is the essence of all instructions. It is as follows:

tan-nāma-rūpa-caritādi-sukīrtanānu-
smṛtyoḥ krameṇa rasanā-manasī niyojya
tiṣṭhan vraje tad-anurāgi janānugāmī
kālaṁ nayed akhilam ity upadeśa-sāram

The essence of all advice is that one should utilize one's full time twenty-four hours a day, in nicely chanting and remembering the Lord's divine name, transcendental form, qualities, and eternal pastimes, thereby gradually engaging one's tongue and mind. In this way, one should reside in Vraja [Goloka Vṛndāvana dhāma] and serve Kṛṣṇa under the guidance of devotees. One should follow in the footsteps of the Lord's beloved devotees, who are deeply attached to His devotional service.

We have to always remain subordinate to the Vrajavāsīs. The banks of Yamunā, the playground for Kṛṣṇa's amorous pastimes, the waters of the Yamunā, the cows, sticks, horns, and flutes are all Vrajavāsīs. They are Vrajavāsīs on the platform of śānta-*rasa* . Raktaka, Citraka, Patraka, and others are Vrajavāsīs on the platform of dāsya-*rasa* . Externally making a show of residing in Vraja while thinking internally about material enjoyment unrelated to Kṛṣṇa cannot be called vrajavāsa, living in Vraja. Vrajavāsīs are those who cannot engage in anything other than Kṛṣṇa's service even in their dreams or while unconscious, and who have natural attachment for Kṛṣṇa. If one is unable to physically live in Vraja, he should live there mentally. This means that he must always keep his mind absorbed in thoughts of Vraja. One has to give up both material enjoyment and dry renunciation. According to *Śrīmad-Bhāgavatam*, an attached householder and a staunch, dry renunciant cannot worship Hari.

We have to follow the gradual path. We must start with hearing the holy names and kṛṣṇa-kathā. Kṛṣṇa's holy name reveals Himself as the Lord's forms, qualities, pastimes, and associates. After hearing, we have to act accordingly. We have to constantly chant whatever we have heard. Then the state of remembrance will come. There are five kinds of remembrance. The final stage of remembrance is called samādhi, uninterrupted remembrance. After the stage of remembrance one attains the stage of self-realization, after which one attains the ultimate goal of life and goes back to Godhead.

One must properly glorify the Lord's name, form, and characteristics. One will not yield any result if one simply makes a pretense of glorifying the Lord. *Śrīmad-Bhāgavatam* (2.8.4) states:

śṛṇvataḥśraddhayā nityaṁ, gṛṇataś ca sva-ceṣṭitam
kālena nātidīrgheṇa, bhagavān viśate hṛdi

Persons who hear *Śrīmad-Bhāgavatam* regularly and are always taking the matter very seriously will have the Personality of Godhead Śrī Kṛṣṇa manifested in their hearts within a short time.

Trying to artificially remember the Lord by giving up one's chanting is not real remembrance. The pretension of remembrance without chanting will leave one meditating on sense objects. The *śāstras* have described two paths, the path of śreyas and the path of preyas. That which we like is the path of preyas, and that which we don't like is the path of śreyas. When śreyas and preyas merge, our hearts will rush toward Śrī Rādhā-Kṛṣṇa' service. In that stage śreyas appears as preyas and preyas as śreyas. This is how exalted devotees think.

The phrase tad anurāgi in the original verse refers to the Vrajavāsīs who are deeply attached to the Lord. The cows, sticks, horns, flute, kadamba trees, and the banks of the Yamunā are deeply attached Vrajavāsīs in śānta-*rasa* . Raktaka, Citraka, and Patraka, who are Nanda's house servants and who serve Kṛṣṇa when He returns from the pasturing ground, are deeply attached Vrajavāsīs in dāsya-*rasa* . Friends like Śrīdāmā or

Sudāmā are deeply attached Vrajavāsīs of viśrambha-sakhya-*rasa* , friendship with love. Arjuna's idea of the Lord is mixed with knowledge of His godhood and is therefore not pure friendship. There is a difference between viśrambha-sakhya-*rasa* and gaurava-sakhya-*rasa* (friendship with awe and reverence). On the platform of viśrambha-sakhya-*rasa* , Kṛṣṇa's friends will climb on Kṛṣṇa's shoulders, feed Him contaminated tāla fruits in the Tālavana forest, fight with Him, and compel Him to carry them on His shoulders. But Arjuna is struck with wonder when he sees Kṛṣṇa's universal form. He says, "O Lord! You are so opulent and great. I have committed an offense by addressing You as friend. Please forgive me." He spoke like this because he was overwhelmed by Kṛṣṇa's opulence.

Personalities like Nanda and Yaśodā are deeply attached Vrajavāsīs in vātsalya-*rasa* . Raghupati Upādhyāya, a disciple of Śrī Mādhavendra Purī said:

śrutim apare smṛtim itare, bhāratam anye bhajantu bhava-bhītāḥ
aham iha nandaṁ vande, yasyālinde paraṁ brahma

Those who are afraid of material existence worship the Vedic literature. Some worship smṛti, the corollaries to the Vedic literature, and others worship the Mahābhārata. As far as I am concerned, I worship Kṛṣṇa's father, Mahārāja Nanda, in whose courtyard the Supreme Personality of Godhead, the Absolute Truth, is playing. (*Padyāvali* 126)

The Vraja gopīs are deeply attached Vrajavāsīs in the topmost *mādhurya-rasa* . When the gopīs, who were afflicted by separation from Kṛṣṇa met Him at Kurukṣetra during the solar eclipse, they said:

āhuś ca te nalina-nābha padāravindaṁ
yogeśvarair hṛdi vicintyam agādha-bodhaiḥ
saṁsāra-kūpa-patitottaraṇāvalambaṁ
gehaṁ juṣām api manasy udiyāt sadā naḥ

Dear Lord whose navel is just like a lotus flower, Your lotus feet are the only shelter for those who have fallen into the deep well of material existence. Your feet are worshiped and meditated upon by great mystic yogīs and highly learned philosophers. We wish that these lotus feet may also be awakened within our hearts, although we are only ordinary persons engaged in household affairs. (*Śrīmad Bhagavatam* 10.82.48)

Materialists are motivated by a desire to become liberated from material existence. Renunciant yogīs practice meditation to realize the subtle object. Surpassing these considerations is the topmost platform of devotional service found in the gopīs of Vraja. The gopīs are not prepared to serve Kṛṣṇa from a distance like the yogīs who practice meditation. Their meditation is spontaneous and natural.

These above mentioned five kinds of *rasas* are found in Goloka and in the Vraja of this world. In Vaikuṇṭha there are two and half kinds of *rasas* , śānta, dāsya, and gaurava-sakhya. Viśrambha-sakhya does not exist there.

In Śrī Rūpa Prabhu's ninth instruction, he determines the best place to perform *bhajana* as follows:

vaikuṇṭhāj janito varā madhu-purī tatrāpi rāsotsavād
vṛndāraṇyam udāra-pāṇi-ramaṇāt tatrāpi govardhanaḥ
rādhā-kuṇḍam ihāpi gokula-pateḥ premāmṛtāplāvanāt
kuryād asya virājato giri-taṭe sevāṁ vivekī na kaḥ

The holy place known as Maṭhurā is spiritually superior to Vaikuṇṭha, the transcendental world, because the Lord appeared there. Superior to Maṭhurāpurī is the transcendental forest of Vṛndāvana, because of Kṛṣṇa's rāsa-līlā pastimes. And superior to the forest of Vṛndāvana is Govardhana Hill, for it was raised by the divine hand of Śrī Kṛṣṇa and was the site of His various loving pastimes. And, above all, the superexcellent Śrī Rādhā-kuṇḍa stands supreme, for it is over-flooded with the ambrosial nectarean prema of the Lord of Gokula, Śrī Kṛṣṇa. Where, then, is that intelligent person who is unwilling to serve this divine Rādhā Kuṇḍa, which is situated at the foot of Govardhana Hill?

As the surrendered maidservants of Śrī Rādhā, we have to constantly live on the banks of Rādhā Kuṇḍa. In the conception of Nārāyaṇa there is no existence of father and mother. Nārāyāṇa is unborn. But when that unborn Lord appears as the son of Devakī and Vasudeva in Maṭhurā, He performs the pastime of taking birth. The Lord of Vaikuṇṭha is unborn. But since that unborn Lord, due to His inconceivable potency, manifested His pastime of taking birth, His position as the Supreme Lord becomes more glorious. Therefore Maṭhurā is superior to Vaikuṇṭha.

Lord Kṛṣṇa appears in the pure mind of a practitioner. That pure mind is also Maṭhurā. Many people consider Maṭhurā a mythical place, a place described in fairy tales. Doing so denies Kṛṣṇa's inconceivable potency. By His inconceivable potency Maṭhurā appears along with Kṛṣṇa in this material world.

Vṛndāvana, where Kṛṣṇa enjoyed the rāsa līlā, is superior to Maṭhurā, where Kṛṣṇa took birth. *Śrī Caitanya-caritāmṛta* (Ādi 1.17) states:

śrīmān rāsa-rasārambhī vaṁśīvaṭa-taṭa-sthitaḥ
karṣan veṇu-svanair gopīr gopī-nāthaḥśriye 'stu naḥ

Śrī Śrīla Gopīnātha, who originated the transcendental mellow of the rāsa dance, stands on the shore in Vaṁśīvaṭa and attracts the attention of the cowherd damsels with the sound of His celebrated flute. May They all confer upon us Their benedictions.

In Maṭhurā Kṛṣṇa enjoys His pastimes as an immature boy. In the rāsa-līlā arena He is a mature boy. Kṛṣṇa enjoyed the rāsa līlā pastimes with His different types of gopī friends. When Śrī Rādhā arrived and saw that the special characteristics of Her service could not be exhibited in a rāsa-līlā that included so many types of gopīs, She left the arena and went to Govardhana. Candrāvalī also arrived. When Śrī Rādhā saw Śrī Kṛṣṇa sitting inside a cave at Govardhana with Candrāvalī, She became very upset. After tactfully deceiving Candrāvali's messenger Śaibyā, Rādhās gopī friends, Tulasī, Dhaniṣṭhā, and others, sent Candrāvalī to Sakhīsthālī. That is why Śrīla Dāsa Gosvāmī Prabhupāda, who was a staunch follower of Śrī Rūpa, offered his obeisances to Sakhīsthālī from a distance. After deceiving Candrāvalī, Śrī Rādhās followers brought Śyāmasundara to Rādhā Kuṇḍa.

Śrī Govardhana, where Śrī Rādhā-Kṛṣṇa's most confidential amorous pastimes take place, is superior to Vṛndāvana. In his prayer to Śrī Govardhana, Śrīla Raghunātha dāsa Gosvāmī wrote (*Stavāvalī*, Vol. 1, text 6):

yasyām-mādhava-nāviko rasavatīm ādhāya rādhām-tarau
madhye cañcala-keli-pāta-valanāt trāsaiḥ stuvatyās tataḥ
svābhiṣṭham-paṇam ādadhe vahati sā yasmin mano-jāhnavī
kas tam-tan nava-dam-pati-pratibhuvam-govardhanam-nāśrayet

Who will not take shelter of Govardhana Hill, where the divine couple enjoy Their rescue-fee pastimes, and where the Mānasa-gaṅgā flows? In the Mānasa-gaṅgā the pilot Mādhava took sweetly beautiful Rādhā on His boat, and when She, frightened by a great storm, prayed that He calm it, He claimed from Her as a rescue-fee the fulfillment of His amorous desires.

Rādhā-kuṇḍa is superior to Govardhana because it is flooded fully with nectarean love of Śrī Kṛṣṇa. Śrī Rūpa-mañjarī, who understood Caitanya Mahāprabhu's confidential intention, instructed that service to

Rādhā-kuṇḍa, the highest object of Śrī Gaurahari's internal mood, is the ultimate goal of all service. Śrī Rādhā-kuṇḍa is totally incomprehensible and unattainable by followers of the Nimbārka-sampradāya, by the followers of any sampradāya under Candrāvalīs guidance, and by the so-called followers of *mādhurya-rasa* who are devoid of devotion to Gaura. Therefore Śrīla Dāsa Gosvāmī wrote in his prayer to Śrī Rādhā-kuṇḍa (*Stavāvalī* text 2)

vraja-bhuvi mura-śatroḥ preyasīnāṁ nikāmair
asulabham api tūrṇaṁ prema-kalpa-drumaṁ tam
janayati hṛdi bhūmau snātur uccair priyaṁ yat
tad ati-surabhi rādhā-kuṇḍam evāśrayo me

May very dear and fragrant Rādhā Kuṇḍa, which, for one who bathes in it immediately creates in the land of the heart a desire tree of pure love rare even among the gopī beloveds of Lord Kṛṣṇa in Vraja, be my shelter.

In his tenth instruction Śrī Rūpa Gosvāmī has ascertained who among the devotees is the best:

karmibhyaḥ parito hareḥ priyatayā vyaktiṁ yayur jñāninas
tebhyo jñāna-vimukta-bhakti-paramāḥ premaika-niṣṭhās tataḥ
tebhyas tāḥ paśu-pāla-paṅkaja-dṛśas tābhyo 'pi sā rādhikā
preṣṭhā tadvad iyaṁ tadīya-sarasī tāṁ nāśrayet kaḥ kṛtī

In the śāstra it is said that of all types of fruitive workers, he who is advanced in knowledge of the higher values of life is favored by the Supreme Lord Hari. Out of many such people who are advanced in knowledge [jñānīs], one who is practically liberated by virtue of his knowledge may take to devotional service. He is superior to the others. However, one who has actually attained prema, pure love of Kṛṣṇa, is superior to him. The gopīs are exalted above all the advanced devotees because they are always totally dependent upon Śrī Kṛṣṇa, the transcendental cowherd boy. Among the gopīs, Śrīmatī Rādhārāṇī is the most dear to Kṛṣṇa. Her kuṇḍa [lake] is as profoundly dear to Lord Kṛṣṇa as this most beloved of the gopīs. Who, then, will not reside at Rādhā-kuṇḍa, and in a spiritual body surcharged with ecstatic devotional feelings [aprākṛta-bhāva], render loving service to the divine couple Śrī Śrī Rādhā-Govinda, who perform Their aṣṭa-kālīya-līlā, Their eternal eightfold daily pastimes. Indeed, those who execute devotional service on the banks of Rādhā-kuṇḍa are the most fortunate people in the universe.

Only the most fortunate live in the most sanctified place, Śrī Rādhā-kuṇḍa, with pure hearts, and worship Kṛṣṇa twenty-four hours a day. Śrī Rādhā-kuṇḍa is the topmost section of Goloka, the most confidential place in the spiritual sky, and the only shelter for devotees on the platform of *mādhurya-rasa* . Planets like Bhū, Bhūvaḥ, and Svaḥ are meant for ambitious householders. Above them are planets like Mahar, Jana, Tapa, and Satya, which are meant for the celibates. Upakurvaṇa-*brahmacārīs* live in Maharloka, naiṣṭhika-*brahmacārīs* attain Janaloka, vānaprasthas attain Tapaloka, and sannyāsīs enjoy in Satyaloka. *Bhagavad-gītā* (8.16) confirms:

ā-brahma-bhuvanāl lokāḥ punar āvartino 'rjuna
mām upetya tu kaunteya punar janma na vidyate

From the highest planet in the material world down to the lowest, all are places of misery wherein repeated birth and death take place. But one who attains to My abode, O son of Kuntī, never takes birth again.

The ecstatic spiritual abode of Vaikuṇṭha is rarely attained even by liberated souls. The Lord's devotees who are free from material desire at once attain that abode after leaving their material bodies. Maṭhurā is superior to Vaikuṇṭha, Vṛndāvana, the abode of the rāsa-līlā, is superior to Maṭhurā, Govardhana is superior to Vṛndāvana, and Rādhā-kuṇḍa is the best of all.

Śrīla Sanātana Gosvāmī Prabhu's explanation that the Lord's abode is three-fourths of the creation is most scientific. The impersonal Brahman is situated beyond the Causal Ocean. Impersonalists think that ultimately there is nothing there. They think all the "imaginary" gods as well as the imaginary form of Brahman will be merged, having become one. The Hayaśīrṣa Pancarātra states:

yā yāśrutir jalpati nirviśeṣaṁ, sā sābhidhatte sa-viśeṣam eva
vicāra-yoge sati hanta tāsāṁ, prāyo balīyaḥ sa-viśeṣam eva

Whatever Vedic mantras describe the Absolute Truth impersonally only prove in the end that the Absolute Truth is a person. The Supreme Lord is understood in two features, impersonal and personal. If one considers the Supreme Personality of Godhead in both features, he can actually understand the Absolute Truth. He knows that the personal understanding is stronger because he can see that everything is full of variety. No one can see anything that is not full of variety.

Śrīman Mahāprabhu says:

nirviśeṣa' tāṅre kahe yei śruti-gaṇa
prākṛta' niṣedhi kare 'aprākṛta' sthāpana

Wherever there is an impersonal description in the Vedas, the Vedas mean to establish that everything belonging to the Supreme Personality of Godhead is transcendental and free of mundane characteristics. (*Śrī Caitanya-caritāmṛta* Madhya 6.141)

Since they think they have defeated material variegatedness, spiritual variegatedness must similarly be rejected. Because they think spiritual variegatedness must be as illusory as material variegatedness, those who pursue this philosophy are called Māyāvādīs. The abode of the impersonal Brahman lies on the other side of the Causal Ocean. The concept of the Brahman effulgence arises after washing off the three modes of material nature. But jyotir abhyantate rupaṁ atulaṁśyāmasundaraṁ: "Within that effulgence is the beautiful and unique form of Lord Śyāmasundara."

Vaikuṇṭha possesses spiritual variegatedness. There are two and half *rasas* found there. The Supreme Lord is omnipotent; both matter and spirit are under His control. This is the philosophy taught by Śrī Rāmānuja. The Lord is the proprietor of the material and spiritual energies.

Questions and Answers:

1: Sometimes we become confused about the goal when we speak with those who do not know the difference between mundane rasa and spiritual rasa. Could you please help us?

Nondevotees want to enjoy the material world, but the devotees want neither to enjoy nor to renounce the world. They want only to serve the Lord. lakṣmī sahasra śata sambhavam sevyamāṁ: "The Lord is always served by hundred of thousands of Lakṣmīs or gopīs."

After achieving perfection and upon giving up the body awarded by our parents, we attain uninterrupted devotional service to the Lord. The Lord is supremely independent and everyone must respect His supreme will. Those who are trying to develop their serving propensity should follow the rules and regulations given by the *ācāryas* . No one should make a pretense. What is the value of making a show of following your constitutional duty if you are still conditioned by your gross and subtle body? Only mundane sahajiyās make such a show.

The descriptions found in ornamental literature like Kāvyaprakāśa or Sāhitya-*darśana* is mundane. Such books describe the affairs between men and women—or a number of men and women together. If the two and half types of *rasas* are applied to the Lord and the other two and half to the abominable experiences lived out by forgetful living entities, the consideration of *rasa* remains incomplete. There are five *rasas* fully manifest in the complete kingdom of God, Goloka. The transcendental gopīs are not concerned with superiority or inferiority or whether they are mature or immature girls. They serve Kṛṣṇa with all their limbs and all their senses. The sages who could not attain perfection in their worship of the Supreme tried to do so by seeing Śrī Rāmacandra's beauty, but since Lord Rāma vowed to accept only one wife, it was impossible for those sages to achieve their goal. Therefore they took birth as gopīs in Vraja. The *Padma Purāṇa* describes this incident. Among them, a few attained perfection at the beginning of the rāsa-lilā pastimes. This is confirmed in the Bṛhad-Vāmana *Purāṇa*. When the personified Upaniṣads were struck with wonder upon seeing the gopīs' good fortune. As a result of their own intense and focused kṛṣṇa-*bhajana*, they too took birth in Vraja as gopīs.

If one considers it from a neutral stance, one will find that the gopīs' love in *mādhurya-rasa* is far superior to and more wonderful than the love of God found in any other *rati*. Of the gopīs Śrī Rādhikā is topmost; She is principal among the group leaders headed by Lalitā and Viśākhā.

By great good fortune one gains entry into Lalitās group. Those who desire to circumambulate Śrī Rādhā Kuṇḍa today try to live on the banks of Lalitā Kuṇḍa with this prayer in their heart. Some people consider Candrāvalī the topmost gopī, but the topmost achievement is to have the opportunity to surrender as Śrī Rādhās maidservant. She is the personification of mahābhāva.

Śrī Rādhās name is secretly mentioned in *Śrīmad-Bhāgavatam* because the author feared this literature would fall into the hands of materialists. But the most magnanimous Śrī Gaurasundara and my spiritual master, Śrī Rūpa Gosvāmī Prabhu, have revealed information about Śrī Rādhā without hiding it from qualified devotees. The *Padma Purāṇa* states:

yathā rādhā priyā viṣṇos tasyāḥ kuṇḍaṁ priyaṁ tathā
sarva-gopīṣu saivaikā viṣṇor atyanta-vallabhā

Just as Śrīmatī Rādhārāṇī is most dear to Kṛṣṇa, Her bathing pond is similarly dear. Of all the gopīs She is the most beloved of the Lord.

Only by Śrī Rādhās mercy can one reside eternally on the banks of Rādhā-kuṇḍa, the topmost place in the entire creation. Therefore Śrī Rūpa Prabhu mentions taking bath in Rādhā-kuṇḍa in his ultimate instruction:

kṛṣṇasyoccaiḥ praṇaya-vasatiḥ preyasībhyo 'pi rādhā
kuṇḍaṁ cāsyā munibhir abhitas tādṛg eva vyadhāyi
yat preṣṭhair apy alam asulabhaṁ kiṁ punar bhakti-bhājāṁ
tat premedaṁ sakṛd api saraḥ snātur āviṣkaroti

Of the many objects of favored delight and of all the lovable damsels of Vrajabhūmi, Śrīmatī Rādhārāṇī is certainly the most treasured object of Kṛṣṇa's love. And, in every respect, Her divine Kuṇḍa is described by great sages as similarly dear to Him. Undoubtedly Rādhā-kuṇḍa is very rarely attained even by the great devotees; therefore it is even more difficult for ordinary devotees to attain. If one simply bathes once within those holy waters, one's pure love of Kṛṣṇa is fully aroused.

"I have taken bath in Rādhā-kuṇḍa"; "I took a dip in Rādhā-kuṇḍa"; "I am a lump of flesh and blood"; "I am my wife's maintainer"; "I am a *sannyāsī*"; "I am a *brāhmaṇa*; *kṣatriya*, *vaiśya*, or a *śūdra*" thinking in any of these ways does not give the qualification to bathe in Rādhā-kuṇḍa. What to speak of such materialistic conceptions, if we are filled with the conception of awe and reverence, we cannot bathe in Rādhā-kuṇḍa. We have to walk the path of Śrī Rādhās maidservants without imitating them (as the *sakhī*-bhekīs do). Simply decorating a male body as if it were female does not qualify one to serve Śrī Rādhā-kuṇḍa.

2: What is the difference between the paramahaṁsas who wear white, and the tridaṇḍa sannyāsīs?

Some devotees who follow the regulative principles are encouraged to accept tridaṇḍa and on the path of attachment to wear white cloth instead of saffron out of respect for the paramahaṁsas. It is improper for devotees on the path of attachment to wear saffron. But if they harbor a cheating propensity in spiritual life, none of the prescribed paths will help. Despite maintaining material attachments, some devotees externally accept the symptoms of tridaṇḍa and wear saffron, deceiving ignorant people.

Śrīla Prabodhānanda Sarasvatī wrote Rādhā-*rasa* -sudhā-nidhī while living at Kāmyavana. He made a show of accepting *sannyāsa*, but was a paramahaṁsa who maintained deep attachment for the Lord in his heart. The point is that one has to give up all material conceptions. The external dress is not important. Those who are truly fixed in transcendence engage in the transcendental service of transcendental Śrī Rādhā in the transcendental Vraja, after attaining the transcendental body of a gopī on the transcendental grove on the bank of transcendental Rādhā-kuṇḍa. A person fixed in transcendence knows himself as one of Śrī Rādhās transcendental maidservants.

Śrīla Jagannātha dāsa Bābājī Mahārāja was a disciple of Śrīla Madhusudana Dāsa, who performed *bhajana* at Surya-kuṇḍa. My spiritual master was a disciple of this Jagannātha dāsa. They had no tinge of a material conception in them. *Śrīmad-Bhāgavatam* (10.84.13) states:

yasyātma-buddhiḥ kuṇape tri-dhātuke
sva-dhīḥ kalatrādiṣu bhauma ijya-dhīḥ
yat-tīrtha-buddhiḥ salile na karhicij
janeṣv abhijñeṣu sa eva go-kharaḥ

One who identifies his self as the inert body composed of mucus, bile, and air, who assumes his wife and family are permanently his own, who thinks an earthen image or the land of his birth is worshipable, or who sees a place of pilgrimage as merely the water there, but who never identifies himself with, feels kinship with, worships or even visits those who are wise in spiritual truth—such a person is no better than a cow or an ass.

By considering ordinary water holy water and the gross material body the self, one can neither see nor bathe in Rādhā-kuṇḍa. Mundane sahajiyās think that by considering the gross bodies the self, by considering their wives and children their own, by considering imaginary objects God, by considering ordinary water sacred, and without understanding that the Lord's pure devotees are their real well-wishers, they can still bathe in Rādhā-kuṇḍa. Śrīman Mahāprabhu said: dīkṣā-kāle bhakta kare ātma-samarpaṇa/ sei-kāle kṛṣṇa tāre kare ātma-sama, sei deha kare tāra cid-ānanda-maya aprākṛta-dehe tāṅra caraṇa bhajaya "At the time of initiation, when a devotee fully surrenders unto the service of the Lord, Kṛṣṇa accepts him to be as good as Himself. When the devotee's body is thus transformed into spiritual existence, the devotee, in that transcendental body, renders service to the lotus feet of the Lord."(*Śrī Caitanya-caritāmṛta* Antya 4.192-93)

One's spiritual body manifests when Vaiṣṇava qualities manifest according to his constitutional propensity. Matter can never become spirit; spirit is eternally spirit. We don't have to bring our original spiritual consciousness down into our gross material conception. If the artificially dressed bodies of the sakhi-bhekis are unclothed, then their natural male bodies will be exposed. The topmost principle in the spiritual kingdom is to bathe in Śrī Rādhā-kuṇḍa.

www.ingramcontent.com/pod-product-compliance
Lightning Source LLC
Chambersburg PA
CBHW070017100426
42740CB00013B/2529